HAMPSHIRE

D1421687

Bromley Libraries

30128 80318 141 4

HAMPSHIRE

through writers' eyes

EDITED BY
ALASTAIR LANGLANDS

Decorations by Matthew Rice

ELAND
London

First published in Great Britain by Eland Publishing Limited
61 Exmouth Market, London EC1R 4QL in 2017

Editorial content © Eland Publishing 2017
Decorations © Matthew Rice

ISBN 978 1 78060 098 7

All rights reserved. This publication may not be reproduced, stored
in a retrieval system or transmitted in any form or by any means,
electronic, mechanical, photocopying, recording, or otherwise, without
permission in writing from the publishers.

Cover image: Moses Mills of Preston Candover
© Hampshire Record Office:
Cosier/Thorp of Preston Candover Collection: 45M86/5/122
Back cover image: *Ringwood, The Millpond* 1900
© The Francis Frith Collection

Text set in Great Britain by James Morris, in Minion, Galliard and Bembo
Printed in Great Britain by Clays Ltd, St Ives plc

Contents

Acknowledgements

The editor thanks Bruce Barnfield, Sam Bibby, David Crane, Ronnie Davidson Houston, Jane Hurst (of the Curtis Museum, Alton), Jane Kirby (librarian at Bedales School), J. C. Langlands, the late Jeremy Lewis, A. B. Rye, Christopher Rye, Tony Weale and Dan Wheeler for their recommendations and offers special thanks to Jane Rye who enthusiastically transcribed much of the text. He also thanks David Rushton, for permission to publish his piece on Kercher's Field, first published in the Northanger Benefice Parish Magazine. He is particularly grateful to his editor, Rose Baring, for the huge contribution she has made.

The publishers would like to thank the following for their permission to reprint copyright material: Rupert Willoughby for permission to publish an extract from his *Basingstoke and Its Contribution to World Culture*; John Murray for permission to use extracts from James Lees-Milne's diaries – *Deep Romantic Chasm, Prophesying Peace* and *Caves of Ice*; Faber & Faber for permission to use an extract from *Edward Thomas – The Last Four Years* by Eleanor Farjeon; Faber & Faber for permission to use the opening of the poem 'Autumn Journal' by Louis MacNeice; Heinemann for permission to use an extract from *The Play Room* by Olivia Manning; Oneworld Publications for permission to use an extract from *Watership Down* by Richard Adams; United Agents on behalf of The Estate of J. B. Priestley for permission to quote from *English Journey*; John Murray (Publishers), a division of Hodder Headline, for permission to use the following poems by John Betjeman – 'The Wykehamist', 'Youth and Age on the Beaulieu River, Hants', 'Aldershot Crematorium'; Johnson & Alcock Ltd on behalf of the Estate of Beryl Bainbridge, 1984, for permission to use extracts from *English Journey: or The Road to Milton Keynes*; Pan Macmillan for permission to use an extract from *Heartstone* by C J Sansom, reproduced with permission of the licensor through PLSclear; Rogers, Coleridge and White on behalf of The Estate of P. G. Wodehouse for permission to use an extract from P. G. Wodehouse's *Damsel in Distress*; Century, a division of Penguin Random House UK, for permission to quote from Edward Rutherfurd's *The Forest*; Curtis Brown on behalf of The Estate of Angus Wilson for permission to use an extract from Angus Wilson's *The Strange Ride of Rudyard Kipling*; Black Spring Press Ltd for permission to quote from Alexander Baron's *From the City, from the Plough*.

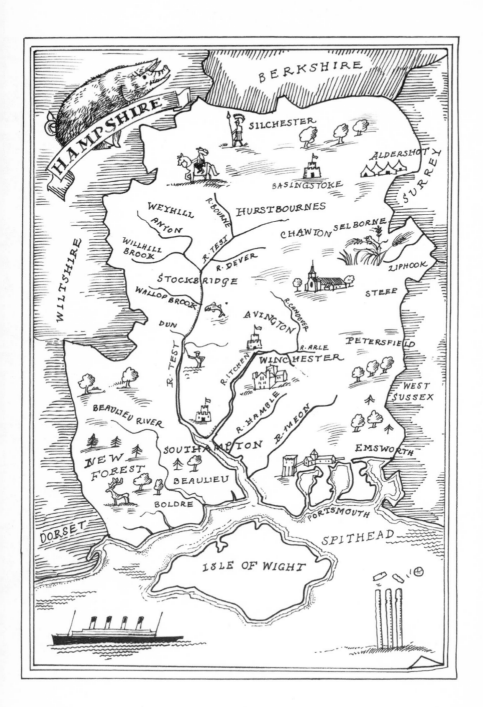

Introduction

When you think of Hampshire, you think of chalk streams and downland, military and naval enterprise, sailing and King Alfred, and Winchester Cathedral. But its literary heritage does not leap to mind. And yet Hampshire has played a surprisingly important role in nurturing the book. For the English novel reached its earliest flowering through the genius of Jane Austen, who was born and lived most of her life here. The world that she depicts in her exquisite novels, and her scintillating and detailed understanding of the human psyche, were born of the county and of her observation of her Hampshire neighbours and friends. But her Hampshire is only part of the story – the largely genteel part which disports itself in country towns and villages. For Hampshire is one of the most densely inhabited of English counties, divided, in fact, between a teeming population largely housed along the southern coast, and two sparsely populated national parks – the New Forest and the South Downs – which account for almost fifty per cent of the land mass.

Many other writers have been drawn here by history, by geography and by necessity. The diarist Pepys earned his living as a naval administrator, travelling frequently to Portsmouth to work, while the poet Keats came to the Isle of Wight for his health, and took mighty inspiration from Winchester's ripe, autumnal water meadows. Charles Kingsley was vicar near Basingstoke, and who cannot believe that the underwater world he depicts in *The Water Babies* is not in some way born of hours gazing into the clear waters of the local chalk streams as a fisherman? Alexander Baron came, as so many have, as a soldier, on his way to the Second World War in Europe. And it was from Hampshire that the precious poet Edward Thomas left for the trenches of northern France, never to return.

But Hampshire's unique gift to literature is nature writing, which began here with Gilbert White in the sleepy village of Selborne. He was, said Flora Thompson, the 'very first of English nature writers, the most

1

sober and modest, yet happiest of men.' A Hampshire man, through and through. From his and all the other contributions gathered here in this collection, a kaleidoscopic, complex, sometimes enchanting, sometimes wistful picture of the county through the ages gradually emerges.

...

I suppose there are few among those who read this book who have not at some time or other made the journey by rail from London to Southampton. Those who have done so and have kept an observant eye may have noticed two things. They may have remarked, first, that after leaving London the train toils heavily uphill with the engine pulling its hardest until Basingstoke in the north of Hampshire is past but then it begins to run downhill, and runs easily and lightly, often with the steam shut off altogether, through Winchester, round the rattling curves of Eastleigh, until the sea-level is reached at Southampton.

Secondly, they may have noted that the country in the Thames Valley is for the most part rich and fertile, green with luxuriant gardens, highly cultivated fields and far-extending woods. But that almost as soon as the Hampshire border is reached, the landscape changes and the scene opens out into a wide expanse of undulating down dotted but sparsely with clumps of trees and human habitations and pierced now and then with railway and roadway cuttings, which reveal deep banks of white-gleaming chalk. This chalky down-land stretches along the line of the rail from Basingstoke in the north to beyond Winchester in the south. And then as Eastleigh is approached another transformation is evident; the chalk is seen no more and the verdant fertility of the Thames Valley seems to have its fellow in the luxuriance in the vale of the Itchen, and the forest splendours of Chilworth and Bassett.

For three thousand years or more the appearance of the southern part of Hampshire has remained in its great general features unchanged; the Test and the Itchen have held their present courses; Southampton Water has existed as an arm of the sea ... the English Channel has divided England from the continent...

I can hardly do better for an introduction to this magnificent county than presenting this description of its shape and variety from F J C Hearnshaw's *A Short History of Southampton* (1910). It has the advantage of eliciting a world now gone but perhaps just within memory, which will, like the rest of this book, encourage a lively imagination.

It also hints at one of Hampshire's defining aspects: its position at the centre of the south coast of England, and its natural potential as a harbour, a place from which to interact with the world, be that by military, civil or mercantile means. From this have grown industries and communities – shipbuilders and sailors, aircraft manufacturers and shippers – whose presence, along with that more recently of holidaymakers and retired folk, has coloured the complexion of the coast.

But let's go back to learn a little, a very little, and that not necessarily trustworthy, of the first people inhabiting this part of England which will be signally important in the development of our nation. Tacitus is almost all we have.

> Who the first inhabitants of Britain were, whether natives or immigrants, remains obscure; one must remember we are dealing with barbarians. But physical characteristics vary, and that very variation is suggestive. The reddish hair and large limbs of the Caledonians proclaim a German origin, the swarthy faces of the Silures, the tendency of their hair to curl and the fact that Spain lies opposite, all lead one to believe that Spaniards crossed in ancient times and occupied the land. The peoples nearest to the Gauls are correspondingly like them. Perhaps the original strain persists, perhaps it is climatic conditions that determine physical type in lands that converge from opposite directions on a single point. On a general estimate, however, we may believe that it was Gauls who took possession of the neighbouring island. In both countries you will find the same ritual, the same religious beliefs. There is no great difference in language, and there is the same hardihood in challenging danger, the same subsequent cowardice in shirking it.

> P Cornelius Tacitus (AD 55–120)
> *Agricola* (AD 97)

Tacitus, Edmund Gibbon's ideal of the historian-philosopher, wrote this account of the natives in his biography of his father-in-law Agricola, who for seven years was Governor of Britain. This passage is an early indication that invasion from Roman Gaul possibly landed in what we know as Hampshire; later historians will wrangle over where continental invaders landed, but in Hampshire their presence is best found in the pre-Roman and Romano-British hill-forts at Ladle Hill, Bury Hill, Danebury Down, Nether Wallop, Buckland Rings and Bramdean as well as their splendid Winchester, Portchester and

Silchester settlements and the six dozen Roman Villas in the county.

Here, next, is something more reliable, in so far as Hugh Trevor Roper describes William Camden as the 'irreplaceable founding father of British Antiquarianism'. His findings are followed closely by many of his successors and in him we find an account of early records of the county's name.

> Next to Wilshire is that country which sometimes the Saxons called Hanteschyr, and is now commonly named Hantshire: of which, one part that beareth farther within the land, belonged, no doubt, to the Belgae, the other which lieth upon the sea appertained, without question, to the Regni, and ancient people of Britaine. On the West it hath Dorsetshire and Wilshire, on the South the Ocean to bound it: on the East it joineth to Sussex and Surrie, and on the North it bordereth upon Berkshire. A small province it is, fruitfull in corne, furnished in some places with pleasant woods thicke and well growen; rich in plenteous pasture, and for all commodities of sea most wealthy and happie. It is thought that it was with the first brought under subjection to the Romans. For, our Histories report, that Vespasian subdued it, and very probable reasons there are inducing us to beleeve the same.
>
> ...
>
> In that booke wherin King William the first made a survey of all England, this whole shire is expressely named Hantscyre and in some places Hentscyre, and the very towne itself for the South situation of it, South-hanton. When all became wasted, by the Danish warres, old Hanton also was left as a pray in the yeere of our Lord 980 to be sacked and rifled by them: and King William the Conqueror in his time had in it but fourescore men and no more in his demaine. But above 200 yeeres since when Edward the Third King of England and Philip Valois bustled for the very Kingdom of France, it was fired by the French and burnt to the ground. Out of the ashes whereof, presently sprung the towne which now is to be seene, but situate in a more commodious place betweene two rivers. Of those two rivers, betweene which this South-anton standeth, that in the West now called Test, and in times past Anton, (as I suppose) springeth out of the forrest of Chat goeth first to Andover, which in the Saxon language is Andeasaran,

that is, The Passage or Ferry over And. Thence glideeth this water streight into Anton Haven, at Arundinis Vadum, as Bede called it and interpreteth it himselfe Reedeford: but now of the bridge where the foord was named, for Redeford, Redbridge. The other river that runneth forth at the East-side of Southamton, may seeme to have been called Alre: For, the mercate towne standing upon the banke thereof, not farre from ponds out of which it issueth, is called Alres-ford, that is, The ford of Alre.

Upon the West banke of this river is situate the most famous Citie of the British Belgians, called by Ptolomee and Antoninus Venta Belgarum, by the Britans of Wales even at this day, Caer Gwent: by the Saxons in old time Wintanceaster, in Latine commonely Wintonia, and by us in these daies of Winchester. The Etymologie of this name Venta, some fetch from Ventus, that is, Wind, others from Vinum, that is, Wine, and some againe from Wina a bishop: who all of them be farre wide, and should doe well to pray for better judgement. Yet like I rather the opinion of Leland: who hath derived it from the British word Guin or Guen, that is, White, so that Caer Guin should signifie as much, as the White Citie. And why not? seeing the old Latines named these their Cities, Alba longa, and Alba regia, of whitenesse: yea and the Grecians also had their Luca, Lucas, and other nations also many places taking name of whitenesse. For, this Venta, like as the other two of the same name, to wit, VENTA SILURUM, and VENTA ICENORUM, are seated all three in a soile that standeth upon chalke and a whitish clay.

This city was the sacred workhouse or shop of embroidering and weaving. And right if his minde is Guidus Pancirolus, who writeth that those Gynaecia were instituted for the weaving of the Princes and souldiers garments of Ship-sailes, of linnen sheets, or coverings and such like cloths, necessarie for the furniture of mansions. But Wolfgangus Lazius was of opinion, that the Procurator aforesaid, had the charge heere of the Emperors dogs. And to say truth, of all the dogs in Europe, ours beare the name; in so much, as Strabo witnesseth, our dogges serve as souldiers, and the ancient Galles made especiall use of them even in their wars. And of all others, they were in most request both for those baitings in the Amphitheaters and also in all other publicke huntings among the Romanes. For, as the same Strabo writeth, they were, that is, of a generous kind and framed naturally for hunting.

William Camden (1551–1623)
Britannia (1586)

Both geographically and temperamentally, the county still centres on this historic jewel – Venta Belgarum or Winchester – which became capital, first of the kingdom of Wessex and then of the nascent nation, under Alfred the Great (849–899), who holds an uncontestable place in the English memory. The city's importance was felt for centuries through the power of its bishops and the commerce of its markets, though now it wears the gentle mien of a county town compared to its more bustling city neighbours – Southampton, Basingstoke and Portsmouth.

But raise your eyes from the streets of Winchester, or walk east until you trip into the clear waters of the river Itchen, and you find Hampshire's glory, her chalky streams and downland, her villages and gentle valleys, her forests and her heaths, all stages for millions of heroic but forgotten lives, like that of the man who adorns the cover of this book. Here lived shepherds and fishermen, blacksmiths and gentlemen and women, farmers, journeymen and rectors. This is the palette used by Jane Austen, and the inspiration for the revolutionary nature writing of Gilbert White.

Chapter 1
Winchester: ancient capital

Without having record to romantic legends, or traditionary
songs it is a sufficient commendation of the antiquity of
Winchester that it extends beyond the reach of every certain
authentic record and is lost in the mist which envelopes the
first population of this island.

Bishop John Milner (1752–1826)

Winchester sits astride the gin-clear water of the River Itchen.
This trout-filled chalk stream sparkles over the long summer
days but in winter sends rolling banks of mist to cloak the ancient
city, enclosed as it is by hills. To the east rise the soft curves of the
South Downs, the start of a green wave of turf that extends hundreds of
miles across south Hampshire and Sussex to the English Channel. The
Itchen, an ancient trade route used by pack animals and river-barges
for thousands of years before rail and motorway seized command
of the traffic, has carved its patient way through these hills, flowing
south towards its junction with the Test at Southampton. To the west
stands Worthy Down, over which climb such ancient roadways as the
Clarendon Way (to Salisbury) and the twenty-five-mile track north to
the empty Roman walls of Silchester.

Winchester is still dominated by its Norman cathedral, a powerful
edifice of stone, surrounded by its associated cloisters, meadows,
bishop's palace and an interconnecting warren of courtyards, lawns and
high flint walls. These are occupied by canons, chapels and a medieval
public school, Winchester College, established in the 14th century
by the then bishop, William of Wykeham. This quarter of the city is
a place apart, hallowed by scholarship and a priestly dignity, which
embraces the world – monarchs, visitors and pilgrims – yet is curiously
separate from the daily life of the bustling market town beside it. For

half of our national history, the bishopric of Winchester was not only the richest in the land, but the bishop was a national figure, more often to be found at court than on his episcopal throne.

The High Street cascades down the length of the city, from the site of the old castle to the banks of the Itchen. As you wander idly past its shops, you are following in the footsteps of our Neolithic ancestors on their track across the water meadows. This went on to become the central avenue of the Iron Age town of Cair Guinntguic, ruled by the Belgae tribe at the time of Christ. As allies, not enemies of Rome, the town grew into Venta Belgarum, literally the meeting-market place of the Belgae, with the Itchen usefully re-directed by Roman engineers to serve as a defensive moat. The Iron Age fort on St Catherine's Hill to the east was never stormed by the legions but morphed into a quiet holy place with its sacred turf maze. Winchester grew into one of the twenty-eight principal cities of Roman Britain, embellished with a cult shrine to the Virgin Goddess, the mistress of the horses. A safe day's march inland from any seaborne Viking raid, it became known to the Saxons as Wintan-Caestre (the fortified market) and the great King Alfred of Wessex chose it as his headquarters, and later as the capital city of an England united by him and his descendants under one crown.

Even the Norman kings after their conquest acknowledged the special claims of Winchester, and were expected to wear their crown here at Easter. But as a graphic demonstration of their power, they tore down the twin Saxon cathedrals (Old Minster and New Minster, filled with the tombs of saints and saintly Saxon kings) and built their own towering structure beside the ruins. It became a beacon for one of the great medieval fairs of Christendom, where a tented city of tens of thousands of traders assembled each year for a fortnight in September. On the eve of St Giles's Day, the great beam for weighing wool sacks was escorted through the city gates to serve the merchants who had travelled from as far as Provence, Lombardy and Moorish Spain to buy our staple cash crop – wool.

As the nearby town of Alresford gradually took over the role of the great sheep market, and the Reformation killed the temporal power of the bishops of Winchester, so began Winchester's five hundred year decline from power to mere gentility. The castle ruins were converted by Wren into a royal summer palace, and later still into a military barracks. Above it was developed a neat triangle of redbrick Victorian order: hospital, jail, police station and cemetery. Yet this long somnolence was a creative literary period for the city, which was walked on, written about and imagined by Keats, Thackeray, Trollope, Jane Austen and Thomas Hardy among many more.

The texts which follow weave a largely chronological pattern, although the literary output of Old Wykehamists demanded a section of its own which begins on page 44.

I leave it to Richard le Gallienne (1866–1947), a prominent literary figures of the 1890s, to bring us to the city. As he said 'There is scarce an event or personality that has been momentous for England that has not at one time touched Winchester – from King Canute to Jane Austen, both Wykehamists in death, for the bones of both rest in the cathedral. Here too rest the bones of Izaak Walton.'

… beyond, it begins to swell and soften and dimple into the round grassy bosoms of the South Downs. Soon one sees that one's road is to lie in those pleasant places, literally in the bosom of the hills; and so strikingly feminine are the contours that one grows almost shy as one approaches them, and, slowly ascending from the plain, is taken in among the soft shadows. 'This earth of the beautiful breasts!'

Once upon the uplands, one is soon conscious of a solitude peculiarly exquisite, and deepening with each mile that brings one nearer Winchester. It is a solitude penetrated, one can hardly tell how, with a sense of antiquity, and that hush of reverence with which very old things seem to fill the air. The land itself seems older than the land in the plains, as the stones in a cathedral seem older than the parent stone in the quarry whence they were hewn. It is that ancient silence which seems to make the grass-grown barrow lonelier than the rest of the meadow, the loneliness of a country of ancient earthworks and Druid stones.

Such a country, of course, it is, and when about eight miles beyond Petersfield, close by a scrap of village called Brookwood, the remains of an old stone circle arrest one at the roadside, one feels that the land is beginning to explain itself. For we are now entering on a region where the names of Saxon kings are still on the lips of peasants, where the battlefields have been green for a thousand years, and the Norman Conquest is spoken of as elsewhere we speak of the French Revolution – a comparatively recent convulsion of politics. Not by our small modern clocks is time measured here, but by the sundial of the stars.

I shall not soon forget the impressiveness of the last three or four miles to Winchester, dreamily ridden in a twilight of fine gold. How strangely spiritual this solid earth, of chalk and nibbling sheep, can sometimes seem; what an expression of diaphanousness it sometimes wears. So a poet's face, long since materialised, will sometimes at evening shine with a boyish starlight, and seem all spirit for a brief elated hour.

The beech trees and the hedges which had somewhat disguised the lines of the land hitherto, had suddenly disappeared, and there was nothing but the long-limbed down lying vast and still beneath the solemn evening sky. The silence seemed like an exquisite vessel of porcelain. One dared scarcely breathe lest it should break. How lonely it was, and yet how little one asked a companion. And there, crowned with a heraldic sunset, lay Winchester in a fold of the down; and, after the hush of those intense uplands, it was almost startling to come upon the sudden sound of the little river Itchen, running with noisy freshness beneath the bridge that is the threshold of the town, and to mingle once more in a warm murmur of men and women.

Here, too, rest the bones of Izaak Walton. But you must ask to see his grave. Else the verger will pass it by, for vergers take small account of literary fame; and what, indeed, can such fame seem to a man in whose sight all day are those carved and gilded chests hoarding the dust of twenty forgotten kings? 'In this tomb rests pious Kind Edred, who nobly governed this land of Britain and died AD 955,' runs the inscription on one of those strange mortuary chests resting on the side screens of the choir; and the guidebook writer adds in brackets: 'Contains many thigh bones and two skulls.' Now a verger realises that no literary man ever had many thigh bones and two skulls. That is only given to kings – and vergers throughout England are unanimously royalist. It is instructive to hear how they speak of Cromwell to this day. The vergers of England at least will never forgive him.

But I must not seem to be disrespectful to vergers, particularly to the courteous and learned verger at Winchester, who so generously and graciously gave me the benefit of historical and architectural acquirements which made me realise neglected opportunities of scholarship with a pang particularly keen. Only to hear him talk of 'apsidal terminations'! He seemed only more familiar with William Rufus, who was carried in here from the New Forest, an arrow in his brain, and was buried in a tomb of basalt, 'many looking on and few grieving.' Yes, as he himself said of the reredos, peopled with the statues of Wincastrian saints and heroes, my verger is a veritable 'mass of history.' You must go and let him tell you the story of Winchester Cathedral. Get him to tell you all I could never tell half so well, and respect with me, not only his learning, but the sentiment of his grateful pride that he has been chosen to be a doorkeeper in this beautiful house of God – and William of Wykeham.

Richard le Gallienne
Travels in England (1900)

Hilaire Belloc is best known for his *Bad Child's Book of Beasts* and his *Cautionary Tales* but as a passionate Sussex man, in 1904 he published an appreciation of the ancient route from Canterbury to Winchester.

Why did the encampment or town upon the Itchen gather round itself a special character, and become the depot into which would stream the lead of the Mendips, the tin of Cornwall, and the armies of all Britain south of Gloucester and west of the Wiltshire Avon?

The answer is The Sea: the necessities and the accidents of the crossing of the Channel; Winchester was made by the peculiar conditions under which the Channel can be passed that is, the passage from the jutting promontory of the Cotentin to the southern cape of the Isle of Wight, which stands so boldly out into the sea, and invites adventure from the French shore.

The estuary of the Seine was not only an obvious outlet, but it gave an opportunity for the early ships to creep under the protection of a windward shore. From the very heart of the country seagoing vessels could go down the stream with a strong tide helping them. They would have calm water as far as the point of Barfleur so long as the wind was south of west, and no danger save the reef of Calvados. Moreover, the trend of the land led them northward in the direction which they knew they had to follow if they were ultimately to find the English coast.

In actual practice, in clear weather, it is but a very short run of fifteen miles or so from the last sight of the French coast to the making of St Catherine's upon the horizon before one.

These considerations, then, the guide and protection of the Cotentin coast, the inlet of the Seine, the narrowing of the sea, the highland upon either side, would of themselves suffice to point this passage out as a natural way from the Continent to England.

Hilaire Belloc (1870–1953)
The Old Road (1904)

And now, some speculation about the Roman Conquest and the later pre-eminence of Winchester.

The Romans would have known all about the impenetrable forest of Andereida. That forest stretched from the open chalk downs of Kent to the open chalk downs of Hampshire and would have been quite impassable for an army. It was impassable even in the eleventh century, for William the Conqueror, when he wanted to go from Hastings to London, had to go round by way of Dover. The Romans would have been likely to do all they could to avoid such an obstacle. I think it probable that there were landings at unexpected places on the coast of Kent, but against all the weight of modern opinion I remain convinced that the main landing of the expedition was made on the coast of Hampshire and was under the direct command of Vespasian.

Why, also, Winchester, having become a strong Roman Camp, and having clear access to the sea via Southampton, would in times of peace be a centrally placed capital of Wessex. Peace was precarious in these islands after the departure of the Romans until the terminal conquest. In 832 the first Danish squadron attacked part of the English coast. The Danes, or Northmen, had begun their ravages in France a few years earlier. For two centuries Scandinavia sent out fleet after fleet of sea-rovers who desolated all the western kingdoms of Europe, and in many cases effected permanent conquests. Wessex was unusual in that it already had a long succession of relatively stable kings and overlords stretching back hundreds of years. It had trade through Southampton, an ecclesiastical power base in Winchester and wealth; perhaps most importantly it had, waiting in the wings, a king who was intelligent, diplomatic and educated, Alfred.

Brian Vesey-Fitzgerald (1900-81)
Hampshire and the Isle of Wight

The historian Aethelweard, in his account of the last year of Alfred's reign, gives a contemporary evaluation of his stature:

In the same year, the magnanimous Alfred passed from the world, king of the Saxons, unshakeable pillar of the western people, a man replete with justice, vigorous in warfare, learned in speech, above all instructed in divine learning. For he had translated unknown numbers of books from rhetorical Latin speech into his own language – so variously and so richly, that his book of Boethius would arouse tearful emotions not only in those familiar with it but even in those hearing it for the first time. For the king died on the seventh day before the feast of all saints; his body lies in peace in Winchester. Now, reader, say "O Christ our Redeemer, save his soul".

The Chronicle of Æthelweard (trans. 1961)

And an account of another King of England buried in Winchester, by the foremost English historian of the time. Unlike Alfred, who was originally buried in the old Saxon Minster, William Rufus, killed by an arrow when hunting in the New Forest in 1125, was buried in the present cathedral, which had been started during the reign of his father, the Conqueror, and was consecrated during his own.

When the king received the wound, he said not a word, but breaking off the shaft of the arrow where it stuck out of his body, he fell upon the ground and thus made more speedy his own death...A few countrymen recovered the body and took it on

15

a cart to the cathedral at Winchester, the blood dripping from it all the way. Here it was committed to the ground within the tower, attended by many of the magnates, but mourned by few. Next year the tower fell but I forbear to mention the different opinions about this lest I should seem to assent too readily to unsupported trifles, the more especially as the building might have fallen through imperfect construction even if he had not been buried there.

William of Malmesbury *(1095?–1143?)*
Chronicle of the Kings of England

Alfred Bowker, once mayor of the city, has imagined a siege of the city during the civil war which beset the troubled reign of King Stephen (1135–54).

The attacking force occupied the convent of St Mary's, which was in close proximity to the northern side of Wolvesey; and from thence they directly assailed the outer walls. They strove to fill in the moat, but for some time the defenders kept them at bay. Armadin however seeing they were greatly outnumbered by the enemy, whose bowmen kept up a continuous hail of arrows upon the battlements, and fearing heavy losses to his none too numerous garrison, was perforce compelled to withdraw his men under cover.

The besiegers now had possession of all the city to the north of the High Street ... it soon became apparent that ere long with the aid of scaling ladders, this portion of the outer defences must fall into the enemy hands. Hubert's resources, however, were not yet exhausted. He had caused immense engines to be constructed such as he had seen in use in Normandy. They were in the nature of catapults, consisting of large beams poised in the centre, the points stretched back so that when one end was released it would hurl heavy stones or other missiles to a great distance.

...

The day upon which Hubert's contrivances were completed was drawing to a close and the attacking force were elated by the knowledge that by nightfall the outer wall on the northern side must yield to their determined assault. At the critical moment when the final attack was about to commence a lurid light lit up the heavens far and wide, and a ball of fire came hissing through the air from the direction of Wolvesey, and struck fair upon the thatched roof of the convent of St Mary's, which afforded the assaulting party protection.

Armadin and the Bishop's troops, under the direction of Hubert, were busily engaged with the immense catapults, and no sooner had the first fireball been sent out into the city on its errand of destruction, than another and another followed, to the consternation of the besiegers. The roof and buildings of many houses nearby had caught alight, and tongues of flame were darting up and up, rising higher every moment. The besiegers, awestruck and paralysed by their immediate danger, at first frantically battled with the flames, vainly attempting to extinguish the fire. The dense volumes of smoke were suffocating, and it was at once obvious that the attack upon the Palace that night was frustrated. The evening had commenced calm and still, but the wind had now risen, and a strong gale was blowing from the south east. And still the vast fireballs, together with the sparks from the fire were flying at a great height through space, borne further upon the wind far out into the doomed town, where the flames spread rapidly. The assailants were fully occupied in the fruitless endeavour to cope with the conflagration, but their efforts proved unavailing. As Armadin gazed upon this sight...he saw that the high wind was carrying the flames in a northerly direction rather than to the westward of the city so that it was possible that the old Cathedral and the castle on the western confines might, with its inmates, go unscathed.

The fire made rapid progress, however. First the good Queen Alswitha's monastery was razed to the ground; the Mint, the Record Office and all the adjacent houses became wrapped in flames. On they sped past the confines of the city, until they reached the great Abbey of Hyde, which was likewise soon enveloped in a sheet of fire... Occasionally, amid the crashing timbers, a sound like thunder betokened the noise of falling masonry; and in such a place, subdued for a moment, the flames would again burst forth with incredible and renewed fury, sounding like the rush of a high and mighty

17

wind through a forest, sweeping and roaring as the devastating fire pressed on.

Alfred Bowker
Armadin or *A Tale of Old Winchester* (1908)

The only royal wedding to take place in Winchester Cathedral was that of the pious Catholic, Mary Tudor, to Philip of Spain in 1554. Here one of Philip's courtiers describes the scene:

His Highness arrived at the church which was well hung with many sumptuous cloth of brocade and crimson and of dark colours and was full of banners and standards and he placed himself on the chair of state which was there, with the ambassadors and noble who came, and there he waited until her majesty the Queen came. She arrived escorted by the lords of this realm. His Highness, being informed, left his chair to receive her and made his bow, and at the time his Highness greeted all the noblewomen and ladies who came with her. The Queen then left his Highness with all the ladies, and went to the chair which was set for her on the left and sat down ... Then the bishop performed the marriage with the same questions and solemnity as in Spain.

Juan de Varaona
Marriage of Philip and Mary (1554)

John Taylor was apprentice to a Thames ferryman, called himself the Water Poet and had 'a great talent for expressing himself in rollicking prose and verse'. He made a series of journeys over his lifetime, each commemorated with a self-published pamphlet:

On 21 August I took Winchester in my way homewards, where I saw an ancient city, like a body without a soul, and I know not the reason of it, but for ought that I perceived, there were almost as many parishes as people. I lodged at the sign of the Cock, being recommended to the host of the house by a token of Salisbury, but mine host died the night before I came, and I, being weary, had more mind to go to bed than to follow him so long a journey to do my message or deliver any commendations. But the whole city seemed almost as dead as mine host, and it may be they were all at harvest work. But I am sure I walked from one end of it to the other, and saw not thirty people of all sorts. So I think that if a man go to Winchester for a goose he might lose his labour for a trader cannot live there by trading such commodities.

John Taylor (1580–1653)
A new discovery by sea with a wherry from London to Salisbury
(1623)

Celia Fiennes began her travels 'to regain my health by variety and change of aire and exercise'. The informative record she left has been a valuable source to many and is often referred to by Nikolaus Pevsner in his *Buildings of England*. The Fiennes family were connected with Winchester through their descent from Agnes Champneys, sister and heiress of William of Wykeham, via her grandson Thomas Wykeham (formerly Perrot) of Broughton. Some members of the Fiennes family took advantage of that Founder's Kin and went to Winchester and New College in privileged circumstances.

I went into the New fforest in Hampshire, thence you go to Alton, thence to Alsford 7 mile, you go along on the hills in sight of the River all wch gives name to those places, its a good Chaulkey way. Thence to Winchester 7 mile – in one mile off the town is Woolsey y^t was formerly ye Bishops house, a large Rambling building like a little town, this is on Maudline hill whereon a Considerable ffaire is kept neare Michelmas, ye Traffique mostly hopps which y^t Country produceth good and Cheese – its noted for a vast many of Waines from Severall parts especially from the West Country…The Bishop's palace stands in a Low Ground or Watry Meadow, its a timber building but so unpleasant that the Bishop lives not at it but at Ffarly Castle about 20 mile off.

The Cathedrall at Winchester is one of ye biggest in England and is to be admired for its Largeness, not its neatness or Curiosity. In the Church there are no good Monuments worth notice… In the town is a new building begun by K. Charles the Second for a Palace when he Came to hunt and for aire and diversions in the Country. I saw ye Modell of it wch was very fine and so would it have been if ffinished; but there is only ye outside shell is set up, there were designed fine apartm^ts and two Chapples but its never like to be finish'd now.

Here is a good Colledge it is on ye same foundation y^t New Colledge in Oxford are; both built and Endowed by Great Willm of Wickam an ancester of ye ffiennes and Lord Say and Seale. So all the founders Kindred by his own Statutes are first to be Chosen and have a Right to many priviledges – its only in default or want of any of his Kindred or of Such and Such Parishes wch he names that any other person ought or Can be Chosen a Child of this Colledg... Y^e Colledge is a good Pile of Building there is a very pretty Chapple in it and a very fine Library wch is in ye Cloysters y^t are very good for walking.

The Warden has built a new appartment for himself wch looks well about a mile or two beyond Winchester, we go by St Cross, a Large hospitall for old men and I thinke most is for ye decayed schollars.

The Masters place is worth 1000 pound a yeare – it used to be annexed to ye Warden of the Colledges place, by their ffoundation they are to give reliefe to any Travellers that call there so farre as a Loafe of bread as big as our two penny bread is and a Draught of beare and a piece of mony. I thinke its ye value of a Groate. Ffrom thence I came to Redbridge, thence to Buckland in the new forest in all 20 mile; ffrom Buckland wch was a Relation's house – Sr Robt Smiths – its a mile to Limington a seaport town – it has some few small shipps belongs to it and some Little trade, but ye Greatest trade is by their Salterns. Y^e Sea water they draw into Trenches and so into Severall ponds y^t are secured in ye bottom to retain it, and it stands for ye Sun to Exhale ye Watry fresh part of it, and if it prove a drye sumer they make the best and most Salt, for ye raine spoyles ye ponds by weakning ye Salt.

Celia Fiennes (1662–1741)
Through England on a Side Saddle in the time of
William and Mary (1888)

Daniel Defoe, now known mainly as the author of *Robinson Crusoe* (1719), published three very successful volumes of travels in Britain between 1724–7. Born in London just before the Plague and the Great

Fire, he was a prolific author of both fiction and non-fiction, as well as trading in woollen goods and wine, and spying for William and Mary. Here he gives us our first glimpse of the medieval Hospital at St Cross, which is to this day an almshouse.

Winchester is a place of no trade, other than is naturally occasion'd by the inhabitants of the city and neighbouring villages, one with another: Here is no manufacture, no navigation; there was indeed an attempt to make the river navigable from Southampton; and it was once made practicable, but it never answer'd the expence, so as to give encouragement to the undertakers.

The hospital on the south of this city, at a mile's distance on the road to, Southampton is worth notice:

How the revenues of this hospital, which should maintain the master and thirty private gentlemen, who they call Fellows, but ought to call Brothers, is now reduc'd to maintain only fourteen, while the master lives in a figure equal to the best gentleman in the country, would be well worth the enquiry of a proper visitor, if such can be nam'd: 'Tis a thing worthy of complaint, when publick charaties, design'd for the relief of the poor, are embezzel'd and depredated by the rich, and turn'd to the support of luxury and pride.

Daniel Defoe (c. 1660–1731)
A Tour thro' the whole island of Great Britain (1720)

Dr Richard Pococke, officially Bishop of the Dioceses of Ossory and Meath in Ireland, seems to have spent most of his time travelling, in Europe, the Near East and throughout the British Isles.

The walls of the town are defended by a deep fossee, and at the south corner of the town are some remains of an old castle, which was likewise encompassed by a deep fosse. The County Hall was the chapel of the castle which is a fine Gothic building as it appears within. It is 110 feet long and 55 and-a-half feet broad. This, with the castle, is said to have been built by King Arthur and at the west end of the outside of the castle I saw some very old pillars. For King Arthur lived at this place. They have a table hung up at the west end of this room, which they call King Arthur's Round Table, but it is supposed to be a table of much later date used in the time of justs and turnaments, being convenient to sit at in order to avoid dispuites in relation to precedency. The names of the twenty four knights are around it: Sr Galahallt, Sr Lancelot Duelake, Sr Gavey, Sr Pibald, Sr Lyonell, Sr Tristram Delyens, Sir Gavetbye, Sir Bedewere, Sr Bibris, Sir Lametemale Tayte, Sir Bicane, Sir Oplomids, Sir Lamirak, Sir Boro de Gamys, Sir Satir, Sir Pellens, Sir Kay, Sir Edorde Marys, Sir Degonet, Sir Degare, Sir Brumear, Sir Lybyns Dillong, Sir Allymore, Sir Mordred.

At the top is the figure of a king, sitting, with these words 'King Arthur'. In the middle a rose is painted with these words round it: 'This is the round table of King Arthur and twenty four of his knights'.

Dr Richard Pococke (1704–65)
The Travels through England (made in 1750–1,
and only published from the manuscript in 1888)

Not everyone who visited was enamoured of Winchester. Horace Walpole, acknowledged arbiter of taste, son of Prime Minister Sir Robert is, like William Cobbett, often quoted because he commented anecdotally, spiritedly and widely on many aspects of society and his outspoken letters are published. Leslie Stephen, father of Virginia Woolf, writes: 'The History of England, throughout a very large segment of the eighteenth century, is simply a synonym for the works of Horace Walpole.' He is writing here to Richard Bentley, a classical scholar and Master of Trinity College, Cambridge. Walpole is best remembered for his Gothic romance, *The Castle of Otranto*, and his settling in Twickenham at Strawberry Hill, his 'little gothic castle'. His devoted friend John Chute had, in 1754, inherited The Vyne, the Tudor house near Basingstoke, now owned by the National Trust, and Walpole first visited as Chute's guest in August, finding the house very damp, so much so, indeed, that he hinted that if he went again in the autumn he would need some persuading not to go there on stilts.

… I was disappointed in Winchester: it is a paltry town and small. King Charles the Second's house is the worst thing I ever saw of Sir Christopher Wren, a mixture of a town hall and a hospital; not to mention the bad choice of the situation in such a country; it is all *ups* that should be *downs*.

Horace Walpole (1717-1797)
Letter September 18th 1755

John Wesley was the Evangelist and leader of Methodism. The prisoners in question were captured during the wide-ranging Anglo-French War which followed France's signing of a treaty of friendship with the United States during the War of Independence.

> At eleven I preached in Winchester, where there are four thousand five hundred French prisoners. I was glad to find they have plenty of wholesome food, and are treated in all respects with great humanity.

John Wesley (1703–91)
Journal October 6th 1780

John Keats had been in Shanklin on the Isle of Wight in search of suitably refreshing sea air and a gentle climate for his fragile health. This was a success at first but he soon felt the attraction of a city and its amenities. It was in Winchester that he found everything required to nurture his towering poetic genius. Sadly, it was only eighteen months before tuberculosis took him, in Rome, in February 1821.

Here he is, writing to his great love Fanny Brawne, from Shanklin in early August, 1819:

> ... This day week we shall move to Winchester; for I feel the want of a Library ... At Winchester I shall get your Letters more readily; and it being a cathedral City I shall have a pleasure always a great one to me when near a Cathedral, of reading them during the service up and down the Aisle ... I long to be off for Winchester.

To Benjamin Bailey
14 August 1819

> We removed to Winchester for the convenience of a Library and find it an exceeding pleasant Town, enriched with a beautiful Cathedrall and surrounded by a fresh-looking

country. We are in tolerably good and cheap Lodgings. Within these two Months I have written 1500 Lines, most of which besides many more of prior composition you will probably see by next Winter. I have written two Tales, one from Boccac(c) io call'd the Pot of Basil; and another call'd St Agnes' Eve on a popular superstition; and a third called Lamia – half finished – I have also been writing parts of my Hyperion and completed 4 Acts of a Tragedy. It was the opinion of most of my friends that I should never be able to write a scene. I will endeavour to wipe away the prejudice…

To Fanny Keats, his younger sister
28 August 1819

…we like it very much: it is the pleasantest Town I ever was in, and has the most recommendations of any. There is a fine Cathedrall which to me is always a source of amusement, part of it built 1400 years ago; and the more modern by a magnificent Man, you may have read of in our History, called William of Wickham. The whole town is beautifully wooded – From the Hill at the eastern extremity you see a prospect of Streets, and old Buildings mixed up with Trees…

There is the Foundation of St Croix about half a mile in the fields – a charity greatly abused. We have a Collegiate School, a Roman Catholic School; a chapel ditto and a Nunnery! And what improves it all is, the fashionable inhabitants are all gone to Southampton. We are qui(e)t…

The delightful weather we have had for two Months is the highest gratification I could receive – no chill'd red noses – no shivering – but fair atmosphere to think in – a clean towel mark'd with the mangle and a basin of clear Water to drench one's face with ten times a day: no need of much exercise – a Mile a day being quite sufficient. My greatest regret is that I have not been well enough to bathe though I have been two Months by the sea side and live now close to delicious bathing – Still I enjoy the Weather I adore fine Weather as the greatest blessing I can have. Give me Books, fruit, French wine and fine whether and a little music out of doors, played by somebody I do not know – not pay the price of one's time for a gig – but a little chance music: and I can pass a summer very quietly without caring much about Fat Louis, Fat Regent or the Duke of Wellington.

To John Taylor, his publisher
5 September 1819

... since I have been at Winchester I have been improving in health – it is not so confined – and there is on one side of the city a dry chalky down where the air is worth sixpence a pint. So if you do not get better at Retford do not impute it to your own weakness before you have well considered the nature of the air and soil – especially as autumn is encroaching: for the autum(n) fogs over a rich land is like the steam from cabbage water – What makes the great difference between dalemen, flatland men, and mountaineers? The cultivation of the earth in a great measure. Our health temperament and dispositions are taken more (notwithstanding the contradiction of the history of Cain and Abel) from the air we breathe than is generally imagined. See the difference between a peasant and a butcher. I am convinced a great cause of it is the difference of the air they breathe.

To George and Georgiana Keats, his brother and sister-in-law
17-27 September 1819

...Now the time is beautiful. I take a walk every day for an hour before dinner and this is generally my walk. I go out at the back door across one street, into the cathedral yard, which is always interesting; then I pass under the trees along a paved path, pass the beautiful front of the cathedral, turn to the left under a stone door way, – then I am on the other side of the building – which leaving behind me I pass on through two college-like squares seemingly built for the dwelling place of Deans and Prebendaries – garnished with grass and shaded with trees. Then I pass through one of the old city gates and then you are in one College Street through which I pass and at the end thereof crossing some meadows and at last a country alley of gardens I arrive, that is, my worship arrives at the foundation of Saint Cross, which is a very interesting old place, both for its gothic tower and alms-square, and for the appropriation of its rich rents to a relation of the Bishop of Winchester. Then I pass across St Cross meadows till you come to the most beautifully clear river – now this is only one mile of my walk I will spare you the other two till after supper when they would do you more good. You must avoid going the first mile just after dinner...

17th September 1819

...This day is a grand day for Winchester – they elect the Mayor. It was indeed high time the place should have some sort of excitement. There was nothing going on – all asleep – Not an old Maids Sedan returning from a card party – and if any old women have got tipsy at christenings they have not exposed themselves in the Street. The first night tho' of our arrival here there was a slight uproar took place at about ten of the clock. We heard distinctly a noise patting down the high street as of a walking cane of the old dowager breed; and a little minute after we heard a less voice observe, 'what a noise the ferril made – it must be loose.' Brown wanted to call the Constables, but I observed 'twas only a little breeze and would soon pass over. The side-Streets here are excessively maiden lady like. The door steps always fresh from the flannel. The Knockers have a very staid, ser(i)ous, nay almost awful qui(e) tness about them. I never saw so quiet a collections of Lions and rams heads – The doors (are) most part black with a little brass handle just above the Key hole – so that you may easily shut yourself out of your own house – he! he! 'There is none of your Lady Bellaston rapping and ringing here – no thundering-Jupiter footmen, no opera-treble-tattoos – but a modest lifting up of the knocker by a set of little wee old fingers that peep through the grey mittens, and a dying fall thereof. The great beauty of Poetry is, that it makes every thing every place interesting – The palatine Venice and the abbotine Winchester are equally interesting. Some time since I began a Poem call'd 'The Eve of St Mark' quite in the spirit of Town quietude. I think it will give you the Sensation of walking about an old county Town in a coolish evening. I know not yet whether I shall ever finish it ...

18th September 1819

…This Winchester is a place tolerably well-suited to me; there is a fine Cathedral, a College, a Roman-Catholic Chapel, a Methodist do, an independent do, - and there is not one loom or any thing like manufacturing beyond bread and butter in the whole City. There are a number of rich Catholic(s) in the place. It is a respectable, ancient aristocratical place – and moreover it contains a nunnery.

To John Hamilton Reynolds
21st September 1819

How beautiful the season is now – How fine the air. A temperate sharpness about it. Really without joking, chaste weather – Dian skies – I never liked the stubble-fields so much as now – Aye better than the chilly green of the Spring. Somehow a stubble-plain looks warm – in the same that some pictures look warm – This struck me so much in my Sunday's walk that I composed upon it.

To Richard Woodhouse
22nd September 1819

You like Poetry better – so you shall have some I was going to give to Reynolds.

Season of mists and mellow fruitfulness,
Close bosom friend of the maturing sun;
Conspiring with him how to load and bless
The vines with fruit that round the thatch eves run;
To bend with apples the moss'd cottage-trees,
And fill all fruit with ripeness to the core;
To swell the gourd, and plump the hazel-shells
With a white kernel; to set budding more,
And still more later flowers for the bees
Until they think warm days will never cease;
For Summer has o'er-brimm'd their clammy cells.

Who hath not seen thee oft amid thy stores?
Sometimes whoever seeks abroad may find
Thee sitting careless on a granary floor,
Thy hair soft-lifted by the winnowing wind;
Or on a half reap'd furrow sound asleep,
Dased with the fume of poppies, while thy hook
Spares the next swath and all its twined flowers;
And sometimes like a gleaner thou dost keep
Steady thy laden head across a brook;
Or by a cyder-press, with patient look,
Thou watchest the last oozings hours by hours.

Where are the songs of Spring? Aye, where are they?
Think not of them, thou hast thy music too.
While barred clouds bloom the soft-dying day
And touch the stubble plains with rosy hue;
Then in a wailful choir the small gnats mourn
Among the river sallows, borne aloft
Or sinking as the light wind lives and dies;
And full grown Lambs loud bleat from hilly bourne;
Hedge-crickets sing, and now with treble soft
The redbreast whistles from a garden croft;
And gathered Swallows twitter in the Skies.

John Keats (1795–1821)
Letters of John Keats (1958)

William Cobbett made his *Rural Rides* in the 1820s. He was a politician, a Member of Parliament with experience in the revolutionary states of America and widely travelled in Britain. He relished opposition to authority and would regularly curse paper money and smoke-filled London. He was possessed of firm opinions, often held as a result of an emotional response. His writing is peppered with superlatives: 'the tops of some of these hills are as fine meadows as I ever saw'; 'the spot is beyond description even now'; 'thus ended the most interesting day, as far as I know, that I ever passed in all my life'.

This being Sunday, I heard, about seven o'clock in the morning, a sort of jangling, made by a bell or two in the cathedral. We were getting ready to be off, to cross the country to Burghclere, which lies under the lofty hills at Highclere, about 22 miles from this city; but hearing the bells of the cathedral, I took Richard to show him that ancient and most magnificent pile, and particularly to show him the tomb of that famous bishop of Winchester, William of Wykham; who was the chancellor and the minister of the great and glorious king, Edward III; who sprang from poor parents in the little village of Wykham, three miles from Botley...

William Cobbett (1763–1835)
Rural Rides (1830)

In 1847–8, the American poet and man of letters Ralph Waldo Emerson toured the British Isles with the eminent Scots historian Thomas Carlyle, C. in the following extract:

Just before entering Winchester, we stopped at the Church of St Cross and, after looking through the quaint antiquity, we demanded a piece of bread and a draught of beer, which the founder, Henry de Blois, in 1136, commanded should be given to every one who should ask it at the gate. We had both, from the old couple who take care of the church. Some twenty people, every day, they said, make the same demand. This hospitality of seven hundred years' standing did not hinder C. from pronouncing a malediction on the priest who receives £2000 a year, that were meant for the poor, and spends a pittance on this small beer and crumbs.

In the Cathedral, I was gratified, at least by the ample dimensions. The length of line exceeds that of any other English church; being 556 feet by 250 in breadth of transept. I think I prefer this church to all I have seen, except Westminster and York. Here was Canute buried, and here Alfred the Great was crowned and buried, and here the Saxon kings: and later, in his own church, William of Wykeham. It is very old: part of the crypt into which we went down and saw the Saxon and Norman arches of the old church on which the present stands, was built fourteen or fifteen hundred years ago. Sharon Turner says, 'Alfred was buried at Winchester, in the Abbey he had founded there, but his remains were removed by Henry I to the new Abbey in the meadows at Hyde, on the northern quarter of the city, and laid under the high altar. The building was destroyed at the Reformation, and what is left of Alfred's body now lies covered by modern buildings, or buried in the ruins of the old.' William of Wykeham's shrine tomb was unlocked for us, and C. took hold of the recumbent statue's marble hands, and patted them affectionately, for he rightly values the brave man who built Windsor, and this Cathedral, and the School here, and New College at Oxford.

Ralph Waldo Emerson (1803–82)
English Traits (1856)

This later appreciation of the marvels of the cathedral comes from the work of Sacheverell Sitwell, art critic and writer on architecture.

But Winchester is marvellous for length of nave, largely, in the state in which we see it now, the work of the famous Bishop William of Wykeham; for its Perpendicular altar screen; but above all for its chantry chapels, which are here in unrivalled number, several of them sited on the feretory or raised platform behind the reredos which was intended for the display of relics. Exceptional, too, and wonderful are the carved and painted ceiling-bosses in the nave at Winchester. As minute and intricate as Japanese netsuke carvings, and more to be admired than those, they show the arms of Bishop Waynflete and the Beaufort portcullis with much else beside, but are indeed only revealed in their full detail through a pair of opera-glasses.

Sacheverell Sitwell (1897–1988)
England (1986)

Florence Marryat, actor and entertainer with George Grossmith, is the daughter of the more famous but less prolific author Captain Marryat. Hilstone, a Trollopian cathedral city, is a version of Winchester where Marryat lived in the 1860s, and the novel contains disguised portraits of leading members of the cathedral community.

Being a market town, Hilstone could boast of a cathedral! And the cathedral towns of our native country possess an individuality exclusively their own, for which all those who do not dwell therein, may be thankful.

Why, in order that a collection of bricks and mortar may attain the height of respectability, it must be imbued with the extreme of dullness, no one has yet been able to determine, but the fact remains, and Hilstone was no exception to the general rule. In vain had a charitable government, in pity for its stagnant condition, established a military depot on the outskirts of the town. The proximity of the red coats had produced no better effect than to put the ecclesiastical party considerably out of temper, and to cause the magic upspringing of half-a-dozen new public houses, to meet the increased demand for liquor.

"Sword and Gown" would not fraternise…Yet, strange to say, the feud was not between the men of each profession. Indeed, nothing pleased Mrs Filmer better than to see the Deanery table or concert-room filled with officers, and she was always especially gracious to the young, unmarried, rich colonel of the Bays, and was known to look with a very lenient eye upon his undisguised flirtation with her only daughter.

But it was the regimental ladies to whom Mrs Filmer and all her satellites bore so unmitigated an aversion…It is hard to say why this female feud existed, or when it had begun; but the ladies of the Bays had been heard to affirm that the occurrence was by no means an unusual one in military experience, and that they would rather be stationed anywhere than near a Cathedral town.

Perhaps they dressed a little too smartly and fashionably to suit the quiet ideas of Hilstone, or, perhaps they had been indiscreet in averring their distaste to the place and its inhabitants, and in comparing its dullness with the remembrance of former gaieties…For although the dullness of Hilstone was an indisputable fact, the natives refused to believe in it, and nothing offended them more than that a stranger should dare to express an opinion in the matter. To them, the old town was a paradise; they revered its shops, its institutions, and its society; it was the healthiest place in the world, the most scientific and the most popular. Nothing that happened in Hilstone could be wrong.

They rested its claims to notice upon the fame which it had acquired in bye-gone days, and were content to let them rest there. Was it not one of the most ancient towns in England? Were not kings and queens buried in gilded coffins in the cathedral, and did it not possess some of the finest antiquities in the country? What could people want more...Was it proposed by some enterprising member of the Town Council to build a public concert room? What could they want better than the Mechanics' Institute, in which the concerts of the Choral Society had been held for so many years? To widen the principal street, and erect new shops? Would they destroy the appearance of a thoroughfare which had stood in its present condition for hundreds of years? To enclose a public field and turn it into a subscription cricket ground! What, deprive the national schoolchildren of their right of way, even though it were as easy for them to go by the road, and the proposal was made for the benefit of the town? Never! The whole place would rise at the mere attempt; and, indeed, on the last occasion the "place," represented by all its worst characters, did rise and threatened to burn down the house of the person who had been so unfortunate as to think of the plan. Hilstone wanted more shops, more gas, more laying on of water, and more carrying off of drains; but the Hilstonians were perfectly contented to let things remain as they were; they liked being cheated, and walking home in the dark, and having a fever break out periodically in the back slums of the town, and refused to believe any of these evils required remedy.

Florence Marryat (1833–99)
Nelly Brooke (1868)

This excerpt from *The History of Henry Esmond* by Thackeray, plunges us into the complex entaglements of the eponymous hero's relationship with his foster family, the Castlewoods, which play out over the years. The novelist George Eliot found it 'the most uncomfortable book you can imagine ... the hero is in love with the daughter all through the book, and marries the mother at the end.' Others, such as Anthony Trollope, thought it a masterpiece.

There was a score of persons in the Cathedral besides the Dean and some of his clergy, and the choristers, young and old, that performed the beautiful evening prayer... and in the stalls, still in her black widow's hood, sat Esmond's dear mistress, her son by her side, very much grown, and indeed a noble-looking youth, with his mother's eyes... When he looked up there were two sapphire beams out of his eyes, such as no painter's palette has the colour to match, I think. On this day there was not much chance of seeing that particular beauty of my young lord's countenance; for the truth is, he kept his eyes shut for the most part, and, the anthem being rather long, was asleep.

But the musick ceasing, my lord woke up, looking about him, and his eye lighting on Mr Esmond, who was sitting opposite him, gazing with no small tenderness and melancholy upon two persons who had had so much of his heart for so many years... Young Castlewood came clambering over the stalls before the clergy were fairly gone, and running up to Esmond, eagerly embraced him...

'It was kind of you to come back to us, Henry,' Lady Esmond said. 'I thought you might come.' She gave him her hand, her little fair hand: there was only her marriage ring on it. The quarrel was over... It was a rapture of reconciliation.

...

My young Lord Viscount was exceedingly sorry when he heard that Harry could not come to the cock-match with him, and must go to London; but no doubt my lord consoled himself when the Hampshire cocks won the match; and he saw every one of the battles, and crowed properly over the conquered Sussex gentlemen.

William Makepeace Thackeray (1811–63)
The History of Henry Esmond (1852)

And here is Becky Sharp, the lively adventuress at the heart of Thackeray's brilliant novel, *Vanity Fair*, on her way to take up her position as governess to the daughters of Sir Pitt Crawley, whose home lies in the vicinity of Winchester. She writes to her bosom friend Amelia Sedley:

I was awakened at daybreak by the charwoman, and having arrived at the inn, was at first placed inside the coach. But, when we got to a place called Leakington, where the rain began to fall very heavily — will you believe it? — I was forced to come outside; for Sir Pitt is a proprietor of the coach, and as a passenger came at Mudbury, who wanted an inside place, I was obliged to go outside in the rain, where, however, a young gentleman from Cambridge College sheltered me very kindly in one of his several great coats.

This gentleman and the guard seemed to know Sir Pitt very well, and laughed at him a great deal. They both agreed in calling him an old screw; which means a very stingy, avaricious person. He never gives any money to anybody, they said (and this meanness I hate); and the young gentleman made me remark that we drove very slow for the last two stages on the road, because Sir Pitt was on the box, and because he is proprietor of the horses for this part of the journey. 'But won't I flog 'em on to Squashmore, when I take the ribbons?' said the young Cantab. 'And sarve 'em right, Master Jack,' said the guard. When I comprehended the meaning of this phrase, and that Master Jack intended to drive the rest of the way, and revenge himself on Sir Pitt's horses, of course I laughed too.

A carriage and four splendid horses, covered with armorial bearings, however, awaited us at Mudbury, four miles from Queen's Crawley, and we made our entrance to the baronet's park in state. There is a fine avenue of a mile long leading to the house, and the woman at the lodge-gate (over the pillars of which are a serpent and a dove, the supporters of the Crawley arms), made us a number of curtsies as she flung open the old iron carved doors, which are something like those at odious Chiswick.

'There's an avenue,' said Sir Pitt, 'a mile long. There's six thousand pound of timber in them there trees. Do you call that nothing?' He pronounced avenue—EVENUE, and nothing—NOTHINK, so droll; and he had a Mr Hodson, his hind from Mudbury, into the carriage with him, and they talked about distraining, and selling up, and draining and subsoiling, and a great deal about tenants and farming—much more than I could understand. Sam Miles had been caught poaching, and Peter Bailey had gone to the workhouse at last. 'Serve him right,' said Sir Pitt; 'him and his family has been cheating me on that farm these hundred and fifty years.' Some old tenant, I suppose, who could not pay his rent. Sir Pitt might have said 'he and his family,' to be sure; but rich baronets do not need to be careful about grammar, as poor governesses must be.

As we passed, I remarked a beautiful church-spire rising above some old elms in the park; and before them, in the midst of a lawn, and some outhouses, an old red house with tall chimneys covered with ivy, and the windows shining in the sun. 'Is that your church, sir?' I said.

'Yes, hang it,' (said Sir Pitt, only he used, dear, A MUCH WICKEDER WORD); 'how's Buty, Hodson? Buty's my brother Bute, my dear—my brother the parson. Buty and the Beast I call him, ha, ha!'

Hodson laughed too, and then looking more grave and nodding his head, said, 'I'm afraid he's better, Sir Pitt. He was out on his pony yesterday, looking at our corn.'

'Looking after his tithes, hang'un (only he used the same wicked word). Will brandy and water never kill him? He's as tough as old whatdyecallum—old Methusalem.'

Mr Hodson laughed again. 'The young men is home from college. They've whopped John Scroggins till he's well nigh dead.'

'Whop my second keeper!' roared out Sir Pitt.

'He was on the parson's ground, sir,' replied Mr Hodson; and Sir Pitt in a fury swore that if he ever caught 'em poaching on his ground, he'd transport 'em, by the lord he would. However, he said, 'I've sold the presentation of the living, Hodson; none of that breed shall get it, I war'nt'; and Mr Hodson said he was quite right: and I have no doubt from this that the two brothers are at variance—as brothers often are, and sisters too. Don't you remember the two Miss Scratchleys at Chiswick, how they used always to fight and quarrel—and Mary Box, how she was always thumping Louisa?

Presently, seeing two little boys gathering sticks in the wood, Mr Hodson jumped out of the carriage, at Sir Pitt's order, and rushed upon them with his whip. 'Pitch into 'em, Hodson,' roared the baronet; 'flog their little souls out, and bring 'em up to the house, the vagabonds; I'll commit 'em as sure as my name's Pitt.' And presently we heard Mr Hodson's whip cracking on the shoulders of the poor little blubbering wretches, and Sir Pitt, seeing that the malefactors were in custody, drove on to the hall.

All the servants were ready to meet us, and . . .

Here, my dear, I was interrupted last night by a dreadful thumping at my door: and who do you think it was? Sir Pitt

Crawley in his night-cap and dressing-gown, such a figure! As I shrank away from such a visitor, he came forward and seized my candle. 'No candles after eleven o'clock, Miss Becky,' said he. 'Go to bed in the dark, you pretty little hussy' (that is what he called me), 'and unless you wish me to come for the candle every night, mind and be in bed at eleven.' And with this, he and Mr Horrocks the butler went off laughing. You may be sure I shall not encourage any more of their visits. They let loose two immense bloodhounds at night, which all last night were yelling and howling at the moon. 'I call the dog Gorer,' said Sir Pitt; 'he's killed a man that dog has, and is master of a bull, and the mother I used to call Flora; but now I calls her Aroarer, for she's too old to bite. Haw, haw!'

Before the house of Queen's Crawley, which is an odious old-fashioned red brick mansion, with tall chimneys and gables of the style of Queen Bess, there is a terrace flanked by the family dove and serpent, and on which the great hall-door opens. And oh, my dear, the great hall I am sure is as big and as glum as the great hall in the dear castle of Udolpho. It has a large fireplace, in which we might put half Miss Pinkerton's school, and the grate is big enough to roast an ox at the very least. Round the room hang I don't know how many generations of Crawleys, some with beards and ruffs, some with huge wigs and toes turned out, some dressed in long straight stays and gowns that look as stiff as towers, and some with long ringlets, and oh, my dear! scarcely any stays at all. At one end of the hall is the great staircase all in black oak, as dismal as may be, and on either side are tall doors with stags' heads over them, leading to the billiard-room and the library, and the great yellow saloon and the morning-rooms. I think there are at least twenty bedrooms on the first floor; one of them has the bed in which Queen Elizabeth slept; and I have been taken by my new pupils through all these fine apartments this morning. They are not rendered less gloomy, I promise you, by having the shutters always shut; and there is scarce one of the apartments, but when the light was let into it, I expected to see a ghost in the room. We have a schoolroom on the second floor, with my bedroom leading into it on one side, and that of the young ladies on the other. Then there are Mr Pitt's apartments—Mr Crawley, he is called—the eldest son, and Mr

Rawdon Crawley's rooms—he is an officer like SOMEBODY, and away with his regiment. There is no want of room I assure you. You might lodge all the people in Russell Square in the house, I think, and have space to spare.

Half an hour after our arrival, the great dinner-bell was rung, and I came down with my two pupils (they are very thin insignificant little chits of ten and eight years old). I came down in your dear muslin gown (about which that odious Mrs Pinner was so rude, because you gave it me); for I am to be treated as one of the family, except on company days, when the young ladies and I are to dine upstairs.

Well, the great dinner-bell rang, and we all assembled in the little drawing-room where my Lady Crawley sits. She is the second Lady Crawley, and mother of the young ladies. She was an ironmonger's daughter, and her marriage was thought a great match. She looks as if she had been handsome once, and her eyes are always weeping for the loss of her beauty. She is pale and meagre and high-shouldered, and has not a word to say for herself, evidently. Her stepson Mr Crawley, was likewise in the room. He was in full dress, as pompous as an undertaker. He is pale, thin, ugly, silent; he has thin legs, no chest, hay-coloured whiskers, and straw-coloured hair. He is the very picture of his sainted mother over the mantelpiece—Griselda of the noble house of Binkie.

'This is the new governess, Mr Crawley,' said Lady Crawley, coming forward and taking my hand. 'Miss Sharp.'

'O!' said Mr Crawley, and pushed his head once forward and began again to read a great pamphlet with which he was busy.

'I hope you will be kind to my girls,' said Lady Crawley, with her pink eyes always full of tears.

'Law, Ma, of course she will,' said the eldest: and I saw at a glance that I need not be afraid of THAT woman. 'My lady is served,' says the butler in black, in an immense white shirt-frill, that looked as if it had been one of the Queen Elizabeth's ruffs depicted in the hall; and so, taking Mr Crawley's arm, she led the way to the dining-room, whither I followed with my little pupils in each hand.

Sir Pitt was already in the room with a silver jug. He had just been to the cellar, and was in full dress too; that is, he had taken his gaiters off, and showed his little dumpy legs in black worsted stockings. The sideboard was covered with glistening old plate—old cups, both gold and silver; old salvers and cruet-stands, like Rundell and Bridge's shop. Everything on the table was in silver too, and two footmen, with red hair and canary-coloured liveries, stood on either side of the sideboard.

Mr Crawley said a long grace, and Sir Pitt said amen, and the great silver dish-covers were removed.

'What have we for dinner, Betsy?' said the Baronet.

'Mutton broth, I believe, Sir Pitt,' answered Lady Crawley.

'Mouton aux navets,' added the butler gravely (pronounce, if you please, moutongonavvy); 'and the soup is potage de mouton a l'Ecossaise. The side-dishes contain pommes de terre au naturel, and choufleur a l'eau.'

'Mutton's mutton,' said the Baronet, 'and a devilish good thing. What SHIP was it, Horrocks, and when did you kill?'

'One of the black-faced Scotch, Sir Pitt: we killed on Thursday.'

'Who took any?'

'Steel, of Mudbury, took the saddle and two legs, Sir Pitt; but he says the last was too young and confounded woolly, Sir Pitt.'

'Will you take some potage, Miss ah—Miss Blunt?' said Mr Crawley.

'Capital Scotch broth, my dear,' said Sir Pitt, 'though they call it by a French name.'

'I believe it is the custom, sir, in decent society,' said Mr Crawley, haughtily, 'to call the dish as I have called it'; and it was served to us on silver soup plates by the footmen in the canary coats, with the mouton aux navets. Then 'ale and water' were brought, and served to us young ladies in wine-glasses. I am not a judge of ale, but I can say with a clear conscience I prefer water.

While we were enjoying our repast, Sir Pitt took occasion to ask what had become of the shoulders of the mutton.

'I believe they were eaten in the servants' hall,' said my lady, humbly.

'They was, my lady,' said Horrocks, 'and precious little else we get there neither.'

Sir Pitt burst into a horse-laugh, and continued his conversation with Mr Horrocks. 'That there little black pig of the Kent sow's breed must be uncommon fat now.'

'It's not quite busting, Sir Pitt,' said the butler with the gravest air, at which Sir Pitt, and with him the young ladies, this time, began to laugh violently.

'Miss Crawley, Miss Rose Crawley,' said Mr Crawley, 'your laughter strikes me as being exceedingly out of place.'

'Never mind, my lord,' said the Baronet, 'we'll try the porker on Saturday. Kill one on Saturday morning, John Horrocks. Miss Sharp adores pork, don't you, Miss Sharp?'

And I think this is all the conversation that I remember at dinner. When the repast was concluded a jug of hot water was placed before Sir Pitt, with a case-bottle containing, I believe, rum. Mr Horrocks served myself and my pupils with three little glasses of wine, and a bumper was poured out for my lady. When we retired, she took from her work-drawer an enormous interminable piece of knitting; the young ladies began to play at cribbage with a dirty pack of cards. We had but one candle lighted, but it was in a magnificent old silver candlestick, and after a very few questions from my lady, I had my choice of amusement between a volume of sermons, and a pamphlet on the corn-laws, which Mr Crawley had been reading before dinner.

So we sat for an hour until steps were heard.

'Put away the cards, girls,' cried my lady, in a great tremor; 'put down Mr Crawley's books, Miss Sharp'; and these orders had been scarcely obeyed, when Mr Crawley entered the room.

'We will resume yesterday's discourse, young ladies,' said he, 'and you shall each read a page by turns; so that Miss a— Miss Short may have an opportunity of hearing you'; and the poor girls began to spell a long dismal sermon delivered at Bethesda Chapel, Liverpool, on behalf of the mission for the Chickasaw Indians. Was it not a charming evening?

At ten the servants were told to call Sir Pitt and the household to prayers. Sir Pitt came in first, very much flushed, and rather unsteady in his gait; and after him the butler, the canaries, Mr Crawley's man, three other men, smelling very much of the stable, and four women, one of whom, I remarked, was very much overdressed, and who flung me a look of great scorn as she plumped down on her knees.

After Mr Crawley had done haranguing and expounding, we received our candles, and then we went to bed; and then I was disturbed in my writing, as I have described to my dearest sweetest Amelia.

Good night. A thousand, thousand, thousand kisses!

Saturday – This morning, at five, I heard the shrieking of the little black pig. Rose and Violet introduced me to it yesterday; and to the stables, and to the kennel, and to the gardener, who was picking fruit to send to market, and from whom they begged hard a bunch of hot-house grapes; but he said that Sir Pitt had numbered every 'Man Jack' of them, and it would be as much as his place was worth to give any away. The darling girls caught a colt in a paddock, and asked me if I would ride, and began to ride themselves, when the groom, coming with horrid oaths, drove them away.

Lady Crawley is always knitting the worsted. Sir Pitt is always tipsy, every night; and, I believe, sits with Horrocks, the butler. Mr Crawley always reads sermons in the evening, and in the morning is locked up in his study, or else rides to Mudbury, on county business, or to Squashmore, where he preaches, on Wednesdays and Fridays, to the tenants there.

A hundred thousand grateful loves to your dear papa and mamma. Is your poor brother recovered of his rack-punch? Oh, dear! Oh, dear! How men should beware of wicked punch!

Ever and ever thine own REBECCA

William Makepeace Thackeray (1811-63)
Vanity Fair: A Novel without a Hero (1847)

Thackeray and Dickens were the same age and admiring rivals as great novelists of the nineteenth century. Thackeray's daughter tells of her little sister, absorbed in her book, suddenly looking up to say, 'Papa, why do you not write books like Nicholas Nickleby?'

The Winchester Assizes, now the Crown Court, have for centuries been an important aspect of the life of the city. Here W. H. Hudson, the naturalist and writer, informs Edward Garnett of their complexion in the early twentieth century.

Oriel Temperance Hotel, Winchester
November 20th 1902

I found your note here to-day when I only came last evening, and am sorry you are suffering from a chill. How this awful cold hasn't killed me during the last two or three days I don't know. I delayed my departure from Silchester to give a lantern-slide exhibition to the school-children, and Tuesday evening was the time fixed by the Rector. I got about 80 slides and had a good room full – all the school-children and a sprinkling of adults. We finished some time after 9 o'clock and I then had to walk over the common – stumbling among the furze bushes in the dark in the face of the wind to get back. Next morning early I packed up and sent the lantern-slides &c. back to town, and went off myself – I had 4 miles to walk to Bramley, wait an hour and a half there for a train; wait again 2 hours at Basingstoke for one to Alton, and an hour and a half there for a train to Winchester! I was half dead with cold when I got here. What I wanted to do here I can't do – take some snapshots of places on the Itchen, so I think of starting tomorrow to Brockenhurst and staying a few days in that part. To-day I have spent the time in the Castle listening to criminals' trials before Mr Justice Day, and in the Cathedral for afternoon choral service. There were some dramatic incidents in Court to-day and I admired the Judge very much. He is a lover of birds and is Mrs Bontine's great friend, so I was inclined to admire him. But he was splendid on the Bench. He spoke with bitterness of the authorities here for keeping men 2 and 4 months in gaol before sending them to trial, and some of his sentences were so lenient that the poor condemned wretches were amazed themselves.

W. H. Hudson
Letters

Tess of the D'Urbervilles, in the haunting Wessex novel of that name, was less fortunate, condemned here to hang for the murder of Alec d'Urberville. Here, she and her man, Angel Clare, are resting at Stonehenge when the constables come for her.

…When they saw where she lay, which they had not done till then, they showed no objection, and stood watching her, as still as the pillars around. He went to the stone and bent over her, holding one poor little hand; her breathing now was quick and small, like that of a lesser creature than a woman. All waited in the growing light, their faces and hands as if they were silvered, the remainder of their figures dark, the stone glistening green-gray, the Plain still a mass of shade. Soon the light was strong, and a ray shone upon her unconscious form, peering under her eyelids waking her.

'What is it, Angel?' she said, starting up. 'Have they come for me?'

'Yes, dearest,' he said. 'They have come.'

'It is as it should be,' she murmured. 'Angel, I am almost glad – yes, glad! This happiness could not have lasted. It was too much. I have had enough; and now I shall not live for you to despise me!'

She stood up, shook herself, and went forward, neither of the men having moved.

'I am ready,' she said quickly.

... The city of Wintoncester, that fine old city, aforetime capital of Wessex, lay amidst its convex and concave downlands in all the brightness and warmth of a July morning. The gabled brick, tile, and freestone houses had almost dried off for the season their integument of lichen, the streams in the meadows were low, and in the sloping High Street, from the West Gateway to the medieval cross, and from the medieval cross to the bridge, that leisurely dusting and sweeping was in progress which usually ushers in an old-fashioned market-day.

From the western gate aforesaid the highway, as every Wintoncestrian knows, ascends a long and regular incline of the exact length of a measured mile, leaving the houses gradually behind. Up this road from the precincts of the city two persons were walking rapidly, as if unconscious of the trying ascent – unconscious through preoccupation and not through buoyancy. They had emerged upon this road through a narrow barred wicket in a high wall a little lower down. They seemed anxious to get out of the sight of the houses and of their kind, and this road appeared to offer the quickest means of doing so. Though they were young they walked with bowed heads, which gait of grief the sun's rays smiled on pitilessly.

One of the pair was Angel Clare, the other a tall budding creature – half girl, half woman – a spiritualised image of Tess, slighter than she, but with the same beautiful eyes – Clare's sister-in-law, 'Liza-Lu. Their pale faces seemed to have shrunk to half their natural size. They moved on hand in hand, and never spoke a word, the drooping of their heads being that of Giotto's 'Two Apostles'. When they had nearly reached the top of the great West Hill the clocks in the town struck eight. Each gave a start at the notes, and, walking onward yet a few steps, they reached the first milestone, standing whitely on the green margin of the grass, and backed by the down, which here was open to the road. They entered upon the turf, and, impelled by a force that seemed to overrule their will, suddenly stood still, turned, and waited in paralysed suspense beside the stone.

The prospect from this summit was almost unlimited. In the valley beneath lay the city they had just left, its more prominent buildings showing as in an isometric drawing – among them the broad cathedral tower, with its Norman windows and immense length of aisle and nave, the spires of St Thomas's, the pinnacled tower of the College, and, more to the right, the tower and gables of the ancient hospice, where to this day the pilgrim may receive his dole of bread and ale. Behind the city swept the rotund upland of St Catherine's Hill; further off, landscape beyond landscape, till the horizon was lost in the radiance of the sun hanging above it.

Against these far stretches of country rose, in front of the other city edifices, a large red-brick building, with level gray roofs, and rows of short barred windows bespeaking captivity, the whole contrasting greatly by its formalism with the quaint irregularity of the Gothic erections. It was somewhat disguised from the road in passing it by yews and evergreen oaks, but it was visible enough up here. The wicket from which the pair had lately emerged was in the wall of this structure. From the middle of the building an ugly flat-topped octagonal tower ascended against the east horizon, and viewed from this spot, on its shady side and against the light, it seemed the one blot on the city's beauty. Yet it was with this blot, and not with the beauty, that the two gazers were concerned.

Upon the cornice of the tower a tall staff was fixed. Their eyes were riveted on it. A few minutes after the hour had struck something moved slowly up the staff, and extended itself upon the breeze. It was a black flag.

'Justice' was done, and the President of the Immortals, in Aeschylean phrase, had ended his sport with Tess. And the d'Urberville knights and dames slept on in their tombs unknowing. The two speechless gazers bent themselves down to the earth, as if in prayer, and remained thus a long time, absolutely motionless: the flag continued to wave silently. As soon as they had strength they arose, joined hands again, and went on.

Thomas Hardy (1840–1928)
Tess of the D'Urbervilles (1892)

WINCHESTER COLLEGE

Founded in the fourteenth century by William of Wykeham to educate men for the clergy and public service, the seventy scholars were expected to continue their education at his foundation, New College, Oxford, and thence go out into the world well prepared. It is the oldest of England's so called Public Schools, a model for the later establishment of Eton. Today, the school has about 700 pupils, still all boys, and is known for its high academic standards. The pupils, known as Wykehamists, still use a unique slang called Notions, some of which can be found in the following pieces.

The following piece, describing the arrival of Matthew Arnold as a pupil at the school, bears out the tradition of scholarship at the college. Arnold (1822-1888) went on to become professor of poetry at Oxford and inspector of schools. His educational, literary and social creed was distinguished by what he called 'sweetness and light', which stands for beauty and intelligence, which he considered the key components of an excellent culture.

An old Wykehamist, who was at Winchester when Matthew Arnold entered in Short Half in 1836, recollects his coming very well and his being placed junior in Senior Part, Fifth Book, which was considered remarkably high. One of the first things he did was to complain to the Doctor [Moberley] that the work of the Senior Part was not sufficiently heavy and that there was nothing to do between 7.30 and 8 a.m. In consequence of this the Doctor promptly ordered that Senior Part should henceforth learn and say portions of Cicero's

Orations during this half hour; and a Commoner-Tutor was brought into school especially to hear this lesson; Arnold's conduct in causing an extra morning lesson to be introduced was resented by many, who thought that the work of the Senior Part was already sufficient.

Of this picaresque novel by Tobias Smollett, George Orwell writes that it is 'frankly pornographic in a harmless way' with 'some of the best passages of sheer farce in the English language'. The eponymous hero, rejected by family, begins a life of his own at Winchester College, much as he means to carry on.

Smollett's *Travels through France and Italy*, full of harsh criticism of foreign ways and means, shows where his heart lies when he reports, 'I hired a return coach-and-four from Pisa to Florence. This road, which lies along to Arno, is very good; and the country is delightful, variegated with hill and vale, wood and water, meadows and cornfields, planted and enclosed like the counties of Middlesex and Hampshire'.

Peregrine gave a loose to his inclinations, and by dint of genius and an enterprising temper, made a figure among the younger classes of heroes in the school.

Before he had been full year at Winchester, he had signalised himself in so many achievements, in defiance to the laws and regulations of the place, that he was looked upon with admiration, and actually chosen *Dux*, or leader, by a large body of his contemporaries...

His behaviour was now no other than a series of licence of effrontery; prank succeeded prank and outrage followed outrage, with surprising velocity. Complaints were every day preferred against him; in vain were admonitions bestowed by the governor in private, and menaces discharged by the master in public; he disregarded the first, despised the latter, divested himself of all manner of restraint, and proceeded in his career to such a pitch of audacity, that a consultation was held upon the subject, in which it was determined that this untoward spirit should be humbled by a severe and ignominious flogging for the very next offence he should commit...

He shook off his boyish connections and fixed his view upon objects which he thought more worthy of his attention... Being one evening at a ball which is always given to the ladies at the time of the races, the person who acted as master of the ceremonies, knowing how fond Mr Pickle was of every opportunity to display himself, came up and told him that there was a fine young creature at the other end of the room, who seemed to have a great inclination to dance a minuet, but wanted a partner, the gentleman who attended her being in boots.

Peregrine's vanity being aroused at this intimation, he went up to reconnoitre the young lady, and was struck with admiration at her beauty... her whole appearance [was] so captivating, that our young Adonis looked and was overcome... [The next day he found out from the young lady] that her habitation was about sixteen miles from Winchester, in a village which she named, and where [as he could easily gather from her discourse] he would be no unwelcome guest... [he] set out early one morning on foot for the village where his charmer lived, at which he arrived at two o'clock in the afternoon; having chosen this method of travelling, that his route might not be so easily discovered, as it might have been had he hired horses, or taken a place in a stage coach... While he remained under the influence of this sweet intoxication, his absence produced great disturbance at Winchester.

The nature of this adventure being unknown to all except those who could be depended upon, everybody who inquired about the cause of Peregrine's absence was told that he had been with a relation in the country, and the Master condescended to overlook his indiscretion... the Commander fearing that Perry was in danger of involving himself in some pernicious engagement, resolved to recall him from the place where he had contracted such imprudent connections, and send him to University where his education might be completed, and his fancy weaned from all puerile amusements... preparations were made for Peregrine's departure to the University, and in a few weeks he set out, in the seventeenth year of his age.

Tobias Smollett (1721-1771)
Peregrine Pickle (1751)

Anthony Trollope's miserable experience at Winchester College, and earlier at Harrow, are thought to have been instrumental in the formation of the prolific novelist, who constructed elaborate imaginary worlds to escape the horror of that in which he found himself. His first successful novel, *The Warden*, is believed to be set at St Cross in Winchester, an institution which many, from Defoe to Ralph Waldo Emerson, declared in need of reform.

When I was twelve there came a vacancy at Winchester College which I was destined to fill. My two elder brothers had gone there, and the younger had been taken away, being already supposed to have lost his chance of New College. It had been one of the great ambitions of my father's life that his three sons, who lived to go to Winchester, should all become fellows of New College. But that suffering man was never destined to have an ambition gratified. We all lost the prize which he struggled with infinite labour to put within our reach. My eldest brother all but achieved it, and afterwards went to Oxford, taking three exhibitions from the school, though he lost the great glory of a Wykamist. He has since made himself well known to the public as a writer in connection with all Italian subjects. He is still living as I now write. But my other brother died early.

...Over a period of forty years, since I began my manhood at a desk in the Post Office, I and my brother, Thomas Adolphus, have been fast friends. There have been hot words between us, for perfect friendship bears and allows hot words. Few brothers have had more of brotherhood. But in those school-days he was, of all my foes, the worst. In accordance with the practice of the college, which submits, or did then submit, much of the tuition of the younger boys from the elder, he was my tutor; and in his capacity of teacher and ruler, he had studied the theories of Draco. I remember well how he used to exact obedience after the manner of that lawgiver. Hang a little boy for stealing apples, he used to say, and other little boys will not steal apples. The doctrine was already exploded elsewhere, but he stuck to it with conservative energy. The result was that, as a part of his daily exercise, he thrashed me with a big stick. That such thrashings should have been possible at a school as a continual part of one's daily life, seems to me to argue a very ill condition of school discipline.

...After a while my brother left Winchester and accompanied my father to America. Then another and a different horror fell to my fate. My college bills had not been paid, and the school tradesmen who administered to the wants of the boys were told not to extend their credit to me. Boots, waistcoats, and pocket-handkerchiefs, which, with some slight superveillance, were at the command of other scholars, were closed luxuries to me. My schoolfellows of course knew that it was so, and I became a Pariah. It is the nature of boys to be cruel. I have sometimes doubted whether among each other they do usually suffer much, one from the other's cruelty; but I suffered horribly! I could make no stand against it. I had no friend to whom I could pour out my sorrows. I was big, and awkward, and ugly, and, I have no doubt, skulked about in a most unattractive manner. Of course I was ill-dressed and dirty. But, ah! How well I remember all the agonies of my young heart; how I considered whether I should always be alone; whether I could not find my way up to the top of that college tower, and from thence put an end to everything? And a worse thing came than the stoppage of the supplies from the shopkeepers. Every boy had a shilling a week pocket money, which we called battels, and which was advanced to us out of the pocket of the second master. On one awful day the second master announced to me that my battels would be stopped. He told me the reason,- the battels for the last half-year had not been repaid; and he urged his own unwillingness to advance the money. The loss of a shilling a week would not have been much, even though pocket-money from other sources never reached me, but that the other boys all knew it! Every now and again, perhaps three or four times in a half-year, these weekly shillings were given to certain servants of the college, in payment, it may be presumed, for some extra services. And now, when it came to the turn of any servant, he received sixty-nine shillings instead of seventy, and the cause of the defalcation was explained to him. I never saw one of those servants without feeling that I had picked his pocket.

When I had been at Winchester something over three years, my father returned to England and took me away. Whether this was done because of the expense, or because my chance of New College was supposed to have passed away, I do not know. As a fact, I should, I believe, have gained the prize, as there occurred in my year an exceptional number of vacancies. But it would have served me nothing, as there would have been no funds for my maintenance at the University till I should have entered in upon the fruition of the founder's endowment, and my career at Oxford must have been unfortunate.

When I left Winchester, I had three more years of school before me...

Anthony Trollope (1815-82)
An Autobiography (1883)

In his penultimate term at Winchester, Lord Alfred Douglas, later famous for his relationship with Oscar Wilde and its repercussions, founded a magazine, *Pentagram*, intended to mock the established school magazine the *Wykehamist*. Its tenth and last edition sold more copies than there were boys in the school. This poem of his is full of Winchester slang.

Triolets

I'm up to books at nine o'clock:
I haven't done my out of school:
Five past! Oh Heavens! What a shock,
I'm up to books at nine o'clock.
My 'toys' are shut? Well burst the lock.
Now my straw hat; 'Play up' you fool!
I'm up to books at five o'clock.
I haven't done my out of school.

You writing lines? Yes. So am I,
For shirking Chapel Sunday last.
Halloa! I hear another sigh:
You writing lines? Yes. So am I;
That's three of us; and here close by
Another scribbling very fast:
YOU writing lines? Yes. So am I,
For shirking Chapel Sunday last.

And here, later, and in nostalgic mood:

A dream of Winchester Days

Creeping backward through the valley of time,
Tracing the tangled skein of lost ways,
Comes my sad soul seeking with a rhyme,
To begin again a palace of dead days.

Very faint at last comes the echo of voices,
Friendly voices, once loud in my ears,
So faint that scarcely my sad soul rejoiced
But rather sighs, half sadly, half with tears

Out the curious byways of memory,
Come many ghosts. Hither come the pale doubt
That quenched a flame of friendship, once so fiery
I had thought only death could put it out.

A crowd of faces are looking at me
Most of these have I loved, all I have known
Whose face is that looking at me wistfully?
Can that be the boy's face that was my own?

Lord Alfred Douglas (1870–1945)

Here, the hero of A. G. Macdonell's satirical novel about English urban and rural society in the 1920s, the Scotsman and journalist Donald visits Winchester, a city the author knew well from his schooldays at the College.

...Donald uttered a loud cry and sprang from his bed, dived into a cold bath, hurled on his clothes, rushed into the street, and drove in a taxi-cab to Waterloo Station and took a train, choosing at random, to the town of Alton.

He walked a bit from Alton, and then lorry-hopped, in army fashion, as far as the straggly, red-tiled village of Alresford, where he got off for a drink of Hampshire beer, and then lorry-hopped again across the high chalky downs until the water-meads of Itchen lay below him on the right, and below him in front, the ancient City of Winchester, city of Alfred, once capital of England, perhaps even the Camelot of Arthur.

Donald got off the lorry at the top of St Giles' Hill and dropped leisurely down into the High Street, at the end of which is the statue of Alfred...

Thence his wanderings took him past the Judges' Lodging and the Deanery and the lovely Canonries and the dusty Elizabethan tithe-barn, through an archway into the outer world of laymen, and through another archway into College Street. The summer term had just begun and the street was crowded with boys and young men, all wearing straw hats...

He visited the College Buildings... the Winchester motto was the extraordinary one of "Manners Makyth Man"...he stopped a small, black-gowned boy, about twelve years of age, and asked politely:

"Can you tell me, please, what that tree is?"

The boy took off his straw hat and replied with equal politeness:

"That is Lord's tree, sir."

"Lord's tree?" said Donald, also taking off his hat. "What is that?"

"It is called that, sir, because only men in Lord's are allowed to sit on the seat at the foot of it," explained the child.

"I am sorry to appear stupid," Donald apologised, "but when you say 'Men in Lord's' do you refer to the Peers of the Realm?"

"By no means," replied the infant. "Men in Lord's are the men in the cricket eleven."

"Oh, I see. The cricket eleven is called Lord's because they go to Lord's to play cricket."

"No, sir. They don't go to Lord's."

"Then why are they called Lord's?" Donald was getting confused.

"Because we used until quite recently to play at Lord's against Eton."

"Ah! Now I begin to understand. Until a few years ago; how many years, by the way?"

"About seventy or eighty, sir."

Donald kept a firm grip upon himself, and tried to speak naturally as he answered: "Quite so. Just the other day. I see.

And the boys in the cricket eleven…"

"Men," interrupted the child firmly.

"I beg your pardon,"

"Men," repeated the child. "We are all men here. There are no boys."

Donald, by now quite dizzy, bowed and thanked the man for his trouble.

"It was a pleasure," replied the man, bowing courteously and removing his hat again and going on his way.

Donald, hat in hand, turned and watched him, and was immensely relieved to see the man halt after going a few yards, and extract a huge and sticky piece of toffee from his trouser-pocket, and cram it into his mouth.

A. G. Macdonell (1895–1941)
England their England (1933)

John Betjeman, poet, broadcaster and architectural campaigner, here describes what he obviously thinks of as an archetypal product of the college, thought to be Richard Crossman, Labour MP and one-time editor of the *New Statesman*, who is best remembered today for his *Diaries of a Cabinet Minister*.

The Wykehamist
(to Randolph Churchill but not about him)

Broad of Church and broad of mind,
Broad before and broad behind,
A keen ecclesiologist,
A rather dirty Wykehamist.
'Tis not for us to wonder why
He wears that curious knitted tie;
We should not cast reflections on
The very slightest kind of don.
We should not giggle as we like
At his appearance on his bike;
It's something to become a bore,
And more than that, at twenty-four.
It's something too to know your wants
And go full pelt for Norman fonts.

Just now the chestnut trees are dark
And full with shadow in the park,
And 'six o'clock' St Mary calls
Above the mellow college walls.
The evening stretches arms to twist
And captivate her Wykehamist.
But not for him these autumn days,
He shuts them out with heavy baize;
He gives his Ovaltine a stir
And nibbles at a 'petit beurre',
And, satisfying fleshly wants,
He settles down to Norman fonts.

John Betjeman (1906–84)

Chapter 2
Southampton: harbour city

Southampton, the largest city in the county, is mother to the word Hampshire. Originally an Anglo-Saxon trading port – Hamtun – strategically placed where the rivers Test and Itchen meet the sea, the hinterland came to be known as 'Hamtunscire', later Hantscire or Southamptonshire.

No historian has been able to explain how it was that Hamtun emerged out of the chaos of the Dark Ages as a fully-fledged trading town in the sixth century. It was clearly wealthy, for more Anglo-Saxon coins have been found here than anywhere else in Britain. It was also confidently laid out like a classical city, with a neat grid of gravelled streets spread over 100 acres. The rectangular dwellings were of a uniform size and contained wells for clean water and waste disposal pits. It was home to a skilled population of three thousand, many of them traders, but it also housed craftsmen working in iron, copper, leather and bone. It may be that industrious Friesians, migrating from the collapsing coastline of northern Europe, made this all possible. Hamtun certainly had many natural advantages as a marketplace. The Solent estuary on which it sits is a flooded river valley, with banks as neatly trimmed as a vast canal, and with a double tide which makes it light work for ships' captains. And sited on the junction of two rivers, it offered not only rich fishing but also a natural trading route into sheep- and cattle-rich Hampshire.

The Danes brought this promising city to bloody ruin in AD 842, and forced civilised life inland, where it took refuge behind the old Roman walls of Winchester. However Southampton is one of several places competing as the site of King Canute's apocryphal parable with the waves. Far from believing his power was such that he could stop the tide, in fact Canute was demonstrating to a band of fawning courtiers that God was more powerful than he and that he had no power over His creation.

The town was only convincingly revived under the strong authority of the Norman crown which ruled both sides of the Channel. South Hamtun boomed, and became a great medieval trading port, shipping out English wool and shipping in French wines. The city had docks, a customs house, an administrative castle and different quarters for the French and English merchants. It was also rich enough to suffer from pirate raids, which explains the magnificent evidence of the city's medieval walls, complete with thirteen extant towers and six gateways, built and rebuilt between the eleventh and fifteenth centuries. These medieval walls are one of the best urban survivals in all of England.

During this period and beyond, English monarchs frequently marched through Hampshire to embark from Southampton on some foreign sally. It was here that Richard the Lionheart set off on the Crusades in 1190, and from here, in 1415, that young King Henry V organised his invasion of France, as Shakespeare's chorus prepares us:

> The king is set from London; and the scene
> Is now transported, gentles, to Southampton:
> There is the play house now, there must you sit;
> And thence to France shall we convey you safe,
> And bring you back, charming the narrow seas
> To give you gentle pass; for if we may,
> We'll not offend one stomach with our play.
> But till the king come forth and not till then
> Unto Southampton do we shift our scene.

During his time in Southampton he discovered a plot against him whilst drinking in the Red Lion Inn, where you can still drink today. To enforce greater obedience, three of his Barons were accused and summarily convicted of treason, before being dragged outside the Bargate to their deaths.

But despite the victory of Agincourt, the old cultural unity between western France and England (under the Norman, Angevin and Plantaganet dynasties) was about to end – and with it the prosperity of Hamtun. By the eighteenth century, the city had decayed into a genteel spa town, where the visiting gentry bathed in rock pools overlooked by romantic medieval ruins. It was just the sort of place where a vicar's widow could find cheap but respectable lodgings, and between 1807–9 the Austen family spent four years here, hiring the upstairs drawing room of The Dolphin coaching inn for Jane Austen's eigheenth birthday party.

The long Victorian peace of the nineteenth century allowed commercial life to flow back to the city. Encouraged by the railway from London which arrived in 1840, and further promoted by the construction of new docks in 1842, prosperity was confirmed when Southampton was chosen as one of two home ports for the fourteen ships of the Royal Mail Packet line. Cunard and P & O followed, fighting a hundred-year war for supremacy of the waves with the Black Ball and White Star lines out of Liverpool. By the '20s and '30s Southampton was pre-eminent, and controlled half the British ocean-going passenger traffic, as well as serving as hub for the flying boats of the brand new Imperial Airways. But such eminence came at a price. When the *Titanic* went down in 1912, four out of five members of the crew came from Southampton. This disaster still catches the imagination of the world, though statistically it was just the tip of the iceberg for Sotonian seamen, who died in huge numbers during the submarine war waged by Germany against British shipping in both the First and Second World Wars.

Southampton, due to its expertise in early aircraft design, was home to the Spitfire, which saved the nation during the Battle of Britain. But this meant that its docks, engineering works and rail yards became a key target for Luftwaffe bombing raids, the shape of the city in blackout neatly defined at night by the moonlight reflecting off the surrounding water. Thus the elegant eighteenth-century city centre was flattened.

But the city managed to reinvent itself in the post-war period. A brand new container port was built in the '60s and it also became home to Esso's giant oil refinery at Fawley. Old liners became vast cruise ships, but they still make their berths at Southampton. The city's football team, the Saints, triumphed over Manchester United in the FA Cup in 1976, and research teams at the university lead the world in oceanography, optoelectronics, sonic and cancer sciences. There are now a quarter of a million Sotonians, the city's bloodline enriched by generation after generation of migrant seamen, including a large Polish community.

...

John Leland, earliest of modern English antiquaries, has been called 'the father of English local history and bibliography'. His *Itinerary* was first published in 1710. Leland was a scholar sponsored, it seems, by Cardinal Wolsey until his fall and then by Thomas Cromwell, who presented him to the living of Laverstoke in Hampshire.

He recommended himself to his King in *A New Year's Gift* (1545) with an account of his 'labyrouse journey: I have so travelid yn yowr dominions booth by the se costes and the middle partes, sparing nother labor nor costes, by the space of these vi. yeres paste, that there is almost nother cape, nor bay, haven, creke or peere, river or confluence of rivers, breches, waschis, lakes, meres, fenny waters, montaynes, valleis, mores, hethes, forsestes, wooddes, cities, burges, castelles, principale manor placis, monasteries, and colleges, but I have seene them; and notid yn so doing a hole worlde of things very memorable'.

The town of Old-Hampton a celebrate thing for fisschar men, and sum merchauntes, stoode a quarter of a mile or ther aboute from New-Hampton by north est and streachyd to the haven syde. The plotte wheryn it stoode berith now good corn and gresse, and is namyid S. Maryfeld by the chirch of S. Mary stonding hard by it. Sum men yet alyve have seene dyvers houses (especially up into the lande of Old-Hampton) withyn the feld self now caullyd S. Maryfeeld. Some thinke that the great suburbe standing yet without the est gate of New-Hampton and joyninge to S. Marie Chirche is part of Old-Hamptoun.

Ther is a chapel of S. Nicholas a poore and smaul thing yet stonding at the est end of S. Marie Chirch in the great cemiterie, wher constant fame is that the old paroche chirch of Old-Hampton stoode. One told me there that the litlenes of this chirch was cause of the erection of the great chirch of our Lady ther now stonding by this occasion: one Matilde, Quene of England, askid what it ment, that a great numbre of people walkyd about the chirch of S. Nicholas, and one answeryd; it is for lak of rome in the chirche. She then ex voto promisid to make ther a new; and this was the originale of S. Marie Chirch. And there be many fair tumbes of marble of marchauntes of New-Hampton buryed in the church of S. Marie, as yn their mother and principale chirch…

The old town of Hampton was brent in tyme of warre, spoyled and rasyd by French pyrates.

This was the cause that the inhabitantes there translatid themself to a more commodious place, and began with the kinges licens and help to builde New-Hampton and to waulle yt yn defence of the enemies.

Ther be yn the fair and right stronge waulle of New-Hampton these gates:

Fyrst Barre gate by north large and welle embatelid. In the upper parte of this gate is domus civica: and undernethe is the toun prison. There is a greate suburbe without this gate, and ther is a great double dike welle waterid on eche hand without it. And so 4. tourres in the waulle, (whereof the 3. as a corner towre is very fair stronge) to the est gate.

The Est gate is strong, but nothing so large as the Barre-gate. There be vj. fair tourres in the walle betwixt the est gate and the south gate: and loke as the town without the waulle is doble dichid from the castelle to Barre-gate, and so to est gate; so it is from est gate almost even to south gate.

The South Gate stondith not even ful south but south est: and ther is ioinyd to it a castelet welle ordinauncid to bete that quarter of the haven.

Ther is a nother meane gate a litle more south caullid Goddeshouse-Gate, of an hospitale yoinid to it.

And not far beyond it is a fair gate caullid the Water gate: without the wich is a faire square key forsid with piles into the haven water for shippes to resort to.

Then a 3. towrres to the west gate.

The West Gate is strong, and even without it is a large key for shippes, as there is without the water gate...

There be 5. paroche chirches withyn the toun of Hampton...

There be 3. principal streates yn Hampton, whereof that that goithe from the barre-gate to the water gate is one the fairest streates that ys yn any town of al England, and it is welle buildid for timbre building...

There cummith fresch water into Hampton by a conduct of leade, and there be certen castelletes onto this conduct withyn the town.

John Leland (1503-52)
The laboryouse journey & serche of Johan Leylande
for Englandes antiquitees (1534-43)

Samuel Pepys, who worked as a civil servant on the Navy Board, and was thus a frequent visitor the naval base at Portsmouth and elsewhere in Hampshire, is the first of many to describe Southampton as having 'one gallant street', a description that continues right up into the twentieth century. Sir Bevis of Hampton (c 1324), whose image he mentions, is a legendary hero. Pepys is best known as a diarist, whose observations of the Restoration, the Great Fire of London and the Plague, have made him the voice of the nation for that period.

26th April 1662

Sir G and I and his clerk, Mr Stephens, and Mr Holt our guide, over to Gosport, and so rode to Southampton. On our way, besides my Lord Southampton's parks and lands, which in one view we could see £6000 per annum, we observed a little churchyard, where the graves are accustomed to be all Sowed with Sage. At Southampton we went to the Mayors, and there dined, and had Sturgeon, of their own catching the last week, which doth not happen in twenty year, and it was well ordered. They brought us also some Caveare, which I attempted to order, but all to no purpose, for they had neither given it salt enough nor are the seeds of the roe broke, but are all in berryes. The towne is all one gallant street – and is walled round with stone, and Bevis's picture upon one of the gates. Many old walls of religious houses, and the Keye well worth seeing. After dinner to horse again, being in nothing troubled but the badness of my hat, which I borrowed to save my beaver.

Samuel Pepys (1633-1703)
Diary (1825)

Celia Fiennes, whose unusually extensive travels through England are an important source of information, was particularly interested in the new, in innovation and in the 'production and manufactures of each place', seemingly constructing an image of the country from its work as well as its geography and buildings. This description of Southampton is typical.

…Southampton is a very neate clean town and the streets well pitch'd and kept so, by their Carrying all their Carriages on sleds as they do in Holland, and permit no cart to go about in ye town, and keep it Clean Swept – this was more strictly observed when the town was full of trade, for it is a good port, but now ye trade has failed and ye town almost forsook and neglected. It's a place of No Strength now, by reason of ye castle being ruined and the fortification neglected and thr Gunns taken thence. Tho' by most its thought the best scittuated port for Shipps to Ride and take their provision in and so Capable of tradeing; but the last 2 Reignes for near 40 year discourag'd it being a proper place for the French to have Seiz'd and Secured for themselves. About 3 leagues off is Cashot Castle just out into the Sea wch does Encompasse it all but a very little point of land Called Horsy Beach that runnes out into the New forrest by Bewly wch was an abby in the fforest, for the Extent of the fforrest is large – Miles long; All round Casholt Castle on the Beach its as full of fine Cockle shells so that they heap them up all round the Castle like a wall.

Celia Fiennes (1662–1741)
Through England on a Side Saddle in the time of William and Mary

Daniel Defoe, travelling a little later, takes Fiennes' interest in commerce and turns it into a genre, 'economic tourism', which becames a staple of the eighteenth and nineteenth centuries.

Southampton is a truly antient town, for 'tis in a manner dying with age; the decay of the trade is the real decay of the town; and all the business of moment that is transacted there, is the trade between us and the islands of Jersey and Guernsey, with a little of the wine trade, and much smuggling: The building of ships also is much stop'd of late; however, the town is large, has many people in it, a noble fair High-Street, a spacious key; and if its trade should revive, is able to entertain great numbers of people: There is a French church, and no inconsiderable congregation, which was a help to the town, and there are still some merchants who trade to Newfoundland, and to the Streights with fish; but for all other trade, it may be said of Southampton as of other towns, London has eaten it up.

Daniel Defoe (1660–1731)
Travels (1720)

In 1808, the Marquess of Lansdowne built a mansion in a Gothic style on the motte of Southampton Castle, using stones from the old keep; known as Lansdowne Castle it provided fine views across the town. The castle was pulled down soon after the Napoleonic wars. William Lisle Bowles, author of the following poem, was a clergyman and better known, or certainly better regarded, as a critic than a poet. He considered nature as the great poetic subject perhaps, as appears here, because in it he finds the hand of God.

Southampton Castle
(inscribed to the Marquis of Lansdowne 1789)

The moonlight is without; and I could lose
An hour to gaze, though Taste and Splendour here,
As in a lustrous fairy palace, reign!
Regardless of the lights that blaze within,
I look upon the wide and silent sea,
That in the shadowy moonbeam sleeps: How still,
Nor heard to murmur, or to move, it lies;
Shining in Fancy's eye, like the soft gleam,
The eve of pleasant yesterdays! The clouds
Have all sunk westward, and the host of stars
Seem in their watches set, as gazing on;
While night's fair empress, sole and beautiful,
Holds her illustrious course through the mid heavens
Supreme, the spectacle, for such she looks,
Of gazing worlds! How different the scene
That lies beneath this arched window's height!
The town, that murmured through the busy day,
Is hushed; the roofs one solemn breadth of shade
Veils; but the towers, and taper spires above,
The pinnets, and the gray embattled walls,
And masts that throng around the southern pier,
Shine all distinct in light; and mark, remote,
O'er yonder elms, St Mary's modest fane,
Oh! If such views may please, to me they shine
How more attractive! But few years have passed,
Since there I saw youth, health, and happiness,
All circling round an aged sire, whose hairs
Are now in peace gone down; he was to me
A friend, and almost with a father's smile
Hung o'er my infant Muse. The cheerful voice
Of fellowship, the song of harmony,
And mirth, and wit were there. That scene is passed:
Cold death and separation have dissolved

The evening circle of once-happy friends!
So has it ever fared, and so must fare,
With all! I see the moonlight watery tract
That shines far off, beneath the forest-shades:
What seems it, but the mirror of that tide,
Which noiseless, 'mid the changes of the world,
Holds its inevitable course, the tide
Of years departing; to the distant eye
Still seems motionless, though hurrying on
From morn till midnight, bearing, as it flows,
The sails of pleasurable barks! These gleam
To-day, to-morrow other passing sails
Catch the like sunshine of the vernal morn.
Our pleasant days are as the moon's brief light
On the pale ripple, passing as it shines!
But shall the pensive bard for this lament,
Who knows how transitory are all worlds
Before His eye who made them! Cease the strain;
And welcome still the social intercourse
That soothes the world's loud jarring, till the hour
When, the universal darkness wrapping all
This nether scene, a light from heaven shall stream
Through clouds dividing, and a voice be heard:
Here only pure and lasting bliss is found!

William Lisle Bowles (1762–1850)

Bowles was educated at Winchester and became chaplain to the Prince Regent. His *Fourteen Sonnets* had a marked effect on young Coleridge. Cadland, his inspiration here, is Capability Brown's smallest surviving pleasure ground, a miniature landscaped park with views across the Solent towards the Isle of Wight.

Cadland, Southampton Water

If ever sea-maid, from her coral cave,
Beneath the hum of the great surge, has loved
To pass delighted from her green abode,
And, seated on a summer bank, to sing
No earthly music; in a spot like this,

The bard might feign he heard her, as she dried
Her golden hair, yet dripping from the main,
In the slant sunbeam. So the pensive bard
Might image, warmed by this enchanting scene,
The ideal form; but though such things are not,
He who has ever felt a thought refined;
He who has wandered on the sea of life,
Forming delightful visions of a home
Of beauty and repose; he who has loved,
With filial warmth his country, will not pass
Without a look of more than tenderness
On all the scene; from where the pensile birch
Bends on the bank, amid the clustered group
Of the dark hollies; to the woody shore
That steals diminished, to the distant spires
Of Hampton, crowning the long lucid wave.
White in the sun, beneath the forest-shade,
Full shines the frequent sail, like Vanity,
As she goes onward in her glittering trim,
Amid the glances of life's transient morn,
Calling on all to view her! Vectis there,
That slopes its greensward to the lambent wave,
And shows through the softest haze its woods and domes,
With gray St Catherine's creeping to the sky,
Seems like a modest maid, who charms the more
Concealing half her beauties. To the East,
Proud yet complacent, on its subject realm,
With masts innumerable thronged, and hulls
Seen indistinct, but formidable, mark
Albion's vast fleet, that, like the impatient storm,
Waits but the word to thunder and flash death
On him who dares approach to violate
The shores and living scenes that smile secure
Beneath its dragon-watch! Long may they smile!
And long, majestic Albion (while the sound
From East to West, from Albis to the Po,
Of dark contention hurtles) may'st thou rest,
As calm and beautiful this sylvan scene
Looks on the refluent wave that steals below.

William Lisle Bowles (1762–1850)

The particular charm of this description of the city by Sir Henry C Englefield is that although he repeats much of what others have previously reported, he stalks the pavements of the city and describes it at the very time that Jane Austen would have seen it.

The town of Southampton is situated on the extreme point of the high gravelly bank which separates the course of the Itchen river from the estuary of the Test, or Anton Water. By this happy choice, the whole town, though almost surrounded by water, enjoys the advantage of the driest situation; and the fall of level, in every direction, keeps the streets constantly free from damp and filth. Besides these essential benefits a great proportion of the houses enjoy a view more or less extensive of the beautiful country adjacent; and as the gravelly soil lies on a bed of clay, numerous wells afford a copious supply of water fit for most domestic purposes, if not always excellent for drinking. As however the principle object of this essay is to point out the objects of antiquity, or other remarkable buildings, which may attract the notice of a stranger, enough has been said on the general situation of the town.

The principle and indeed the only approach to the town from the land, is by an extensive and well-built suburb, in which nothing occurs worthy of remark excepting a large Elm tree on the left side of the road which is still called the Pound Elm, from the ancient pound of the town which once occupied that spot. This suburb was separated from the town by a very broad and deep ditch which has been filled up within the memory of several persons yet living.

…On the shore between the high and low water mark, near the platform, stood the Admiralty Gallows belonging to the local jurisdiction of the town.

From the tower and gate the wall runs in a direction nearly west for about one hundred and twenty yards having the sea washing its foot till it meets the Great or East Quay. In this length it is defended by one large and high turret at which it makes a little bend to the northward. An ancient gate with a low pointed arch, with a groove for a portcullis, and machicolations over it, opens on this quay; which projects into the river about one hundred and thirty yards and is evidently as ancient (at least in part) as the town itself. This water gate has been so defaced by houses built against it on every side, that it not easy to make out its original form; nor can we now trace the manner in which it was connected to the wall to the south east of it, the line of which projects at least thirty feet beyond the outer front of the gate. The demolition of an old house built against it has lately brought down all the machicolations; and in its present mutilated state no one but a staunch antiquary could much lament its total removal; which is seriously talked of and which would essentially conduce to the convenience of the commerce carried on upon the quay. Just beyond the northern part of this gate, two machicolations appear in the wall which perhaps defended another gate or postern opening on the quay for the more convenient carrying on the trade of it.

At the bottom of the High Street, on the right hand, we enter Porter's-lane which is so narrow and closed by overhanging old houses that it is difficult to view the front of a very considerable and most curious edifice which has much the appearance of having been a magnificent dwelling or palace.

The walk to the Itchen ferry at high water is very beautiful commanding a view of the opposite steep and woody shore and enlivened with a multitude of vessels of different sizes, laid up or under repair. The little round building called the Cross-house, erected for the accommodation of passengers waiting for the boat has marks of considerable antiquity, and is not an ugly edifice.

The hamlet of Northam which stands directly opposite to Bittern on the southern bank of the Itchen was probably in some degree inhabited at the same period as coins are said to have been found there. It is probable that the mouth of the Itchen was at that time, and long afterwards, much wider than it is now, and that the water flowed in nearly a straight line from Northam to St Mary's churchyard and from thence to the present south gate, in a curve, not far from the line of the town wall, covering the whole marsh and the site of the buildings on the same level now called Orchard-lane, Spring-gardens etc Nothing indeed but artificial embankments, prevents the sea at high water from inundating these places at the present day.

In this line the distance from Northam to St Mary's is not great and the springs of Houndwell would naturally draw the inhabitants of Northam from a spot without water to one so well supplied with that most necessary article, and at least equally well situated for fishing, or other nautical occupations. This probably was the state of things until Saxon conquerors of the kingdom having formed permanent establishments in the country from which they had nearly swept its ancient inhabitants began to wage perpetual intestine wars and of course to fortify the most important posts after the manner of their own nation. The establishments of the Romans which seem to have been seated in general in low situations, and near streams, did not at all suit with the northern system of fortresses; which, particularly in the earliest times, affected elevated sites, with high towers, secured from surprise by the view they commanded of the country around them; and from assault by the steep ascent of the natural or artificial mount on which they were founded. The peculiar advantages of the narrow and rather high point of land on which Southampton now stands, commanding at once the Itchen and Test, and very easily fortified on the land side, could not escape their notice; and from the high circular hill on which the keep of the castle formerly stood and the curved line of its yet remaining wall, we have probable grounds for supposing it to be among the most ancient of Saxon castles. But besides the existing fortifications there is great reason to suspect that the northern ditch of the town, filled up within the memory of man, and of uncommon breadth and depth, was continued quite across until it met the Itchen, and completely insulated the castle and the present town.

Sir Henry C Englefield (1752–1822)
A Walk through Southampton (1801)

Some two years before ill health sent the poet Keats again to the Isle of Wight in search of a healthy sea air, he came to Southampton in 1817 on his way there, looking for a place where he could work in solitude on *Endymion*, the first line of which had already come to him. In his luggage were seven volumes of Shakespeare, to which he refers below, evidently with his island destination in mind. 'There's my Comfort' would seem to be a reference to Stephano's line about the bottle in his hand in *The Tempest*: 'Here's my comfort'.

To George and Thomas Keats
Tuesday April 15 1817

My dear Brothers,
I am safe at Southampton – after having ridden three stages outside and the rest in for it began to be very cold. I did not know the Names of any of the towns I passed through all I can tell you is that sometimes I saw dusty Hedges sometimes Ponds – then nothing – then a little Wood with trees look you like Launce's Sister 'as white as a Lilly and as small as a Wand' – then came houses which died away into a few straggling Barns then came hedge trees aforesaid again. As the Lamp light crept along the following things were discovered. 'long heath brown furze' – Hurdles here and there half a Mile – Park palings when the Windows of a House were always discovered by reflection – One Nymph of Fountain N.B Stone – lopped Trees – Cow ruminating – ditto Donkey – Man and Woman going gingerly along – William seeing his Sisters over the Heath – John waiting with a Lanthen for his Mistress – Barber's Pole – Doctor's Shop – However after having had my fill of these I popped my Head out just as it began to Dawn – N.B. this tuesday Morn saw the sun rise – of which I shall say nothing at present – I felt rather lonely this Morning at breakfast so I went and unbox'd a Shakespeare – 'There's my Comfort' – I went immediately after Breakfast to the Southampton Water where I enquired for the Boat to the Isle of Wight as I intend seeing that place before I settle – it will go at 3 so shall I after having taken a Chop – I know nothing of this place but that it is long – tolerably broad – has bye streets – two or three Churches – a very respectable old Gate with two Lions to guard it – the Men and Women do not materially differ from those I have been in the Habit of seeing – I forgot to say that from dawn till half past six I went through a most delightful Country – some open Down but for the most part thickly wooded. What surprised me most was an immense quantity of blooming Furze on each side the road cutting a most rural dash – The Southampton water when I saw it just now was no better than a low Water.

Water which did no more than answer my expectations – it will have mended its manners by 3 – From the W(h)arf are seen the shores on each side stretching to the Isle of Wight …

John Keats
Selected Letters (2002)

The American novelist Nathaniel Hawthorne, author of *The Scarlet Letter*, came to England after the success of the novel as United States Consul at Liverpool, a lucrative post which he held for four years. In the following passage, S stands for Sophia, Nathaniel's wife. Their children are U – Una, J – Julian and R – Rose.

October 11th. We all left London on Sunday morning, between ten and eleven, from the Waterloo station, and arrived in Southampton about two, without meeting with anything very remarkable on the way. We put up at Chapple's Castle Hotel, which is one of the class styled 'commercial,' and, though respectable, not such a one as the nobility and gentry usually frequent. I saw little difference in the accommodation, except that young women attended us instead of men, – a pleasant change. It was a showery day, but J– and I walked out to see the shore and the town and the docks, and, if possible, the ship in which S– was to sail [to Lisbon with Rose]. The most noteworthy object was the remains of an old castle, near the water-side; the square, gray, weed-grown, weird keep of which shows some modern chimney-pots above its battlements, while remaining portions of the fortress are made to seem as one of the walls for coal-depots, and perhaps for small dwellings. The English characteristically patch new things into old things in this manner, materially, legally, constitutionally, and morally. Walking along the pier, we observed some pieces of ordnance, one of which was a large brass cannon of Henry VIII's time, about twelve feet long, and very finely made. The bay of Southampton presents a pleasant prospect, and I believe it is the great rendezvous of the yacht-club. Old and young seafaring people were strolling about, and lounging at corners, just as they do on Sunday afternoons in the minor seaports of America.

From the shore we went up into the town, which is handsome, and of a cheerful aspect, with streets generally wide and well paved, – a cleanly town, not smoke-begrimed. The houses, if not modern, are, at least with few exceptions, new fronted. We saw one relic of antiquity – a fine medieval gateway across the principal street, much more elevated than the gates of Chester, with battlements at the top, and a spacious apartment over the great arch for the passage of carriages, and the smaller one on each side for foot-passengers. There were two statues in armour or antique costume on the hither side of the gateway, and two old paintings on the other. This, so far as I know, is the only remnant of the old wall of Southampton.

On Monday the morning was bright, alternating with a little showeriness. U–, J–, and I went into the town to do some shopping before the steamer should sail; and a little after twelve we drove down to the dock.

Nathaniel Hawthorne (1804–64)
Southampton: an account of his visit to the city in 1854

Walter White was a cabinet-maker who published accounts of his holiday walks and here gives us, in little, a busy, personal, ninety minutes of his time.

Arriving at Southampton some passengers are made to wait an hour and a half for a train to carry them on to Dorsetshire. I spent the interval in a walk round the docks, where a number of that grand fleet of steamers, the names of which were then in everyone's mouths, were then lying. I saw the *Atrata*, the *La Plata*, the *Orinoco,* and others, ready to sail or in the eager bustle of preparation; and there too was the *Himalaya*, which had only that morning got off the mud bank that stopped her for a day or two in the Solent. A crowd had gathered to look at the noble vessel, and that she had sustained no damage was a subject of general congratulation, for who was there did not anticipate with pride the services the swift ship was yet to render in the war.

Walter White (1811–93)
A Londoner's Walk to Land's End (1861)

In this political novel, *Beauchamp's Career*, George Meredith satirises the Conservative establishment, of which Cecilia and her father are examples. Bevisham is the name given to Southampton. Of all his works, this was Meredith's favourite.

Sir Arthur Conan Doyle paid Meredith homage in the short-story *The Boscombe Valley Mystery*, when Sherlock Holmes says to Dr Watson, during the discussion of the case, 'And now let us talk about George Meredith, if you please, and we shall leave all minor matters until tomorrow.'

Beauchamp was requested by Cecilia to hold the reins. His fair companion in the pony-carriage preferred to lean back musing. They came to the fir-heights overlooking Bevisham. Here the breezy beginning of a South-western autumnal gale tossed the ponies' manes and made threads of Cecilia's shorter locks of beautiful auburn by the temples and the neck, blustering the curls that streamed in a thick involution from the silken band gathering them off her uncovered clear-swept ears.

'Bevisham looks well from here. We might make a north-western Venice of it, if we liked.'

'Papa told you it would be money sunk in mud.'

'Did I mention it to him? Thoroughly Conservative! So he would leave the mud as it is. They insist on our not venturing anything – those Tories – exactly as though we had gained the best of human conditions, instead of counting crops of rogues, malefactors, egoists, noxious and lumbersome creatures that deaden the country. Your town down there is one of the ugliest and dirtiest in the kingdom: it might be the fairest.'

'I have often thought that of Bevisham, Nevil.'

He drew a visionary sketch of quays, embankments, bridged islands, public buildings, magical emanations of patriotic architecture, with a practical air, an absence of that enthusiasm which struck her with suspicion when it was not applied to landscape or the Arts; and she accepted it, and warmed, and even allowed herself to appear hesitating when he returned to the similarity of the state of mud-begirt Bevisham and our great sluggish England.

George Meredith (1828–1909)
Beauchamp's Career (1897)

J. B. Priestley was a popular wireless broadcaster during the war after which wrote a number of popular plays the most successful of which is *An Inspector Calls.*

I had been to Southampton before, many times, but always to or from a ship. The last time I sailed for France during the war was from there, in 1918, when half a dozen of us found ourselves the only English officers in a tall crazy American ship bursting with doughboys, whose bands played ragtime on the top deck. Since then I had sailed for the Mediterranean and New York from Southampton, and had arrived there from Quebec. But it had no existence in my mind as a real town, where you could buy and sell and bring up children; it existed only as a muddle of railway sidings, level crossings, customs houses and dock sheds: something to have done with as soon as possible. The place I rolled into down the London Road was quite different, a real town. This is a fine approach, very gradual and artful in its progression from country to town. You are still staring at the pleasant Hampshire countryside when you notice that it is beginning to put itself into some order, and then the next minute you find that it is Southampton Common and that the townsfolk can be seen walking there; and, the minute after, the road is cutting between West Park and East Park, and on either side the smaller children of absent pursers and chief stewards are running from sunlight to shadow, and there are pretty frocks glimmering among the trees; and now, in another minute, the town itself is all round you, offering you hats and hams and acrobats at the Palace Theatre. It would be impossible to say where Southampton itself really began, though I should like to believe that the true boundary is that corner of East Park where there is a memorial to the lost engineers of the *Titanic*, to prove that there are dangerous trades here too.

Further down, the London Road changes into Above Bar Street; then the traffic swirls about the Bar Gate itself, which is very old but has so many newly-painted armorial decorations that it looks as gaudy as the proscenium of a toy theatre; and then once through or round Bar Gate, you are in High Street. Another quarter of a mile or so, at the bottom of High Street, you must go carefully; otherwise you may lose England altogether and find yourself looking at the Woolworth building or table mountain. One could write a story of a man who walked down this long straight street, on a dark winter's day, and kept on and on until at last he saw that he had walked into a panelled smoke room, where he settled down for a pipe, only to discover soon that Southampton had quietly moved away from him and that his smoke room was plunging about in the Channel. For, you see, you can catch the *Berangeria* or the *Empress of Britain* at the end of this High Street.

This one road, which begins as if it had been lately cut out of the New Forest and ends in the shadow of the great liners, is Southampton's main artery. You walk up and down it, shop in it, eat and drink and entertain yourself in it. We hear a good deal about Southampton's comparative prosperity; and this main street is the symbol of it. When I looked at it, the sun was shining and the day was as crisp as a good biscuit. The pavement on each side was crowded with neat smiling people, mostly women, and the mile of shops seemed to be doing a brisk trade. Here at last was a town that had not fallen under the evil spell of our times.

Its figures, I knew, were up, not down. It had recently opened the largest graving dock in the world, big enough for the monsters that have as yet only been planned and not built. The town was making money. At first I felt like a man who had walked into a fairy tale of commerce. The people who jostled me did not look as if they had just stepped out of an earthly paradise; there was no Utopian bloom upon them; but nevertheless they all seemed well-fed, decently clothed, cheerful, almost gay. The sun beamed upon them, and so did I. Their long street was very pleasant. I noticed that it shared the taste of Fleet Street and the Strand for wine bars. I went into one of these; and it had a surprising succession of Ye Olde panelled rooms, in one of which I drank a shilling glass of moderate sherry and listened to four citizens talking earnestly about German nudist papers, their supply having recently been cut off by Hitler. Their interest in these papers was genuine but not of a kind to commend itself to the leaders of the nudist movement. Though it was only the middle of the day, there were plenty of people drinking in these rooms, though few of them were taking wine. There was a fair sprinkling of respectable women, mostly having a glass with their men. I had lunch in another of these places, and it was full and the food reasonably good of its kind.

When you are nearing the end of this street, with Southampton water sparkling in the middle distance, you notice that the shops dwindle and become more nautical, until at last you can turn in at almost any doorway and buy a flag or two, charts, ropes and all the yachtsman's paraphernalia. I turned to the right at the bottom and followed the old town wall. There I saw the memorial marking the place from which the Pilgrim Fathers first set sail, in a ship about as big as the cocktail bar in which some of their descendants now sail back to this shore. I saw the old West Gate, through which the troops marched when they were on their way to Crécy and Agincourt. In short, I saw historical Southampton whose population, that day, consisted of a few old men, sitting and spitting. I soon left it to return to the Town Quay. Here the present was dominating the past, just as these giant liners themselves were dominating not only the sheds and wharves that tried to enclose them but the very town itself. Against a porcelain sky of palest blue, their black-and-crimson and buff funnels were enormous, dazzling. It did one's heart good to see them. I longed to go aboard. They seemed to me, as indeed they have always seemed to me, these giant liners, to be things not only of formidable size and power but also of real beauty, genuine creations of man the artist. Let us have our laugh, as I have had mine both in and out of print, at the nonsense inside them, their Louis Quinze drawing-rooms and Tudor smoke-rooms, but let us also ask ourselves what we have built to compare with them in majesty since the medieval cathedrals. Their very names have an epic roll, suggesting an ample and noble life. (If another Gibbon describes our decline and fall, what play he will make with these names!) Unlike the cathedrals, these ships have not been built to glorify God; they are of this world; they were not even designed to glorify the Commonwealth but only to earn dividends; but having arrived at a time when men have a passion – perhaps the purest of their passions – for machines, these ships are creations of power and beauty. I am glad to have lived in their age, to have seen them grow in strength and comeliness, these strange towns of painted steel that glide up to and away from this other town of motionless brick. They would not be here at all, nor would the High Street look so prosperous nor all the women dart in and out of the shops, if there were not an odd narrowing of the English Channel between Portland Bill and Cap de la Hague near Cherbourg. It is this bottling of the water that gives Southampton its double high tides, practically three hours of high water, which is time and tide enough for the manoeuvring of these enormous ships. They ought to empty a glass now and again in the wine bars to Portland Bill and Cap de la Hague.

...It may simply have been further acquaintance with the town and a sharper vision, but whatever it was, the fact remains that Southampton did not look quite so bright and prosperous when I came to look at it again. Once off that long High Street, I found myself in some very poor quarters. The only thing to be said in favour of these squalid little sidestreets of Southampton is that they did not seem as devastatingly dismal as the slums of the big industrial towns. There was still a sea sparkle in these people's lives. They were noisy and cheerful, not crushed. Perhaps it is impossible to live a completely colourless existence on the edge of such blue water. There were brown faces to be seen. The air in the narrow brick gullies, thickened as it was by the reek of overcrowded rooms, bad food, piles of old junk, had not entirely lost its salt and savour. Gramophones were scratching out those tunes concocted by Polish Jews fifteen storeys above Broadway. Cheap food and drink and tobacco and gossip were to be had; the men could guffaw round the entrance to the old junk yards; the girls knew how to powder their noses; the children could always wander to the water's edge. It might have been much worse. But it could be – and at first I thought it was – much better.

Not a bad town, this. That fine approach and the heartening spread of common and park; the long bright bustling street; the genial air of the place, with its hint of a festive Jack's-in-port life; the gigantic new graving dock: here was a town that had not let the universal depression master it and that was contriving to enjoy its unique situation, between forest and heath and deep blue water, a lovely bay window upon the wide world. It was not bad at all. Given a job to do and a bit of money in our pockets, you and I could live there and be reasonably happy. They are rather proud of themselves down there, for though that deep water outside, with London only a couple of hours away, was simply so many fathoms of luck for them, they have had the wit and energy to make the commercial most of it. Nevertheless, Southampton has not been able, just as their very owners have not been able, to live up to those great ships it harbours. They are the soul of the place. Their coming and going light it up. The citizens are knowledgeable and proud of these visiting giants, but they have not succeeded yet in building a town or planning a life worthy of such majestic company. What a Southampton that would be!

J. B. Priestley (1894–1984)
English Journey (1935)

Nevil Shute wrote this prophetic novel, *What Happened to the Corbetts*, as a warning, just before the start of the Second World War, aware, as others were not, what the experience of war might be.

… Before dinner they had planned a new position for the sweet pea hedge, taking it off the wall and putting it between the garage and the lilac tree. She had showed him that the magnolia was coming out; they had talked about the errors of omission of the gardener, who came once a week. Then he had read the paper for a little; he remembered having heard during the day that all leave had been cancelled for the Fleet over at Portsmouth, because of the tension on the Continent. But there was always tension on the Continent, and leave had been cancelled many times before. There didn't seem to be anything particularly alarming in the paper.

The first bomb fell soon after that, before midnight.

The concussions were considerable – they must have been, because he could remember nothing from the time that he put out his light and settled down to sleep till he was standing at the window with Joan, his arm round her shoulders, peering out into the rainy night. The bursts, distant as they were, were rocking the house and setting things tinkling in the room.

'Peter, what can it be?' she had asked. 'They wouldn't be firing guns for practise at this time of night, would they?'

He had shaken his head. 'Not on a night like this. There's nothing for them to see.'

And suddenly she had cried: 'Oh, Peter! Look!'

He had looked, and he had seen a sheet of yellow flame perhaps a quarter of a mile away, outlining the roof-tops in silhouette. With that there came a shattering concussion, and another, and another, nearer every time.

'Oh, Peter!' she had cried. 'It hurts my ears!'

He had hurried her from the window; they crouched down on the floor beside the wardrobe at the far side of the room. 'Keep your hands pressed tight over your ears,' he had said. 'I think this must be an air-raid.'

That salvo passed; as soon as it was over she had insisted upon going upstairs to quieten the children and the nurse.

He went down the garden to the garage, got the car, and drove to his office in Cumberland Place. He was appalled at what he saw. In Westwood Road he passed a house that had suffered a direct hit; above the first floor there was very little left of it. He went on, sober and a little sick, and stopped once more to inspect a crater in the road where there had been a motor-car.

... There was a tendency to chalk up such notices as BUSINESS AS USUAL.

Southampton was itself again, busy and enterprising.

He went into an ironmonger's where he was known, to buy a Primus stove. 'I'm sorry, Mr Corbett,' said the man, 'but I'm right out. Haven't got a Primus in the place. Regular run on Primuses there's been this morning, what with the gas being off and all. I'm sorry.'

'Do you know where I could get one?'

The man suggested one or two other places. 'Would you like me to save you a gallon of paraffin, Mr Corbett?'

'Is that short?'

'There's been a great run on it this morning. We shall be out very soon.'

He bought a can, had it filled with paraffin, and took it with him to the office.

Then he went out again.

He got a Primus stove with difficulty at a ship chandler's

down by the docks. After trying half a dozen stores, he got some very large candles irreverently at an ecclesiastical suppliers. Fresh milk was unobtainable; it seemed that very little milk had come into Southampton that morning. He got a few tins of condensed milk at a grocer's shop.

… Corbett said: 'I may want to go out to Hamble this afternoon. Will that be all right?'

'No, sir, it won't be all right. You'll not be able to go beyond the borough boundary, just this side of Netley Common. Not without you have a pass from the Chief Constable's office.'

'Why is that?'

'I couldn't say, sir,' said the man impassively. 'Them's the orders that we've got. You can pass along for Sholing now.'

They drove through. Corbett said: 'Let's go on and have a look at Netley Common.'

They went on down the road to Bursledon.

… Next morning it was raining heavily. Corbett had breakfast; then Joan rowed him on shore to the car to go into Southampton.

He had left the car parked in the open. Trying to start it, he discovered that the tank was empty; the drain-plug and the washer were placed neatly on the running-board. Petrol in Hamble was at a premium. He replaced the drain-plug angrily and went back on board to fetch a can out of his store, returned to the car, filled it into his tank, and got going on the road to Southampton.

… At Norham Bridge, before entering the city proper, there was a barricade guarded by police. He was stopped and asked where he was going to. He told the constable his house and his office.

'You'll have to go round by the other bridge, sir,' said the man. 'You know it, of course?'

Corbett nodded, 'Why is that?'

The man hesitated. 'It's Mr Corbett, isn't it? The solicitor?'

'That's right.'

The constable said, 'We've got our orders not to allow any traffic in the Northern district. On account of the sickness, and that.'

'Is it the cholera?'

The man hesitated for a little. 'Well – we've got orders, not to talk about it, sir. Spreading alarm, if you take my meaning.'

'I understand. It's pretty bad, is it?'

'I did hear it was better this morning, getting under control, like. It's typhoid now that they're more upset about.'

Corbett nodded. 'That's bad.'

'It is, sir.'

Nevil Shute (1899–1960)
What Happened to the Corbetts (1938)

John Arlott, later the voice of Test Match Special on the BBC, was also a poet and attracted the attention of John Betjeman, who became a mentor for Arlott's literary ambitions. His description of Southampton during the war, rather unusually talking about himself in the third person, shows Nevil Shute's uncanny prescience.

... War broke out... At the same time, an attachment to Dawn Rees, a nurse at the Royal South Hants Hospital, became serious and led to engagement and eager anticipation of marriage...

Dawn's mother, daughter of the wealthy owner of a chain of butchers' shops, estranged herself from her family by marrying a Welsh-born Canadian army dispatch rider. However, she did her best to bring up her three children, of whom Dawn was the eldest, in snobbery. She greeted her daughter's marriage in 1940 with a telegram regretting that she had married beneath her, which was little cheer for a wartime bride... Dawn had qualified as a state Registered Nurse and became night sister at the Southampton Children's Hospital. J.A's duties in the police emergency department were from nine to half past six and, also, every other night, he was required to sleep in Police Headquarters on air-raid emergency duty. All this meant that they spent much less time together than most young couples in normal circumstances, and they were desperately grateful for the time they were together, indeed for the very fact that they were together.

Soon, too, the air-raids became more frequent. It is difficult to piece together, or at least to evaluate, the emotions, developments, events of that time. Love of a young wife was mixed with fear, chiefly for her: never knowing whether she would be there, or even alive, at the end of a tour of duty. Southampton, as a matter of historic fact, had more 'incidents' – and air-raid warnings – than any other place in Britain. The first air-raid on the town came by day, when the couple were at home. After some dithering, they took cover; then could not resist coming out to look, and were rewarded for that piece of madness by seeing the legendary Polish fighter squadron drive away the German bombers, an event which produced an euphoric effect, to be rapidly dispelled by the well-organised, systematic and heavy night bombing. In the same raid a huge food store in Southampton Docks was hit, it was full of butter and burnt for several days, while an appalling mess of molten yellow fat ran across the dockside to clot in the sea. Within weeks, the new flat which had been a young couple's pride was in truth very near to the receiving end. It was not a direct hit, which was a considerable comfort because it meant that the contents remained intact, apart from the glass and other splinters embedded in the furniture. Fortunately, too, both were on night duty when the bomb, fourth in a 'stick' of six, fell. It was a chilling experience to return 'home' – by luck within two or three minutes of each other – to contemplate the destruction of a superficial dream. It was no more than a trifle; it was not possible to come back from the death and maiming of the raids and regard damage to property as a matter of real importance. What was important was that they were both alive. Now they needed to find somewhere to live before nightfall: that proved simple as did so many problems in that period when such difficulties were seen as everyday.

... So, no sooner bombed out but rehoused. It was a pleasant, modern, semi-detached house in Bassett Green Road, with ample rooms... It was an odd, unnatural existence, between nursing duties, police duty and air-raid stand-by... It was a bicycle life: riding home, generally through the blackout in that 1940-41 winter, wondering whether one would find one's spouse there, or any company at all. Rations were stretched, augmented from the garden and the preserve cupboard at Basingstoke – where he visited as often as he could take his wife with him.

When bombs fell, everything was activity, though it soon became completely orderly, controlled activity – as a rule. One night he left his office as the alert sounded to stroll, as usual, unhurriedly over to the control room in the Civic Centre. On the way he passed young George Brown, son of the great Hampshire and England cricketer, a constable in the mobile section. 'What are you up to, then, George?'

'Got to drive the Chief Constable up to Red Lodge; he doesn't like it down here when it gets hot.'

'Lucky chap, enjoy it.'

As he entered the Civic Centre, a bomb dropped a few yards away. The three or four men who were inside the door dived for cover: the stick of four – big ones – thundered on. As the dust slowly settled they gratefully made their way into the control room. That personable, young George Brown, though, was dead; a direct hit on his car – before the Chief Constable reached it.

Southampton was, indeed, hard hit; the great V of the Test and Itchen rivers of Southampton Water was a simple, even inviting, target for any bombing aircraft. First the incendiaries marked it in detail and then the heavy stuff pounded down, magnifying the destruction and spreading the fires. The police in the target-area towns were under instruction that in the event of any military withdrawal they would remain behind, to render support of a pacific kind to the occupying force to control and protect the civilian population: though not too much was said about that. At one juncture, though, it was decided, after four days of intensive night attack, and with buildings burning steadily, that, if the bombers came again, the town should be abandoned. It was a gut-racking piece of knowledge. That night one couple took a tender and terrified farewell; when the alert sounded, it seemed that the end of all things was near. The bombers did not come – not that night – and for the rest of the war life seemed, if not safer, richer, a bonus.

John Arlott (1914–91)
Basingstoke Boy

Bulldog Drummond was one of the most famous British fictional characters of the first half of the twentieth century. The creation of H C McNeile, who published under the pen name of Sapper, he was based on McNeile himself, on his friend Gerard Fairlie and on the idea of the English gentlemen of that time, tempered by war. When McNeile died in 1937, Fairlie continued the series of Bulldog Drummond novels himself.

The *New York Times* critic observed that 'if you like a good knock-down-and-drag-out yarn with excitement and violence on nearly every page, you can't go wrong on Bulldog Drummond'. Ian Fleming stated that James Bond was 'Sapper from the waist up and Mickey Spillane below'. Drummond himself advertised himself thus: 'Demobilised officer finding peace incredibly tedious would welcome diversion. Legitimate if possible; but crime, if of a comparatively humorous description, no objection. Excitement essential.' Here, as ever, he's facing his own extinction.

> The yacht *Gadfly* was lying in Southampton Water and he had decided to go on board in the late afternoon. His two invalids would be carried on stretchers; an ambulance was even now in readiness below to take them to the coast. They would be unconscious – a matter which presented little difficulty to Mr Robinson. And the Professor would never regain consciousness. He had served his purpose, and all that mattered as far as he was concerned was to dispose of him as expeditiously as possible. With Drummond things were a little different. In spite of what he had said to Freyder downstairs, the scheme was too big to run any unnecessary risks, and though it went against his grain to kill him in his present condition, he quite saw that he might have to. Drummond might remain in his present condition for months, and it was manifestly impossible to wait for that length of time to obtain his revenge. It might be, of course, that when he woke up he would have recovered his reason, and if so… Mr Robinson's eyes gleamed at the thought. In anticipation he lived through the minute when he would watch Drummond, bound and weighted, slip off the deck into the sea…
>
> 'You have your orders,' he remarked curtly. 'If Drummond makes a sound – gag him. I shall be on board myself in about two hours.'

He closed the doors, leaving the two men inside, and the car started. It was impossible to see out of either window owing to the curtains, and the ostentatious production of a revolver by one of the men removed any thought Drummond might have of trying to use the razor-blade. 'Mad or not, take no chances,' was the motto of his two guards, and when on top of everything else, though he hadn't made a sound, they crammed a handkerchief half down his throat, he almost laughed.

He judged they had been going for about an hour, when the diminished speed of the car and the increased sounds of traffic indicated a town. It felt as if they were travelling over cobbles, and once they stopped at what was evidently a level crossing, for he heard a train go by. And then came the sound of a steamer's siren, to be followed by another and yet a third.

A seaport town, obviously, he reflected, though that didn't help much. The only comfort was that a sea-port town meant a well-used waterway outside. And if he could get free, if he could go overboard with the Professor, there might be a shade more chance of being picked up. Also there would almost certainly be curious loungers about as they were carried aboard.

The car had stopped; he could hear the driver talking to someone. Then it ran forward a little and stopped again. And a moment or two later a curious swaying motion almost pitched him off the bunk. Surely they couldn't be at sea yet. The car dropped suddenly, and with a sick feeling of despair he realised what had happened. The car had been hoisted bodily on board; his faint hope of being able to communicate with some onlooker had gone.

Once again the car became stationary, save for a very faint and almost imperceptible movement. From outside came the sounds of men heaving on ropes, and the car steadied again. They were actually on board, and the car was being made fast.

Still the two men sat there with the doors tight shut, and the windows hermetically sealed by the blinds of them. They seemed to be waiting for something, and suddenly, with a sigh of relief, one spoke.

'She's off.'

It was true: Drummond could feel the faint throb of the propeller.

'The specimens are on board,' laughed the other man, 'and I guess it will be safe to open the doors in about a quarter of an hour or so, and get a bit of air. This damn thing is like a Turkish bath.'

He rose and peered cautiously through a slit in the curtain, but he made no movement to open the door until the throbbing of the propeller had ceased, and the harsh rattle of a chain showed that they were anchoring. Then and not until then did he open the doors with a sigh of relief.

Cautiously, Drummond raised his head and stared out. Where were they? He had followed every movement in his mind since he had come on board, but he was still as far as ever from knowing where they were. And luckily one glance was enough. It didn't need even the glimpse he got of a huge Cunarder about a half-mile away: he recognised the shore. They were in Southampton Water, and though the knowledge didn't seem to help very much, at any rate it was something to have one definite fact to start from.

Sapper (Gerard Fairlie) (1899–1983)
The Third Round 1950

In 1983, Beryl Bainbridge brings her novelist's ear to the tasking of finding England, by retracing the route of J. B. Priestley's *English Journey* (quoted above). In doing so she captures the changes that fifty years have wrought on the country, concluding that they have not helped the working class.

....No porters at Waterloo, and I had to walk miles, carrying two suitcases, my handbag, typewriter, notebook and Sunday papers, before finding a carriage which allowed smoking.

....No porters at Southampton either. One thing was certain, I had too much luggage. Once installed in a taxi on the way to the hotel I sat on the edge of my seat determined to miss nothing of my surroundings, and had time to observe a massage parlour and an Allied Carpets showroom before we swung past a curved pink building, its clock tower wrapped in a green fishing net, and immediately entered an avenue of tall trees bounded on either side by parkland. Glimpsed a group of elderly Sikhs playing football and a further fifty or more sitting cross-legged under an oak tree. No sign of banks or shops or monumental edifices to Cunard or the Blue Funnel Line, just long stretches of parched grass and numerous Alsatian dogs padding in and out of bushes.

This long hot summer and the still blazing sun has turned Britain into a foreign country. I might as well be in Yugoslavia. The leaves are falling from the trees and the grass is turning brown. How disconcerting to see cars flash past with apparently naked drivers at the wheel. Perhaps this is the beginning of the 'greenhouse effect', that warming up of the atmosphere which scientists predict will turn Durham into a grape-growing region and Southern Europe into a desert within the next thousand years. It's a bad sign, large dogs roaming without owners. I ask the taxi driver where Southampton is and he says this is it.

My hotel is half-way down the avenue, set back from the road. The neighbourhood reminds me of one of those small-town main streets seen in old American movies. Not exactly rocking-chairs on the back porch, but there don't seem to be any hedges or gates and I half expect a crew-cut youth to pedal past on a bike, hurling newspapers onto withered lawns. The hotel is a Victorian house improved beyond hope. It has an airport lounge built on at the front and conference facilities at the side. The carpeting could strike one blind. In the foyer is an intricate plastic vase designed to look as though cast in bronze, and a large model of a galleon. The ship is obviously built of genuine lead because it's slung from the ceiling on wire hawsers and there is a card saying it weighs four tons and that it lights up at night.

I decided to go for a walk before unpacking and crossed the avenue only to find myself in a forest of oak and sycamore. Tried to climb a tree to see if the city was anywhere in sight but deterred by nettles. The whole world wobbles in sunshine. Sounds of bird-song and the continuous whine of traffic like the noise of a humming top. I imagine the entire population is spinning past in cars, searching for Southampton.

Tonight we all had dinner together in a roadhouse further up the Avenue. There are a lot of us – Jimmy Dewar, the producer, and his assistant Alison Jelf, John Warwick, the camera man, and his assistant Richard Rankin, and Eric Woodward, the sound-man. Eric doesn't have any assistance. We have two directors, David Pritchard and Bernard Hall, but only David is with us at the moment. Bernard will be joining us in Birmingham.

The bars and restaurants are crowded and it was almost ten o'clock before we sat down at a table. I can't eat so late at night, not unless I'm allowed to lie full length and watch television. Nor do I like eating and drinking at the same time. It's wasteful; it takes ages on a full stomach to get any benefit from drink.

August 15th

Today we went into Southampton by trawler, surely the best way to enter a seaport. We began further down the river at a place called Hamble, which has a Marina, and ended up alongside the quay where the *Titanic* had berthed. I didn't know what to make of the Marina. An armada of pleasure boats – catamarans, sailing ships, cabin cruisers, yachts – stretching along the river in either direction, each and every one painted and polished as though it had come from the boatyard an hour before; not an unfurled sail, a speck of rust or a barnacle in sight. There weren't any people about save for two old men, one stripped to the waist and the other looking like Captain Birdseye, taking something from the boot of a car. Perhaps the recession has by-passed Hamble. It must be expensive to own a boat, what with mooring fees and insurance and sophisticated equipment to ensure one doesn't go adrift in a fog, not to mention the price of fuel. Also you have to keep lifting them out of the water to scrape their bottoms. There were so many of them that if they had all set sail at once there wouldn't have been enough water to float them.

I had to walk down to the jetty and be seen leaping aboard the trawler. It was our first day of filming. I had a sound box tied round my waist and a small microphone taped to my chest. The box sticks out and I worry lest people think I have had a colostomy. I shall be wearing it, on and off, for the next fifty-six days. It is astonishing the difference between walking for oneself, as it were, and walking for the camera. In theory all one has to do is shift one leg after the other as in real life, but in practice it's about as simple as dancing on a trampoline. I couldn't help staring straight ahead as though there was a gun at my back. Perhaps it showed, because I was asked to do it again. This time I held on to the rail of the jetty and looked casually down into the water. There was a large bass flickering in the shallows. In hot weather fish grow dozy and don't realise how close they've come to the shore. If I'd had a butterfly net, or very long arms, I could have scooped it out as easily as plucking apples from a tree. The two old men overtook me. They had obviously been having words because Captain Birdseye said, 'Now, dear boy, if you can't be civil, stay mute', and the other one snorted.

...What a mess we make of our surroundings. Travelling by car I hardly notice what I'm driven through. We move like ants, along cracks and crevices. I only glimpse doorways and ground-floor windows, unless the car happens to be going up hill. This morning, distanced by water, I saw the top and bottom of it, the whole wretched no-man's-land of industrial development, engineering works, chemical plants, pylons and railway sidings – mile after ugly mile of ingenious clutter sprawling along the

banks of the river towards Southampton. Yet I suppose it was a prosperous sight; and what did it matter if the land was ripped up and laid waste when the sky was so broad and so dazzlingly blue. The white domes of the BP oil containers appeared to quiver in the heat; the domes hold petroleum, cooking oil and nuclear fuel. One can only hope they're labelled correctly.

... I had been so busy sorting the clams that I hadn't noticed how near we'd come to Southampton. One moment we had the river to ourselves and the next we were in the middle of ferry boats and hydrofoils, bulk ships and container boats, and a whole fleet of barges belonging to the US army, painted green and shaped like giant bath tubs, not going anywhere, just parked in lines. Ahead of us reared the monstrous stern of the supertanker *Burmah Endeavor*, built during the Suez crisis to take oil the long way round and stranded in the Solent because she's no longer needed and there's nothing else she's fit for. Her salvation would be another crisis, another war. Whoever owns her pays a thousand pounds a week to keep her rusting in the water. Further up there's another one, not quite as large, called the *Tantalus*.

The river began to look as littered as the land. Two years ago a bulk ship rammed the end of the Royal Pier, snapping the wooden piles and sliding the Mayflower Hall sideways into the waves, its dance floor peeled up and the planks sticking up like oars. The Dance Hall was named in memory of the voyage of the Pilgrim Fathers, though they didn't get very far. Their boat sprang a leak a mile out of Southampton and they had to put into Portsmouth for repairs.

The *Burmah Endeavor* blotted out the sun – two hundred foot high and the length of five football pitches. She's painted in bathing-costume bands of fleshy pink and wishy-washy blue, and there was a moment as we slipped beneath the nipped-in waist of her bows – a minnow rounding a whale – when she curved away from us like a fat lady on a seaside post-card. Out of her ample shadow we were in the docks, alongside the twisted girders of the Ocean Terminal, built in the glory days of the great *Queens* and now being smashed into rubble. There weren't any proper ships doing ship-worthy jobs, just a destroyer turned into a museum and three sailing boats, one in use to teach the handicapped about the sea, a line of crutches dangling in a frill from the side, and something Jack called a yacht but which bore more resemblance to a space craft. It belongs to an Arab Sheikh, and Jack said it was being refitted at a cost of forty million pounds. The mind boggles. On the quayside, where the bulldozers were knocking the Ocean Terminal to smithereens, an old man sat under a drizzle of dust, napping on a deckchair.

Back again to Hamble. We lay on the deck among the buckets of clams and ate Cornish pasties. Eric, the sound man, said real Cornish pasties have meat one end and jam the other.

No sooner had we disembarked from the trawler than we returned immediately to Southampton, travelling by car through that avenue of trees between East Park and West Park. At the corner of East Park we got out to look at the monument to the *Titanic*. It was splendidly sculpted and showed sturdy men in wellington boots attending to some boilers. The inscription beneath said it was dedicated to the memory of 'The Engineer Officers of the *Titanic* who did their duty'. I felt there was a whiff of reproach in the wording, a slight implication that the rest of the staff had run like hell for the life-boats. No more than a few feet away stood a large circular cage so heavily meshed with wire that it was difficult to see inside. It housed a querulous collection of parrots, canaries and farmyard hens. I supposed it was a bird sanctuary, if a somewhat eccentric one. A piece of rubber painted to look like a fried egg hung from a string in the roof.

August 16th
In the evening we drove to the Royal Pie again to board the supertanker *Tantalus*. We would have preferred the *Burmah Endeavour*, but it wasn't allowed. We arrived early because John Warwick, the camera man, wanted to film the quay at sunset. The *Tantalus* was riding high in the water with her propeller-blade sticking up like the fin of a shark. I squatted on the quay among the debris of the Ocean Terminal, peering through the arch of her stern where it curved up and out to meet the rudder, and saw a little sailing boat slapping along the horizon. There was a ripple of golden light as the sun slipped to the edge of the sky and then the river turned grey and the boat had gone.

The watchmen on board the *Tantalus* told me they were grieved that such a fine vessel had been abandoned and left to rot. It was time marching on, they said. There were two of them guarding her because a forgotten ship is full of ghosts and shadows.

There wasn't much to see save for that great expanse of deck and some pieces of old machinery. God knows what was happening in the oily holds beneath. She was in better condition than I had imagined, though there were blisters of rust pushing up the paintwork. The crew quarters were at the stern. Most of the doors were either locked or jammed. Through the windows I could see basins of rat poison on the floors. All the clocks had stopped at a quarter to four. The only shadows were cast by starlings coming home to roost on the superstructure; they flew in a ragged arrow over the bashed-in roof of the Ocean Terminal and swooped upwards into the darkening sky.

Afterwards we went to the Juniper pub down by the West Gate to see Paulette, a topless fire-eater. The pub was Elizabethan, built in 1930. It had been the haunt of sailors and hard cases and was now patronised by lorry drivers and holiday makers. The governor was a frail man called Harry who had a dicky heart; his Mum and Dad were over from Ireland to keep an eye on him. He introduced me to his brother-in-law, Brian, who had worked on the liners. I asked Brian if he had known Mr Vincent but he didn't recall the name. He said did I know that Jane Austen had lived as a girl in a house at the bottom of the garden. I looked out of the mullioned windows and there was nothing out there save a scrap of yard and a clothes line pegged with dish towels.

Harry took me through to the back to meet Paulette. Her dressing room was the pub kitchen. She wore a fish-net vest and a flame-coloured shawl with tassels, and she sat at a table crowded with pots of mustard and bottles of H.P. Sauce. A friend, she said, had taught her to fire-eat. At first it was just something to do for a lark and then it became a livelihood. Normally she likes to use the wheel, but they won't let her, on account of the timber beams. She's very busy this week, doubling up at the pub over the road because the stripper there is off sick. Paulette looked frail too, as though a breath would blow her out. Fire-eating was in her blood, she said. Her father was a Russian dancer. 'Ballet?' I asked. 'Russian,' she said. Once she had set fire to her hair and often she had burnt her lips. I began to think that everyone on Southampton was in thrall to Haphaestus.

Though it wasn't my cup of tea I found her act interesting, and her dance, such as it was, gracefully done. She was accompanied on one of those hi-fi contraptions manipulated by a disc jockey. He sat on a stool and worked the controls – skilfully, I thought. When she whirled the fire sticks above her head, the music was suitably flickering, or perhaps that was an illusion created by the coloured lights bouncing round the walls. There was a hiss from the amplifier when she drew the flame between her legs, then a sizzling roar as she whipped it up her belly, in which the audience joined, brought to their feet and urging her on. When it was over she put on her fish-net vest and darted off to the pub over the road.

We should have gone home then, but I wanted to know, apart from fire-eating, how people in Southampton earned their living. I knew that the engineering works and Fawley Refinery and British Petroleum were mostly automated industries. It was difficult to get any information. The bar was full to the doors and the glasses of whisky kept coming. It didn't help that most of our party seemed to be from Dublin, and those that weren't were either retired or on the dole. Harry's Mum said Southampton was in decline, but really, looking at the sun-flushed, roaring throng it was hard to believe that people were feeling the pinch. The old *Queens* were mentioned and the *Titanic*. A man called Will, who worked on the Dublin ferries, asked if anyone had seen the film *History is Made at Night*, with Charles Boyer. Boyer had played either a fellow on his honeymoon or someone skedaddling from a murky past. He thought it was the latter because, at the end, didn't he redeem himself by giving away his life-jacket to a poor Irish girl from the lower decks? 'I remember,' he said, 'the phosphorescent glow of the iceberg as it drifted to the stern, and that fellow Boyer standing at the rail with the tears in his marvellous eyes. Did none of you see it?' None of us had. Someone said the negligence of the owners in the matter of the life-boats was criminal. And the poor sods in third class had stayed below because they knew their proper station in life. Will said there hadn't been any hint of that in the film, and even if there had it would have gone over his head. What had concerned him was the lack of grappling-irons on board. We looked at him. 'Do you not follow me?' he said. 'They could have attached themselves to the iceberg and hung on until the rescue boats arrived.' We were too far gone to know if this was feasible or not. Some said the cold would be killing, others that body heat would melt the iceberg.

I got back to the hotel in the small hours of the morning. All that I had known of Southampton until three days ago was that she had once rivalled Liverpool as a port, had surpassed her, taken her trade and done her in. I had expected Southampton to be like Liverpool, grim and grand and dark, and found her hardly a city at all, more of a holiday village set between a forest and a river. Not a bad place to live, whether one went down to the sea in ships or stayed at home making chocolate cakes and thinking of the past. An ordinary place inhabited by ordinary people, publicans and tramps, fishermen and fire-eaters.

It had been a long day.

Beryl Bainbridge (1932–2010)
English Journey, or The Road to Milton Keynes (1984)

Chapter 3
Portsmouth: first line of defence

Portsmouth stands apart from Hampshire, for it is literally an island city, surrounded by a maze of marshy tidal estuaries and low-lying islands. For some five hundred years it has been home to the British Navy, the ships framed by this moody marine landscape of mud-creeks, ancient moorings, gravel beaches, forgotten ditches, walls, moats and forts. It is full of the scent of the sea and the cry of gulls, yet despite the presence of such genteel coastal resorts at Southsea (and the distant terraces of Osborne Palace on the Isle of Wight) it is not a pretty place. Like a brood sister to Victorian London, or a northern city transplanted to the south, its neat terraces of red-brick houses, built for dockyard workers, are set off by flamboyant pubs and cut through by train tracks efficiently linking the busy docks to the rest of England.

To the north, the chalk slopes of Portsdown Hill look like a wonderful pastoral Arcadia, though they are in fact riddled with half a dozen vast subterranean brick-built Victorian artillery fortresses and contemporary naval research stations. The southern horizon is entirely filled by the Isle of Wight, a geographical shield which protects the harbour of Portsmouth from storm and delays enemy fleets. The third, hidden explanation for Portsmouth's destiny is a submerged sand bank, some fourteen miles long and four miles wide, which occupies the centre of the Solent waters. This is the Spithead, one of the great roadsteads of England, where whole fleets can be safely anchored and patiently assembled, protected from storms but able to use winds from any direction to make their passage.

At the end of a muddy creek in the north-western corner of Portsmouth harbour stands Portus Adurni (Porchester Castle), the most intact Roman fortress to survive north of the Alps. It was first raised by a Roman admiral, the Count of the Saxon Shore, as part of a system of naval defences that ringed the south-eastern coast of Britannia. For a long time it was assumed that it was built as a defence against North

Sea pirates, but it is now thought that it was probably the opening salvo in his campaign to become a usurper Emperor. Porchester Castle then passed like a bloody orb of dominion into the hands of every invader of England – be they late Roman, Saxon, Dane, Viking, Norman or French – just as it served as the base for every English war-party set for France, be it led by a Richard, by John, by Edward III or Henry V.

The Tudors provided the historical turning point in Portsmouth's history. During the fifteenth century the old flat-bottomed Frisian Cogs (which had dominated the medieval trade routes for a thousand years and could be decorated fore and aft with wooden towers to turn them into warships) were replaced in a revolution in ship design and warfare. Every Renaissance monarch with an eye to survival needed to master the art of casting cannon, which were mounted on the new ocean-going three-masted carracks or the raised terraces of an artillery fortress. So Henry VII and Henry VIII shifted their naval base to a narrow strait on the south-western tip of Portsea where they ordered the construction of castles, shipyards, foundries and a dry dock beside these deeper waters. At Southsea Castle and at the preserved shipwreck of the *Mary Rose* you can still see for yourself the Tudor birth of this new city.

As the British Empire expanded over the next five hundred years, Portsmouth also grew, rippling ever further out to cover the entire low, flat island of Portsea. It became the naval workshop of Britain, and specialised not so much in shipbuilding (which happened at Chatham) but in refitting the fleets of the Royal Navy: adding new sails, renewing the rigging, copper sheathing their bottoms, replacing the masts and ever upgrading the armaments. The city boomed in wartime and shrunk in peace, and became the home of a proudly insular and hard-drinking working-class culture. Pompey men tended to be rowdy, patriotic, and always more interested in football and the pub than writing or the theatre. A dynasty of local brewers (which evolved into the Bonham-Carter and Martineau families) greatly prospered in this milieu and dominated town politics in the liberal interest.

The city was never short of drama. The Duke of Buckingham was stabbed in the heart in The Greyhound pub on August 23rd, 1628; Colonel Goring threatened to blow up this naturally Parliamentarian town during the Civil War; and Portsmouth very nearly achieved a Puritan coup d'état before Charles II's Restoration. All our naval heroes, be they Captain Cook, Lord Hood, William Bligh or Horatio Nelson, waved goodbye to England from Portsmouth, where their wrecked bodies would be returned and their wounded battleships repaired.

In the heyday of Empire, the Spithead review of the Royal Navy (which had started in the reign of George III) became a mainspring of foreign policy. In case they needed reminding, Russian Tsars, Prussian Kaisers, Ottoman Sultans, French Presidents and Persian Shahs were solemnly escorted by the reigning monarchs to see for themselves the strength of the Royal Navy. To protect the naval base from a surprise attack from the land, Lord Palmerston created the most heavily fortified city on earth in the nineteenth century. This Pax Britannica lasted from 1815 to 1914, but Portsmouth's greatest test came in the middle of the twentieth century. The city was hit by sixty-seven bombing raids during the Blitz, yet survived to assist in the arming of the largest Armada on earth – the eight hundred ships marshalled for D-day on June 6th, 1944.

The relentless postwar decline of both Empire and Royal Navy gutted the economic base of the city, which has survived by diversifying into electronic systems. In the same postwar period old Mrs Borthwick-Norton refused to profit by selling any of the 7,000 acres of her Southwick estate to the north-west of the city, so speculative builders were forced to expand north-eastwards, creating a string of suburbs: Havant, Leigh and Waterlooville. In the centre of the city the damage done by the Blitz was trebled by urban planners in the 1960s. This did however allow the city fathers to push a motorway right down to the ferry ports, and so beat their traditional rival (Southampton) and dominate this ancient trade. The city remains proud of its grammar school, its football team, its pubs and its historical heritage, including such extraordinary, and touchable, icons of British history as HMS *Victory* and HMS *Warrior*.

...

The following description of Porchester Castle, imagined at the time when England was consumed with fighting Napoleon, was written by Walter Besant, the Victorian novelist and historian who was born in Portsmouth, and gives a sense of the load of history carried by this city.

The Castle, which, now that the long wars are over, one hopes for many years, is silent and deserted, its ruined courts empty, its crumbling walls left to decay, presented a different appearance indeed in the spring of the year 1802. For in those days it was garrisoned by two regiments of militia, and was occupied by the prodigious number of eight thousand prisoners.

I am told that there are other ancient castles in the country even more extensive and more stately than Porchester; but I have never seen them, and am quite satisfied to believe that for grandeur, extent, and the awe of antiquity, there can be none which can surpass, and few which can pretend to equal, this monument. It is certainly ruinous in parts, yet still so strong as to serve for a great prison, but it is not overthrown, and its crumbling walls, broken roofs, and dismantled chambers surround the place with a solemnity which affects the most careless visitor.

It is so ancient that there are some who pretend that parts of it may belong to British times, while it is certain that the whole of the outer wall was built by the Romans. In imitation of their camps, it stands foursquare, and has hollow round towers in the sides and at the corners. The spot was chosen, not at the month of the harbour, the Britons having no means of attacking ships entering or going out; but at the very head of the harbour, where the creek runs up between the shallows, which are banks of mud at low water. Hither came the Roman galleys, laden with military stores, to land them under the protection of the Castle. When the Romans went away, and the Saxons came, who loved not fighting behind walls, they neglected the fortress, but built a church within the walls, and there laid their dead. When in their turn the Normans came, they built a castle after their own fashion, within the Roman walls. This is the stronghold, containing four-square towers and a fortified entrance. And the Normans built the water-gate and the gate tower. The rest of the great space became the outer bailly of the castle. They also added battlements to the wall, and dug a moat, which they filled with sea-water at high tide.

The battlements of the Normans are now broken down or crumbling away; great patches of the rubble work have fallen here and there. Yet one can walk round the narrow ledge designed for the bowmen. The wall is crowned with waving grass and wallflowers, and up the sides grow elder-bushes, blackberry, ivy, and bramble, as luxuriantly as in any hedge beyond Portsdown. If you step out through the water-gate, which is now roofless, with little left to show its former splendour, except a single massive column, you will find, at high tide, the water lapping the lowest stones of the towers, just as it did when the Romans built them. Instead of the old galleys, which must have been light in draught, to come up Porchester Creek, there are now lying half a dozen boats, the whole fleet of the little village. On the other side of the water are the wooded islets of Great and Little Horsea, and I suppose they look today much as they did a thousand years ago. On this side you look towards the east; but if you get to the south side of the Castle, and walk across a narrow meadow which lies between the wall and the sea, you have a very different view. For you look straight across the harbour to its very mouth, three miles away; you gaze upon a forest of masts and upon ships of every kind, from the stately man-o'-war to the saucy pink, and, twenty years ago, of every nation – because, in those days, we seemed at war with half the world – from the French-built frigate, the most beautiful ship that floats, to the Mediterranean xebecque, all of them prizes. Here they lie, some ready for sea, some just arrived, some battered by shot, some newly repaired and fresh from the yard; some – it seems a cruel fate for ships which have fought the battles of their country – converted into hulks for convicts and for prisoners; some store-ships – why, there is no end to the number and the kind of the ships lying in the harbour. They could tell, if they could speak, of many a battle and many a storm; some of them are as old as the days of Admiral Benbow; one poor old hulk is so old that she was once a man-o'-war in the old Dutch wars of Charles II and carried on board, it is said, the Duke of York himself.

In the dockyard, within the harbour, the wooden walls of England are built; here they are fitted up; from this place they go forth to fight the French. Heavens! how many ships we sent forth every year! How many were built in the yard! How many brave fellows were sacrificed year after year before the insatiable rage for war which possessed one man, and through him all Europe, could be overcome, and the tyrant confined in his cage, like a wild beast, until he should die! Standing under those walls, I say, we could look straight down the harbour to the forts which guard its entrance; we could see in the upper part the boats plying backwards and forwards; we could hear the booming of the salutes; we could even see the working of the semaphore, by whose mysterious arms news is conveyed to London in half an hour. And the sight of the ships, the movement of the harbour, the distant banging of the guns, made one, even one who lived in so quiet a village as Porchester, feel as if one was taking part in the great events which shook the world. It was a hard time to many, and an anxious time for all; a time full of lavish expenditure for the country; a time when bread was dear and work scarce, with trade bad and prospects uncertain. Alas with what beating of heart did we wait for news, and gather together to listen when a newspaper was brought to the village. For still it seemed as if, defeat his navies though we might, and though we chased his cruisers off the seas, and tore down the French flag from his colonies, the Corsican Usurper was marching from one triumph to another, until the whole of Europe, save Russia and England, was subjugated and laid prostrate at his feet.

Walter Besant (1836–1901)
The Holy Rose (1886)

The *Mary Rose*, Henry VIII's great warship, was built in Portsmouth in 1511, and was fully fitted and heavily armed with four hundred men, when on July 19th 1545 she suddenly sank with almost total loss of life during an engagement with the French in the Solent.

A survivor claims that 'the disaster was caused by their not having closed the lowest row of gun ports on one side of the ship. Having fired the guns on that side, the ship was turning, in order to fire from the other, when the wind caught her sails so strongly as to heel her over, and plunge her open gunports beneath the water, which flooded and sank her.'

After almost twenty years of searching and underwater archaeology, the hull of the *Mary Rose* was brought to the surface in October 1982, and can now be visited in its own, purpose-built museum.

...The *Mary Rose* was sunk 'by so much foly...for she was laden with much ordinances, and the ports left open, which were low...so that when the ship should turne, the water entered, and sodainly she sanke.'

From *Hall's Chronicle* (1548)

'one of the King's shippes, called the *Marye Rose*, was drowned in the myddest of the haven, by reason that she was overladen with ordinaunce, and had the ports lefte open, which were very lowe, and the great artillerie unbreeched, so that when the ship shoolde tourne, the water entred, and soddainely she sunke. In hir was Sir George Carewe, knight, and foure hundredth souldioures undrr his guidyng. There escaped not paste fortie persons of all the number.'

From *Holinshed's Chronicle* (1577)

In C J Sansom's historical mystery, Shardlake, a private eye, finds himself aboard the *Mary Rose* as she sinks.

As the smoke cleared I saw the galleys were undamaged. The *Mary Rose* began turning to port, fast and steeply. I heard a cracking of sails. Then through the doorway, I felt a sudden strong gust of wind.

'That's too fast,' one of the sailors said.

The ship heeled to starboard. I thought it would be like the earlier manoeuvre and she would right herself, but she tilted more and more. The soldiers on the port side, which rose high as the starboard side dipped lower, clung to the side of the portholes; their guns began slipping back through them and crashing down the decks. Looking through the doorway I saw a man fall off the topmast into the web of rigging, swivel guns fall from the topdeck railing, into the sea. I heard crashing and shouting below the netting and closing the weatherdeck as men and equipment slid and fell. All this took only seconds, but the time seems to stretch out in my memory, detail after terrible detail. All the soldiers on our deck, and their guns, were now tumbling and crashing against the starboard side. The long cannon on the port side, too, began slipping from its mount.

'Get out of here!' the sailor beside us shouted to his fellow. They went down on hands and knees and began crawling rapidly out onto the walkway above the netting, grasping the sides for the ship was tilted at such an angle now it was impossible to walk. Under the netting men were screaming. I saw hands reaching up through the mesh...I began crawling after the sailors, gritting my teeth against the pain in my shoulder... We got out on to the walkway. Men were hacking frantically up at the stout netting with their knives. A hand reached up and grasped my arm, a frantic voice shouted, 'Help us!' but then the water crashed over us, the cold a sudden shock, and I felt myself carried outwards. In the seconds I rode the top of the onrushing water I saw dozens of soldiers falling from the aftercastle through open or broken blinds. I saw the red of Pygeon's heavy brigandyne as he fell past me like a stone, eyes wide with horror, and Snodin's plump form, arms windmilling frantically, mouth open and screaming. The men threw up great splashes as they hit the sea, then disappeared, the weight of their clothing and helmets taking them at once to the bottom. All those men, all of them. And from the hundreds trapped below the netting, and on the lower decks, I heard a terrible screaming. Then the cold waters closed over my head and I thought, this is it, the end I feared, drowning. And suddenly all the pains in my body were gone.

C J Sansom
Heartstone (2010)

The deeply unpopular favourite of James I, the Duke of Buckingham, who went on to hold office as Lord High Admiral under Charles I, was murdered by John Felton in Portsmouth in August 1628. Buckingham was so unpopular, after a number of wildly unsuccessful expeditions, that Felton was acclaimed by the public as a hero.

In a letter from Whitehall dated June 9th 1626, Charles I writes:

Buckingham I command you to draw my armie together to Porchemouth to the end that I may send them speedli to Rochel. I shall send after you directions how and whaire to billett them until the tyme when ye will be able to shipp them for the doing whereof this shall be sufficient warrant it being the command of your loving faithfull constant frend.

Here, the Duke's contemporary, Sir Henry Wotton, describes his death.

The Duke's fame was more and more in obloquy amongst the mass of people, whose judgments are only reconciled with good successes.

John Felton by nature of a deep melancholy, silent and gloomy constitution but bred in the active way of a soldier, this was the man that closely within himself had conceived the duke's death. But what may have been the immediate or greatest motive of that felonious conception is even yet in the clouds. He went and stood expecting till the Duke of Buckingham should pass through a kind of lobby between that room and the next where were divers attending him; towards which passage, as I conceive somewhat darker than the chamber, which he avoided, while the duke came in with Sir Thomas Fryer close at his ear in the very moment as the said knight withdrew himself from the duke, the assassin gave him with a back blow a deep wound into his left side, leaving the knife in his body, which the duke himself pulling out, in a sudden effusion of spirits, he sunk down under the table in the next room, and immediately expired.

Sir Henry Wotton (1568–1639)
A short view of the life and death of George Villiers
Duke of Buckingham

And here Felton's contemporary Zouch Townley, salutes his action in a poem:

'Let the duke's name solace and crown thy thrall
All we for him did suffer, thou for all!
And I dare boldly write, as thou dar'st die,
Stout Felton, England's ransom, here doth lie!'

Expecting to be killed in the act of assassination, Felton had pinned inside his hat:

That man is cowardly and base and deserveth not the name of a gentleman that is not willing to sacrifice his life for the honor of his God, his king, and his country. Let no man commend me for doing it, but rather discommend themselves as to the cause of it, for if God had not taken away our hearts for our sins, he would not have gone so long unpunished.

The diary of John Evelyn (1620–1706), which did not come into the public realm until around 1820, has been somewhat eclipsed by that of his contemporary Pepys, though it has proved a mine of information on seventeenth-century life and events. Here the Royalist sympathiser describes the siege of Portsmouth, at which the Royalist garrison under Goring was routed by the Parliamentarians.

> … the next day to see the siege of Portsmouth. For now was that bloody difference between the King and parliament broken out which ended in the fatal tragedy so many years after. It was on the day of its being rendered to Sir William Waller; which gave me an opportunity of taking my leave of Colonel Goring, the Governor, now embarking for France. That day was fought the signal battle of Edgehill.

Samuel Pepys refers in his now famous *Diary* to his business here as 'clerk of the king's ships'. This diary remained in cipher until an undergraduate John Smith at Magdalene College, Cambridge, Pepys's college, laboured to transcribe it for three years, miserably unaware that the key to the shorthand was, close at hand, in the library. He completed the work in 1822. In response to the question of whether Pepys intended it to be read, Robert Louis Stevenson claims: 'Pepys was not such an ass, but he must have perceived, as he went on, the extraordinary nature of the work he was producing'. The latest, best and indeed only edition to read is Robert Latham's of 1970.

1661
January 2nd
Coach for Portsmouth. The Queenes things were all in White-hall Court, ready to be sent away, and her Majesty ready to be gone in an hour after to Hampton-court tonight, and so to be at Portsmouth on Saturday next.

11th *office day.*
This day comes news by letters from Portsmouth that the Princess Henriette is fallen sick of the measles on board the *London*, after the Queene and she were under sail – and so was forced to come back again into Portsmouth harbour. And in their way, was by negligence of the Pilott run upon Horse-sand. The Queene and she continue aboard, and do not entend

to come on shore till she sees what will become of the young Princesse. This news does make people think something endeed; that three of them should fall sick of the same disease one after another. This morning likewise, we have an order to see guards set in all the King's yards; and so we do appoint who and who shall go to them. Sir Wm Batten to Chatham – Collonell Slingsby and I to Deptford and Woolwich – Portsmouth, being a garrison, needs none.

May 1st

Up earely and baited at Petersfield, in the room which the King lay in lately at his being there.

Here very merry and played, us and our wifes at bowles. Then we set forth again; and so to Portsmouth, seeming to me a very pleasant and strong place. And we lay at the Red lyon, where Haslerigg and Scott and Walton did hold their Councell when they were here, against Lambert and the committee of safety.

Several officers of the Yard came to see us tonight; and merry we were, but troubled to have no better Lodgeings.

May 2nd

Up; and Mr Creed and I to walk round the town upon the Walls. Then to our Inne; and there all the officers of the Yard to see me with great respect and I walked with them to the Dock and saw all the Stores, and much pleased with the sight of the place.

Back, and brought them all to dinner with me and treated them handsomely; and so after dinner by water to the Yard, and there we made sale of the old provisions. Then we and our wifes all to see the *Mountagu*, which is a fine ship. And so to the town again by water; and then to see the room where the Duke of Buckingham was killed by Felton.

So to our lodgings and to supper and to bed.

1662
April 23rd

Up earely and to Petersfield, and there dined well; and thence got a contry-man to guide us by Havan, to avoid going through the forrest; but he carried us much out of the way.

No news of the Queene at all. So to dinner and then to the pay all the afternoon. Then Sir W. Penn and I walked to the King's-yard, and there lay at Mr Tippet's, (master shipwright of the yard) where exceeding well treated.

By coach to Portsmouth, and there visited the Mayor Mr Timbrell our Anchorsmith, who showed us the present they have for the Queene; which is a salt-sellar of silver, the walls Christall, with four Eagles and four grayhounds standing up at top to bear up a dish – which is indeed one of the neatest pieces of plate that ever I saw – and the case is very pretty also.

April 25th
All the morning at Portsmouth at the pay; and then to dinner and again to the pay.

April 29th
At the pay all the morning, and so to dinner and then to it again in the afternoon.

April 30th
… And so I took leave of Sir W. Penn – he desiring to know whither I went, but I could not tell him. I went to the ladies, and there took them and walked to the Mayors (to show them the present) and then to the Dock where Mrs Tippets made much of them and thence back again, the Doctor being come to us to their Lodgeings, whither came our supper by my appointment, and we very merry, playing at cards and laughing very merry, till twelve o'clock at night. And so having stayed so long (which we had resolved to stay till they bid us be gone) which yet they did not do; but by consent we bid them goodnight. And so passed the guards and went to the Doctor's lodgings, and there lay with him – our discourse being much about the Quality of the lady with Mrs Pierce, she being some old and handsome and painted and fine, and hath a very handsome maid with her – which we take to be the marks of a bawd. But Mrs Pierce says she is a stranger to her and met by chance in the coach, and pretends to be a dresser. Her name is Eastwood. So to sleep in a bad bed, about one a'clock in the morning.

This afternoon, after dinner, comes Mr Steventon one of the burgesses of the town, to tell me that the Mayor and burgesses did desire my acceptance of a Burgessshipp and were ready at the Mayor to make me one. So I went and there they were all ready and did with much civility give me my oath. All, after the oath, did by custom shake me all by the hand. So I took them to a tavern and made them drink; and paying the reckoning, went away – they having first in the tavern made Mr Wraith also a burgesse, he coming in while we were drinking. It cost me a piece in gold to the Town Clerke and 10s to the bayliffes, and spent 6s.

1666
October 20th
...there comes to me Comissioner Middleton whom I took on purpose to walk in the garden with me and to learn what he observed when the fleet was at Portsmouth. He says that the fleet was in such a condition as to discipline, as if the Devil had commanded it – so much wickedness of all sorts.

Enquiring how it came to pass that so many ships miscried this year, he tells me that he enquired, and the pilots do say that they dare not do nor go but as the captains will have them; and if they offer to do otherwise, the captains swear they will run them through.

Samuel Pepys (1633–1703)
Diary (1660–69)

Percy Francis Westerman was born in Portsmouth in 1876 and educated at Portsmouth Grammar School before taking up a clerical appointment at Portsmouth Dockyard at the age of twenty. He went on to become a hugely successful author for children. The excerpt is taken from *A Lad of Grit*, his first book, which is set during the reign of Charles II. The *Royal Oak* alluded to here was burned by the Dutch when they raided the Medway in 1667.

On the morrow following my arrival I, in company with my cousin Maurice, was taken by my uncle to the dockyard.

Here all was activity and noise. Most of the fleet – amongst which were pointed out to me the *Yarmouth*, *Swiftsure*, *London*, and *Ruby* – lay at anchor at some distance from the wharves, while close alongside were the *Naseby*, her name being changed to the *Royal Charles*, and the *Montague*.

There was but one dry dock, and in it lay the *Providence*; and on a slip, being nearly fit for launching, stood a large ship of seventy-six guns, her name having but recently been changed to the *Royal Oak*.

While we were looking on with astonishment at this busy scene, a short, thick-set man, whose portly body was ill-supported by a pair of bandy legs, came towards the place where we stood. He wore a blue uniform, with three-cornered hat, and carried at his side a sword that trailed behind him as he walked, and even threatened to become entangled between his legs.

'Ha! Captain Duce of the Lizard! Stand aside, boys, while I have speech with him.'

The captain was in a rage.

'A pretty pass! Here lie I ready to weigh and make sail, but ne'er a loaf of bread aboard!'

'I cannot help you, Captain,' replied my uncle. 'I can only refer you to the Commissioner.'

'Hang the Commissioner!' roared the irate officer. 'First I am directed to apply to him; he sends me to you; you thereupon give me cold comfort by sending me again to the Commissioner. How can I take my ship to sea lacking bread and flour? Ah! Here, sirrah!' he broke off, noticing a man passing by. 'Here, sirrah! You're the person I want.'

The man addressed came across to where the captain and my uncle were debating. His calling was apparent, he being covered from head to foot with flour.

'Well, Hunt, how is it Captain Duce can get no supplies from you?'

The baker shook his head. 'Over a thousand pounds are due to my partner and me,' said he. 'We were to be paid monthly, but have received nothing since September last. Verily, I am afraid to go abroad lest I am arrested by my creditors, whom I cannot pay, as the Navy Commissioners will not pay me!'

Without waiting to hear further, for complaints of arrears of payment were a common occurrence, Maurice and I stole away and wandered towards the slip where the *Royal Oak* was nearing completion.

A noble sight she made, this immense yellow-painted hull, with her double tier of gunports and her towering stern, richly ornamented with gilded quarter badges and richly carved galleries. Little did we know that a short seven years hence would see the ship, the pride of the king's navy, a battered and fire-swept wreck – but I anticipate.

Percy F Westerman (1876-1959)
A Lad of Grit 1909

Daniel Defoe was author of *Robinson Crusoe* (1719) and *Diary of the Plague Year* (1722), both vivid and compelling novels and still enormously popular after three centuries. As we have heard from earlier chapters, he was also a pioneer of economic travel writing, and his panoramic travels in Britain provide an economic picture of the islands on the eve of the Industrial Revolution.

From hence we descend gradually to Portsmouth. The situation of this place is such, that it is chosen, as may well be said, for the best security to the navy above all the places in Britain; the entrance into the harbour is safe, but very narrow, guarded on both sides by terrible platforms of cannon. Before any ships attempt to enter this port by sea, they must also pass the cannon of the main platform of the garrison, and also another at South-Sea-Castle; so that it is next to impossible that any ships could match the force of all those cannon, and be able to force their way into the harbour; in which I speak the judgment of men well acquainted with such matters, as well as my own opinion, that the mouth or entrance into Portsmouth is narrow, and may be lock'd up with booms, which before the ships could break, and while they were lying at them to break them away, they would be torn in pieces by the battery at the Point: That the guns on the said battery at the Point at Portsmouth, are defended as above, with ambruziers, and the gunners stand cover'd, so that they cannot so soon be beaten from their guns; that the greatest fleet of ships that ever were in the hands of one nation at a time, would not pretend, if they had not an army also on shore, to attack the whole work, to force their entrance into the harbour at Portsmouth.

As to the strength of the town by land, the works are very large and numerous, and besides the battery at the

Point aforesaid, there is a large hornwork on the south-side, running out towards South-Sea Castle; there is also a good counterscarp, and double mote, with ravelins in the ditch, and double pallisadoes, and advanced works to cover the place from any approach, where it may be practicable...

The town of Portsmouth, besides its being a fortification, is a well inhabited, thriving, prosperous corporation; and hath been greatly enrich'd of late by the fleet's having so often and so long lain there, as well as large fleets of merchant-men, as the whole navy during the late war; besides the constant fitting out of men here, and the often paying them at Portsmouth, has made a great confluence of people thither on their private business, with other things, which the attendance of those fleets hath required: These things have not only been a great advantage to the town, but has really made the whole place rich, and the inhabitants of Portsmouth are quite another sort of people than they were a few years before the Revolution; this is what Mr Camden takes notice of, even so long ago as the reign of Queen Elizabeth; that 'Portsmouth was populous in time of war, but not so in time of peace': but now the business of the navy is so much encreased, and so much of it always done here, that it may be said, there is as much to do at Portsmouth now in time of peace, as there was then in time of war, and more too...

From Portsmouth west, the country lyes low and flat, and is full of creeks and inlets of the sea and rivers, all the way to Southampton, so that we ferry over three times in about eighteen miles; besides going over one bridge, namely, at Tichfield: The first of these ferries is that at Portsmouth itself, (viz.) cross the mouth of the harbour... to Gosport; from thence we ride to Tichfield, as above, where we pass the river Alre, which rises in the same county at Alresford, or near it, which is not above twenty-two miles off; and yet it is a large river here, and makes a good road below, call'd Tichfield Bay: Thence at about four miles we pass another river at Busselton, narrow in breadth, but exceeding deep, and eminent for its being able to carry the biggest ships: Here is a building yard for ships of war, and in King William's time, two eighty gun ships were launched here. It seems the safety of the creek, and the plenty of timber in the country behind it, is the reason of building so much in this place... Many of the king's ships were built hereabouts, besides abundance of large merchant ships, which were about that time built at Southampton, at Redbridge, and at Bursleton.

Colonel Norton also, a known gentleman, whose seat at Southwick is within six miles of Portsmouth, and within three miles of the water carriage; this gentleman they told me had an immense quantity of timber, some growing within sight of the very docks in Portsmouth: Farther west it is the like, and as I rode through New-Forest, I cou'd see the antient oaks of many hundred years standing, perishing with their wither'd tops advanced up in the air, and grown white with age, and that could never yet get the favour to be cut down, and made serviceable to their country.

Daniel Defoe (1661?–1731)
A Tour thro' the whole island of Great Britain (1720)

William Gilpin (1724-1804) was rector of Boldre in the New Forest. He was, Pevsner tells us, 'the most influential of all writers on picturesque travelling, telling his readers what to look for, how to look, and how to create picturesque landscape effects.' Gilpin went so far as to suggest that 'a mallet judiciously used' might render the insufficiently ruinous gable of Tintern Abbey even more picturesque.

From the top of Portsdown Hill, where we soon arrived, we had a grander view in its kind than perhaps any part of the globe can exhibit. Beneath our feet lay a large extent of marshy ground which is covered with water when the tides flow high and adorned with innumerable islands and peninsulas. About a mile from the eye this marsh is joined by the island of Portsea distinguished by its peculiar fertility and the luxuriance of its woods; among which the town of Portsmouth appears to rise at the distance of five miles. The island is nearly of a triangular form but here it seems to be a long stretch of land forming a boundary to the harbour which like a land-locked bay runs up between it and the marshy grounds we had just surveyed. Far to the right and at the very end of the harbour stands Portchester castle, the massy towers of which showed themselves to advantage at this distance. The harbour of Portsmouth which would contain all the shipping in Europe was the grand feature in this view. Besides innumerable skiffs and smaller vessels plying about this ample bason we counted between fifty and sixty sail of the line. Some of them appeared lying unrigged in the water others in commission with their colours flying. Beyond Portsmouth we had a view of the sea which is generally crowded with ships especially the road of St Helens where some men of war are commonly waiting for the wind. Beyond all appeared the Isle of Wight the high grounds of which bounded the prospect. This whole view from Portsdown Hill was picturesque as well as amusing. The parts were rather large indeed but they were distinct and well connected.

Having surveyed this extensive landscape we descended the hill and soon entered the isle of Portsea through a small fortification. The sea at full tide flows into the ditches that surround it and just brings it within the definition of an island. The whole is a perfect flat but the road winding through luxurious inclosures and shaded by noble oaks is agreeable. In this island we travelled about four miles to Portsmouth.

At Portsmouth we were recommended to the civilities of a very worthy gentleman though but indifferently qualified to satisfy our curiosity. He was so deaf that we were obliged to repeat our question four or five times and when we had made it intelligible he stammered so exceedingly that the question was lost before the answer could be obtained. His company however opened a free access to everything we wished to examine.

William Gilpin (1724-1804)
Observations on the coasts of Hampshire (1774)

The *Royal George*, at the time of her launch in 1756, was the largest warship in the world; she sank undergoing routine maintenance work whilst anchored off Portsmouth on August 29th 1782, with the loss of more than 800 lives including women and children who were visiting the great vessel. William Cowper was one of the most popular poets of his day, a prolific composer of hymns and a fervent anti-slavery campaigner.

On the Loss of the Royal George

Toll for the brave—
The brave! that are no more:
 All sunk beneath the wave,
Fast by their native shore.
 Eight hundred of the brave,
Whose courage well was tried,
 Had made the vessel heel
And laid her on her side;
 A land-breeze shook the shrouds,
And she was overset;
 Down went the Royal George,
With all her crew complete.

Toll for the brave—
Brave Kempenfelt is gone,
 His last sea-fight is fought,
His work of glory done.
 It was not in the battle,
No tempest gave the shock,
 She sprang no fatal leak,
She ran upon no rock;
 His sword was in the sheath,
His fingers held the pen,
 When Kempenfelt went down
With twice four hundred men.

Weigh the vessel up,
Once dreaded by our foes,
 And mingle with your cup
The tears that England owes;
 Her timbers yet are sound,
And she may float again,
 Full charg'd with England's thunder,
And plough the distant main;
 But Kempenfelt is gone,
His victories are o'er;
 And he and his eight hundred
Must plough the wave no more.

William Cowper (1731–1800)

Here a young and promising captain, twenty-eight-year-old Horatio Nelson (1758–1805), shows that he was not always in control of his destiny. He was about to take command of HMS *Boreas*, bound for the Caribbean where he would meet his wife, Fanny, on Nevis. Towards the end of Nelson's life, Admiral Frank Austen, Jane's eldest brother, wrote of the puny, fragile, half-blind man with the empty sleeve, 'I never heard of his equal, nor do I expect to see such a man.'

Letter to William Locker, Esq.,
Portsmouth, April 21st, 1784

My dear Sir,

Since I parted from you, I have encountered many disagreeable adventures. The day after I left you, we sailed at daylight, just after high water. The d----d Pilot – it makes me swear to think of it – ran the Ship aground, where she lay with so little water that the people could not walk round her till next high water. That night and part of the next day, we lay below the Nore with a hard gale of wind and snow; Tuesday I got into the Downs: on Wednesday I got into a quarrel with a Dutch Indiaman who had English on board, which we settled after some difficulty. The Dutchman has made a complaint against me; but the Admiralty fortunately have approved my conduct in the business, a thing they are not very guilty of where there is a likelihood of a scrape. And yesterday, to complete me, I was riding a blackguard horse that ran away with me at Common, carried me round all the Works into Portsmouth, by the London gates, through the Town out at the gate that leads to Common, where there was a wagon in the road – which is so very narrow, that a horse could barely pass. To save my legs, and perhaps my life, I was obliged to throw myself from the horse, which I did with great agility: but unluckily upon hard stones, which has hurt my back and my leg, but done no other mischief. It was a thousand to one that I had not been killed. To crown all, a young girl was riding with me; her horse ran away with mine; but most fortunately a gallant young man seized her horse's bridle a moment before I dismounted, and saved her from the destruction which she could not have avoided...

Give my compliments to Madam Bradley, etc. and rest assured I am yours, most sincerely,

Horatio Nelson

In the spring of 1797, the Spithead anchorage, was sight of a naval mutiny which lasted for a month. Since the country was at war with Revolutionary France at the time, the mutineers promised to act immediately if French ships were seen heading for England, but in the meantime were demanding a rise in pay to keep pace with the inflation of the preceding decades, better food, more shore leave and compensation for sickness and injury. After two weeks negotiations had broken down, but:

To the mutineers at Spithead 1797 came the news that Lord Howe, the idol of the Channel fleet, and the King's personal friend, was about to start for Portsmouth. Whether the idea originated with George III or with Pitt, it was a most happy inspiration. The King and Howe were the only two men in authority whom the sailors really trusted; and when Howe came to them with full power from the crown to treat with them, and to grant the royal pardon at his discretion, bringing with him moreover the desired act of Parliament, the mutineers felt that at last their negotiation was based on solid rock, and that they were no longer at the mercy of deceitful men.

Howe's popularity was well deserved. Although at times he could be stern and exacting, yet ever since the Seven Years' War, when as Captain of the Magnanime he won the title of the 'sailor's friend' by granting leave of absence to all his crew, watch by watch, he had never failed to show kindness to the seamen under his command. His mediation was the one thing needed to bring the mutiny quietly and happily to an end. He arrived in Portsmouth early on the 11th. In spite of his gout and his seventy-one years, he began his business at once. By noon he was at St Helens, on board *The Royal George*; and on the same day he visited *The Queen Charlotte*, his old flagship, and *The Duke*, and talked to the delegates of some other ships. He spoke in a conciliatory way, as became his character. Howe's procedure was to tell the mutineers that the government had all the time intended

115

to grant them everything promised by the Admiralty, and that as they knew, the act for the increase of their wages and provisions had already been passed before he left London. He impressed them with a due sense of their misconduct in renewing the mutiny through idle suspicion; and when they had expressed their regret and contrition, he talk to every wounded man, sitting by the side of their cradles, and constantly ordering his live-stock and wines to be applied to their use at the discretion of the surgeon, and at all times for the sick on board. Howe's kindness and courage, together with the memory of his great victory of 1794, gave him a moral authority over the seamen which belonged to no other admirals of the time, except perhaps St Vincent, Duncan and Nelson.

For four days he continued this treatment, and contrived in that time to visit every one of the mutinous ships. Howe's speeches made a favourable impression — his presence alone must have had a considerable effect in subduing the mutiny.

But still the mutineers were not satisfied. They insisted that the officers against whom the ships' companies had individual complaints should not be allowed to return. It was an extraordinary demand, and a very important principle was involved in it. If the Lords of the Admiralty complied, they would be tacitly admitting that they had allowed a too harsh administration of the Articles of War; and their compliance would be an earnest that discipline should be more lenient in future. They would be setting up a strange precedent, too, in dismissing, at the instance of common seamen, officers whose appointment they had themselves approved. But however unhappy the circumstances might be, the Board were forced to agree to the dismissal of these officers. Howe found that it was the only means of bringing about a peaceful settlement. The seamen refused to serve under officers who had not treated them fairly; the officers themselves had no wish to be foisted on crews which would not obey them; and Howe 'judged fit to acquiesce in what was now the mutual desire of both officers and seamen in that fleet.' Although he was quite exhausted with his efforts Howe was characteristically unwilling to resign his charge without a final act of reconciliation. Accordingly the whole of May 15th was devoted to feasting and processions. In the early morning a large number of boats came to the Sally Port, and the townspeople were roused by the reiterated airs of 'God Save the King' and 'Rule Britannia,' played by the massed bands of the fleets and the whole morning was spent in a tour of the fleet.

Conrad Gill (1883–1968)
The Naval Mutinies of 1797 (1913)

Patrick O'Brien's well-regarded and popular naval novels, set during the Napoleonic Wars, featured Captain Jack Aubrey and his ship's surgeon Stephen Maturin, whose natural inclinations are captured here:

This morning when I was walking beside the coach as it laboured up Portsdown Hill and I came to the top, with all Portsmouth Harbour suddenly spread below me, and Gosport, Spithead and perhaps half the Channel fleet glittering there – a powerful squadron moving out past Haslar in line ahead, all studdingsails abroad – I felt a longing for the sea. It has a great cleanliness. There are moments when everything on land seems to me tortuous, dark, and squalid; though to be sure, squalor is not lacking aboard a man-o'-war.

Patrick O'Brian (1914–2000)
Post Captain (1972)

Another naval series set during the Napoleonic Wars featured Horatio Hornblower, who rises from junior captain to Admiral of the Fleet in the Royal Navy over the course of the books. Here the bracing bravery and heroism of the navy comes ringing through the prose:

'Are you going back to fight, Father?' Richard asked.

He said one more goodbye to Barbara; it was not easy. If he had good fortune he might be home in a week, but he could not tell her that, for it might reveal too much the nature of his mission. This little bit of deception helped to shatter the mood of unity and union; it made him a little cold and formal again. Hornblower had had a strange feeling as he turned away from her of something lost forever. Then he climbed into the chaise with Browen beside him and rolled away, skirting the autumnal Downs to Guildford in the gathering evening, and then down the Portsmouth Road – the road along which which he had driven on so many momentous occasions – through the night. The transition was brief from luxury to hardship. At midnight he set foot in the *Porta Coeli*, welcomed by Freeman, square, stocky, and swarthy as ever, with black hair hanging to the cheeks, gipsy-fashion; one noted almost with surprise that there were no rings in his ears. Not more than ten minutes was necessary to tell Freeman, under seal of secrecy, the mission upon which the *Porta Coeli* was to be despatched; in obedience to his orders received four hours earlier Freeman already had the brig ready for sea, and at the end of that ten minutes the hands were at the capstan getting in the anchor.

'It's going to be a dirty night, sir' said Freeman out of the darkness beside him. 'Glass is still dropping.'

'I expect it will be, Mr Freeman.'

Freeman suddenly raised his voice to one of the loudest bellows that Hornblower had ever heard – that barrel-shaped chest could produce a surprising volume of sound.

'Mr Carlow! Have all hands shorten sail. Get that maintopmast stays'l in! Have another reef in the tops'ls! Southeast by south, quartermaster.'

'Southeast by south, sir.'

C S Forester (1899–1966)
Lord Hornblower (1952)

The heroine of Jane Austen's novel *Mansfield Park*, Fanny Price, is returning to her modest family home in Portsmouth after living with her much grander uncle, Sir Thomas Bertram, for some seven years at Mansfield Park. Sir Thomas is impatient with Fanny who has refused an offer of marriage from the rich (and untrustworthy) Henry Crawford, being secretly in love with her cousin Edmund. Fanny's brother William, who is making his way in the Royal Navy, accompanies her on the journey.

Jane Austen, with two brothers of her own trained in Portsmouth, was well-informed about the great sea port and matters naval. Her brother Frank joined the navy in 1788 as a fourteen-year-old, and rose through the ranks to become Sir Francis Austen, Admiral of the Fleet.

Chapter VII

… With such thoughts as these among ten hundred others, Fanny proceeded in her journey, safely and cheerfully, and as expeditiously as could rationally be hoped in the dirty month of February. They entered Oxford, but she could take only a hasty glimpse of Edmund's College as they passed along, and made no stop anywhere, till they reached Newbury, where a comfortable meal, uniting dinner and supper, wound up the enjoyments and fatigues of the day.

The next morning saw them off again at an early hour; and with no events and no delays they regularly advanced, and were in the environs of Portsmouth while there was yet daylight for Fanny to look around her, and wonder at its new buildings. They passed the Drawbridge, and entered the town; and the light was only beginning to fail, as, guided by William's powerful voice, they were rattled into a narrow street, leading from the high street and drawn up before the door of a small house now inhabited by Mr Price.

Fanny was all agitation and flutter – all hope and apprehension. The moment they stopt, a trollopy-looking maid-servant, seemingly in waiting for them at the door, stept forward,

and more intent on telling the news, than giving them any help, immediately began with, 'the *Thrush* is gone out of harbour, please Sir, and one of the officers has been here to' – She was interrupted by a fine tall boy of eleven years old, who rushing out of the house, pushed the maid aside, and while William was opening the chaise door himself, called out, 'you are just in time. We have been looking for you this half hour. The *Thrush* went out of harbour this morning. I saw her. It was a beautiful sight. And they think she will have her orders in a day or two. And Mr Campbell was here at four o'clock, to ask for you; he has got one of the *Thrush*'s boats, and is going off to her at six, and hoped you would be here in time to go with him.'

A stare or two at Fanny, as William helped her out of the carriage, was all the voluntary notice which this brother bestowed; but he made no objection to her kissing him, though still entirely engaged in detailing further particulars of the *Thrush*'s going out of harbour, in which he had a strong right of interest, being to commence his career of seamanship in her at this very time.

Another moment, and Fanny was in the narrow entrance-passage of the house, and in her mother's arms, who met her there with looks of true kindness, and with features which Fanny loved the more, because they brought her aunt Bertram's before her; and there were her two sisters, Susan, a well-grown fine girl of fourteen, and Betsey, the youngest of the family, about five – both glad to see her in their way, though with no advantage of manner in receiving her. But manner Fanny did not want. Would they but love her, she should be satisfied. She was then taken into a parlour, so small that her first conviction was of its being only a passage-room to something better, and she stood for a moment expecting to be invited on; but when she saw there was no other door, and that there were signs of habitation before her, she called back her thoughts, reproved herself, and grieved lest they should have been suspected. Her mother, however, could not stay long enough to suspect any thing. She was gone again to the street door, to welcome William. 'Oh! My dear William, how glad I am to see you. But have you heard about the *Thrush*? She is gone out of harbour already, three days before we had any thought of it; and I do not know what I am to do about Sam's things, they will never be ready in time; for she may have her orders tomorrow, perhaps. It takes me quite unawares. And now you must be off for Spithead too. Campbell has been here, quite in a worry about you; and now, what shall we do? I thought to have had such a comfortable evening with you, and here everything comes upon me at once.'

Her son answered cheerfully, telling her that every thing was always for the best; and making light of his own inconvenience, in being obliged to hurry away so soon. 'To be sure, I had much rather she had stayed in harbour, that I might have sat a few hours with you in comfort; but as there is a boat ashore, I had better go off at once, and there is no help for it. Whereabouts does the *Thrush* lay at Spithead! Near the Canopus? But no matter – here's Fanny in the parlour, and why should we stay in the passage? – Come, mother, you have hardly looked at your own dear Fanny yet.'

In they both came, and Mrs Price having kindly kissed her daughter again, commented a little on her growth, began with very natural solicitude to feel for their fatigues and wants as travellers.

'Poor dears! How tired you must both be! – and now what will you have? I began to think you would never come. Betsey and I have been watching for you this half hour. And when did you get anything to eat? And what would you like to have now? I could not tell whether you would be for some meat, or only a dish of tea after your journey, or else I would have got something ready. And now I am afraid Campbell will be here, before there is time to dress a steak, and we have no butcher at hand. It is very inconvenient to have no butcher in the street. We were better off in our last house. Perhaps you would like some tea, as soon as it can be got.'

They both declared they would prefer it to anything. 'Then, Betsey, my dear, run into the kitchen, and see if Rebecca has put the water on; and tell her to bring in the tea-things as soon as she can. I wish we could get the bell mended – but Betsey is a very handy little messenger.'

Betsey went with alacrity; proud to shew her abilities before her fine new sister. 'Dear me!' continued the anxious mother, 'what a sad fire we have got, and I dare say you are both starved with cold. Draw your chair nearer, my dear. I cannot think what Rebecca has been about. I am sure I told her to bring some coals half an hour ago. Susan, you should have taken care of the fire.'

'I was upstairs, mamma, moving my things;' said Susan, in a fearless, self-defending tone, which startled Fanny. 'You know you had but just settled that my sister Fanny and I should have the other room; and I could not get Rebecca to give me any help.'

Further discussion was prevented by various bustles; first, the driver came to be paid – then there was a squabble between Sam and Rebecca, about the manner of carrying up his sister's trunk, which he would manage all his own way; and lastly in walked Mr Price himself, his own loud voice preceding him, as with something of the oath kind he kicked away his son's portmanteau, and his daughter's band-box in the passage, and called out for a candle; no candle was brought, however, and he walked into the room. Fanny, with doubting feelings, had risen to meet him, but sank down again on finding herself undistinguished in the dusk, and unthought of. With a friendly shake of his son's hand, and an eager voice, he instantly began – 'Ha! Welcome back, my boy. Glad to see you. Have you heard the news? The *Thrush* went out of harbour this morning. Sharp is the word, you see. By G-, you are just in time. The doctor has been here enquiring for you; he has got one of the boats, and is to be off for Spithead by six, so you had better go with him. I have been to Turner's about your mess; it is all in a way to be done. I should not wonder if you had your orders to-morrow; but you cannot sail with this wind, if you are to cruize to the westward; and Captain Walsh thinks you will certainly have a cruize to the westward, with the Elephant. By G-, I wish you may. But old Scholey was saying just now, that he thought that you would be sent first to the Texel. Well, well, you are ready, whatever happens. But by G-, you lost a fine sight by not being here in the morning to see the *Thrush* go out of harbour. I would not have been out of the way for a thousand pounds. Old Scholey ran in at breakfast time, to say she had slipped her moorings and was coming out. I jumped up, and made but two steps to the platform. If ever there was a perfect beauty afloat, she is one; and there she lays at Spithead, and anybody in England would take her for an eight-and-twenty. I was upon the platform two hours this afternoon, looking at her. She lays close to the *Endymion*, between her and the *Cleopatra*, just to the eastward of the sheer hulk.'

'Ha!' cried William, 'that's just where I should have put her myself. It's the best berth in Spithead. But here is my sister, sir, here is Fanny;' turning and leading her forward; 'it is so dark you do not see her.'

With an acknowledgement that he had quite forgot her, Mr Price now received his daughter: and, having given her a cordial hug, and observed that she was grown into a woman, and he supposed would be wanting a husband soon, seemed very much inclined to forget her again.

Fanny shrunk back to her seat, with feelings sadly pained by his language and his smell of spirits; and he talked on only to his son, and only of the *Thrush*, though William, warmly interested, as he was, in that subject, more than once tried to make his father think of Fanny, and her long absence and long journey.

After sitting some time longer, a candle was obtained; but, as there was still no appearance of tea, nor, from Betsey's reports from the kitchen, much hope of any under a considerable period, William determined to go and change his dress, and make the necessary preparations for his removal on board directly, that he might have his tea in comfort afterwards.

As he left the room, two rosy-faced boys, ragged and dirty, about eight and nine years old, rushed into it just released from school, and coming eagerly to see their sister, and tell that the *Thrush* was gone out of harbour; Tom and Charles: Charles had been born since Fanny's going away, but Tom she had often helped to nurse, and now felt a particular pleasure in seeing again. Both were kissed very tenderly, but Tom she wanted to keep by her, to try to trace the features of the baby she had loved, and talk to him of his infant preference of herself. Tom, however, had no mind for such treatment: he came home, not to stand and be talked to, but to run about and make noise; and both boys had soon burst away from her, and slammed the parlour door till her temples ached.

She had now seen all that were at home; there remained only two brothers between herself and Susan, one of whom was clerk in a public office in London, and the other midshipman on board an Indiaman. But though she had seen all the members of the family, she had not yet heard all the noise they could make.

Another quarter of an hour brought her a great deal more. William was soon calling out from the landing-place of the second storey, for his mother and for Rebecca. He was in distress for something that he had left there, and did not find again. A key was mislaid, Betsey accused of having got at his new hat, and some slight, but essential alteration of his uniform waist-coat, which he had been promised to have done for him, entirely neglected.

Mrs Price, Rebecca, and Betsey, all went to defend themselves, all talking together, but Rebecca loudest, and the job was to be done, as well as it could, in a great hurry; William trying in vain to send Betsey down again, or keep her from being troublesome as she was; the whole of which, as almost every door in the house was open, could be plainly distinguished in the parlour, except when drowned at intervals by the superior noise of Sam, Tom, and Charles chasing each other up and down stairs, and tumbling about and hallooing.

Fanny was almost stunned. The smallness of the house, and thinness of the walls, brought everything so close to her, that, added to the fatigue of her journey, and all her recent agitation, she hardly knew how to bear it. Within the room all was tranquil enough, for Susan having disappeared with the others, there were soon only her father and herself remaining; and he taking out a newspaper – the accustomary loan of a neighbour, applied himself to studying it, without seeming to recollect her existence. The solitary candle was held between himself and the paper, without any reference to her possible convenience; but she had nothing to do, and was glad to have the light screened from her aching head, as she sat in bewildered, broken, sorrowful contemplation.

She was at home. But alas! It was not such a home, she had not such a welcome, as – she checked herself; she was unreasonable. What right had she to be of importance to her family? She could have none, so long lost sight of! William's concerns must be dearest – they always had been – and he had every right. Yet to have so little said or asked about herself – to have scarcely an enquiry made about Mansfield! It did pain her to have Mansfield forgotten; the friends who had done so much – the dear, dear friends! But here, one subject swallowed up all the rest. Perhaps it must be so. The destination of the *Thrush* must be now pre-eminently interesting. A day or two might shew the difference. She only was to blame. Yet she thought it would not have been so at Mansfield. No, in her uncle's house there would have been consideration of times and seasons, a regulation of subject, a propriety, an attention towards every body which there was not here.

The only interruption which thoughts like these received for nearly half an hour, was from a sudden burst of her father's, not at all calculated to compose them. At a more than ordinary pitch of thumping and hallooing in the passage, he exclaimed, 'Devil take those young dogs! How they are singing out! Ay, Sam's voice louder than all the rest! That boy is fit for a boatswain. Holla – you there – Sam – stop your confounded pipe, or I shall be after you.'

This threat was so palpably disregarded, that though within five minutes afterwards the three boys all burst into the room together and sat down, Fanny could not consider it as a proof of any thing more than their being for the time thoroughly fagged, which their hot faces and panting breaths seemed to prove – especially as they were still kicking each other's shins, and hallooing out at sudden starts immediately under their father's eye.

The next opening of the door brought something more welcome; it was for the tea-things, which she had begun almost to despair of seeing that evening. Susan and an attendant girl, whose inferior appearance informed Fanny, to her great surprise, that she had previously seen the upper servant, brought in every thing necessary for the meal; Susan looked as she put the kettle on the fire and glanced at her sister, as if divided between the agreeable triumph of shewing her activity and usefulness, and the dread of being thought to demean herself by such an office. 'She had been into the kitchen,' she said, 'to hurry Sally and help make the toast, and spread the bread and butter – or she did not know when they should have got tea – and she was sure her sister must want something after her journey.'

Fanny was very thankful. She could not but own that she should be very glad of a little tea, and Susan immediately set about making it, as if pleased to have the employment all to herself; and with only a little unnecessary bustle, and some few injudicious attempts at keeping her brothers in better order than she could, acquitted herself very well. Fanny's spirit was as much refreshed as her body; her head and heart were soon the better for such a well-timed kindness. Susan had an open, sensible countenance; she was like William – and Fanny hoped to find her like him in disposition and good will towards herself.

In this more placid state of things William re-entered, followed not far behind by his mother and Betsey. He, complete in his Lieutenant's uniform, looking and moving all the taller, firmer, and more graceful for it, and with the happiest smile over his face, walked up directly to Fanny – who, rising from her seat, looked at him for a moment in speechless admiration, and then threw her arms round his neck to sob out her various emotions of pain and pleasure.

Anxious not to appear unhappy, she soon recovered herself: and wiping away her tears, was able to notice and admire all the striking parts of his dress – listening with reviving spirits to his cheerful hopes of being on shore some part of every day before they sailed, and even of getting her to Spithead to see the sloop.

The next bustle brought in Mr Campbell, the Surgeon of the Thrush, a very well behaved young man, who came to call for his friend, and for whom there was with some contrivance found a chair, and with some hasty washing of the young tea-maker's, a cup and saucer; and after another quarter of an hour of earnest talk between the gentlemen, noise rising upon noise, and bustle upon bustle, men and boys at last all in motion together, the moment came for setting off; every thing was ready, William took leave, and all of them were gone – for the three boys, in spite of their mother's intreaty, determined to see their brother and Mr Campbell to the sally-port; and Mr Price walked off at the same time to carry back his neighbour's newspaper.

Something like tranquillity might now be hoped for, and accordingly, when Rebecca had been prevailed on to carry away the tea-things, and Mrs Price had walked about the room some time looking for a shirt sleeve, which Betsey at last hunted out from a drawer in the kitchen, the small party of females were pretty well composed, and the mother having lamented again over the impossibility of getting Sam ready in time, was at leisure to think of her eldest daughter and the friends she had come from.

A few enquiries began; but one of the earliest – 'How did her sister Bertram manage about her servants? Was she as much plagued as herself to get tolerable servants?' – soon led her mind away from Northamptonshire, and fixed it on her own domestic grievances; and the shocking character of all the Portsmouth servants, of whom she believed her own two were the very worst, engrossed her completely. The Bertrams were all forgotten in detailing the faults of Rebecca, against whom Susan had also much to depose, and little Betsey a great deal more, and who did seem so thoroughly without a single recommendation, that Fanny could not help modestly presuming that her mother meant to part with her when her year was up.

'Her year!' cried Mrs Price; 'I am sure I hope I shall be rid of her before she has staid a year, for that will not be up till November. Servants are come to such a pass, my dear, in Portsmouth, that it is quite a miracle if one keeps them more than half-a-year. I have no hope of ever being settled; and if I was to part with Rebecca, I should only get something worse. And yet, I do not think I am a very difficult mistress to please – and I am sure the place is easy enough, for there is always a girl under her, and I often do half the work myself.'

Fanny was silent; but not from being convinced that there might not be a remedy found for some of these evils. As she now sat looking at Betsey, she could not but think particularly of another sister, a very pretty little girl, whom she had left there not much younger when she went into Northamptonshire, who had died a few years afterwards. There had been something remarkably amiable about her. Fanny, in those early days, had preferred her to Susan; and when the news of her death had at last reached Mansfield, had for a short time been quite afflicted. The sight of Betsey brought the image of little Mary back again, but she would not have pained her mother by alluding to her, for the world. While considering her with these ideas, Betsey, at a small distance, was holding out something to catch her eyes, meaning to screen it at the same time from Susan's. 'What have you got there, my love?' said Fanny, 'come and shew it to me.'

It was a silver knife. Up jumped Susan, claiming it as her own, and trying to get it away; but the child ran to her mother's protection, and Susan could only reproach, which she did very warmly, and evidently hoping to interest Fanny on her side. 'It was very hard that she was not to have her own knife; it was her own knife; little sister Mary had left it to her upon her death-bed, and she ought to have had it to keep herself long ago. But mamma kept it from her, and was always letting Betsey get hold of it; and the end of it would be that Betsey would spoil it, and get it for her own, though mamma had promised her that Betsey should not have it in her own hands.'

Fanny was quite shocked. Every feeling of duty, honour, and tenderness was wounded by her sister's speech and her mother's reply. 'Now, Susan,' cried Mrs Price in a complaining voice, 'now, how can you be so cross? You are always quarrelling about that knife. I wish you would not be so quarrelsome. Poor little Betsey; how cross Susan is to you! But you should not have taken it out, my dear, when I sent you to the drawer. You know I told you not to touch it, because Susan is so cross about it. I must hide it another time, Betsey. Poor Mary little thought it would be such a bone of contention when she gave it to me to keep, only two hours before she died. Poor little soul! She could but just speak to be heard, and she said so prettily, 'Let sister Susan have my knife, mamma, when I am dead and buried.' Poor little dear! she was so fond of it, Fanny, that she would have it lay by her in bed, all through her illness. It was the gift of her good godmother, old Mrs Admiral Maxwell, only six weeks before she was taken for death. Poor little sweet creature! Well, she was taken away from evil to come. My own Betsey, (fondling her), you have not the luck of such a good godmother. Aunt Norris lives too far off, to think of such little people as you.'

Fanny had indeed nothing to convey from aunt Norris, but a message to say she hoped her god-daughter was a good girl, and learnt her book. There had been at one moment a slight murmur in the drawing-room at Mansfield Park, about sending her a Prayer-book; but no second sound had been heard of such a purpose. Mrs Norris, however, had gone home and taken down two old Prayer-books of her husband, with that idea, but upon examination, the ardour of generosity went off. One was found to have too small a print for a child's eyes, and the other to be too cumbersome for her to carry about.

Fanny fatigued and fatigued again, was thankful to accept the first invitation of going to bed; and before Betsey had finished her cry at being allowed to sit up only one hour extraordinary in honour of sister, she was off, leaving all below in confusion and noise again, the boys begging for toasted cheese, her father calling out for his rum and water, and Rebecca never where she ought to be.

There was nothing to raise her spirits in the confined and scantily-furnished chamber that she was to share with Susan. The smallness of the rooms above and below indeed, and the narrowness of the passage and staircase, struck her beyond her imagination. She soon learnt to think with respect of her own little attic at Mansfield Park, in that house reckoned too small for anybody's comfort.

Chapter VIII

Could Sir Thomas have seen all his niece's feelings, when she wrote her first letter to her aunt, he would not have despaired; for though a good night's rest, a pleasant morning, the hope of soon seeing William again, and the comparatively quiet state of the house, from Tom and Charles being gone to school, Sam on some project of his own, and her father on his usual lounges, enabled her to express herself cheerfully on the subject of home, there were still to her own perfect consciousness, many drawbacks suppressed. Could he have seen only half that she felt before the end of the week, he would have thought Mr Crawford sure of her, and been delighted with his own sagacity.

Before the week ended, it was all disappointment. In the first place, William was gone. The *Thrush* had had her orders, the wind had changed, and he was sailed within four days from their reaching Portsmouth; and during those days, she had seen him only twice, in a short and hurried way, when he had come ashore on duty. There had been no free conversations, no walk on the ramparts, no visit to the dock-yard, no acquaintance with the *Thrush* – nothing of all that they had planned and depended on. Every thing in that quarter failed her, except William's affection. His last thought on leaving home was for her. He stepped back again to the door to say, 'Take care of Fanny, mother. She is tender, and not used to rough it like the rest of us. I charge you, take care of Fanny.'

William was gone; - and the home he had left her in was – Fanny could not conceal it from herself – in almost every respect, the very reverse of what she could have wished. It was the abode of noise, disorder, and impropriety. Nobody was in their right place, nothing was done as it ought to be. She could not respect her parents, as she had hoped. On her father, her confidence had not been sanguine, but he was more negligent of his family, his habits were worse, and his manners coarser, than she had been prepared for. He did not want abilities; but he had no curiosity, and no information beyond his profession; he read only the newspaper and the navy-list; he talked only of the dock-yard, the harbour, Spithead, and the Motherbank; he swore and he drank, he was dirty and gross. She had never been able to recall anything approaching to tenderness in his former treatment of herself. There had remained only a general impression of roughness and loudness; and now he scarcely ever noticed her, but to make her the object of a coarse joke.

Her disappointment in her mother was greater; there she had hoped much, and found almost nothing. Every flattering scheme of being of consequence to her soon fell to the ground. Mrs Price was not unkind – but, instead of gaining on her affection and confidence, and becoming more and more dear, her daughter never met with greater kindness from her, than on the first day of her arrival. The instinct of nature was soon satisfied, and Mrs Price's attachment had no other source. Her heart and her time were already quite full; she had neither leisure nor affection to bestow on Fanny. Her daughters never had been much to her. She was fond of her sons, especially of William, but Betsey was the first of her girls whom she had ever much regarded. To her she was most injudiciously indulgent. William was her pride; Betsey, her darling; and John, Richard, Sam, Tom, and Charles, occupied all the rest of her maternal solicitude, alternately her worries and her comforts. These shared her heart; her time was given chiefly to her house and servants. Her days were spent in a kind of slow bustle; always busy without getting on, always behindhand and lamenting it, without altering her ways; wishing to be an economist, without contrivance or regularity; dissatisfied with her servants, without skill to make them better...

Jane Austen (1775–1817)
Mansfield Park (1814)

Charles Dickens was born in Portsmouth but the family moved to London when he was only two, and his formative years were spent in Kent. Dickens returned to Portsmouth to give Penny Readings but only once involved the county and the city in his novels.

'Now listen to me, Smike,' said Nicholas, as they trudged with stout hearts onwards. 'We are bound for Portsmouth.' Smike nodded his head and smiled, but expressed no other emotion; for whether they had been bound for Portsmouth or Port Royal would have been alike to him, so they had been bound together.

'I don't know much of these matters,' resumed Nicholas; 'but Portsmouth is a seaport town, and if no other employment is to be obtained, I should think we might get on board some ship. I am young and active, and could be useful in many ways. So could you.'

'I hope so,' replied Smike. 'When I was at that – you know where I mean?'

'Yes, I know,' said Nicholas. 'You needn't name the place.'

'Well, when I was there,' resumed Smike; his eyes sparkling at the prospect of displaying his abilities; 'I could milk a cow, and groom a horse, with anybody.'

'Ha!' said Nicholas, gravely. 'I am afraid they don't keep many animals of either kind on board ship, Smike, and even when they have horses, that they are not very particular about rubbing them down; still you can learn to do something else, you know. Where there's a will, there's a way.'

'And I am very willing,' said Smike, brightening up again.

The knowledge that they were drawing near their place of destination, gave them fresh courage to proceed; but the way had been difficult, and they had loitered on the road, and Smike was tired. Thus, twilight had already closed in, when they turned off the path to the door of a roadside inn, yet twelve miles short of Portsmouth.

'Twelve miles,' said Nicholas, leaning with both hands on his stick, and looking doubtfully at Smike.

'Twelve long miles,' repeated the landlord.

'Is it a good road?' inquired Nicholas.

'Very bad,' said the landlord. As of course, being a landlord, he would say.

'I want to get on,' observed Nicholas, hesitating. 'I scarcely know what to do.'

'Don't let me influence you,' rejoined the landlord. 'I wouldn't go on if it was me.'

'Wouldn't you?' asked Nicholas, with the same uncertainty.

'Not if I knew when I was well off,' said the landlord. And having said it he pulled up his apron, put his hands into his pockets, and, taking a step or two outside the door, looked down the dark road with an assumption of great indifference…

And when they arrive in the city…

There is no lack of comfortable furnished apartments in Portsmouth, and no difficulty in finding some that are proportionate to very slender finances; but the former were too good, and the latter too bad, and they went into so many houses, and came out unsuited, that Nicholas seriously began to think he should be obliged to ask permission to spend the night in the theatre, after all.

Eventually, however, they stumbled upon two small rooms up three pair of stairs, or rather two pair and a ladder, at a tobacconist's shop, on the Common Hard; a dirty street leading down to the dock-yard. These Nicholas engaged, only too happy to have escaped any request for payment of a week's rent beforehand.

Charles Dickens (1812–70)
Nicholas Nickleby (1839)

An early adopter of the motor car, at this stage John James Hissey (1847–1921) is still travelling by horse and cart.

...A little further on...we noticed the keep of Warblington Castle, a very picturesque feature in the landscape and the only picturesque one we had seen since we had left quaint, old-world Bosham. Perhaps it may have been the contrast of the places we passed through, with the beauties of Bosham, that made them seem somewhat commonplace. Havant succeeded Emsworth, with the usual strip of semi-country between, and there we pulled up at the 'Bear', and baited our horses and refreshed ourselves. On a table of the landing of our inn stood an excellent model of an old-fashioned three-decker, made of bone, the waitress told us, by the French prisoners confined at Porchester Castle, during the Napoleonic wars. It was at that time, and at that castle, by the way, that these same prisoners invented ox-tail soup. It appears that ox-tails were given to the Frenchmen as being of but little value, but they managed to convert the despised tails into a delicious soup, so much so, that when the officer appointed to inspect the food at the prison tasted it, he demanded angrily how it was such luxuries were provided for them.

From Havant our road maintained much the same character as the first part of the stage only perhaps there were more green fields than houses on the way. To our left we had a fine view over Langstone harbour with its sluggish, winding waterways, and dreary stretches of mudflats. Then Portsmouth became dimly visible ahead, half hidden as it was by its own smoke, above which, in the clearer air, the masts of several huge men-o'-war were visible. To our right was the long line of the Downs, with massive Portsdown forts arranged at intervals along the top. The sudden transition from the placid, peaceful country to this land bristling with fortifications was almost startling, to say nothing of the ironclads at anchor in the bay.

Passing through Cosham and crossing at the same time the old London and Portsmouth coach road, we came to another salt-water creek running far inland the mimic waves of which washed our very wheels as we drove along. Soon afterwards the gray weather-beaten keep of Porchester Castle came into sight, an interesting ruin showing both Roman and Norman work. From the top of the keep is a comprehensive view of Portsmouth harbour, the ships therein, and the town. Porchester Castle would be a most delightful spot were it not for the presence of noisy excursionists and picnic parties from Portsmouth that effectively prevent all romancing there or quiet enjoyment of the place.

After Porchester the scenery began gradually to improve, and almost became pretty.

John James Hissey (1847–1921)
On Southern English Roads (1896)

In this semi-autobiographical short story, Rudyard Kipling's parents are about to return to India where the family have all lived happily together and to abandon him and his sister for five years in Southsea with people they have never met before. The desolation only gradually dawns on the boy.

Seaside towns on the south coast were a favourite venue for such abandonments, and through much of the nineteenth and twentieth centuries grown men and women avoided them and the memories of wretched childhoods which they evoked.

'Let us go away,' said Punch. 'This is not a pretty place.' But Mamma and Papa and Judy had left the cab, and all the luggage was being taken into the house. At the doorstep stood a woman in black, and she smiled largely, with dry chapped lips. Behind her was a man, big, bony, grey, and lame as to one leg – behind him a boy of twelve, blackhaired and oily in appearance. Punch surveyed the trio, and advanced without fear, as he had been accustomed to do in Bombay when callers came and he happened to be playing in the veranda.

... 'I don't like these people,' said Punch. 'But never mind. We'll go away soon. We have always went away soon from everywhere. I wish we was gone back to Bombay *soon.*' The wish bore no fruit. For six days Mamma wept at intervals, and showed the woman in black all Punch's clothes – a liberty which Punch resented. 'But p'raps she's a new white *ayah,*' he thought. 'I'm to call her Antirosa, but she doesn't call *me* Sahib. She says just Punch,' he confided to Judy. 'What is Antirosa?' Judy didn't know. Neither she nor Punch had heard anything of an animal called an aunt. Their world had been Papa and Mamma, who knew everything, permitted everything, and loved everybody – even Punch when he used to go into the garden at Bombay and fill his nails with mould after the weekly nail-cutting, because, as he explained between two strokes of the slipper to his sorely-tried father, his fingers 'felt so new at the ends.'

In an undefined way Punch judged it advisable to keep both parents between himself and the woman in black and the boy with black hair. He did not approve of them. He liked the grey man, who had expressed a wish to be called 'Uncle-harri.' They nodded at each other when they met, and the grey man showed him a little ship with rigging that took up and down.

'She is a model of the *Brisk* – the little *Brisk* that was sore exposed that day at Navarino.' The grey man hummed the last words and fell into a reverie. 'I'll tell you about Navarino, Punch, when we go for walks together; and you mustn't touch the ship, because she's the *Brisk*.'

Long before that walk, the first of many, was taken, they roused Punch and Judy in the chill dawn of a February morning to say Good-bye; and of all people in the wide earth to Papa and Mamma – both crying this time. Punch was very sleepy and Judy was cross.

'Don't forget us,' pleaded Mamma. 'Oh, my little son, don't forget us, and see that Judy remembers too.'

'I've told Judy to bemember,' said Punch, wriggling, for his father's beard tickled his neck. 'I've told Judy – ten – forty – 'leven thousand times. But Ju's so young – quite a baby – isn't she?'

'Yes,' said Papa, 'quite a baby, and you must be good to Judy, and make haste to learn to write and – and – and – '

Punch was back in his bed again. Judy was fast asleep, and there was the rattle of a cab below. Papa and Mamma had gone away...

When a matured man discovers that he has been deserted by Providence, deprived of his God, and cast without help, comfort, or sympathy, upon a world which is new and strange to him, his despair, which may find expression in evil living, the writing of his experiences, or the more satisfactory diversion of suicide, is generally supposed to be impressive. A child, under exactly similar circumstances as far as its knowledge goes, cannot very well curse God and die. It howls till its nose is red, its eyes are sore, and its head aches. Punch and Judy, through no

135

fault of their own, had lost all their world. They sat in the hall
and cried; the black-haired boy looking on from afar.

Rudyard Kipling (1865–1936)
Baa Baa Black Sheep (1888)

Here Angus Wilson, the novelist, who also wrote a searching biography
of Kipling, gives a few more details:

In 1871 the Kipling family, now including his younger sister
Alice (always called Trix), Rudyard's only sibling, returned to
England on leave. On their return to India the parents left their
children with people in Southsea, now part of Portsmouth,
who had advertised their services in caring for the children of
English parents in India. It was a usual practice for the children
of the English in India to be thus separated from their parents,
but Rudyard and his sister were not prepared for the event. 'We
had had no preparation or explanation', Kipling's sister wrote;
'it was like a double death, or rather, like an avalanche that had
swept away everything happy and familiar'. Nor is it known why
the parents chose to put them in the hands of paid guardians
rather than with one or more members of Alice Kipling's
family. One sister was married to Alfred Baldwin, a prosperous
manufacturer: their child, about the same age as Rudyard, was
Stanley Baldwin, afterwards prime minister; another sister had
married Sir Edward Burne-Jones, the painter; a third sister had
married Sir Edward Poynter, who became president of the Royal
Academy. By 1871 all of these families would have been able and
willing to receive the Kipling children.

Instead they went to Southsea, to a house now notorious as
the House of Desolation (so-called in Kipling's 'Baa baa, black
sheep'). Kipling was not yet six years old; Trix was three. Here
he attended 'a terrible little day-school'. The woman who
cared for them, Mrs Pryse Agar Holloway, is, in Kipling's
account of her as Aunty Rosa, a monster. Deliberately cruel
and unjust, she tries to set sister against brother, systematically
humiliates the young Kipling, allows her son to terrorise him
mentally and physically, and denies him simple pleasures.
She also introduces a Calvinistic protestantism into Kipling's

experience: 'I had never heard of Hell, so I was introduced to it in all its terrors'. He took refuge in reading. One of his punishments was to be compelled to read devotional literature: in this way he acquired a mastery of biblical phrase and image. The Kipling children remained with Mrs Holloway for five and a half years: towards the end of that time, Kipling's eyesight began to fail... Kipling's mother returned from India in April 1877, and for the rest of the year her children lived with her. At the beginning of the next year Kipling went off to public school; Trix returned to the care of Mrs Holloway.

The truth of Kipling's description of his childhood has been doubted: Mrs Holloway was not cruel but misunderstood by a spoiled, preternaturally imaginative child; 'Baa baa, black sheep' is fiction, not autobiography; or, if autobiography, then shamelessly self-indulgent. And how can one explain Trix's return to Southsea? We cannot now know the facts.

Angus Wilson (1913–1991)
The Strange Ride of Rudyard Kipling (1977)

Sir Arthur Conan Doyle came to Portsmouth in June 1882 and set up a medical practice at 1 Bush Villas in Elm Grove, Southsea. When he arrived in the town, he had less than £10 in his pocket; when he left, eight years later, he was married and a famous writer. A prolific writer of stories such as this, it was the creation of Sherlock Holmes that made his name and fortune. The first two Holmes stories were written while Conan Doyle was living in Porstmouth.

My story is one which you may well treasure up in your memories, and tell again to others, for it is not likely that in this whole county of Hampshire, or even perhaps in all England, there is another left alive who is so well able to speak from his own knowledge of these events, or who has played a more forward part in them.

...I was born then in the year 1664, at Havant, which is a flourishing village a few miles from Portsmouth off the main London road, and that is where I spent the greater part of my youth. It is now as it was then, a pleasant, healthy spot, with a hundred or so brick cottages scattered along in a single irregular street, each with its little garden in front, and maybe a fruit-tree or two at the back. In the middle of the village stood the old church with the square tower, and the great sun-dial like a wrinkle upon its grey, weather-blotched face... As to the Independents, of whom my father was one, they also were under the ban of the law, but they attended conventicle at Emsworth, whither we would trudge, rain or shine, on every Sabbath morning. There were Papists, too, amongst us, who were compelled to go as far as Portsmouth for their Mass. Thus, you see, small as was our village, we were a fair miniature of the whole country, for we had our sects and our factions, which were all the more bitter for being confined in so narrow a compass...

My childhood was...a gloomy one. Now and again when there chanced to be a fair at Portsdown Hill, or when a passing rare showman set up his booth in the village, my dear mother would slip a penny or two from her housekeeping money into my hand, and with a warning finger upon her lip would send me off to see the sights...

Now and again upon a holiday I was permitted to walk down to Portsmouth – once I was even taken in front of my father upon his pad nag, and there I wandered with him through the streets with wondering eyes, marvelling over the strange sights around me. The walls and the moats, the gates and the sentinels, the long High Street with the great Government buildings, and the constant rattle of drums and blare of trumpets; they made my little heart beat quicker beneath my sagathy stuff jacket. Here was the house in which some thirty years before the proud Duke of Buckingham had been struck down by an assassin's dagger.

Sir Arthur Conan Doyle (1859–1930)
Micah Clarke (1889)

The Play Room is the last work of Olivia Manning who was born in Portsmouth in 1908 and lived, she writes, 'in the longest, dreariest avenue in England'. Her novel is a vision of the decline of Portsmouth and the wretched end to the admiration and devotion which Laura displays for Vicky: a late-twentieth-century adolescent education in a rapacious adult world of seedy gentility. As a child Manning's favourite book was *The Water Babies*. She was best known for her *Fortunes of War* series of six novels, described by Anthony Burgess as 'the finest fictional record of the war produced by a British writer', and which grew out of married life in the Levant with her husband who worked for the British Council. Despite all her travelling, she died, not far away from Portsmouth, on the Isle of Wight, in 1980.

Laura was home early but her mother jumped up at the sight of her, saying in relief: 'So there you are!' as though she had perhaps been killed by a bus or raped in broad daylight.

For a while there was peace but Laura, the complainer, was plotting more complaints.

She was putting her troubles down to the fact that she lived in Rowantree Avenue. It was, she decided, the longest and dreariest road in Camperlea and in the whole of its long dreary length there was not one presentable boy of the right age.

When she had not been invited to Gilda Hooper's Christmas party, she concluded it was a case of out-of-sight, out-of-mind. Living half-way down this mile-long road, she was always too far away. How could she hope to participate in the great events of life? When this had first occurred to her, she asked why on earth her parents ever thought of coming to live here.

She was told they had married in the early fifties when there were few houses to be found. Camperlea, a residential neighbour of Portsmouth, had suffered for its nearness to the naval dockyard. Half the houses were damaged and still unrepaired. 'We had to be glad to get anything,' said Mrs Fletcher.

'But that was years ago,' Laura protested: 'There's nothing to stop us moving now,'

'Oh, yes, there's plenty to stop us. We can't afford the new houses and we wouldn't get much for this one. Besides, there's the mortgage. That's not paid up yet.'

...Her father had retired and married... When on active service, he had crowds of friends and never thought of marriage. 'He was having too good a time,' Mrs Fletcher said with a significant nod. When he took Tom and Laura out on Sunday walks, he told them much the same thing. Naval life, he said, was just what he wanted. He was always off somewhere and when he came back, full of experiences and funny stories, he was welcome everywhere. The only bills he had to worry about were mess bills and his account with the naval tailor on

Portsmouth Hard. He dressed well. He was a handsome man, not tall but well built and light on his feet. When he married, even though late in life, it came as a shock to a number of women. People were always telling Mrs Fletcher how popular he had been at naval dances where he swept round the floor on his light dancing feet. That did not please her much.

...The bus meandered through the long main street where changes had taken place during the last five years. Shops that had not altered in half a century were being rebuilt, or given a modern polish, not for the sake of the North Camperlea residents but to tempt the newcomers, the factory workers at Salthouse, who were reputed to 'have so much money they don't know what to do with it'. Though at street level there was redecorating and buying up of neighbours and opening of self-service stores that dazzled the eyes with light, the upper storeys were still the old house-tops of dark brick corbelled with painted stone.

That was Camperlea, Laura thought. Even when they reached South Camperlea and came into a region of turreted houses massed about with firs and evergreens, there was still the wine dark brick with the rendered parts painted the colour of custard. But in sight of the front where the sky broadened and the light seemed to grow lighter, the streets widened and there were plain, white-painted houses and elegant shops. Everything seemed to open up and reflect the windy brightness of the sea.

'Why can't we live here?' Laura grumbled, knowing the answer as well as anyone. Tom, relaxed in his seat, shrugged with philosophical calm and said: 'Can't afford it.'

If anything happened in Camperlea, it happened in South Camperlea. South Camperlea had developed before the war when the navy set up an experimental sea-plane base. Mr Fletcher often spoke of the rollicking days when the hotels were full of officers, and smart bars and clubs and tea-rooms had started up along the front. The Town Council, thinking the town all set to rival Southsea, constructed a promenade and laid out the Flamingo Lake area of large houses. Camperlea's first-ever block of flats was built at that time. Plans had been in mind to construct a new pier, but the glory did not last long enough. The Navy lost interest in sea-planes. The base was dismantled and all that remained of it was the hangar...

…She (Laura) wanted Vicky but she also wanted Vicky's lustre. Vicky was aureoled with romantic tragedy. Her brother had been thrown off his motor-bicycle and killed and her mother, ill with grief, had had to have Vicky at home to attend her. Because Mrs Logan was never really well again, the Logans went on winter holidays to places like Marrakesh and the Canary Islands…

Laura had been a little girl when there was so much talk about Ronnie Logan's accident. People had said how shocking it was that the young man had been killed, while the motor-bicycle was unscratched. Then, two or three years after the accident, there had been all the fuss about Mr Logan's design for the Camperlea reading room.

People wrote to the *Camperlea Herald* to say the room was much too large. It was painted in impracticable colours and had a black ceiling which was described in the paper as 'unheard of'. The long sofa seats had no backs but were upholstered in shades of fuchsia and shocking pink. One wall was entirely of glass but all this glass looked on to nothing more than a corner of the park given over to a compost heap, a potting shed and a dozen wheel-barrows.

The letters filled two pages of the paper. In reply Mr Logan said that while Camperlea remained moribund within the limited, class-ridden concepts of the thirties, an artistic revolution had revivified the outside world. People wanted brilliance and colour: they wanted space and light. The reading room was designed to answer the demands of the modern world.

Still, nobody liked it, except, of course, Laura. Mr and Mrs Fletcher, members of the Ratepayers' Association, disapproved the room without ever going…

Laura had not been to Salthouse for three years. She was reluctant to return there but could not remember why. Salthouse had changed and seemed frightening, perhaps, merely because unfamiliar. Years ago, when Mr Fletcher had gone with the children for Sunday walks, they used to take the bus to the level crossing and then find themselves in a country district, adventurous with tumble-down neglect. There had been clay pits and a brickworks and the great hangar where the sea-planes were serviced. But the whole of Salthouse was now in the hands of the developers. The downland slopes had been eaten up by the housing estate. The road had ceased to be a country road and had become a highway for the factory lorries that went up to join the Brighton road above. The last time she was there the factory foundations had just been laid. It was an important factory that made plastic and plastic goods. A whole population had been brought to Salthouse during the last three years. What had been a playground for North Camperlea was now a township of council houses and plain utilitarian buildings.

The *Camperlea Herald* had spoken of the 'new, raw, unconventional Salthouse community'. Well and good. The trouble was not that the Salthouse people were new, raw and unconventional but that they had so much money to spend. The women, large, loud bursting girls in slacks and high-heeled shoes, would come to the High Street on Saturday afternoons and go back laden with meat, poultry, fruit, tinned vegetables, cakes and sweetmeats. Their homeward cavalcade was a vision of abundance that astounded the Camperlea pensioners. Still carefully making do themselves, they scarcely knew that prosperity had overtaken other places.

Laura, ready to take any view so long as it was opposed to the Camperlea view, defended the Salthouse spendthrifts ('If they have the money, why shouldn't they enjoy it') while distrusting them. Salthouse, though another world, was not the world she wanted...

A worker at the factory, Clarrie, seemed to see some especial virtue in knowing what he wanted and wanting what he did want. Laura...thought that Clarrie was not merely dull, he was a man without resonance: a bore and a boor...

'You want to come with me, don't you? All right. I'll pick you up at your house, if you like.'

'Grief, no. My mother's funny about motor-cycles.'

'At the end of the road, then. Seven sharp... You'll see, we'll have a fabulous time. It'll be mad. I'll make Clarrie introduce you to everyone.'

...Early on Saturday evening, when the shops were shutting and the pavements were dusty and paper-strewn, Vicky and Laura rode out of the town, passing the gas-works and crossing the channel that divided Camperlea from Salthouse. Topping the bridge, that was railway- and foot-bridge, Laura, on the pillion, looked over the broad, shallow mud basin of Salthouse Creek and saw in the distance the black shape of Salthouse hangar.

The tide was out. The basin was nothing now but interfolding curves of mud...

... They reached the lane where Mr Fletcher had taken Tom and Laura for Sunday walks. Clarrie slowed to a pause and put his feet down. 'Where's this go, then?' Vicky did not know. Laura, who did know, felt, for no reason she could recall, an acute unwillingness to visit the lane again.

'There's nothing down there,' she said; 'it only leads to the Creek,' but Clarrie took no notice of her.

He dragged the front wheel round and the machine bumped and bounced them along the rough track between abandoned allotments and the flat dispiriting turnip field. No one worked the land now. It had been sold for development and soon the factories and houses would spread and cover it.

In the old days, when it had been country, unusual flowers could be found here, but now the urban grime was killing everything. Only dandelions, groundsel, white convolvulus and coarse grass bordered the track. People had dumped mattresses in the field and hillocks of old tin cans. The whole place was like some big untidy backyard.

The sky had misted over and there was something disturbing about the white, refracted light. Although it was Saturday, the day dedicated to pleasure, Laura expected to hear the bells of Salthouse church. Remembering the insistent bell-beating frustrations of childhood, she remembered the last time she had been down the lane and suddenly knew why she had been unwilling to return.

It was three years before, when Camperlea people still came out on the bus to walk in their Sunday clothes. Laura, alone for some reason, had come upon a group of people standing about a small white object on the ground. When she got nearer she saw the object was a puppy. The puppy was unconscious but shivering violently and the stout woman who stood over it, wailed: 'This keeps happening. I can't take any more of it. I'd finish the poor thing off if I could.'

143

A young man spoke up briskly: 'I'd do it. Give me a brick and I'd finish it off in a jiffy.'

Laura wanted to cry 'Don't kill it' but she dared not speak in front of all those grown-up people. For all she knew, the right thing might be to put the animal out of its misery. The young man had gone to the brickfield and seeing him coming back with his weapon, Laura had run away. Mrs Fletcher, who loved dogs, cried out indignantly when she heard this story: 'It was only a puppy fit. They often have them. The little thing would have got over them if they'd let it live.'

The lane had looked bleak enough in the livid light; now it looked bleaker as Laura saw it in the light of her remembered cowardice. She felt as though it had been her task to save the dog; and she had failed.

'What's this?' said Clarrie, slowing down to stare at the brickworks' chimney.

'They used to make bricks here,' Laura said. Her father had told her that tramps who slept against the brick kiln for warmth were found dead in the morning. Though the kiln had been cold for years, the Fletcher children had seen it as sinister and they would dare each other to go near it. Beyond the brickfield were the clay pits: a region of artificial hills and ponds where rats ran about and Laura had once fallen into the water when trying to reach some bullrushes.

Mr Fletcher said that long ago there had been a country house beside the Creek. The house had been pulled down but part of the garden wall remained and there were two cottages where the outdoor servants had lived. Sometimes he was too tired to go farther than the cottages but when he had the energy, he would take them as far as the hangar which was built out into the creek. The hangar was always the ultimate point of the walk. At the Creek the track turned north and ran up through dull country to join the main road above.

These walks had been a delight to the children. Their father, who kept in the background at home, used to talk all the time, treating of some splendid subject such as the nature of the stars or the navy or the places he had seen abroad. He showed them that the world was wide and full of marvels and one event led to another. He told them that the Salthouse land had been bought by speculators and one day it would all be built over. Even the

Creek, he said, would be drained and built over. These projects had seemed to the children visionary in the extreme, yet he had been right about the Salthouse land. No one ever came here from Camperlea now. The Sunday playground had changed into a town and become the preserve of strangers.

After the ruined cottages there was the long run down to the Creek.

'What's that, then?' said Clarrie Piper, as the hangar appeared black in the distance.

'It's a hangar,' Laura said.

'A what?'

'There used to be sea-planes on the Creek and that's where they were serviced. The Navy left a lot of stuff behind.'

'Hah!' Clarrie put on speed as though imagining he might find something of value in the hangar.

The track turned and twisted, passing through an ancient orchard. The trees were bare of leaves, fruitless, distorted, grey-green with lichen and all bent towards the north as though a killer wind had swept over them and left behind nothing but phosphorescent corpses. There was a mile or more of this tree cemetery before the sea-wall came in sight. It was high tide and the water had spread up among the reeds and the coarse grasses that tufted the edge of the downs.

Clarrie stopped opposite the hangar and propped up the BSA. They leant against the wall and surveyed the Creek that, shallow and unnavigable by anything bigger that a row-boat, looked now like a great waterway separating Camperlea from Salthouse. There was one little island. It had a hut from which, Mr Fletcher said, the excise men used to watch for smugglers.

Vicky had never been here before and she was astonished by the extent of the Creek and the desolation surrounding it. Clarrie looked at the hangar, his expression spiteful and calculating as though he disliked the big black structure and was wondering how to get the better of it...

Suddenly he threw down his cigarette, trod it out with a decisive movement and turned again to the hangar. He said, 'Let's see, then,' and swung himself over the wall. He began to cross the grass with a sauntering swagger but the ground was sea marsh and his feet sank into mud. Unable to maintain the swagger, he began to make antic movements for Vicky's entertainment.

145

'What's inside?' he shouted.

Vicky did not know. Laura was not saying.

The hangar, being a naval artefact, had been built to last. At the top, where roof joined sides, the wind had pulled the canvas from the struts, but the building was sound. It had a formidable air as though, standing there for thirty solitary years, it had acquired a place in the world and its own reason for existence. Laura felt, as she had felt in childhood, that the great black blank face was keeping watch on them and their intrusion must not go too far.

Clarrie went round to the right. The girls did not try to follow him but they knew he expected to be watched. When he reached the water's edge, he stared down at the muddy bottom, then he bent his knees as though about to lower himself in at the water's edge.

Laura shouted: 'The mud's very soft.' Whether he heard her or not, he gave up the idea of wading to the front of the hangar and crossed to the side where there was a ledge just under the water surface. With his hands pressed to the canvas, he stretched out a foot but he could not reach the ledge. He risked falling in and this time Vicky shouted: 'Oh, Clarrie, don't.'

Laura told her: 'He doesn't need to go in the front. There's a door on the other side.' Before Vicky could call out again, he suddenly stepped back from the hangar, stared at it, then, making a rush at it, threw himself upon the fabric and began beating on it with his hands. The fabric held. Knowing no other way in, he was trying to break through the side and seemed distraught that he could not do so. When he could make no impression with his fists, he began kicking at the fabric with his feet. The girls could hear him screaming in fury as he banged and kicked in a performance so futile, it looked insane.

'Shall I tell him about the entrance?'

Vicky was observing Clarrie with a strange smile and said: 'I don't think I would if I were you.' Laura, disturbed by both of them, moved away. A few yards to the left there was a gap in the wall and she was able to reach the hangar over a flint ridge which formed a path to the door. She knew the door well. If it were not held open, it fell shut and one had to feel one's way through semi-darkness to the platform at the back of the hangar.

She knew the way to the platform. Standing on it, she

could see out through the end of the hangar which was open to the Creek. Not much light came in even on a fine day. Now it was scarcely possible to make out the cat-walks that ran along on either side. A glint came from the floor which was under water at high tide so the hangar became a dock and the planes could be floated in for servicing.

Laura looked out on a view of the Camperlea gas-works on the far side of the Creek: a scene as dismal as a steel engraving, framed by the mourning blackness of the hangar's edge.

This prospect had been the final event for the Fletcher children in the ever eventful walk down the lane. Looking down on the in-washing sea, she remembered how she and Tom had planned to turn the hangar into a theatre. The platform was as wide as a stage. They would write their own plays, of course, and produce them so splendidly that the whole of Camperlea would come to see them. The lane would be alive with cars and buses and pedestrians. Walking home, they discussed with their father the problems of lighting the stage and seating the audience. He treated the project seriously and seriously answered all their questions. Tom thought people could come by boat, rowing into the hangar on one tide and rowing out on the next. Between the tides they would sit in the boats to watch the play. He was disconcerted to learn that the interval between tides was nearly twelve and a half hours.

'We could serve refreshments before they left,' he said.

Had Mrs Fletcher been there she would have dismissed the whole idea as ridiculous but their father let them talk, knowing that time would defeat their designs just as it had defeated his own.

No sound came from outside the hangar, Clarrie must have given up his attempt to batter it down. The door opened; an arrow of light fell towards the platform, and Vicky called: 'Come on, Laura. We're going back to the dance.'

Clarrie, his face sullen, was already on the saddle. He started off before Laura had properly got a grip on the centre of the handle-bar. She was thrown to one side…

'…keep your head down if you don't want to lose it.'

It was obvious when he started off that this time he knew exactly where he was going. He turned into Salthouse Lane, taking the turn at an angle that nearly threw Laura off her perch. She held on obstinately, feeling his desire to be rid of her, and knowing if she fell, he would not stop to retrieve her. They passed the allotments and the brickfield, then Clarrie slowed and looked about him. When they came to the cottages, he stopped and pushing at Laura's shoulder, said: 'This is where you get off.'

'Why?'

'We want to talk private, see? You wait here.'

'I don't want to wait here.'

'You don't want to do nothing, do you?' Clarrie's irony was venomous. He gave Laura another push to hasten her descent but she gripped the tank with her knees, tightened her hold on the handle-bars, and said: 'I'm not leaving Vicky.'

Clarrie put his hands to her waist and lifted her up from the tank as he might lift a cup from a hook. Afraid if he dropped her, she would fall face to the ground, she was forced to lift one foot over the tank. In a moment she was standing in the road.

She turned and appealed to Vicky who had watched her swift displacement with bewildered eyes. 'Vicky, you told me to stay with you. Do you want me to wait here?'

'We can't leave her here alone.' Vicky made a move to get off the pillion but she was too slow. Clarrie shot away and she had to cling to him to save herself from falling.

Looking back, Clarrie shouted: 'We won't be long.' Now that he had got what he wanted, he sounded hilarious and, reassured by his tone, Laura watched the machine swerve round the bend and out of sight; then listened to the throb of the engine as it faded in the distance. She supposed they would stop at the Creek and lean over the Creek wall and talk intimately together. If they were not to be long, she did not mind waiting here. Freed from the hateful, overhanging nearness of Clarrie, she could even enjoy solitude.

The lowering sunlight fell richly over the dead orchard. The brick of the orchard wall had a garnet glow. It was always just here, at this point, with the Creek still a mile away, that the sky seemed to open up and became higher and wider than other skies. Even in cloudy weather, Laura had felt that the light over the undulating orchard increased the spaciousness of space. But this evening the illusion could not last much longer. Already the sky was growing yellow; damp was rising and the close, misty air seemed to shut out sound.

Now there was nothing to be heard, Laura went to the cottages and looked for diversion. A few yards behind them were the remains of a walled-in kitchen garden where Tom and she, climbing about among the crumbling brickwork, had found gooseberries and currants growing in a tangle of undergrowth. There might be some now but she feared, if she were out of sight, Vicky and Clarrie would go on, thinking she had walked back to Salthouse.

The last occupants of the cottages had padlocked the doors and shuttered the windows; all to no purpose. They had been empty so long, the roofs had fallen in. Now the front door had been broken open, the shutters had dropped on their hinges and the rooms were open to intruders. Laura, looking in through a window frame, saw nothing but dust and shadow. At the side of one cottage there was a fig tree covered with small green bottle shapes. Dozens more had fallen to the ground. She gathered a handful and amused herself by biting them open and finding the miniature seeds inside. She tried with her tongue to recognise some recondite fig flavour but they were not even bitter. They tasted of nothing and she threw them one by one into an upper window.

A smell of autumn had come into the air and the twilight was gathering. She began to grow tired of solitude and sat down on the grass verge, feeling she had waited long enough. The silence was oppressive. The sensible thing, she knew, would be to start walking back while there was still light. Probably the others would catch up on her. She thought about it but could not leave the spot where Vicky had left her. She had to be found waiting exactly where Vicky expected to find her. It was not just a question of loyalty. She wanted Clarrie to know that Vicky had a vigilant friend.

When the ground felt chilly beneath her, she rose and walked to the bend in the road round which the motor-cycle had passed from view. Dusk had fallen but a ghostly light still hung over the orchard grass and the trees looked incandescent. She could see the roof of the distant hangar. She thought of walking on in the hope of meeting Vicky and Clarrie, but if she did not meet them, she would have that much farther to walk back. She returned to the cottages, knowing it was now so late, even if she set out to walk the night would overtake her long before she reached Salthouse. She began to think of Mrs Fletcher's hints and warnings about 'bad men'. She trembled, feeling cold, and listened and longed for Vicky to come, and remembered fearful stories about haunted roads.

When it was almost dark she heard a motor-bicycle in the remote distance and her nerves leapt in relief. They were coming at last. But the sound trickled away from her and when it was lost in the distance, she saw a light raying and moving upwards where the lane joined the main road. She watched it until it disappeared.

That could only be Vicky's BSA for no other traffic had come along the lane. They must have decided to return by the main road. She could not bear to think they had forgotten her. She told herself they just could not imagine she would wait here all the time. They thought she had walked back to Salthouse. Anyway, here she was, abandoned, alone.

Surely, when they found she was not in the dance hall, they would return for her, all the more surprised at her tenacity.

But it was too late for fantasies now. Something rustled in the grass. People said that after dark the rats ran in packs over the old allotments. At the thought of walking back past the brickfields and the chalk-pits and the rat-infested fields, fear rose in her like a sickness.

Still, she had to get home. She did not know the time but she had a sinking sense that hours had passed since they left her there. Hours and hours. At the thought of her mother's anxiety, the rats seemed innocuous. She started back to Salthouse at a run.

The moon, edging up from the horizon like a coin pressing into a slot, gave enough light to mark the path but it was indefinite light. Several times she found herself lost in the long grass with the rats and spiders.

The moon, a gibbous moon, horribly blacked out on one side, rose quickly and lightened the brickfield and the brickfield chimney, a threatening phallus, and the distant greyish clay hills.

Olivia Manning (1908–1980)
The Play Room (1969)

Alfred, Lord Tennyson instructed his son that this, possibly his last poem, should stand at the end of every edition of his work. It was written in 1889 while he was returning to his home of Farringford on the Isle of Wight, and he told his son that evening that 'it came in a moment'. 'The bar' is the sandbank which had to be negotiated on that journey from Portsmouth.

Crossing the bar

Sunset and evening star,
　　And one clear call for me!
And may there be no moaning of the bar,
　　When I put out to sea,

But such a tide as moving seems asleep,
　　Too full for sound and foam,
When that which drew from out the boundless deep
　　Turns again home.

Twilight and evening bell,
　　And after that the dark!
And may there be no sadness of farewell,
　　When I embark;

For tho' from out our bourne of Time and Place
　　The flood may bear me far,
I hope to see my Pilot face to face
　　When I have crost the bar.

Lord Tennyson (1809–1892)

Chapter 4
The New Forest

The New Forest is vast area of ancient wilderness, right next to three of the biggest cities in Southern England: Southampton, Bournemouth and Portsmouth. This precious two-hundred-and-nineteen-square-mile pair of lungs is a place of enchantment for many, rich in childhood memories of summer camps, family caravan holidays, long-distance hikes, pony treks and romantic picnics. On its periphery are most of the best hotels and restaurants in Hampshire. Although beloved by locals, it has never achieved the celebrity of national parks like Dartmoor or the Peak district. It is a flat heathland composed of clay, sand and gravel, broken by woods and forests. No canyons, mountains or waterfalls here. Yet there are parts of it which seem never to have been disturbed by the hand of man, and which suggest the primal heathland that emerged out of the last ice age some 12,000 years ago. This is a landscape that supports its own native species – most famously the indigenous breed of New Forest wild ponies – and all three varieties of our native snakes. It is a place to explore gradually, burrowing into the depths of it where, as in some slow-building orchestral movement, you push through areas of mixed native woodland into impressive forests of Scotch pine, beech and oak. In the lateral light of dusk and dawn, these majestic trees can seem touched by the divine.

The New Forest is also overpoweringly full of stories. Like so many places in England with the epithet 'New', it actually means the exact opposite. Archaeologists tell us that men have struggled to make a living from this awkward, acid-rich soil for many thousands of years. But the primal tale of the New Forest is one of violent dispossession, when the Norman king, William the Conqueror, and his even more brutal son, William Rufus, emptied the landscape of people in order to make a royal hunting forest for their sole use. It became a place dedicated to the five animals of the medieval chase: the hart, the hind,

153

the boar, the hare and the wolf, touched by pagan associations with Odin's wild hunt.

The story that I was told as a child, walking through these woods, is an Anglo-Saxon version of the Highland clearances, where women and children were driven off the land by the flat blades of soldiers, village churches were desecrated and the humble cottages of traditional farmers burnt over their heads if they were too slow to move. The menfolk were brutally punished if they dared return to attempt to farm or graze, let alone hunt, over their own land. There are terrible stories of the punishments meted out by the forest wardens, assisted by a man-pack of rangers, foresters, surveyors and sergeants. Trespassers would be hung or mutilated by due process of royal law, but much darker are the tales of poachers who were never brought before these forest tribunals. Instead, their hands were tied behind their backs and they were sewn into the hides of deer, set loose and then hunted by hounds who would tear them apart. Such brutality calls down its own curse. Within decades, three royal princes died in the New Forest. The first to fall was William the Conqueror's son, Richard, followed by one of his grandsons who, like Absalom, was caught in the natural noose of a branch. Most famously, wicked King William Rufus died in the heart of the forest, struck by a mysterious arrow. The site of his assassination is still commemorated, even celebrated, by the Rufus Stone. This tale burnt brightly in the hands of sixteenth-century bishops and seventeenth-century lawyers, as a metaphor for how the indigenous liberties of the proud Anglo-Saxons had been suppressed by foreign tyrants, but could be regained by either the establishment of the Church of England and by the supremacy of Parliament.

The policing of the New Forest was undeniably brutal in the first hundred years, but within a few generations it had evolved into a more pliable institution. Villagers on the periphery regained the right to graze the land with their ponies, horses and cattle (but not sheep), to glean firewood, to cut peat, to dig for clay, to gather bracken (for stable litter) and to fatten their pigs for sixty days before Christmas on the fallen acorns. These rights were never absolute, and always seasonal, but the harsher forest laws were curtailed under the Magna Carta, and in 1217 by the Charter of the Forest.

The political turbulence of the Wars of the Roses eroded the Royal Forests as a separate institution, and our Tudor monarchs were wise enough to interest themselves in just the oak forests suitable for shipbuilding. To this we owe the fact that the New Forest, so conveniently close to the naval dockyard at Portsmouth and the shipyards of Southampton, was preserved in its entirety. Other royal forests melted back into the land, especially during the desperate sell-off pursued by such cash-strapped monarchs as James I and Charles I. By the seventeenth century, providing the naval oak forests were respected, the three New Forest Courts of Swainmote (held on the feast days of St Michael, St Martin and St John) upheld, rather than restricted, the rights of those villagers who had inherited rights of usage over the forest. It effectively became a National Park centuries before such a concept was invented. There is nowhere else like it in Britain. It is a place true to itself, a place apart, ripe for colonisation by the imagination of novelists, as this selection of writings will reveal.

...

Contrary to the preferences of his readers today, *The White Company* was Sir Arthur Conan Doyle's own favourite among his work, historical fiction being his preferred genre. The eponymous Company was modelled on a Free Company of Archers, mercenaries during the Hundred Years' War (1347–1453) under command of Sir John Hawkwood, whose huge portrait is painted on the north wall of the cathedral in Florence. It is towards this company that the hero novice, John of Hordle, hurtles down the Lyndhurst Road at the end of this piece.

Beaulieu's Cistercian Abbey was founded by King John in 1204 and consecrated in 1246 in presence of Henry lll. The refectory, now the church, and the remains of the Abbey walls still stand.

Chapter I
How the Black Sheep came forth from the fold

The great bell of Beaulieu was ringing. Why should the great bell of Beaulieu toll when the shadows were neither short nor long?
    ...A stranger who knew nothing either of the Abbey or of its immense resources might have gathered from the appearance of the brothers some conception of the varied duties which they were called upon to perform, and of the busy, wide-spread life which centred in the old monastery. As they swept gravely in by twos and by threes, with bended heads and muttering lips, there were few who did not bear upon them some signs of their daily toil. Here were two with wrists and sleeves all spotted with

155

the ruddy grape juice. There again was a bearded brother with a broad-headed axe and a bundle of faggots upon his shoulders, while beside him walked another with the shears under his arm and the white wool still clinging to his whiter gown. A long, straggling troop bore spades and mattocks while the two rearmost of all staggered along under a huge basket o' fresh-caught carp, for the morrow was Friday, and there were fifty platters to be filled and as many sturdy trenchermen behind them. Of all the throng there was scarce one who was not labour-stained and weary, for Abbot Berghersh was a hard man to himself and to others.

… 'Where is the master of the novices?'

'He is without, most holy father.'

'Send him hither.'

The sandalled feet clattered over the wooden floor, and the iron-bound door creaked upon its hinges. In a few moments it opened again to admit a short square monk with a heavy, composed face and an authoritative manner.

'You have sent for me, holy father?'

'Yes, brother Jerome, I wish that this matter be disposed of with as little scandal as may be, and yet it is needful that the example should be a public one.' The Abbot spoke in Latin now, as a language which was more fitted by its age and solemnity to convey the thoughts of two high dignitaries of the order.

… 'This plaint is thine, as I learn, brother Ambrose,' said he. 'May the holy Benedict, patron of our house, be present this day and aid us in our findings! How many counts are there?'

'Three, most holy father,' the brother answered in a low and quavering voice.

'Have you set them forth according to rule?'

'They are here set down, most holy father, upon a cantle of sheep-skin.'

'Let the sheep-skin be handed to the chancellor. Bring in brother John, and let him hear the plaints which have been urged against him.'

At this order a lay-brother swung open the door, and two other lay-brothers entered leading between them a young novice of the order. He was a man of huge stature, dark-eyed and red-headed, with a peculiar half-humorous, half-defiant expression upon his bold, well-marked features. His cowl was thrown back upon his shoulders, and his gown, unfastened at the top, disclosed a round, sinewy neck, ruddy and corded like the bark of the fir. Thick, muscular arms, covered with a reddish down, protruded from the wide sleeves of his habit, while his white shirt, looped up upon one side, gave a glimpse of a huge knotty leg, scarred and torn with the scratches of brambles. With a bow to the Abbot, which had in it perhaps more pleasantry than reverence, the novice strode across to the carved prie-dieu which had been set apart for him, and stood silent and erect with his hand upon the gold bell which was used in the private orisons of the Abbot's own household. His dark eyes glanced rapidly over the assembly, and finally settled with a grim and menacing twinkle upon the face of his accuser.

The chancellor rose, 'Charges brought upon the second Thursday after the Feast of the Assumption, in the year of our Lord thirteen hundred and sixty-six, against brother John, formerly known as Hordle John, or John of Hordle, but now a novice in the holy monastic order of the Cistercians…

'Item, that between nones and vespers on the feast of James the Less the said brother John was observed upon the Brockenhurst road, near the spot which is known as Hatchett's Pond in converse with a person of the other sex, being a maiden of the name of Mary Sowley, the daughter of the King's verderer. Item, that after sundry japes and jokes the said brother John did lift up the said Mary Sowley and did take, carry, and convey her across a stream, to the infinite relish of the Devil and the exceeding detriment of his own soul, which scandalous and wilful falling away was witnessed by three members of our order.'

… 'And the woman?' asked the Abbot. 'Did she not break into lamentation and woe that a brother should so demean himself?'

'Nay, she smiled sweetly upon him and thanked him. I can vouch it and so can brother Porphyry.'

… 'What hast thou to say, brother John, upon these weighty things which are urged against you?'

'Little enough, good father, little enough,' said the novice, speaking English with a broad West Saxon drawl. The brothers, who were English to a man, pricked up their ears at the sound of the homely and yet unfamiliar speech; but the Abbot flushed red with anger, and struck his hand upon the oaken arm of his chair.

'...As regards the maid, too, it is true that I did heft her over the stream, she having on her hosen and shoon, whilst I had but my wooden sandals, which could take no hurt from the water. I should have thought shame upon my manhood, as well as my monkhood, if I had held back my hand from her.' He glanced around as he spoke with the half-amused look which he had worn during the whole proceedings.

'There is no need to go further,' said the Abbot. 'He has confessed to all. It only remains for me to portion out the punishment which is due to his evil conduct.

... 'John of Hordle,' he thundered, 'you have shown yourself during the two months of your novitiate to be a recreant monk, and one who is unworthy to wear the white garb which is the outer symbol of the spotless spirit. That dress shall therefore be stripped from thee...Ho there! lay-brothers—Francis, Naomi, Joseph—seize him and bind his arms! Drag him forth, and let the foresters and the porters scourge him from the precincts!'

As these three brothers advanced towards him to carry out the Abbot's direction, the smile faded from the novice's face, and he glanced right and left with his fierce brown eyes, like a bull at a baiting. Then, with a sudden deep-chested shout, he tore up the heavy oaken prie-dieu and poised it to strike, taking two steps backward the while, that none might take him at a vantage.

'By the black rood of Waltham!' he roared, 'if any knave among you lays a finger-end upon the edge of my gown, I will crush his skull like a filbert!' With his thick knotted arms, his thundering voice, and his bristle of red hair, there was something so repellent in the man that the three brothers flew back at the very glare of him... Springing forward, he hurled his unwieldy weapon at brother Ambrose, and, as desk and monk clattered on to the floor together, he sprang through the open door and down the winding stair. Sleepy old brother Athanasius, at the porter's cell, had a fleeting vision of twinkling feet and flying skirts; but before he had time to rub his eyes the recreant had passed the lodge, and was speeding as fast as his sandals could patter along the Lyndhurst Road.

Sir Arthur Conan Doyle (1859–1930)
The White Company (1891)

Some corroboration for the outrage among the brothers that 'after sundry japes and jokes the said brother John did lift up the said Mary Sowley and did take, carry, and convey her across a stream' can be found in Chapter XXIII of *Tess of the D'Urbervilles*, by the ensuing sexual ecstasy of the four maids whom Angel Clare carries, one at a time, through the pool. Hardy tells us that that evening 'the air of the sleeping chamber seemed to palpitate with the hopeless passion of the girls. They writhed feverishly under the oppressiveness of an emotion thrust on them by cruel Nature's law – an emotion they neither expected nor desired'.

This tale is set in an indeterminate time of magic and witchcraft. The narrator warns: 'my story will take you into times and spaces alike rude and uncivil. Blood will be spilt, virgins suffer distresses; the horn will sound through woodland glades; dogs, wolves, deer, and men, Beauty and the Beasts will tumble each other seeking life or death with their proper tools. You will have wandered with Isoult, and will know why she was called La Desirous, with Prosper le Gai, and will understand how a man may fall in love with his own wife.'

The author, Maurice Hewlett, was called to the bar but this, his first novel, was such a success that he gave up law and took to writing short stories, plays, essays, records of his travels and ten more novels.

...All his heart laughed. Prosper was merry. Whither he should go, what find, how fare, he knew not at all... Prosper was very certain that at twenty-three it is a great thing to be hale and astride a horse.

The country was split into bleak ravines, a pell-mell of rocks and boulders, and a sturdy crop of black pines between them. An overgrowth of brambles and briony ran riot over all. Prosper rode up a dry river-bed, keeping steadily west, so far as it would serve him; found himself quagged ere a dozen painful miles, floundered out as best he might, and by evening was making good pace over a rolling bit of moorland through which ran a sandy road. It was the highway from Wanmouth to Market Basing and the north, if he had known.

Riding forward carelessly, with a loose rein, he slept that night in the woods. Next day he rode fast and long without meeting a living soul, and so came at last into Morgraunt Forest, where the trees shut out the light of the day, and very few birds sing. He entered the east purlieus in the evening of his fifth day from Starning, and slept in a rocky valley. Tall black trees stood all round him, the vanguards of the forest host.

He espies a wretched-looking girl who is accused of witchcraft, and muses:

'If I leave her she gains death, or life (which is worse), and if I take her with me it can only be one way. What then! A man can lay down his life in many ways, giving it for the life that needeth. And if by any deed of mine I pluck this child out of the mire, put clear light into her eyes (which now are all dark), and set the flush on her grey cheeks which she was assuredly designed to carry there; and if she breathe sweet air and grow in the grace of God and sight of men—why then I have done well, however else I do.' He thought no more, but took the girl's hand again in both of his. 'Well, Isoult,' he said cheerfully, 'thou shalt not be hanged yet awhile, nor shall that worse thing befall thee. I will wed thee as soon as I may. At cock-crow we two will seek a priest.'

Isoult la Desiree's humbleness suggests that he has married beneath him. The couple endure hardships faithfully together; she, however, is not what she seems and the enchantment of the Forest itself has a notable influence on them both.

Towards the grey of the morning, seeing that the whole forest was at peace, with no sign of dogs or men all that night, and now even a rest from the far howling of the wolves, Prosper's head dropt to his breast. In a few seconds he slept profoundly. Isoult awoke and saw that he slept: she lay watching him, longing but not daring. When she saw that he looked blue and pinched about the cheek-bones, that his cheeks were yellow where they should be red, and grey where they had been white, she knew he was cold; and her humbleness was not proof against this justification of her desires. She crept out of her snug nest, crawled towards her lord and felt his hands: they were ice. 'Asleep he is mine,' she thought. She picked up the cloak, then crept again towards him, seated herself behind and a little above him, threw the cloak over both and snuggled it well in.

She put her arms about him and drew him close to her bosom. His head fell back at her gentle constraint; so he lay like a child at the breast. The mother in her was wild and throbbing. Stooped over him she pored into his face. A divine pity, a divine sense of the power of life over death, of waking over sleep, drew her lower and nearer. She kissed his face – the lids of his eyes, his forehead and cheeks. Like an unwatched bird she foraged at will, like a hardy sailor touched at every port but one. His mouth was too much his own, too firm; it kept too much of his sovereignty absolute. Otherwise she was free to roam; and she roamed, very much to his material advantage, since the love that made her rosy to the finger-tips, in time warmed him also. He slept long in her arms.

She began to be very hungry.

'He too will be hungry when he wakes,' she thought; 'what shall I do? We have nothing to eat.' She looked down wistfully at his head where it lay pillowed. 'What would I not give him of mine?' The thought flooded her. But what could she do?

She heard the pattering of dry leaves, the crackle of dry twigs snapt, and looking up, saw a herd of deer feeding in a glade not very far off.

Idly as she watched them, it came home to her that there were hinds among them with calves. One she noticed in particular feed a little apart, having two calves near her which had just begun to nibble a bit of grass. Vaguely wondering still over her plight, she pictured her days of shepherding in the downs where food had often failed her, and the ewes perforce mothered another lamb. That hind's udder was full of milk: a sudden thought ran like wine through her blood.

She slid from Prosper, got up very softly, took her cup, and went towards the browsing deer. The hind looked up (like all the herd), but did not start nor run. A brief gaze satisfied it that here was no enemy, neither a stranger to the forest walks; it fell-to again, and suffered Isoult to come quite close, even to lay her hand upon its neck. Then she stood for a while stroking the red hind, while all the herd watched her.

She knelt before the beast, clasping both arms about its neck; she fondled it with her face, as if asking the boon she would have. Some message passed between them, some assurance, for she let go of the hind's neck and crawled on hands and knees towards the udder. The deer never moved, though it turned its head to watch her. She took the teat in her mouth, sucked and drew milk. The herd stood all about her motionless; the hind nozzled her as if she had been one of its own calves; so she was filled.

Next she had to fill her cup. This was much more difficult. The hind must be soothed and fondled again, there must be no shock on either side. She started the flow with her mouth; then she knelt against the animal with her hand pressed to its side, took the teat in her hand and succeeded. She filled the cup with Prosper's breakfast. She got up, kissed the hind behind the eyes, stroked its neck many times, and went tiptoe back to her lord and master. She found him still sound asleep, so sat quietly watching him till he should awake, with the cup held against her heart to keep it warm.

Broad daylight and a chance beam of sun through the trees woke him at last. It would be about seven o'clock. He stretched portentously, and sat up to look about him; so he encountered her tender eyes before she had been able to subdue their light.

'Good-morning, Isoult,' said he. 'Have I been long asleep?'

'A few hours only, lord.'

'I am hungry. I must eat something.'

He took the cup she tendered, looking at her.

'Drink first, my child,' he said.

'Lord, I have drunk already.'

He drained the cup without further ado.

'Good milk,' he said when he had done. He took these things, you see, very much as they came.

His next act was to kneel face to the sun and begin his prayers. Something made him stop; he turned him to his wife.

'Hast thou said they prayers, Isoult?'

'No, lord,' said she, reddening.

'Come then and pray with me. It is a good custom.'

She obeyed him so far as to kneel down by his side…

Maurice Hewlett (1861–1923)
The Forest Lovers 1898

Capt Marryat's wonderful childrens' book, *The Children of the New Forest*, celebrates the ineffable superiority of English children, and especially Royalist children, sequestered in the seventeenth-century forest. The manor of Arnewood is mentioned in the Domesday Book; Jacob's cottage seems to be in the neighbourhood of the village of Sway in the New Forest.

It was in the month of November in the year 1647 that King Charles, accompanied by Sir John Berkley, Ashburnham, and Legg, made his escape from Hampton Court and rode as fast as the horses could carry them towards that part of Hampshire which led to the New Forest. The king had expected that his friends had provided a vessel in which he might escape to France; but in this he was disappointed. There was no vessel ready, and after riding for some time along the shore, he resolved to go to Titchfield, a seat belonging to the Earl of Southampton. After a long consultation with those who attended him, he yielded to their advice, which was to trust to Colonel Hammond, who was governor of the Isle of Wight for the Parliament, but who was supposed to be friendly to the king. Whatever might be the feelings of commiseration of Colonel Hammond towards a king so unfortunately situated, he was firm in his duties towards his employers, and the consequence was that King Charles found himself again a prisoner in Carisbrooke Castle.

A short distance from the town of Lymington, which is not far from Titchfield, where the king took shelter, but on the other side of Southampton Water, and south of the New Forest, to which it adjoins, was a property called Arnwood, which belonged to a Cavalier of the name of Beverley. It was at that time a property of considerable value, being very extensive; it abutted on the New Forest, and might have been supposed to have been a continuation of it. This Colonel Beverley, as we must call him, for he rose to that rank in the king's army, was a valued friend and companion of Prince Rupert's, and at last fell in his arms at the battle of Naseby. Colonel Beverley had married into the family of the Villiers, and the issue of his marriage was two sons and two daughters; but his zeal and his sense of duty had induced him, at the commencement of the war, to leave his wife and family at Arnwood, and he was fated never to meet them again. The news of his death had such an effect on Mrs Beverley, already worn with anxiety on her husband's account, that a few months afterwards she followed him to an early tomb, leaving the four children under the charge of an elderly relative till such time as the family of the Villiers could protect them; but, as will appear by our history, this was not at that period possible. The life of a king and many other lives were in jeopardy, and the orphans remained at Arnwood, still under the care of their elderly relation, at that time that our history commences.

The New Forest, my readers are perhaps aware, was first enclosed by William the Conqueror as a royal forest for his own amusement. Since that time to the present day, it has continued a royal domain. At the period of which we are writing, it had an establishment of verderers and keepers, paid by the crown, amounting to some forty or fifty men. At the commencement of the civil war they remained at their posts, but soon found, in the disorganised state of the country, that their wages were no longer to be obtained; and then, when the king had decided upon raising an army, Beverley, who held a superior office in the forest, enrolled all the young and athletic men who were employed in the forest and marched them away with him, to join the king's army. Some few remained, their age not rendering their services of value, and among them was an old and attached servant of Beverley's, a man of above sixty years of age, whose name was Jacob Armitage, and who had obtained the situation through Colonel Beverley's interest. Those who remained in the forest lived in cottages many miles asunder, and indemnified themselves for the non-payment of their salaries by killing the deer for sale and for their own subsistence.

The cottage of Jacob Armitage (forest ranger) was situated on the skirts of the New Forest about a mile and a half from the mansion of Arnwood... He promised the colonel that he would watch over the family.

...

Jacob knew that Arnwood was to be burned down that night and that it would be necessary to remove the family...

The next morning, Jacob, who was most anxious to learn the news, saddled the pony, having first given his injunctions to Edward how to behave in case any troopers should come to the cottage. He told him to pretend that the children were in bed with the smallpox, as they had done the day before. Jacob then travelled to Gossip Allwood's, and he there learnt that King Charles had been taken prisoner, and was at the Isle of Wight, and that the troopers were all going back to London as fast as they came. Feeling that there was now no more danger to be apprehended from them, Jacob set off as fast as he could for Lymington. He went to one shop and purchased two peasant dresses which he thought would fit the two boys, and at another he bought similar apparel for the two girls. Then, with several other ready-made articles, and some other things which were required for the household, he made a large package, which he put upon the pony, and, taking the bridle, set off home, and arrived in time to superintend the cooking of the dinner, which was this day venison fried in a pan, and boiled potatoes.

When dinner was over he opened his bundle, and told the little ones that now they were to live in a cottage they ought to wear cottage clothes, and that he had brought them some to put on, which they might rove about the woods in, and not mind tearing them. Alice and Edith went into the bedroom, and Alice dressed Edith and herself, and came out quite pleased with their change of dress. Humphrey and Edward put theirs on in the sitting-room, and they all fitted pretty well, and certainly were very becoming to the children.

'Now, recollect, you are all my grandchildren,' said Jacob; 'for I shall no longer call you Miss and Master – that we never do in a cottage. You understand me, Edward, of course?' added Jacob.

Edward nodded his head, and Jacob telling the children that they might go out of the cottage and play, they all set off, quite delighted with clothes which procured them their liberty.

We must now describe the cottage of Jacob Armitage, in which the children have in future to dwell. As we said before, it contained a large sitting-room, or kitchen, in which were a spacious hearth and chimney, table, stools, cupboards, and dressers; the two bedrooms which adjoined it were now appropriated, one for Jacob, and the other for the two boys; the third, or inner bedroom, was arranged for the two girls, as being more retired and secure. But there were outhouses belonging to it; a stall in which White Billy, the pony, lived during the winter; a shed and pig sty rudely constructed, with an enclosed yard attached to them; and it had, moreover, a piece of ground of more than an acre, well fenced in to keep out the deer and game, the largest portion of which was cultivated as a garden and potato-ground, and the other, which remained in grass, contained some fine old apple and pear trees. Such was the domicile. The pony, a few fowls, a sow and two young pigs, and the dog Smoker, were the animals on the establishment. Here Jacob Armitage had been born – for the cottage had been bought by his grandfather – but he had not always remained at the cottage. When young he had for several years served in the army. His father and brother had lived in the establishment at Arnwood, and he was constantly there as a boy. The chaplain of Arnwood had taken a fancy to him, and taught him to read – writing he had not acquired. As soon as he grew up, he served in the troop commanded by Colonel Beverley's father; and after his death, Colonel Beverley had procured for him the situation of forest ranger, which had been held by his father, who was then alive, but too aged to do the duty. Jacob Armitage married a good and devout young woman, with whom he lived several years, when she died; after which, his father being also dead, Jacob Armitage had lived alone until the period at which we have commenced this history.

Captain Marryat (1792–1846)
Children of the New Forest (1847)

Sir Arthur Conan Doyle's eponymous hero Micah Clarke, as we learned earlier, is from Havant, near Portsmouth, and 'a kinsman of Joseph Clarke, the old Roundhead of that town'. He becomes eagerly involved in Monmouth's Rebellion (1685) but, gradually repelled by the extreme opinions he encounters, he declares ultimately for toleration.

We had passed through Fareham and Botley ... and were now making our way down the Bishopstoke road. The soil changes about here from chalk to sand, so that our horses' hoofs did but make a dull subdued rattle, which was no bar to our talk – or rather to my companion's, for I did little more than listen. In truth, my mind was so full of anticipations of what was before us, and of thoughts of the home behind, that I was in no humour for sprightly chatter. The sky was somewhat clouded, but the moon glinted out between the rifts, showing us the long road which wound away in front of us.

... The patch of light in the east had increased and broadened, and the sky was mottled with little pink feathers of cloud. As we passed over the low hills of Chandler's Ford and Romsey we could see the smoke of Southampton to the south-east, and the broad dark expanse of the New Forest with the haze of morning hanging over it. A few horsemen passed us, pricking along, too much engrossed in their own errand to enquire ours. A couple of carts and a long string of pack-horses, laden principally with bales of wool, came straggling along a by-road, and the drivers waved their broad hats to us and wished us God-speed. At Dunbridge the folk were just stirring and paused in taking down the cottage shutters to come to the garden railings and watch us pass. As we entered Dean, the great red sun pushed its rosy rim over the edge of the horizon, and the air was filled with the buzz of insects and the sweet scent of the morning. We dismounted at this latter village, and had a cup of ale while resting and watering the horses...

At the end of a week or two news came of the fugitives. Monmouth, it seems, had been captured by Portman's yellow-coats when trying to make his way to the New Forest, whence he hoped to escape to the Continent. He was dragged, gaunt, unshaven, and trembling, out of a bean-field in which he had taken refuge, and was carried to Ringwood, in Hampshire.

Sir Arthur Conan Doyle
Micah Clarke (1889)

Contrasting Micah's youth and innocence, Finnemore below presents Ferrers's maturity and command in the same vengeful days. The Duke of Monmouth, illegitimate son of Charles ll, unwillingly challenged the Catholic James ll's claim to the throne. Abandoned by his army, Monmouth was led to the scaffold and his supporters severely punished.

Early on a fine August morning in the year 1685 I rode through Winchester on my way home from London. Some miles out of town I entered on a long stretch of open road and saw at the far end of the level causeway bright sparkles and flashes as of the sun falling on burnished armour. Soon I made out a troop of cavalry advancing at a walk. As we drew near each other I knew the regiment by the facings and next I knew the officer riding before them. Lieutenant Poyntz recognised me at the same moment.

'What! Ferrers?' he called out as he rode over to my side of the road, then drew rein, and we greeted each other. But the next moment my eyes were drawn to the detachment which followed and I understood the slow pace of the horsemen. Six troopers rode two by two and with them walked a tall, ruddy-faced man in the corduroys and top boots of a farmer. His round red English face was set and grim, his bright blue eyes stared proudly before him but alas his arms were bound at his back, and a rope stretched from his wrists to the bonds of those that walked next. Two by two after him came eight other stalwart brown faced fellows, ploughmen and the like by their looks, but dirty and dishevelled, their clothes torn and stained, and one or two bandaged as if suffering from wounds. Now for the first time the sickening sense of what this futile Monmouth rebellion meant to our west-country lads came home to my heart. I was fresh from London where the most dreadful threats of vengeance were filling the air. The intention of the Privy Council to give to the west country a terrible lesson had already leaked out and I looked with heavy eyes at the poor fellows tramping along roped one to the other like a gang of desperate criminals to whom it is hopeless to show mercy.

Such a glorious morning as this was their birthright. They should have been, sickle in hand, among the corn, now painting the landscape with patches of bright gold. The farmer should have been at their head, or pounding the road to market on his stout cob. On many and many such a morning had I ridden that road and seen such men straightening their backs to scan the passing traveller, and to give their honest simple greeting; had drawn rein to pass the time of day with such-and-such a farmer, and speak of crops and the outlook of the season...

'There is word in London that Jeffreys will come down to try them.'

My companion shrugged his shoulders.

'A short shrift and a long rope, eh?'

· · ·

Fifty yards down from the ridge we entered an oak wood through the heart of which ran two roads. Where they crossed a signpost was set up to guide travellers. I was passing it when a frightened voice called out behind me.

'Captain! Master George! Look there. Look at the signpost!'

I looked, and gave such a start as to jerk the reins and bring my steed up instantly. The signpost was surmounted by an iron spike, and from this spike a ghastly, gory head looked down upon us, a venerable grey head, the silver hairs clotted with blood and clinging stiffly about the skull. The distorted face was pale as wood ashes, except where it was marked with blotches of blood, which was now dark and dried and peeling in the heat. I was shocked utterly and beyond telling. It was John Woodley the old game-keeper...

Shortly afterwards, Ferrers stumbles upon the young lovers of the title hiding in the bushes. They are, as often in these New Forest tales, fugitives. In this case it is the bloody retribution of Judge Jeffreys which terrifies them.

J E Finnemore
The Lover Fugitives: A Romance (1901)

The ubiquitous Celia Fiennes gives her ha'pence worth:

...Ffrom Limmington to Lindhurst is 6 mile, where is a house of ye Kings w^n he comes to hunt in the new fforest... There is a Bow man wch is to provide ye King wth Bow and arrow when he Comes into ye fforest – they have some priviledge also but ye shooteing by bow and arrow being Left off, y^t office is not regarded.

Celia Fiennes (1662–1741)
Through England on a Side Saddle in the time of William and Mary (1888)

And so, tangentially, does Tobias Smollett, the Scots poet, traveller and novelist, author of *Peregrine Pickle* (1751) and *Humphrey Clinker* (1771).

I shall not pretend to describe the castle or palace of Fontainbleau, of which I had only a glimpse in passing; but the forest, in the middle of which it stands, is a noble chase of great extent, beautifully wild and romantic, well stored with game

of all sorts, and abounding with excellent timber. It put me in
mind of the New Forest in Hampshire.

Tobias Smollett (1721–1771)
Travels through France and Italy (1766)

William Cobbett, a conservative Radical farmer stuffed with
indignation and hyperbole (as witness his varied emotions in the
course of this one day), toured England on horseback commenting
on what he witnessed. He fiercely cursed certain causes of what he
deemed the deplorable state of the land: paper money, taxes, national
debt, absentee landlords; above all he took aim at the 'Great Wen' with
which name he heaped insults on London.

Weston Grove
October 18th 1826

....The New Forest formerly extended, westward, from
Southampton Water and the river Oux to the river Avon,
and northward from Lymington Haven to the borders of
Wiltshire. We know that this was its utmost extent; and
we know also that the towns of Christchurch, Lymington,
Ringwood, and Fordingbridge, and the villages of Bolder,
Fawley, Lyndhurst, Dipden, Eling, Minsted, and all the other
villages that now have churches; we know, I say (and pray
mark it), that all these towns and villages existed before the
Norman Conquest: because the Roman names of several of
them (all the towns) are in print, and because an account of
them all is to be found in Doomsday Book, which was made
by this very William the Conqueror.
...at the distance of half a mile from the water-side we came
out again upon the intolerable heath, and went on for seven
or eight miles over that heath, from the village of Beaulieu to
that of Marchwood, having a list of trees and enclosed lands
away to our right all the way along, which list of trees to the
southwest side of that arm of the sea which goes from Calshot
castle to Redbridge, passing by Southampton, which lies on
the northeast side. Never was a more barren tract of land than
these seven or eight miles. We had come seven miles across
the forest in another direction in the morning; so that a poorer

spot than this New Forest there is not in all England; nor, I believe, in the whole world.

... The moon shone very bright by the time that we mounted Town-hill common; and now, skirting the enclosures upon the edge of the common, we passed several of those cottages which I so well recollected, and in which I had the satisfaction to believe that the inhabitants were sitting comfortably with bellies full by a good fire. It was eight o'clock before we arrived at Weston Grove. To those who like water-scenes (as nineteen-twentieth of people do) it is the prettiest spot, I believe, in all England.

William Cobbett (1763–1835)
Rural Rides (1830)

Moody, like novelists before and after him, presents the forest as a place of mystery and treachery.

Beside the heaths, lawns and woods, of which the forest is composed, there is another kind of surface found in many parts, which comes under none of these denominations, and that is the bog. Many parts of the forest abound in springs; and as these lands have ever been in a state of nature, and of course undrained, the moisture drains itself into the low grounds where, as usual in other rude countries, it becomes soft and spongy and generates bogs. These in some places are very extensive. In the road between Brockenhurst and Ringwood, at a place called Longslade-bottom, one of these bogs extends three miles, without interruptions, and is the common drain of all those parts. It has in general the appearance of common verdure. But the traveller must be on his guard. These tracts

171

of deceitful ground are often dangerous, to such as leave the beaten roads, and traverse the paths of forest. A horse track is not always a mark of security. It is perhaps only beaten by the little forest horse which will venture into a bog in quest of better herbage; and his lightness will secure him in a place, where a larger horse, under the weight of a rider, would flounder.

Henry Moody
Antiquarian and topographical sketches of
Hampshire: New Forest (1846)

And similarly, for Charles Kingsley, it's a place in which the worst can happen:

In the New Forest: a ballad (1847)

Oh she tripped over Ocknell plain,
And down by Bradley Water;
And the fairest maid on the forest side
Was Jane, the keeper's daughter.

She went and went through the broad gray lawns
As down the red sun sank,
And chill as the scent of a new-made grave
The mist smelt cold and dank.

'A token, a token!' that fair maid cried,
'A token that bodes me sorrow;
For they that smell the grave by night
Will see the corpse to-morrow.

'My own true love in Burley Walk
Does hunt to-night, I fear;
And if he meet my father stern,
His game may cost him dear.

'Ah, here's a curse on hare and grouse,
A curse on hart and hind;
And a health to the squire in all England,
Leaves never a head behind.'

Her true love shot a mighty hart
Among the standing rye,
When on him leapt that keeper old
From the fern where he did lie.

The forest laws were sharp and stern,
The forest blood was keen;
They lashed together for life and death
Beneath the hollies green.

The metal good and the walnut wood
Did soon in flinders flee;
They tost the orts to south and north,
And grappled knee to knee.

They wrestled up, they wrestled down,
They wrestled still and sore;
Beneath their feet the myrtle sweet
Was stamped to mud and gore.

Ah, cold pale moon, thou cruel pale moon,
That starest with never a frown
On all the grim and the ghastly things
That are wrought in thorpe and town:

And yet, cold pale moon, thou cruel pale moon,
That night hadst never the grace
To lighten two dying Christian men
To see one another's face.

They wrestled up, they wrestled down,
They wrestled sore and still,
The fiend who blinds the eyes of men
That night he had his will.

Like stags full spent, among the bent
They dropped a while to rest;
When the young man drove his saying knife
Deep in the old man's breast.

The old man drove his gunstock down
Upon the young man's head;
And side by side, by the water brown,
Those yeomen twain lay dead.

They dug three graves in Lyndhurst yard;
They dug them side by side;
Two yeomen lie there, and a maiden fair
A widow and never a bride.

Charles Kingsley (1819–1875)
In the New Forest: a ballad (1847)

Caroline Anne Bowles (1786–1864) married the poet Robert Southey shortly before he died. Her private education was mainly at the hands of the writer and artist William Gilpin. Caroline spent summers with her uncle at Calshot Castle, near the village of Boldre on the edge of the New Forest where Gilpin was vicar. William Gilpin (1724–1804) is best known as father of the picturesque – 'that kind of beauty which is agreeable in a picture'.

The Birth-day

Farther a-field we journeyed, Jane and I,
When summer days set in, with their long, light
Delicious evenings. Then, most happy child!
Most favoured! — I was sent a frequent guest,
Secure of welcome, to the loveliest home
Of all the country, o'er whose quiet walls
Brooded the twin-doves, Holiness and Peace:
There with thine aged partner didst thou dwell,
Pastor and master! servant of thy Lord,
Faithful as he, the labours of whose love
Recorded by thy pen, embalm for aye
The name of Gilpin heired by thee — right heir
Of the saint's mantle. Holy Bernard's life,
Its apostolic graces unimpaired,
Renewed in William's, virtuous parish priest !
Let me live o'er again, in fond detail,
One of those happy visits. Leave obtained,

Methought the clock stood still. Four hours past noon,
And not yet started on our three mile walk !
And six the vicarage tea hour – primitive,
And I should lose that precious hour, most prized,
When in the old man's study, at his feet,
Or nestling close beside him, I might sit
With eye, ear, soul intent on his mild voice,
And face benign, and words so simply wise
Framed for his childish hearer. 'Let us go !'
And like a fawn I bounded on before,
When lagging Jane came forth, and off we went.
Sultry the hour, and hot the dusty way,
Though here and there by leafy screen o'erarched —
And the long broiling hill! and that last mile
When the small frame waxed weary! the glib tongue
Slackening its motion with the languid limbs.
But joy was in my heart, howe'er suppressed
Its outward show exuberant ; and, at length,
Lo! the last turning — lo! the well-known door,
Festooned about with garlands picturesque,
Of trailing evergreens. Who's weary now ?
Sounding the bell with that impatient pull
That quickens Mistress Molly's answering steps
To most unusual promptness. Turns the lock —
The door uncloses — Molly's smiling face
Welcomes unasked. One eager, forward spring,
And farewell to the glaring world without ;
The glaring, bustling, noisy, parched-up world !
And hail repose and verdure, turf and flowers,
Perfume of lilies, through the leafy gloom
White gleaming; and the full, rich, mellow note
Of song-thrush, hidden in the tall thick bay
Beside the study window !
The old house,
Through flickering shadows of high-arching boughs,
Caught gleams of sunlight on its time-stained walls,
And frieze of mantling vine; and lower down,
Trained among jasmines to the southern bow,
Moss roses, bursting into richest bloom,
Blushed by the open window. There she sate,

The venerable lady, her white hair
White as the snowy coif, upon her book
Or needlework intent; and near at hand
The maiden sister friend — a lifelong guest —
At her coarse sempstresship — another Dorcas,
Unwearying in the work of charity.
Oh! kindest greeting! as the door unclosed
That welcomed the half-bold half-bashful guest,
And brought me bounding on at a half word
To meet the proffered kiss. Oh, kindest care!
Considerate of my long, hot, dusty walk,
Of hat and tippet that divested me,
And clinging gloves; and from the glowing cheek
And hot brow, parted back the clustering curls,
Applying grateful coolness of clear lymph,
Distilled from fragrant elder — sovereign wash
For sunburnt skin and freckled! Kindest care,
That followed up those offices of love
By cautionary charge to sit and rest
'Quite still till tea time.' Kindest care, I trow,
But little relished. Restless was my rest,
And wistful eyes, still wandering to the door,
Revealed 'the secret of my discontent,'
And told where I would be. The lady smiled,
And shook her head, and said, —
   'Well! go your ways
And ask admittance at that certain door
You know so well.' All weariness was gone —
Blithe as a bird, thus freed, away I flew.
And in three seconds at the well-known door
Tapped gently; and a gentle voice within
Asking 'Who's there?'
'It's me' I answered low,
Grammatically clear.
   'Let me come in,'
The gentle voice rejoined; and in I stole,
Bashfully silent, as the good man's smile,
And hand extended, drew me to his chair;
And there all eye and ear, I stood full long,
Still tongueless, as it seemed; love-tempering awe

Chaining my words up. But so kindly his,
His aspect so benign, his winning art
So graciously conforming; in short time
Awe was absorbed in love, and then unchained
By perfect confidence, the little tongue
Questioned and answered with as careless ease
As might be, from irreverent boldness free.
True love may cast out fear, but not respect,
That fears the very shadow of offence.
How holy was the calm of that small room!
How tenderly the evening light stole in,
As 'twere in reverence of its sanctity!
Here and there touching with a golden gleam
Book-shelf or picture -frame, or brightening up
The nosegay set with daily care — love's own —
Upon the study table. Dallying there
Among the books and papers, and with beam
Of softest radiance, starring like a glory
The old man's high bald head and noble brow,
There still I found him, busy with his pen —
Oh pen of varied power! found faithful ever,
Faithful and fearless in the one great cause —
Or some grave tome, or lighter work of taste —
His no ascetic, harsh, soul-narrowing creed —
Or that unrivalled pencil, with few strokes,
And sober tinting slight, that wrought effects
Most magical — the poetry of art!
Lovely simplicity! — true wisdom's grace —
That, condescending to a simple child,
Spread out before me hoards of graphic treasures;
Smiling encouragement as I expressed
Delight or censure — for in full good faith
I played the critic — and vouchsafing mild
To explain or vindicate; in seeming sport
Instructing ever; and on graver themes
Winning my heart to listen, as he taught
Things that pertain to life. Oh precious seed!

Caroline Anne Bowles (1786–1864)
Poems (1867)

William Wilkie Collins *The Woman in White*, according to the author, 'is the story of what a woman's patience can endure and what a man's resolution can achieve'. The mystery attached to Blackwater Park, represents something of the suspicion with which Victorians viewed this savage, sparsely populated area, not to mention the suspicion with which Laura views her new husband, Sir Percival Glyde. Here Laura's half-sister, Marion, shares her first impressions. There is still a Blackwater House near the mouth of the Beaulieu river.

The house is situated on a dead flat, and seems to be shut in — almost suffocated, to my north-country notions, by trees. I have seen nobody but the man-servant who opened the door to me, and the housekeeper, a very civil person, who showed me the way to my own room, and got me my tea. I have a nice little boudoir and bedroom, at the end of a long passage on the first floor. The servants and some of the spare rooms are on the second floor, and all the living rooms are on the ground floor. I have not seen one of them yet, and I know nothing about the house, except that one wing of it is said to be five hundred years old, that it had a moat round it once, and that it gets its name of Blackwater from a lake in the park...
I began my sight-seeing, of course, with the house. The main body of the building is of the time of that highly-overrated woman, Queen Elizabeth. On the ground floor there are two hugely long galleries, with low ceilings lying parallel with each other, and rendered additionally dark and dismal by hideous family portraits — every one of which I should like to burn. The rooms on the floor above the two galleries are kept in tolerable repair, but are very seldom used. The civil housekeeper, who acted as my guide, offered to show me over them, but considerately added that she feared I should find them rather out of order. My respect for the integrity of my own petticoats and stockings infinitely exceeds my respect for all the Elizabethan bedrooms in the kingdom, so I positively declined exploring the upper regions of dust and dirt at the risk of soiling my nice clean clothes. The housekeeper said, 'I am quite of your opinion, Miss,' and appeared to think me the most sensible woman she had met with for a long time past.
So much, then, for the main building. Two wings are added at either end of it. The half-ruined wing on the left

(as you approach the house) was once a place of residence standing by itself, and was built in the fourteenth century. One of Sir Percival's maternal ancestors — I don't remember, and don't care which — tacked on the main building, at right angles to it, in the aforesaid Queen Elizabeth's time. The housekeeper told me that the architecture of 'the old wing,' both outside and inside, was considered remarkably fine by good judges. On further investigation I discovered that good judges could only exercise their abilities on Sir Percival's piece of antiquity by previously dismissing from their minds all fear of damp, darkness, and rats. Under these circumstances, I unhesitatingly acknowledged myself to be no judge at all, and suggested that we should treat 'the old wing' precisely as we had previously treated the Elizabethan bedrooms. Once more the housekeeper said, 'I am quite of your opinion, Miss,' and once more she looked at me with undisguised admiration of my extraordinary common-sense.

We went next to the wing on the right, which was built, by way of completing the wonderful architectural jumble at Blackwater Park, in the time of George II.

This is the habitable part of the house, which has been repaired and redecorated inside on Laura's account. My two rooms, and all the good bedrooms besides, are on the first floor, and the basement contains a drawing-room, a dining-room, a morning-room, a library, and a pretty little boudoir for Laura, all very nicely ornamented in the bright modern way, and all very elegantly furnished with the delightful modern luxuries. None of the rooms are anything like so large and airy as our rooms at Limmeridge, but they all look pleasant to live in. I was terribly afraid, from what I had heard of Blackwater Park, of fatiguing antique chairs, and dismal stained glass, and musty, frouzy hangings, and all the barbarous lumber which people born without a sense of comfort accumulate about them, in defiance of the consideration due to the convenience of their friends. It is an inexpressible relief to find that the nineteenth century has invaded this strange future home of mine, and has swept the dirty 'good old times' out of the way of our daily life.

I dawdled away the morning — part of the time in the rooms downstairs, and part out of doors in the great square which is formed by the three sides of the house, and by the lofty iron railings and gates which protect it in front. A large circular fishpond with stone sides, and an allegorical leaden monster in the middle, occupies the centre of the square. The pond itself is full of gold and silver fish, and is encircled by a broad belt of the softest turf I ever walked on. I loitered here on the shady side pleasantly enough till luncheon-time, and after that took my broad straw hat and wandered out alone in the warm lovely sunlight to explore the grounds.

Daylight confirmed the impression which I had felt the night before, of there being too many trees at Blackwater. The house is stifled by them. They are, for the most part, young, and planted far too thickly. I suspect there must have been a ruinous cutting down of timber all over the estate before Sir Percival's time, and an angry anxiety on the part of the next possessor to fill up all the gaps as thickly and rapidly as possible. After looking about me in front of the house, I observed a flower-garden on my left hand, and walked towards it to see what I could discover in that direction.

On a nearer view the garden proved to be small and poor and ill kept. I left it behind me, opened a little gate in a ring fence, and found myself in a plantation of fir-trees.

A pretty winding path, artificially made, led me on among the trees, and my north-country experience soon informed me that I was approaching sandy, heathy ground. After a walk of more than half a mile, I should think, among the firs, the path took a sharp turn — the trees abruptly ceased to appear on either side of me, and I found myself standing suddenly on the margin of a vast open space, and looking down at the Blackwater lake from which the house takes its name.

The ground, shelving away below me, was all sand, with a few little heathy hillocks to break the monotony of it in certain places. The lake itself had evidently once flowed to the spot on which I stood, and had been gradually wasted and dried up to less than a third of its former size. I saw its still, stagnant waters, a quarter of a mile away from me in the hollow, separated into pools and ponds by twining reeds and rushes, and little knolls of earth. On the farther bank from me the trees rose thickly again, and shut out the view, and cast their black shadows on the sluggish, shallow water. As I walked down to the lake, I saw that the ground on its farther side was damp and marshy, overgrown with rank grass and dismal willows. The water, which was clear enough on the open sandy side, where the sun shone, looked black and poisonous opposite to me, where it lay deeper under the shade of the spongy banks, and the rank overhanging thickets and tangled trees. The frogs were croaking, and the rats were slipping in and out of the shadowy water, like live shadows themselves, as I got nearer to the marshy side of the lake. I saw here, lying half in and half out of the water, the rotten wreck of an old overturned boat, with a sickly spot of sunlight glimmering through a gap in the trees on its dry surface, and a snake basking in the midst of the spot, fantastically coiled and treacherously still. Far and near the view suggested the same dreary impressions of solitude and decay, and the glorious brightness of the summer sky overhead seemed only to deepen and harden the gloom and barrenness of the wilderness on which it shone. I turned and retraced my steps to the high heathy ground, directing them a little aside from my former path towards a shabby old wooden shed, which stood on the outer skirt of the fir plantation, and which had hitherto been too unimportant to share my notice with the wide, wild prospect of the lake.

On approaching the shed I found that it had once been a boat-house, and that an attempt had apparently been made to convert it afterwards into a sort of rude arbour, by placing inside it a firwood seat, a few stools, and a table. I entered the place, and sat down for a little while to rest and get my breath again.

I had not been in the boat-house more than a minute when it struck me that the sound of my own quick breathing was very strangely echoed by something beneath me. I listened intently for a moment, and heard a low, thick, sobbing breath that seemed to come from the ground under the seat which I was occupying. My nerves are not easily shaken by trifles, but on this occasion I started to my feet in a fright — called out — received no answer — summoned back my recreant courage, and looked under the seat.

There, crouched up in the farthest corner, lay the forlorn cause of my terror, in the shape of a poor little dog — a black and white spaniel. The creature moaned feebly when I looked at it and called to it, but never stirred. I moved away the seat and looked closer. The poor little dog's eyes were glazing

181

fast, and there were spots of blood on its glossy white side. The misery of a weak, helpless, dumb creature is surely one of the saddest of all the mournful sights which this world can show. I lifted the poor dog in my arms as gently as I could, and contrived a sort of make-shift hammock for him to lie in, by gathering up the front of my dress all round him. In this way I took the creature, as painlessly as possible, and as fast as possible, back to the house.

Finding no one in the hall I went up at once to my own sitting-room, made a bed for the dog with one of my old shawls, and rang the bell. The largest and fattest of all possible house-maids answered it, in a state of cheerful stupidity which would have provoked the patience of a saint. The girl's fat, shapeless face actually stretched into a broad grin at the sight of the wounded creature on the floor.

'What do you see there to laugh at?' I asked, as angrily as if she had been a servant of my own. 'Do you know whose dog it is?'

'No, Miss, that I certainly don't.' She stooped, and looked down at the spaniel's injured side — brightened suddenly with the irradiation of a new idea — and pointing to the wound with a chuckle of satisfaction, said, 'That's Baxter's doings, that is.'

I was so exasperated that I could have boxed her ears. 'Baxter?' I said. 'Who is the brute you call Baxter?'

The girl grinned again more cheerfully than ever. 'Bless you, Miss! Baxter's the keeper, and when he finds strange dogs hunting about, he takes and shoots 'em. It's keeper's dooty Miss, I think that dog will die. Here's where he's been shot, ain't it? That's Baxter's doings, that is. Baxter's doings, Miss, and Baxter's dooty.'

I was almost wicked enough to wish that Baxter had shot the housemaid instead of the dog. Seeing that it was quite useless to expect this densely impenetrable personage to give me any help in relieving the suffering creature at our feet, I told her to request the housekeeper's attendance with my compliments. She went out exactly as she had come in, grinning from ear to ear. As the door closed on her she said to herself softly, 'It's Baxter's doings and Baxter's dooty — that's what it is.'

...The poor little dog! I wish my first day at Blackwater
Park had not been associated with death, though it is only the
death of a stray animal.

Wilkie Collins (1824–1889)
The Woman in White (1859)

Thomas Love Peacock, in sublime contrast to the world of the ghostly
The Woman in White, provides an idyllic scene for the amusing and ideal
battle of the sexes. Peacock's leisurely and deliberate yet informative long
first sentence sets the style for his seven sophisticated novels. They are
full of allusions and quotations and (as with the poetry of T S Eliot fifty
years later) the reader is sent to the library to refer to great, especially
classical, authors. Amusing certainly; he affectionately encourages
laughter, though Mr Falconer's premonition of the destruction of the
forest introduces momentarily a melancholy note. Peacock's half dozen
novels consist of an unusual quantity of conversation, of which Lewis
Carroll's Alice would approve. The philosophical discussions at table
must be characteristic of the kinds of salon held in the more cultivated
parts of Hampshire like The Vyne, Broadlands, Bramshill, Highclere
Castle, Avon Tyrrell, The Grange, Cranbury Park, Hackwood Park,
Mottisfont Abbey, Blackmoor House and Rotherfield Park. Peacock's
elder daughter married George Meredith and during the last year of his
life Peacock rejoiced in discovering the novels of Dickens.

Chapter II

Gregory Gryll, Esq., of Gryll Grange in Hampshire, on the
borders of the New Forest, in the midst of a park which was a
little forest in itself, nearly reaching to the sea, and well stocked
with deer, having a large outer tract, where a numerous light-
tenanted and well-conditioned tenantry fattened innumerable
pigs, considered himself well located for what he professed to
be, *Epicuri de grege porcus*, (a pig from the herd of Epicurus)
and held, though he found it difficult to trace the pedigree,
that he was lineally descended from the ancient and illustrious
Gryllus, who maintained against Ulysses the superior
happiness of other animals to that of the life of man...
     He liked to dine well, and withal to dine quietly, and to
have quiet friends at his table, with whom he could discuss

questions which might afford ample room for pleasant conversation and none for acrimonious dispute...

Chapter III

...The Reverend Doctor Opimian, the worthy divine, dwelt in an agreeably situated vicarage, on the outskirts of the New Forest. A good living, a comfortable patrimony, a moderate dowry with his wife, placed him sufficiently above the cares of the world to enable him to gratify all his tastes without minute calculations of cost. His tastes in fact were four: a good library, a good dinner, a pleasant garden and rural walks. He was an athlete in pedestrianism. He took no pleasure in riding, either on horseback or in a carriage... Beyond the limits of his ordinary but within those of his occasional range was a solitary round tower on an eminence backed with wood, which had probably in old days been landmark for hunters; but having in modern days no very obvious use, was designated, as many such buildings are, by the name of the Folly.

One fine Midsummer day, with a southerly breeze and a cloudless sky, the Doctor, having taken an early breakfast... set out with a good stick in his hand and a Newfoundland dog at his heels for one of his longest walks, such as he could only take in the longest days.

Arriving at the Folly, which he had not visited for a long time, he was surprised to find it enclosed...He was aroused by the approach of a young gentleman from within the enclosure...The stranger led the way across an open space in the wood, to a circular hall, from each side of which a wide passage led, on the left hand to the tower, and on the right hand to the new building, which was so masked by the wood, as not to be visible except from within the glade. It was a square structure of plain stone, much in the same style as that of the tower. The young gentleman took the left-hand passage, and introduced the doctor to the lower floor of the tower.

'I have divided the tower,' he observed, 'into three rooms: one on each floor. This is the dining-room; above it is my bedroom; above it again is my library. The prospect is good from all the floors, but from the library it is most extensive, as you look over the woods far away into the open sea.'

'A noble dining-room,' said the Doctor. 'The height is well proportioned to the diameter. That circular table well becomes the form of the room, and gives promise of a fine prospect in its way'...'This building,' thought he, 'might belong to the age of chivalry.' But the library brought him back to other days. The walls were covered with books, the upper portion accessible by a gallery, running entirely round the apartment. The books of the lower circle were all classical; those of the upper, English, Italian, and French, with a few volumes in Spanish...

A French clock in the library struck two... 'At this time of the year,' said the young gentleman, 'I lunch at two...I hope you will partake with me.'

'I accept with pleasure.'

'Now you must know,' said the young gentleman, 'I have none but female domestics. You will see my two waiting maids.' He rang the bell, and the specified attendants appeared: two young girls about sixteen and seventeen; both pretty, and simply, but very becomingly, dressed...Of the provision set before him the Doctor preferred some cold chicken and tongue...The dog, who had behaved throughout with exemplary propriety, was not forgotten. The Doctor rose to depart...

'My name is Theophilus Opimium. I am a Doctor of Divinity and the incumbent of Ashbrook-cum-Ferndale'.

'I am simply,' said the other, 'Algernon Falconer. I have inherited some money but no land. Therefore having the opportunity, I made this purchase, to fit it up in my own fashion, and live in it in my own way.'

The Doctor preparing to depart, Mr Falconer proposed to accompany him part of the way, and calling out another Newfoundland dog, who immediately struck up a friendship with his companion, he walked away with the Doctor, the two dogs gambolling before them.

...

The Reverend Doctor Opimium. '...but here is a charming piece of forest scenery. Look at that old oak with the deer under it; the long and deep range of fern running up from it to that beech-grove on the upland, the lights and shadows on the projections and recesses of the wood, and the blaze of foxglove in its foreground. It is a place in which a poet might look for a glimpse of a Hamadryad.'

Mr Falconer. 'Very beautiful for the actual present – too beautiful for the probable future. Some day or other the forest will be disforested; the deer will be either banished or destroyed; the wood will be either shut up or cut down. Here is another basis for disappointment. The more we admire it now, the more we shall regret it then. The admiration of sylvan or pastoral scenery is at the mercy of an inclosure act, and instead of the glimpse of a Hamadryad you will sometimes see a large board warning you off the premises under penalty of rigour of law.'

...There was within moderate distance a deep dell, in the bottom of which ran a rivulet, very small in dry weather, but in heavy rains becoming a torrent, which had worn itself a high-banked channel, winding in fantastic curves from side to side of its narrow boundaries. Above this channel the old forest tree rose to a great height on both sides of the dell. The slope every here and there was broken by promontories which during centuries the fall of the softer portions of the soil had formed; and on these promontories were natural platforms, covered, as they were more or less accessible to the sun, with grass and fern and moss and foxglove, and every variety of forest vegetation. These platforms were favourite resorts of deer, which imparted to the wild scene its own peculiar life.

This was a scene in which, but for the deeper and deeper wear of the floods and the bolder Falls of the promontories, time had made little change. The eyes of the twelfth century had seen it much as it appeared to those of the nineteenth. The ghosts of departed ages might seem to pass through it in succession, with all their changes of faith and purpose and manners and costume. To a man who loved to dwell in the past, there could not be a more congenial scene. One old oak stood in the centre of one of the green platforms, and a portion of its gnarled roots provided a convenient seat. Mr Falconer had frequently passed a day here when alone. The deer had become too accustomed to him to fly at his approach, and the dog had been too well disciplined to molest them. There he had sat for hours at a time, reading his favourite poets. There was no great poet with some of whose scenes this scenery did not harmonise.

...

The winter set in early. December began with intense frost... Algernon Falconer did not allow his impatience to require that the horses should be put to extraordinary speed. He found something tranquillising in the movement of a postillion in a smart jacket, vibrating on one horse upwards and downwards, with one invariable regulated motion like the cross-head of a side-lever steam-engine, and holding the whip quietly arched over the neck of the other. The mechanical monotony of the movement seemed less in contrast than in harmony with the profound stillness of the wintry forest: the leafless branches heavy with rime frost and glittering in the sun: the deep repose of nature, broken now and then with the traversing of deer, or the flight of wild birds: the highest and loudest among them the long line of rooks: but for the greater part of the way one long deep silence, undisturbed but by the rolling of the wheels and the iron tinkling of the hoofs on the frozen ground. By degrees he fell in to a reverie...

Thomas Love Peacock (1785–1866)
Gryll Grange (1860)

R D Blackmore is one of those popular Victorian novelists who is now known only for a single work, *Lorna Doone*. Like his contemporary Thomas Hardy, he was a west-country man with a strong sense of place in his writing. Nowelhurst, the house in this novel, is based on an Elizabethan house in Burley in the New Forest.

Within the New Forest, and not far from its western boundary, as defined by the second perambulation of the good King Edward I, stands the old mansion of the Nowells, the Hall of Nowelhurst. Not content with mere exemption from all feudal service, their estate claims privileges, both by grant and custom. The benefit of Morefall trees in six walks of the forest, the right of digging marl, and turbary illimitable, common of pannage, and license of drawing akermast, pastime even of hawking over some parts of the Crown land,—all these will be catalogued as claims quite indefensible, if the old estates come to the hammer, through the events that form my story. With many of these privileges the Royal Commissioners will deal in a spirit of scant courtesy, when the Nowell influence is lost in the neighbouring boroughs; but as yet these claims have not been treated like those of some poor commoners.

'Pooh, pooh, my man, don't be preposterous: you know, as well as I do, these gipsy freedoms were only allowed to balance the harm the deer did.'

And if the rights of that ancient family are ever called in question, some there are which will require a special Act to abolish them. For Charles II, of merry memory (saddened somewhat of late years), espied among the maids of honour an uncommonly pretty girl, whose name was Frances Nowell. He suddenly remembered, what had hitherto quite escaped him, how old Sir Cradock Nowell—beautiful Fanny's father—had saved him from a pike–thrust during Cromwell's 'crowning mercy'. In gratitude, of course, for this, he began to pay most warm attentions to the Hampshire maiden. He propitiated that ancient knight with the only boon he craved—craved hitherto all in vain—a plenary grant of easements in the neighbourhood of his home. Soon as the charter had received the royal seal and signature, the old gentleman briskly thrust it away in the folds of his velvet mantle. Then taking the same view of gratitude which his liege and master took, home he went without delay to secure his privileges. When the king heard of his departure, without any kissing of hands, he was in no wise disconcerted; it was the very thing he had intended. But when he heard that lovely Fanny was gone in the same old rickety coach, even ere he began to whisper, and with no leave of the queen, His Majesty swore his utmost for nearly half an hour. Then having spent his fury, he laughed at the 'sell', as he would have called it if the slang had been invented, and turned his royal attention to another of his wife's young maidens.

Nowelhurst Hall looks too respectable for any loose doings of any sort. It stands well away from the weeping of trees, like virtue shy of sentiment, and therefore has all the wealth of foliage shed, just where it pleases, around it. From a rising ground the house has sweet view of all the forest changes, and has seen three hundred springs wake in glory, and three hundred autumns waning. Spreading away from it wider, wider, slopes 'the Chase', as they call it, with great trees stretching paternal arms in the vain attempt to hold it. For two months of the twelve, when the heather is in blossom, all that chase is a glowing reach of amaranth and purple. Then it fades away to pale orange, dim olive, and a rusty brown when Christmas shudders over it; and so throughout young green and russet, till the July tint comes back again. Oftentimes in the fresh spring morning the blackcocks—'heathpoults' as they call them—lift their necks in the livening heather, swell their ruffing breasts, and crow for their rivals to come and spar with them. Below the chase the whiskers of the curling wood converge into a giant beard, tufted here and there with hues of a varying richness; but for the main of it, swelling and waving, crisping, fronding, feathering, coying, and darkening here and there, until it reach the silver mirror of the spreading sea. And the seaman, looking upwards from the war–ship bound for India, looking back at his native land, for the last of all times it may be, over brushwood waves, and billows of trees, and the long heave of the gorseland: 'Now, that's the sort of place', he says, as the distant gables glisten; 'the right sort of berth for our jolly old admiral, and me for his butler, please God, when we've licked them Crappos as ought to be'.

South–west of the house, half a mile away, and scattered along the warren, the simple village of Nowelhurst digests its own ideas. In and out the houses stand, endwise, crossways, skewified, anyhow except upside down, and some even tending that way. It looks like a game of dominoes, when the leaves of the table have opened and gape betwixt the players. Nevertheless, it is all good English; for none are bitterly poor there; in any case of illness, they have the great house to help them, not proudly, but with feeling; and, more than this, they have a parson who leads instead of driving them. There are two little shops exceedingly anxious to under–sell each other, and one mild alehouse conducted strictly upon philosophic principles. Philosophy under pressure, a caviller would call it, for the publican knows, and so do his customers, that if poachers were encouraged there, or any uproarious doings permitted (except in the week of the old and new year), down would come his licence–board, like a flag hauled in at sunset.

Pleasant folk, who there do dwell, calling their existence 'life', and on the whole enjoying it more than many of us do; forasmuch as they know their neighbours far better than themselves, and perceive each cousin's need of trial, and console him when he gets it. Not but what we ourselves partake the first and second advantages, only we miss the fruition of them, by turning our backs on the sufferer.

Nowelhurst village is not on the main road, but keeps a straggling companionship with a quiet parish highway which requires much encouragement. This little highway does its best to blink the many difficulties, or, if that may not be, to compromise them, and establish a pleasant footing upon its devious wandering course from the Lymington road to Ringwood. Here it goes zig to escape the frown of a heavy-browed crest of furzery, and then it comes zag when no soul expects it, because a little stream has babbled at it. It even seems to bob and dip, or jump, as the case may be, for fear of prying into an old oak's storey or dusting a piece of grassland. The hard-hearted traveller who lives express, and is bound for the train at Ringwood, curses, too often, uphill and down dale, the quiet lane's inconsistency. What right has any road to do anything but go straight on end to its purpose? What decent road stops for a gossip with flowers—flowers overhanging the steep ascent, or eavesdropping on the rabbit-holes? And as for the beauty of ferns—confound them, they shelter the horse-fly—that horrible forest-fly, whose tickling no civilised horse can endure. Even locusts he has heard of as abounding in the New Forest; and if a swarm of them comes this very hot weather, good-bye to him, horse and trap, newest patterns, sweet plaid, and chaste things.

And good-bye to thee, thou bustling 'traveller'—whether technically so called or otherwise,—a very good fellow in thy way, but not of nature's pattern. So counter-sunk, so turned in a lathe, so pressed and rolled by steam-power, and then condensed hydraulically, that the extract of flowers upon thy shirt is but as the oil of machinery. But we who carry no chronometer, neither puff locomotively—now he is round the corner—let us saunter down this lane beyond the mark-oak and the blacksmith's, even to the sandy rise whence the Hall is seen. The rabbits are peeping forth again, for the dew is spreading quietude: the sun has just finished a good day's work and is off for the western waters. Over the rounded heads and bosses, and then the darker dimples of the many-coloured foliage—many-coloured even now with summer's glory fusing it — over heads and shoulders, and breasts of heaving green, floods the lucid amber, trembling at its own beauty— the first acknowledged leniency of the July sun. Now every moment has its difference. Having once acknowledged that he may have been too downright in his ride of triumph, the sun, like every generous nature, scatters broadcast his amends. Over holt, and knoll, and lea, and narrow dingle, scooped with shadow where the brook is wimpling, and through the breaks of grass and gravel, where the heather purples, scarcely yet in prime flush, and down the tall wood overhanging, mossed and lichened, green and grey, as the grove of Druids—over, through, and under all flows pervading sunset. Then the birds begin discoursing of the thoughts within them—thoughts that are all happiness, and thrill and swell in utterance. Through the voice of the thicket–birds—the mavis, the whinchats, and the warblers—comes the tap of the yaffingale, the sharp, short cry of the honey–buzzard above the squirrel's cage, and the plaining of the turtle–dove.

But from birds and flowers, winding roads and woods, and waters where the trout are leaping, come we back to the only thing that interests a man much—the life, the doings, and the death of his fellow–men.

R. D. Blackmore (1825–1908)
Cradock Nowell – A Tale of the New Forest (1866)

Robert Louis Stevenson wrote this tale with Lloyd Osbourne, an American author who was also Stevenson's stepson. It was a childhood map drawn by Lloyd Osbourne that had led to the invention of *Treasure Island*, and the happy pleasure given so many by that rollicking story.

The train travelled forth into the world... it passed Christchurch by the sea, Herne with its pinewoods, Ringwood on its mazy river. A little behind time, but not much for the South-Western, it drew up at the platform of a station, in the midst of the New Forest, the real name of which (in case the railway company 'might have the law of me') I shall veil under the alias of Browndean.

Many passengers put their heads to the window and among the rest an old gentleman... pulled his bare, grey head back into the carriage, and the train smoked under the bridge, and forth, with ever quickening speed, across the mingled heaths and woods of the New Forest.

Not many hundred yards beyond Browndean, however, a sudden jarring of brakes set everybody's teeth on edge, and there was a brutal stoppage. Morris Finsbury was aware of a confused uproar of voices, and sprang to the window. Women were screaming, men were tumbling from the windows on the track, the guard was crying to them to stay where they were; at the same time the train began to gather way and move very slowly backward toward Browndean; and the next moment, all these various sounds were blotted out in the apocalyptic whistle and the thundering onslaught of the down express.

The actual collision Morris did not hear. Perhaps he fainted. He had a wild dream of having seen the carriage double up and fall to pieces like a pantomime trick; and sure enough, when he came to himself, he was lying on the bare earth and under the open sky. His head ached savagely; he carried his hand to his brow, and was not surprised to see it red with blood. The air was filled with an intolerable, throbbing roar, which he expected to find die away with the return of consciousness; and instead of that it seemed but to swell the louder and to pierce the more cruelly through his ears. It was a raging, bellowing thunder, like a boiler-riveting factory.

And now curiosity began to stir, and he sat up and looked about him. The track at this point ran in a sharp curve about a wooded hillock; all of the near side was heaped with the wreckage of the Bournemouth train; that of the express was mostly hidden by the trees; and just at the turn, under clouds of vomiting steam and piled about with cairns of living coal, lay what remained of the two engines, one upon the other. On the heathy margin of the line were many people running to and fro, and crying aloud as they ran, and many others lying motionless like sleeping tramps.

Morris suddenly drew an inference. 'There has been an accident' thought he, and was elated at his perspicacity.

R. L. Stevenson (1850–94) and Lloyd Osbourne (1868–1947)
The Wrong Box (1889)

Heywood Sumner was a painter, designer of stained glass windows and illustrator, in the company of the Arts and Crafts fellowship. In his mid-forties he moved to Cuckoo Hill, near Fordingbridge in Hampshire, and spent the rest of his life exploring and recording the natural history, archaeology and folklore of his surroundings.

The Forest suggests trees; green tracks through interminable trees; no clear sky; but above, waving branches, below, tree trunks and tangle; shadowy gloom as the trees descend the valleys, and a broken vision of multitudinous tree-tops on wooded hills. Up and down, trees, trees, innumerable trees. But this does not describe our side of the Forest. Here, on the Northern side – and the Ringwood and Romsey road may be taken as the boundary between the North and South sides of the Forest – here, we have long rolling hills of heather, fern, and furze, worn into five parallel ridges and furrows by the streams that trickle in dry, and rush in wet weather down gravelly courses to the broad valley of the Avon. Here and there are thickets of holly, thorn, yew and crab-apple. Here and there are old woods of oak, beech, yew, holly, thorn and whitebeam. Here and there are enclosures of Scots fir, oak and sweet chestnut. But the main features of our side of the New Forest are, heather uplands, winding moorland streams, and scattered woods. The open country is never far distant. Afoot or a-wheel you may learn the same thing. The tracks from Highwood, and Ogdens and Frogham to Fritham, and the roads from Ringwood and Fordingbridge and Downton to Cadenham, all give far views over wild foregrounds to distant cultivation. They reveal the vision of a primeval waste, set in the midst of an older and more fertile formation; of heathlands surrounded by the chalk hills of Dorset, Wilts, Hants, and the Isle of Wight; and they tell that the Bagshot Beds, on which you stand, are deposited over a great trough of chalk that dips from Badbury and Pentridge to the island, and from Purbeck to the Hampshire South Downs.

...

The old method of mud-walling – puddle clay and rushes – is excellent, when it is well done, but the chances are against good work. For this reason. The wall is raised – like concrete in boarded 'rearings'; 1 ft 6 in: at a 'rearing'. Four men meet, puddle, and raise a 'rearing', then they leave the job for a fortnight while it dries. They meet again; and if there has been drying weather meantime, the next 'rearing' goes up on a firm lower course: not so however if there has been broken weather, yet in such an event the temptation is great for men who have met by arrangement to put in a day's work – probably they go on with the next 'rearing', and the result is a weak wall that 'bags' with the weight which it is not ready to bear. And this is the cause of most of the failures in mud-walling. There is very little mud-walling done now here-abouts, and the craft is dying out.

...

For the first 3 years of our life at Cuckoo Hill we were undisturbed by heath fires on Ibsley Common. Occasionally, furze bushes were set alight on Gorley Hill, but they only made a grand blaze, and, after creating mild excitement, died down leaving but a small blackened patch in the morning as record of what seemed to be a great fire on the preceding night. Fires also we had seen every Spring far up in the Forest, or across the valley on the Plumley, Verwood, and StIves heath-lands; some authorised burnings, such as the great Furze Fire on Latchmoor on Easter Monday 1905, some unauthorised – by accident, on purpose - ; but never had the fires come near us, nor did we know the dangerous speed of a heath fire running before the wind, till the spring of 1906 when Ibsley common was burnt across from end to end – from the top of Brogenslade to Newlands – and this is how it came about. Furze-hill was the starting point. Furze-hill is rightly named, and of late years the commoners were complaining that the furze had made too much growth. It was encroaching on the feed.

Accordingly, we arranged a convenient day, and on Saturday, March 31 we all assembled at 9 o'clock in the morning, and with solemn publicity began to set fire to the furze patches along the Huckles brook. They behaved just like the furze fires on Gorley Hill, the flames blazed up furiously, and then abruptly died down without any attempt at spreading. And so each man went about with burning furze brands setting light to the straggling patches. Furze Hill soon was smoking with in-numerable fires. (Women with their babies stood watching on the lew side; the children were scared by the crackle and roar of the flames, & really behaved with remarkable caution; while

Lizzie Thomas made strange inarticulate sounds whenever the fires seemed dangerously near to their Fern rick.) From Furze-Hill we burnt our fiery way up Brogenslade, and all went well till we got to the deep rutted drokes at top; here the furze brakes are thickly fringed with heather & long sage grass; and here we found to our cost that we had lit more fires than we could control. A brisk North Wester too sprang up & the fire began running, across the droke, up the hill, and away over the plain: followed by a fringe of beaters: about ten of us; and by dint of persistent beating with fir boughs we succeeded in keeping the running fire within some bounds, but failed to stop is till it reached Ladywell; and here, at the deep droke, leading to North Hollow bridge, we finally beat out the fire. By 3 o'clock we could safely leave the charred ground...we could slake our thirsty, smoke dried throats, & and feel well pleased at the success of the first authorised burning of the Common within the memory of man.

Our pleasure was short-lived. At night unauthorised fires sprang up, first in several places on Gorley & then beyond Mockbeggar. The latter was a very big blaze...and this fire blazed furiously from 9 o'clock to the small hours of Sunday morning. The wind was high and was blowing more westerly than in the morning. The result of this fire was that all the hills between Mockbeggar and Newlands and a large piece of the Whitefield plain were burnt to a cinder ground. The turf cutters grumbled at the loss of a specially good turf-ground, while the keepers – wholly disclaiming the fire – approved the result, as it would save them the trouble in looking for outlying pheasants' nests.

Then followed a week of warnings and nightly watchings... Throughout the week we continued on the watch...A strange incident of these fires on Ibsley Common was the running accompaniment of explosions that here and there followed the flames. They were caused by soldiers' cartridges which had been dropped during the manoeuvres of 1898...and tested after years of exposure in the moss and heather.

Two young men from 'up along', Witt and Goudge by name, were caught lighting furze on Gorley Hill, and they got 2 months apiece for thus misusing a matchbox, but the fires on Ibsley Common kept their own secret.

The Common quickly recovered from its blackened state. In three weeks' time green blades were pushing up through the ashes and the ponies and the sheep were nibbling the tender tops of the young sage grass.

Heywood Sumner (1853–1940)
Cuckoo Hill: The book of Gorley (1910)

During World War II the novelist Nevil Shute wore his other hat, as an engineer, developing secret weapons, in a mysterious entity rather similar to Force J.

Throughout the autumn and the winter activity increased in the Beaulieu area, and with it came mysteries. Lepe House, the mansion at the entrance to the river, was taken over by the Navy and became full of very secretive naval officers; it became known that this was part of a mysterious naval entity called Force J. Near Lepe House and at the very mouth of the river a construction gang began work in full strength to make a hard, sloping concrete platform running down into the water where the flat-bottomed landing craft could beach to refuel and let their ramps down to embark the vehicles or tanks... A mile or so along the coast a country house was occupied by a secret naval party who did strange things with tugs and wires and winches, and with what looked like a gigantic reel of cotton floating in the sea; this was 'Pluto', Pipe Line Under The Ocean, which was to lay pipes from England to France to carry petrol to supply the armies which were due to land in Normandy. On a bare beach nearby a thousand navvies were camped making huge concrete structures known as 'Phoenix', one of many such sites all along the coast. It was not till after the invasion that it became known that these were a part of the artificial harbour 'Mulberry' on the north coast of France.

Inland it was the same. Every wood was littered with dumps of shells and ammunition in little corrugated-iron shelters, thousands and thousands of them spaced at regular intervals. There were radar stations upon Beaulieu Common and Bofurs guns at Bucklers Hard; there was radio everywhere, the slim antennae pointing up from hedges, from haystacks, and from trucks. Over the whole countryside as winter merged into spring there was continuously the roar of aircraft, symbol of modern military power.

They turned back to Beaulieu as the sun was going down, and now they saw the whole fleet getting under way. The whole stretch of water between the Isle of Wight and the mainland was crowded with landing craft and ships of every sort, and all in turn were getting short their anchors, weighing, and moving off. In the deep channels were the Infantry Landing Ships, cross-Channel steamers and small liners with landing craft hanging on their davits; in the shallows were the LCTs loaded with vehicles and tanks and men, moving off towards the eastern entrance at Spithead in great flotillas, shepherded by their MLs. Coming down Southampton Water was a great fleet of Tank Landing Ships, big American vessels with a double door that opened in the bow. Overhead the fighters circled in the evening light, the inner patrol positioned to catch any German aircraft that penetrated the outer guard of fighters over the Channel. The evening was thunderous with the roar of engines on the sea and overhead.

Nevil Shute (1899–1960)
Requiem for a Wren (1955)

The novelist Edward Rutherfurd invents fictional families and tells the stories of members of those families through the centuries. Using this framework, he chronicles the history of a place, often from the beginning of civilisation to modern times. Dottie Pride is one such character, a Pride from *The Forest*, whose family, through time, has been involved with all the places and events laid out beneath her.

High over Sarum the small plane flew. Below, the graceful cathedral with its soaring spire rested on the sweeping green lawns like a huge model. Beyond the cathedral precincts, the medieval city of Salisbury lay peacefully in the sun. Earlier that morning there had been an April shower, but now the sky was clear, a pale washed blue. A perfect day, thought Dottie Pride, to fly a reconnaissance mission. Not for the first time, she was grateful for the fact she worked in television.

...

197

From Sarum, the beautiful Avon valley continued due south through lush green meadows for over twenty miles until it reached the sheltered waters of Christchurch harbour. On its western side lay the rolling ridges of Dorset; to the east, the huge county of Hampshire with its ancient capital of Winchester and great port of Southampton. Dottie glanced at the map. There were only two small market towns on the Avon between here and the sea. Fordingbridge, eight miles south, and Ringwood, another five beyond that. A few miles below Ringwood, she noted, there was a place called Tyrrell's Ford.

They had not even reached Fordingbridge before the plane banked and turned towards the south-east. They passed a low ridge, crested with oak trees. And there it was below them; huge, magnificent, mysterious. The New Forest.

...

They flew over plantation and brown heather for ten miles. The terrain was wilder and barer than she had expected; but as they came to Lyndhurst, at the forest centre, the landscape changed. Groves of oak, green glades, open lawns cropped by stocky little New Forest ponies; pretty thatched cottages with brick or white-washed walls. This was the New Forest she knew from picture postcards. They followed the line of the old road that led south through the middle of the Forest. The oak woods were thick below them. In a glade, she caught sight of some deer. They passed over a village in a huge clearing, its open green lawns dotted with ponies. Brockenhurst. A small river appeared now, flowing south through a lush valley with steep sides. Here and there she saw pleasant houses with paddocks and orchards. Prosperous. On a high knoll on the wooded valley's eastern side, she saw a squat little parish church, obviously ancient. Boldre church. She should visit that.

A minute later they were over the harbour town on Lymington and its crowded marina. To the right, on the edge of some marshes, a sign on a large boathouse proclaimed: SEAGULL'S BOATYARD.

The English Channel lay a few miles away to the west. Beneath them was a pleasant stretch of Solent water with the green slopes of the Isle of Wight beyond. As they flew eastwards now she looked from the map to the coastline.

...

'Do you want to fly over Beaulieu?'

'Of course.' This would be the setting for the opening sequence. Far below them the lovely old abbey precincts lay tranquil in the sun. Behind, screened by trees, was the famous Motor Museum. They circled it once, then headed north again towards Lyndhurst.

They had just passed Lyndhurst and were flying north-west towards Sarum when Dottie asked the pilot to circle again. Peering down, it took her a few moments to locate her target; but there could be no mistaking it.

A single stone, set near the edge of a woodland glade. A couple of cars were parked in the little gravel car park nearby and she could see their occupants standing by the small monument.

'The Rufus Stone,' she said.

'Ah. I've heard of that,' said the pilot.

Few of the hundreds of thousands who went to wander or camp in the New Forest each year failed to pay the curious site a visit. The stone marked the spot where, according to the nine-hundred-year-old tale, King William Rufus, the Norman King – called Rufus on account of his red hair – had been killed by an arrow in mysterious circumstances while hunting deer. After Stonehenge, it was probably the most famous standing stone in southern England.

'Wasn't there a tree there once?' asked the pilot. 'The arrow glanced off it and hit the king?'

'That's the story.' Dottie saw another car make its way into the gravel car park. 'Only it seems,' she said, 'that he wasn't shot there at all.'

Edward Rutherfurd (1948–)
The Forest (2000)

Chapter 5
Hinterland

'Of all situations for a constant residence, that which appears to me most delightful is a little village far in the country; a small neighbourhood, not of fine mansions finely peopled, but of cottages and cottage-like houses...

'Nothing is so delightful as to sit down in a country village with one of Miss Austen's delicious novels, quite sure before we leave it to become intimate of every spot and every person it contains; or to trample with Mr White over his own parish of Selborne, and form a friendship with the fields and coppices, as well as with the birds, mice and squirrels, which inhabit them.'

Mary Russell Mitford of Alresford (1787–1855)

Beyond the major historic cities, the coast and the emptiness of the New Forest, lies rolling agricultural land – some of it vast agro-industrial wheat fields, some intimate valleys preserving the traditional combination of meadow pastureland and small-scale farming around Hampshire's famous chalk streams. Dotted with villages and county towns like Alton and Alresford, Petersfield and Stockbridge, the central belt of the county contains the South Downs National Park, an area of chalk uplands grazed by sheep and appreciated by hikers. Towards the north of the county, beyond the ever-growing city of Basingstoke, the land becomes sandier, the close-cropped grass of the downs replaced by firs and birch, gorse and ferns.

As well as the diaries and letters of two of England's most famous villagers – Gilbert White and Jane Austen, who lived within three miles of each other in Selborne and Chawton – we also have fictional takes on the Hampshire countryside from Sherlock Holmes and P G Wodehouse, Thomas Hardy on Weyhill Fair, Richard Adams on Watership Down, Gilbert White on the part he played in the ruination of Netley Abbey, John Arlott on the Basingstoke of his childhood and the irrepressible appetite of James Lees-Milne, crisscrossing the county in his role as 'unqualified historic buildings secretary' for the National Trust, then in its infancy.

…

Despite her fame now, during her lifetime Jane Austen was little known, her novels mostly being published anonymously. It was not until the publication of this memoir, by her nephew, fifty-two years after her death, that her admiring readership learned much about her. It had an immediate and incalculable effect on the public's view of Jane Austen.

Here James Edward Austen-Leigh begins by describing the rectory of Steventon, where her father, George Austen, was vicar and where Jane was born and lived throughout her childhood.

The house itself stood in a shallow valley, surrounded by sloping meadows, well sprinkled with elm trees, at the end of a small village of cottages, each well provided with a garden, scattered about prettily on either side of the road. It was sufficiently commodious to hold pupils in addition to a growing family, and was in those times considered to be above the average of parsonages; but the rooms were finished with less elegance than would now be found in the most ordinary dwellings. No cornice marked the junction of wall and ceiling; while the beams which supported the upper floors projected into the rooms below in all their naked simplicity, covered only by a coat of paint or whitewash: accordingly it has since been considered unworthy of being the Rectory house of a family living, and about forty-five years ago it was pulled down for the purpose of erecting a new house in a far better situation on the opposite side of the valley.

North of the house, the road from Deane to Popham Lane ran at a sufficient distance from the front to allow a carriage drive, through turf and trees. On the south side the ground rose gently, and was occupied by one of those old-fashioned gardens in which vegetables and flowers are combined, flanked and protected on the east by one of the thatched mud walls common in that country, and overshadowed by fine elms. Along the upper or southern side of this garden, ran a terrace of the finest turf, which must have been in the writer's thoughts when she described Catharine Morland's childish delight in 'rolling down the green slope at the back of the house.'

But the chief beauty of Steventon consisted in its hedgerows. A hedgerow, in that country, does not mean a thin formal line of quickset, but an irregular border of copse-wood and timber, often wide enough to contain within it a winding footpath, or a rough cart track. Under its shelter the earliest primroses, anemones, and wild hyacinths were to be found; sometimes, the first bird's-nest; and, now and then, the unwelcome adder. Two such hedgerows radiated, as it were, from the parsonage garden. One, a continuation of the turf terrace, proceeded westward, forming the southern boundary of the home meadows; and was formed into a rustic shrubbery, with occasional seats, entitled 'The Wood Walk.' The other ran straight up the hill, under the name of 'The Church Walk,' because it led to the parish church, as well as to a fine old manor-house, of Henry VIII's time, occupied by a family named Digweed, who have for more than a century rented it, together with the chief farm in the parish. The church itself—I speak of it as it then was, before the improvements made by the present rector—a little spireless fane, just seen above the woody lane, might have appeared mean and uninteresting to an ordinary observer; but the adept in church architecture would have known that it must have stood there some seven centuries, and would have found beauty in the very narrow early English windows, as well as in the general proportions of its little chancel; while its solitary position, far from the hum of the village, and within sight of no habitation, except a glimpse of the gray manor-house through its circling screen of sycamores, has in it something solemn and appropriate to the last resting-place of the silent dead. Sweet violets, both purple and white, grow in abundance beneath its south wall. One may imagine for how many centuries the ancestors of those little flowers have occupied that undisturbed, sunny nook, and may think how few living families can boast of as ancient a tenure of their land. Large elms protrude their rough branches; old hawthorns shed their annual blossoms over the graves; and the hollow yew-tree must be at least coeval with the church.

But whatever may be the beauties or defects of the surrounding scenery, this was the residence of Jane Austen for twenty-five years. This was the cradle of her genius. These were the first objects which inspired her young heart with a sense of the beauties of nature. In strolls along those wood-walks, thick-coming fancies rose in her mind, and gradually assumed the forms in which they came forth to the world. In that simple church she brought them all into subjection to the piety which ruled her in life, and supported her in death.

J E Austen Leigh (1798–1884)
A Memoir of Jane Austen (1869)

In this selection of correspondence to her beloved sister Cassandra, Jane Austen talks candidly and wittily about her life in Steventon. The letters are often sent to Godmersham in Kent, where Cassandra was staying with their brother Edward. Neither of the girls married, although four of their five brothers did. Jane Austen's life among the gentry of this corner of Hampshire saw her socialising with the Biggs at Manydown, the family of the MP William Chute, who lived at The Vyne, one of the great houses of Hampshire, and the banknote-manufacturer John Portal who had built a mansion at Laverstock. Jane went to balls at Kempshott Park, Hackwood Park and Hurstbourne Park, and spent many evenings dancing at the Assembly Rooms in Basingstoke.

Brother James lives in Deane, a village neighbouring Steventon, with his wife Mary, who is expecting a baby as these extracts begin.

Saturday 27–Sunday 28 October 1798
…I cannot send you quite so triumphant an account of our last day's Journey as of the first and second. Soon after I had finished my letter from Staines, my Mother began to suffer from the exercise and fatigue of travelling so far, she was a good deal indisposed from that particular kind of evacuation which has generally preceded her Illnesses. She had not a very good night at Staines, and felt a heat in her throat as we travelled yesterday morning, which seemed to foretell more Bile. She bore her Journey however much better than I had expected, at Basingstoke where we stopped more than half an hour, received much comfort from a Mess of Broth, and the sight of Mr Lyford, who recommended her to take 12 drops of Laudanum when she went to Bed, as a Composer, which she accordingly did. It is by no means wonderful that her Journey should have produced

some Kind of visitation; I hope a few days will entirely remove it. James called on us just as we were going to Tea, and my Mother was well enough to talk very cheerfully to him, before she went to Bed. Lyford has promised to call, in the course of a few days, and then they will settle about the Dandelion Tea; the receipts for which were shewn him at Basingstoke, he approved of them highly; they will only require some slight alteration to be better adapted to my Mother's Constitution. James seems to have taken to his old Trick of coming to Steventon inspite of Mary's reproaches, for he was here before breakfast, is now paying us a second visit. Mary is quite well he says, and uncommonly large; they were to have dined here to day, but the weather is too bad. I have had the pleasure of hearing that Martha is with them; James fetched her from Ibthorpe on Thursday, she will stay with them till she removes to Kintbury. We met with no adventures at all on our Journey yesterday, except that our Trunk had once nearly slipt off, we were obliged to stop at Hartley to have our wheels greazed.

...There has been a great deal of rain here for this last fortnight, much more than in Kent; indeed we found the roads all the way from Staines most disgracefully dirty. Steventon lane has its full share of it, I do not know when I shall be able to get to Deane.

Saturday 17–Sunday 18 November 1798
...My mother desires me to tell you that I am a very good housekeeper, which I have no reluctance in doing, because I really think it my peculiar excellence, and for this reason – I always take care to provide such things as please my own appetite, which I consider as the chief merit in housekeeping. I have had some ragout veal, and I mean to have some haricot mutton tomorrow. We are to kill a pig soon. There is to be a ball at Basingstoke next Thursday. Our assemblies have very kindly declined ever since we laid down the carriage, so that dis-convenience and dis-inclination to go have kept pace together.

...I went to Deane with my father two days ago to see Mary, who is still plagued with the rheumatism, which she would be very glad to get rid of, and still more glad to get rid of her child, of whom she is heartily tired. Her nurse is come, and has no particular charm either of person or manner; but as all the Hurstbourne world pronounce her to be the best nurse that ever was, Mary expects her attachment to increase. What fine weather this is! Not very becoming perhaps early in the morning, but very pleasant out of doors at noon, and very wholesome – at least everybody fancies so, and imagination is everything. To Edward, however, I really think dry weather of importance. I have not taken to fires yet. I believe I never told you that Mrs Coulthard and Anne, late of Manydown, are both dead, and both died in childbed. We have not regaled Mary with this news. Harry St John is in Orders, has done duty at Ashe, and performs very well. I am very fond of experimental housekeeping, such as having an ox-cheek now and then; I shall have one next week, and I mean to have some little dumplings put into it, that I may fancy myself at Godmersham.

Saturday 1–Sunday 2 December 1798
I was at Deane yesterday morning. Mary was very well, but does not gain bodily strength very fast. When I saw her so stout on the third and sixth days, I expected to have seen her as well as ever by the end of a fortnight... Letty is with Mary at present, of course exceedingly happy, and in raptures with the child. Mary does not manage matters in such a way as to make me want to lay in myself. She is not tidy enough in her appearance; she has no dressing-gown to sit up in; her curtains are all too thin, and things are not in that comfort and style about her which are necessary to make such a situation an enviable one, Elizabeth was really a pretty object with her nice clean cap put on so tidily and her dress so uniformly white and orderly. We live entirely in the dressing-room now, which I like very much; I always feel so much more elegant in it than in the parlour.

Tuesday 18–Wednesday 19 December 1798
I enjoyed the hard black Frosts of last week very much, and one day while they lasted I walked to Deane by myself. I do not know that I ever did such a thing in my life before.

Monday 24 December 1798
I was to have dined at Deane to day, but the weather is so cold that I am not sorry to be kept at home by the appearance of Snow.

Wednesday – The Snow came to nothing yesterday, so I did go to Deane, returned home at 9 o'clock at night in the little carriage – without being very cold.

Friday 28 December 1798
Mrs Lefroy has just sent me word that Lady Dorchester means to invite me to her Ball on the 8th of January, which tho' an humble Blessing compared with what the last page records, I do not consider as any Calamity.

Tuesday 8 January 1799
Charles [another brother] is not come yet, but he must come this morning, or he shall never know what I will do to him. The ball at Kempshott is this evening, and I have got him an invitation, though I have not been so considerate as to get him a partner... I am not to wear my white satin cap to-night, after all; I am to wear a mamalone [should read 'mamalouc'] cap instead, which Charles Fowle sent to Mary, and which she lends me. It is all the fashion now; worn at the opera, and by Lady Mildmays at Hackwood balls. I hate describing such things, and I dare say you will be able to guess what it is like ... My gown is made very much like my blue one, which you always told me sat very well, with only these variations: the sleeves are short, the wrap fuller, the apron comes over it, and a band of the same completes the whole.

Continuing the letter the next day, she writes:

... I wore my green shoes last night, and took my white fan with me... I spent a very pleasant evening, chiefly among the Manydown party. There was the same kind of supper as last year, and the same want of chairs. There were more dancers than the room could conveniently hold, which is enough to constitute a good ball at any time. I do not think I was very much in request. People were rather apt not to ask me till they could not help it; one's consequence, you know, varies so much at times without any particular reason. There was one gentleman, an officer of the Cheshire, a very good-looking young man, who, I was told, wanted very much to be introduced to me, but as he did not want it quite enough to take much trouble in effecting it, we never could bring it about.

I danced with Mr John Wood again, twice with a Mr South, a lad from Winchester, who, I suppose, is as far from being related to the bishop of that diocese as it is possible to be, with G. Lefroy, and J. Harwood, who, I think, takes to me rather more than he used to do. One of my gayest actions was sitting down two dances in preference to having Lord Bolton's eldest son for my partner, who danced too ill to be endured. The Miss Charterises were there, and played the parts of the Miss Edens with great spirit. Charles never came. Naughty Charles! I suppose he could not get superseded in time.

Saturday 24 October 1800
We have been exceedingly busy ever since you went away. In the first place we have had to rejoice two or three times every day at your having such very delightful weather for the whole of your Journey; in the second place we have been obliged to take advantage of the delightful weather ourselves by going to see almost all our Neighbours. On Thursday we walked to Deane, Yesterday to Oakley Hall and Oakley, and to day to Deane again. At Oakley Hall we did a great deal – ate some sandwiches all over mustard, admired Mr Bramston's Porter and Mrs Bramston's Transparencies, and gained a promise from the latter of two roots of hearts-ease, one all yellow and the other all purple, for you. At Oakley we bought ten pair of worsted stockings, and a shift. The shift is for Betty Dawkins, as we find she wants it more than a rug. She is one of the most grateful of all whom Edward's charity has reached, or at least she expresses herself more warmly than the rest, for she sends him a 'sight of thanks.' This morning we called at the Harwoods, and in their dining-room found Heathcote and Chute for ever – Mrs Wm Heathcote and Mrs Chute – the first of whom took a long ride yesterday morning with Mrs Harwood into Lord Carnarvon's Park and fainted away in the evening, and the second walked down from Oakley Hall attended by Mrs Augusta Bramston.

They had meant to come on to Steventon afterwards, but we knew a trick worth two of that. If I had thought of it in time, I would have said something civil to her about Edward's never having had any serious idea of calling on Mr Chute while he was in Hampshire; but unluckily it did not occur to me; Mrs Heathcote is gone home to day; Catherine had paid her an early visit at Deane in the morning, and brought a good account of Harris. James went to Winchester fair yesterday, bought a new horse...

Sunday 30 November–Monday 1 December 1800
...Part of the money and time I spent at Andover were devoted to the purchase of some figured cambric muslin for a frock for Edward – a circumstance from which I derive two pleasing reflections; it has in the first place opened to me a fresh source of self-congratulation on being able to make so munificent a present, secondly it has been the means of informing me that the very pretty manufacture in question may be bought for 4s.6d. pr yd – yard & half wide. Martha has promised to return with me, & our plan is to [have] a nice black frost for walking to Whitchurch, & there throw ourselves into a postchaise, one upon the other, our heads hanging out at one door, our feet at the opposite.
...By the bye, there will not be any Ball, because Delmar lost so much by the Assemblies last winter that he has protested against opening his rooms this year. I have charged my Myrmidons to send me an account of the Basingstoke Ball; I have placed my spies at different places that they may collect the more; & by so doing, by sending Miss Bigg to the Townhall itself, & posting my Mother at Steventon I hope to derive from their various observations a good general idea of the whole.

In 1800, Jane's father retired from the clergy and moved his family to Bath, where he died in 1804. The next five years were unsettled for his widow and two unmarried daughters, but between 1806 and 1809 they lived in Southampton, where their naval-officer brother, Frank, lived with his family.

Wednesday 7–Thursday 8 January 1807
...We did not take our walk on Friday, it was too dirty, nor have we yet done it; we may perhaps do something like it to-day, as after seeing Frank skate, which he hopes to do in the meadows by the beach, we are to treat ourselves with a passage over the ferry. It is one of the pleasantest frosts I ever knew, so very quiet. I hope it will last some time longer for Frank's sake, who

is quite anxious to get some skating; he tried yesterday, but it would not do. Our acquaintance increase too fast. He was recognised lately by Admiral Bertie, & a few days since arrived the Admiral & his daughter Catherine to wait upon us. There was nothing to like or dislike in either. To the Berties are to be added the Lances, with whose cards we have been endowed, & whose visit Frank & I returned yesterday. They live about a mile & three-quarters from S. to the right of the new road to Portsmouth, & I believe their house is one of those which are to be seen almost anywhere among the woods on the other side of the Itchen. It is a handsome building, stands high, & in a very beautiful situation. We found only Mrs Lance at home, & whether she boasts any offspring besides a grand pianoforte did not appear. She was civil and chatty enough, & offered to introduce us to some acquaintance in Southampton, which we gratefully declined. I suppose they must be acting by the orders of Mr Lance of Netherton in this civility, as there seems no other reason for their coming near us. They will not come often, I dare say. They live in a handsome style & are rich, & she seemed to like to be rich, & we gave her to understand that we were far from being so; she will soon feel therefore that we are not worth her acquaintance. You must have heard from Martha by this time. We have had no accounts of Kintbury since her letter to me. Mrs F. A. has had one fainting fit lately; it came on as usual after eating a hearty dinner, but did not last long. I can recollect nothing more to say. When my letter is gone I suppose I shall.

In 1809, it was the turn of their brother, Edward, to offer a solution, as related here, in her 1938 biography of the novelist, by Elizabeth Jenkins:

An independent establishment for them with their mother and Martha Lloyd was desirable, and Edward wanted it to be near him. He offered his mother a choice of two small houses, one near the grounds of Godmersham, the other at Chawton, opposite the Great House. There were many reasons for their preferring the latter. Jane called their branch of the family 'the Hampshire-born Austens,' and it was an attractive proposal that they should be once more settled near to Steventon and Deane.

She longed to go to Chawton, as soon as it was decided that they should. Cassandra was at Godmersham in December 1808, and Jane's letters were frequently interspersed with talk of what they should do in their new home. They would certainly have a piano, as good a one as could be got for thirty guineas, and Jane promised herself to practise country dances, to be able to provide amusements for the nephews and nieces.

Elizabeth Jenkins
Jane Austen: a biography (1938)

But the matter is not yet settled in October 1808, as the following extracts from the sisters' correspondence makes clear:

Saturday 1–Sunday 2 October 1808
...Mr Choles is gone to drive a Cow to Brentford, & his place is supplied to us by a Man who lives in the same sort of way by odd jobs, and among other capabilities has that of working in a garden, which my Mother will not forget, if we ever have another garden here. In general however she thinks much more of Alton, and really expects to move there. Mrs Lyell's 130 Guineas rent have made a great impression. To the purchase of furniture, whether here or there, she is quite reconciled, & talks of the Trouble as the only evil. I depended upon Henry's liking the Alton plan, & expect to hear of something perfectly unexceptionable there, through him.

Sunday 20 November 1808
...There are six Bedchambers at Chawton; Henry wrote to my Mother the other day, & luckily mentioned the number – which is just what we wanted to be assured of. He speaks also of Garrets for Storeplaces, one of which she immediately planned fitting up for Edward's Manservant – & now perhaps it must be for our own – for she is already quite reconciled to our keeping one. The difficulty of doing without one, had been thought of before. His name shall be Robert, if you please...

Friday 9 December 1808
...A larger circle of acquaintance & an increase of amusement is quite in character with our approaching removal. Yes – I

211

mean to go to as many Balls as possible, that I may have a good bargain. Every body is very much concerned at our going away, & every body is acquainted with Chawton & speaks of it as a remarkably pretty village, and every body knows the House we describe – but nobody fixes on the right. I am very much obliged to Mrs Knight for such a proof of the interest she takes in me – & she may depend upon it, that I will marry Mr Papillon, whatever may be his reluctance or my own. I owe her much more than such a trifling sacrifice. Our Ball was rather more amusing than I expected, Martha liked it very much, & I did not gape till the last quarter of an hour. It was past nine before we were sent for, & not twelve when we returned. The room was tolerably full, & there were perhaps thirty couple of Dancers;

...We want to be settled at Chawton in time for Henry to come to us for some Shooting, in October at least; but a little earlier, & Edward may visit us after taking his boys back to Winchester; suppose we name the 4 th of Sept – will not that do? I have but one thing more to tell you. Mrs Hill called on my Mother yesterday while we were gone to Chiswell & in the course of the visit asked her whether she knew anything of a Clergyman's family of the name of Alford who resided in our part of Hampshire. Mrs Hill had been applied to, as likely to give some information of them, on account of their probable vicinity to Dr Hill's Living – by a Lady, or for a Lady, who had known Mrs and the two Miss Alfords in Bath, whither they had removed it seems from Hampshire – & who now wishes to convey to the Miss Alfords some work, or trimming, which she has been doing for them – but the Mother & Daughters have left Bath, & the Lady cannot learn where they are gone to.- While my Mother gave us the account, the probability of its being ourselves, occurred to us, & it had previously struck herself...

Monday 11 – Tuesday 12 October 1813
...Poor Basingstoke Races! – there seem to have been two particularly wretched days on purpose for them;- & Weyhill week does not begin much happier.

It was while living at Chawton that Jane was finally published with success: *Sense and Sensibility* (1811), *Pride and Prejudice* (1813) *Mansfield Park* (1814) and *Emma* (1816). Some 160 years later, and the house in Chawton where this unassuming genius lived, is visited by James Lees-Milne:

Monday 29ᵗʰ October 1979
... Drove to Chawton and went over Jane Austen's house. Quite a few relics of hers, and some furniture which she owned, or so the visitor is led to believe. Some vagueness as to whether a writing desk belonged to Jane, or *might* have done.

James Lees-Milne (1908–97)
Romantic Chasm: Diaries 1979–81

At the other end of Jane Austen's century, the novelist Charlotte M Yonge wrote this rambling account of the village of Otterbourne, near Winchester, for her descendants to appreciate their history and sense of place. What she writes here could be an account of any one of the hundreds of Hampshire villages.

Not many of us remember Otterbourne before the Railroad, the Church, or the Penny Post. It may be pleasant to some of us to try to catch a few recollections before all those who can tell us anything about those times are quite gone.

To begin with the first that is known about it, or rather that is guessed. A part of a Roman road has been traced in Otterbourne Park, and near it was found a piece of a quern, one of the old stones of a hand mill, such as was used in ancient times for grinding corn; so that the place must have been inhabited at least seventeen hundred years ago. In the last century a medallion bearing the head of a Roman Emperor was found here, sixteen feet beneath the surface. It seems to be one of the medallions that were placed below the Eagle on the Roman Standards, and it is still in the possession of the family of Fitt, of Westley.

Dane Lane... is said to be the road by which the Danes made their way to Winchester, being then a woodland path. ...It is worth noting that the tenure of the lands descended by right to the youngest son in a family instead of the eldest.

213

Such 'cradle fiefs' exist in other parts of England, and in Switzerland, on the principle that the elder ones go out into the world while their father is vigorous, but the youngest is the stay of his old age.

...Merdon Castle seems to have been dismantled as quickly as it had been built.

...Good men had come to think that founding colleges was the very best thing they could do for the benefit of the Church, and William of Waynflete, who was made Bishop of Winchester in 1447, founded another college at Oxford in honour of St Mary Magdalen. To this College he gave large estates for its maintenance, and in especial a very large portion of our long, narrow parish of Otterbourne

...What happened here in the Great Rebellion we do not know. An iron ball was once dug up in the grounds at Otterbourne House, which may have come from Oliver's Battery; but it is also said to be only the knob of an old pump handle—

'When from the guarded down / Fierce Cromwell's rebel soldiery kept watch o'er Wykeham's town, / They spoiled the tombs of valiant men, warrior, and saint, and sage; / But at the tomb of Wykeham good angels quenched their rage.' Colonel Nathanael Fiennes prevented harm from being done to the College or the monuments in the Cathedral; but there was some talk of destroying that holy place, for I have seen a petition from the citizens of Winchester that it might be spared. It is said that some loyal person took out all the stained glass in the great west window, hid it in a chest, and buried it; but when better times came, it could not be restored to what it was before, and was put in confusedly, as we now see it.

...There is an odd, wild story, that Cromwell sunk all his treasure in the great well at Merdon Castle, in Hursley Park, 300 feet deep. It was further said, if it were drawn up again, that no one must speak till it was safe, otherwise it would be lost. A great chest was raised to the mouth of the well, when one of the men said, 'Here it comes!' The rope broke, it fell back, and no one ever saw it more.

...There must have been a great quickening of activity in Otterbourne soon after the Restoration, for it was then that the Itchen canal or barge river, as it used to be called, was dug, to convey coals from Southampton, and, of course, this much improved the irrigation of the water meadows. This canal was one of the first made in England, and was very valuable for nearly two hundred years, until the time of railways.

...The family of Smythe, Roman Catholics, long held Brambridge, and they endowed a little Roman Catholic Chapel at Highbridge. At one time, a number of their tenants and servants were of the same communion, and there is a note in the parish register by the curate to say that there were several families at Allbrook and Highbridge whose children he had not christened, though he believed they had been baptised by the Roman Catholic priest. One of the daughters of the Smythe family was the beautiful Mrs Fitz-Herbert, whom the Prince of Wales, afterwards George IV, was well known to have privately married. He never openly avowed this.

...All through the time of the long war with France there was here, as well as everywhere else around the coast, fear of a landing of the French. The flat-bottomed boats to bring the French over were actually ready at Boulogne, and the troops mustered to come across in them. On our side, volunteers were in training in case of need, and preparations were made for sending off the women and children inland on the first news of the enemy landing. Not very many years ago there were still to be seen in a barn at Hursley the planks prepared to fit as seats into the waggons that were to carry them away.

...With the activity that followed upon the peace came a great deal of road-making. The present high road between Winchester and Southampton was then made, and the way cut through the hills—Otterbourne Hill and Compton Hill on either side. This led to the main part of the inhabitants settling in the village street, instead of round the old Church as before. Another great road was made at the same time— that which crosses Golden Common and leads ultimately to Portsmouth. It used to be called Cobbett's Road, because William Cobbett, a clever, self-taught man, had much to do with laying it out. Cobbett had a good many theories which he tried to put into practice, some sensible, others mistaken.

These roads were for the coaches. Young folks, who never saw anything nearer approaching to a stage coach than the drags some gentlemen keep, can hardly fancy what these stage coaches were—tall vehicles, holding four inside passengers and at least twelve outside and quantities of luggage. ...There was also a guard, who in mail coaches took care of the post bags, and dropped them at the places where they were intended for. In the days when highwaymen infested the roads the guard had carried pistols ...It is odd to look back at an old article in a quarterly review describing coach travelling as something so swift and complete that it could not be surpassed in its perfection. Yet accidents with the spirited horses and rapid driving were not uncommon, and a fall from an overloaded coach was a dangerous thing.

There was a company in London that carried letters from one part of that town to another for twopence apiece, and this was the cheapest post in England. A letter from London to Otterbourne cost eightpence, and one from Winchester either threepence or fourpence, one from Devonshire elevenpence, and this was paid not by the sender, but by the receiver. It was reckoned impolite to prepay a letter.

There was no post office in Otterbourne till between 1836 and 1840; for, of course there were few letters written or received, and thus it did not seem to many persons worthwhile for village children to learn to write. If they did go into service at a distance from home, their letters would cost more than their friends could afford to pay. This was a sad thing, and broke up and cut up families... Travelling was so expensive that visits could seldom be made, and servants could not go to their homes unless they were within such a short distance as to be able to travel by coach or by carrier's cart, or even walking all the way, getting a cast now and then by a cart.

Charlotte M Yonge (1823-1901)
Old Times at Otterbourne (1891)

Gilbert White was born in his grandfather's vicarage at Selborne in Hampshire. He was educated at Oriel College, Oxford, ordained in 1749 and subsequently held several curacies in Hampshire including Selborne's neighbouring parishes of Newton Valence and Farringdon, as well as Selborne itself. In 1752-3 he returned to Oxford as Dean of Oriel.

After the death of his father in 1758, White moved back into the family home at The Wakes in Selborne, which he eventually inherited in 1763, remaining there until his death. In 1789 he published his *Natural History of Selborne*, which consists of letters to Thomas Pennant and to Daines Barrington. His letters tend to concentrate on the natural life of the village and the surrounding countryside, though he is interested in the part played by humans in this story as well. For more of his nature writing, you should turn to Chapter Seven – *Gilbert White and the Green Laboratory*.

Letter I : To Thomas Pennant
The parish of Selborne lies in the extreme eastern corner of the county of Hampshire, bordering on the county of Sussex, and not far from the county of Surrey; it is about fifty miles south-west of London, in latitude 51, and near midway between the towns of Alton, and Petersfield. Being very large and extensive, it abuts on twelve parishes, two of which are in Sussex, viz., Trotton and Rogate. If you begin from the south and proceed westward, the adjacent parishes are Emshot, Newton Valance, Faringdon, Hartley Mauduit, Great Wardleham, Kingsley, Hedleigh, Bramshot, Trotton, Rogate, Lysse, and Greatham. The soils of this district are almost as various and diversified as the views and aspects. The high part to the south-west consists of a vast hill of chalk, rising three hundred feet above the village; and is divided into a sheep down, the high wood, and a long hanging wood called the Hanger. The covert of this eminence is altogether beech, the most lovely of all forest trees, whether we consider its smooth rind or bark, its glossy foliage, or graceful pendulous boughs. The down or sheep-walk, is a pleasing park-like spot, of about one mile by half that space, jutting out on the verges of the hill-country, where it begins to break down into the plains, and commanding a very engaging view, being an assemblage of hill, dale, wood-lands, heath, and water. The prospect is bounded to the south-east and east by a vast range of mountains called the Sussex-downs, by Guild-down near Guildford, and by the Downs round Dorking, and Ryegate in Surrey, to the north-east, which altogether, with the country beyond Alton and Farnham, form a noble and extensive outline.

At the foot of this hill, one stage or step from the uplands, lies the village, which consists of one single street, three-quarters of a mile in length, in a sheltered vale, and running parallel with the Hanger. The houses are divided from the hill by a vein of stiff clay (good wheat-land), yet stand on a rock of white stone, little in appearance removed from chalk; but seems so far from being calcareous, that it endures extreme heat. Yet that the freestone still preserves somewhat that is analogous to chalk, is plain from the beeches, which descend as low as those rocks extend, and no farther, and thrive as well on them, where the ground is steep, as on the chalks.

The cart-way of the village divides, in a remarkable manner, two very incongruous soils. To the south-west is a rank-clay, that requires the labour of years to render it mellow; while the gardens to the north-east, and small enclosures behind, consist of a warm, forward, crumbling mould, called black malm, which seems highly saturated with vegetable and animal manure; and these may perhaps have been the original site of the town; while the wood and coverts might extend down to the opposite bank.

At each end of the village, which runs from south-east to north-west, arises a small rivulet: that at the north-west end frequently fails; but the other is a fine perennial spring, little influenced by drought or wet seasons, called Well-head. This breaks out of some high grounds joining to Nore-hill, a noble chalk promontory, remarkable for sending forth two streams into two different seas.

The one to the south becomes a branch of the Arun, running to Arundel, and so falling into the British Channel: the other to the north. The Selborne stream makes one branch of the Wey; and meeting the Black-down stream at Hedleigh, and the Alton and Farnham stream at Tilford-bridge, swells into a considerable river, navigable at Godalming from whence it passes to Guildford, and so into the Thames at Weybridge; and thus at the Nore into the German ocean.

...Still on to the north-east, and a step lower, is a kind of white land, neither chalk nor clay, neither fit for pasture nor for the plough, yet kindly for hops, which root deep into the freestone, and have their poles and wood for charcoal growing just at hand. This white soil produces the brightest hops.

As the parish still inclines down towards Wolmer-forest, at the juncture of the clays and sand the soil becomes a wet, sandy loam, remarkable for timber, and infamous for roads. The oaks of Temple and Blackmoor stand high in the estimation of purveyors, and have furnished much naval timber; while the trees on the freestone grow large, but are what workmen call shakey, and so brittle as often to fall to pieces in sawing. Beyond the sandy loam the soil becomes a hungry lean sand, till it mingles with the forest; and will produce little without the assistance of lime and turnips.

Letter IV: To Thomas Pennant
...The freestone of this place...is in great request for hearth-stones and the beds of ovens: and in lining of lime-kilns it turns to good account; for the workmen use sandy loam instead of mortar; the sand of which fluxes and runs by the intense heat, and so cases over the whole face of the kiln with a strong vitrified coat like glass, that is well preserved from injuries of weather, and endures thirty or forty years. When chiselled smooth, it makes elegant fronts for houses, equal in colour and grain to the Bath stone; and superior in one respect, that, when seasoned, it does not scale. Decent chimney-pieces are worked from it of much closer and finer grain than Portland; and rooms are floored with it; but it proves rather too soft for this purpose.

Letter V: To Thomas Pennant
Among the singularities of this place the two rocky hollow lanes, the one to Alton, and the other to the forest, deserve our attention. These roads, running through the malm lands, are, by the traffic of ages, and the fretting of water, worn down through the first stratum of our freestone, and partly through the second; so that they look more like water-courses than roads; and are bedded with naked rag for furlongs together. In many places they are reduced sixteen or eighteen feet beneath the level of the fields; and after floods, and in frosts, exhibit very grotesque and wild appearances, from the tangled roots that are twisted among the strata, and from torrents rushing down their broken sides; and especially when those cascades are frozen into icicles, hanging in all the fanciful shapes of frost-work. These rugged gloomy scenes affright the ladies when they peep down into them from the paths above, and

219

make timid horsemen shudder while they ride along them; but delight the naturalist with their various botany, and particularly with their curious filices with which they abound.

...The village of Selborne, and large hamlet of Oakhanger, with the single farms, and many scattered houses along the verge of the forest, contain upwards of six hundred and seventy inhabitants. We abound with poor; many of whom are sober and industrious, and live comfortably in good stone or brick cottages, which are glazed, and have chambers above stairs: mud buildings we have none.

Besides the employment from husbandry the men work in hop gardens, of which we have many; and fell and bark timber. In the spring and summer the women weed the corn; and enjoy a second harvest in September by hop-picking. Formerly, in the dead months they availed themselves greatly by spinning wool.

Letter IX: To Thomas Pennant
...General Howe turned out some German wild boars and sows in his forests, to the great terror of the neighbourhood; and, at one time, a wild bull or buffalo: but the country rose upon them and destroyed them.

I have been informed also, from undoubted authority, that some ladies (ladies you will say of peculiar taste) took a fancy to a toad, which they nourished summer after summer, for many years, till he grew to a monstrous size, with the maggots which turn to flesh flies. The reptile used to come forth every evening from an hole under the garden-steps; and was taken up, after supper, on the table to be fed. But at last a tame raven, kenning him as he put forth his head, gave him such a severe stroke with his horny beak as put out one eye. After this accident the creature languished for some time and died.

Letter XXV: To Daines Barrington
We have two gangs or hordes of gypsies which infest the south and west of England, and come round in their circuit two or three times in the year.

...With regard to these peculiar people, the gypsies, one thing is very remarkable, and especially as they come from warmer climates; and that is, that while other beggars lodge in barns, stables, and cow-houses, these sturdy savages seem to pride themselves in braving the severities of winter, and in living sub dio the whole year round. Last September was as wet a month as ever was known; and yet during these deluges did a young gypsy-girl lie-in in the midst of one of our hop-gardens, on the cold ground, with nothing over her but a piece of blanket extended on a few hazel-rods bent hoop-fashion, and stuck into the earth at each end, in circumstances too trying for a cow in the same condition: yet within this garden there was a large hop-kiln, into the chambers of which she might have retired, had she thought shelter an object worthy her attention…

Letter XXVII: To Daines Barrington
We had in this village more than twenty years ago an idiot-boy, whom I well remember, who, from a child, showed a strong propensity to bees; they were his food, his amusement, his sole object. And as people of this cast have seldom more than one point of view, so this lad exerted all his few faculties on this one pursuit. In the winter he dosed away his time, within his father's house, by the fireside, in a kind of torpid state, seldom departing from the chimney corner; but in the summer he was all alert, and in quest of his game in the fields, and on sunny banks. Honey-bees, humble-bees, and wasps, were his prey wherever he found them: he had no apprehensions from their stings, but would seize them *nudis manibus*, and at once disarm them of their weapons, and suck their bodies for the sake of their honey-bags. Sometimes he would fill his bosom between his shirt and his skin with a number of these captives; and sometimes would confine them in bottles. He was a very merops apiaster, or bee-bird; and very injurious to men that kept bees; for he would slide into their bee-gardens, and, sitting down before the stools, would rap with his finger on the hives, and so take the bees as they came out. He has been known to overturn hives for the sake of honey, of which he was passionately fond. Where metheglin was making he would linger round the tubs and vessels, begging a glass of what he called bee-wine. As he ran about he used to make a humming noise with his lips, resembling the buzzing of bees. This lad was lean and sallow, and of a cadaverous complexion; and,

except in his favourite pursuit, in which he was wonderfully adroit, discovered no manner of understanding...

When a tall youth he was removed from hence to a distant village, where he died, as I understand, before he arrived at manhood.

Letter XXVIII: To Daines Barrington

It is the hardest thing in the world to shake off superstitious prejudices: they are sucked in as it were with our mother's milk; and growing up with us at a time when they take the fastest hold and make the most lasting impressions, become so interwoven into our very constitutions, that the strongest good sense is required to disengage ourselves from them. No wonder therefore that the lower people retain them their whole lives through, since their minds are not invigorated by a liberal education, and therefore not enabled to make efforts adequate to the occasion...

...In a farmyard near the middle of this village stands, at this day, a row of pollard-ashes, which by the seams and long cicatrices down their sides, manifestly show that, in former times, they have been cleft asunder. These trees, when young and flexible, were severed and held open by wedges, while ruptured children, stripped naked, were pushed through the apertures, under a persuasion that, by such a process, the poor babes would be cured of their infirmity. As soon as the operation was over, the tree, in the suffering part, was plastered with loam, and carefully swathed up. If the parts coalesced and soldered together, as usually fell out, where the feat was performed with any adroitness at all, the party was cured; but, where the cleft continued to gape, the operation, it was supposed, would prove ineffectual. Having occasion to enlarge my garden not long since, I cut down two or three such trees, one of which did not grow together.

We have several persons now living in the village, who, in their childhood, were supposed to be healed by this superstitious ceremony, derived down perhaps from our Saxon ancestors, who practised it before their conversion to Christianity.

At the south corner of the Plestor, or area, near the church, there stood, about twenty years ago, a very grotesque hollow pollard-ash, which for ages had been looked on with no small veneration as a shrew-ash. Now a shrew-ash is an ash whose twigs or branches, when gently applied to the limbs of cattle, will immediately relieve the pains which a beast suffers from the running of a shrew-mouse over the part affected: for it is supposed that a shrew-mouse is of so baneful and deleterious a nature, that wherever it creeps over a beast, be it horse, cow, or sheep, the suffering animal is afflicted with cruel anguish, and threatened with the loss of the use of the limb. Against this accident, to which they were continually liable, our provident fore-fathers always kept a shrew-ash at hand, which, when once medicated, would maintain its virtue for ever. A shrew-ash was made thus: Into the body of the tree a deep hole was bored with an auger, and a poor devoted shrew-mouse was thrust in alive, and plugged in, no doubt, with several quaint incantations long since forgotten. As the ceremonies necessary for such a consecration are no longer understood, all succession is at an end, and no such tree is known to subsist in the manor, or hundred.

As to that on the Plestor, 'the late vicar stubb'd and burnt it' when he was way-warden, regardless of the remonstances of the by-standers, who interceded in vain for its preservation, urging its power and efficacy...

Letter XXXVIII: To Daines Barrington
In a district so diversified as this, so full of hollow vales, and hanging woods, it is no wonder that echoes should abound. Many we have discovered that return the cry of a pack of dogs, the notes of a hunting-horn, a tunable ring of bells, or the melody of birds, very agreeably: but we were still at a loss for a polysyllabical, articulate echo, till a young gentleman, who had parted from his company in a summer evening walk, and was calling after them, stumbled upon a very curious one in a spot where it might least be expected. At first he was much surprised, and could not be persuaded but that he was mocked by some boy; but, repeating his trials in several languages, and finding his respondent to be a very adroit polyglot, he then discerned the deception.

This echo in an evening, before rural noises cease, would repeat ten syllables most articulately and distinctly, especially if quick dactyls were chosen.

...All echoes have some one place to which they are returned stronger and more distinct than to any other; and that is always the place that lies at right angles with the object of repercussion, and is not too near, nor too far off.

Buildings, or naked rocks, re-echo much more articulately than hanging wood or vales; because in the latter the voice is as it were entangled, and embarrassed in the covert, and weakened in the rebound.

The true object of this echo, as we found by various experiments, is the stone-built, tiled hop-kiln in Galley-lane, which measures in front 40 feet, and from the ground to the eaves 12 feet. The true *centrum phonicum*, or just distance, is one particular spot in the King's-field, in the path to Nore-hill, on the very brink of the steep balk above the hollow cart way. In this case there is no choice of distance; but the path, by mere contingency, happens to be the lucky, the identical spot, because the ground rises or falls so immediately, if the speaker either retires or advances, that his mouth would at once be above or below the object.

Gilbert White (1720–93)
The Natural History of Selborne (1789)

And this, from his journal:

Sept. 25 1789
Men bag their hops; & house seed-clover. A fern-owl plays round the Plestor. As we were walking this day, Sept. 22nd: being the King's coronation, on Nore-hill at one o'clock in the afternoon, we heard great guns on each side of us, viz. from the S. & from the N.E, which undoubtedly were the cannons of Portsmouth & Windsor; the former of which is at least 26 miles distant, & the latter 30. If the guns heard from the N.E were not from Windsor, they must be those of the Tower of London.

Gilbert White (1720–93)
Journals

Close by to Selborne lies the village of Blackmoor. Here, a century after Gilbert White, we get a slice of Victorian village life.

Except when he will have to go to Balmoral, as Minister in attendance on the Queen, the Lord Chancellor will pass his comparatively short holiday at Selborne, his place on the Hampshire downs. It is not twenty-five years ago that Sir Roundell Palmer bought this property. It was then a ferny wilderness, but he was not daunted, and, having taken a fancy to the spot, he determined to create a country house there, and at once proceeded to build, to plant and to adorn. Now there is a handsome house, surrounded by trim lawns, with beautiful gardens and terraces, the kitchen gardens and glasshouses being remarkably extensive and complete. The rhododendrons are very luxurious in the grounds and the conservatory contains some enormous fuchsias. Blackmoor Church, which is near at hand, was not only built by Lord Selborne [the Palmer family title] at the cost of £10,000, but he has endowed it with £150 a year. The views all round are magnificent and the country richly wooded.

Speaking at a festive gathering of the people of his parish, Lord Selborne said that he believed that they did take great interest in his fortunes, but he was afraid that perhaps their minds were addressed to the 'honour' and less to the 'responsibility'. He trusted that God would so direct his thoughts that he would not care for these mere honours, but that he would look upon all earthly dignities, all worldly distinctions, as useful only for the sake of the country and the welfare of all mankind ...He was not ambitious for place, he was not ambitious for power, for well he knew that all earthly things faded, and he was only anxious to do some good in the world, ere he was called upon to take that final step, which, if it leads but to the lowest place in the Master's kingdom, is far beyond all other honours, and, if it leads not to that place, then nothing here below is worth striving for.

And here is another brilliant nature writer W. H. Hudson, who was born in the wild open plains of Argentina and settled in England in 1874. He produced a series of ornithological studies, including *Argentine Ornithology* (1888–1899) and *British Birds* (1895), and later achieved fame with his books on the English countryside, including *Hampshire Days* (1903), *Afoot in England* (1909) and *A Shepherd's Life* (1910), which helped foster the back-to-nature movement of the 1920s and 1930s. He was a founding member of the Royal Society for the Protection of Birds.

> I do not, however, say that all new and large churches raised in small rustic centres appear discordant things; there is a new and comparatively large one which moves one to admiration – the church of Blackmoor. Here the vegetation and surroundings are unlike those which accord best with the small typical structures, the low tower and shingled spire. The tall, square tower of Blackmoor, of white stone roofed with red tiles, rises amid the pines of Wolmer Forest, simple and beautiful in shape, and gives a touch of grace and grateful colour to that darker, austere nature. From every point of view it is a pleasure to the eye, and because of its enduring beauty the memory of the man who raised it is like a perfume in the wilderness.

> W. H. Hudson (1841–1922)
> *Hampshire Days* (1903)

It's well worth seeking out the reclusive village of Priors Dean today, untouched, it seems, since W. H. Hudson visited.

> …When calling to mind the churches known to me in this part of Hampshire, I always think with peculiar pleasure of the smaller ones, and perhaps with the most pleasure of the smallest of all – Priors Dean. It happened that the maps which I use in my Hampshire rambles and which I always considered the best – Bartholomew's two miles to the inch – did not mark Priors Dean, so that I had to go and find it for myself. I went with a friend one excessively hot day in July, by Empshott and Hawkley through deep by-roads so deep and narrow and roofed over with branches as to seem in places like tunnels. On that hot day in the silent time of the year it was strangely still, and gave one the feeling of being in a country long deserted by man. Its only inhabitants now appeared to be the bullfinches. In these deep shaded lanes one constantly hears the faint plaintive little piping sound, the almost inaudible alarm note of the concealed bird; and at intervals, following the sound, he suddenly dashes out, showing his sharp-winged shape and clear grey and black upper plumage marked with

white for a moment or two before vanishing once more in the overhanging foliage.

We went a long way round, but at last coming to an open spot we saw two cottages and two women and a boy standing talking by a gate, and of these people we asked the way to Priors Dean. They could not tell us. They knew it was not far away – a mile perhaps; but they had never been to it, nor seen it, and didn't well know the direction. The boy when asked shook his head. A middle-aged man was digging about thirty yards away, and to him one of the women now called, 'Can you tell them the way to Priors Dean?'

The man left off digging, straightened himself, and gazed steadily at us for some moments. He was one of the usual type – nine in every ten farm labourers in this corner of Hampshire are of it – thinnish, of medium height, a pale, parchment face, rather large straightish nose, pale eyes with little speculation in them, shaved mouth and chin, and small side whiskers as our fathers wore them. The moustache has not yet been adopted by these conservatives. The one change they have made is, alas! in their dress – the rusty black coat for the smock frock.

When he had had his long gaze, he said, 'Priors Dean?'

'Yes, Priors Dean,' repeated the woman, raising her voice.

He turned up two spadefuls of earth, then asked again 'Priors Dean?'

'Priors Dean!' shouted the woman. 'Can't you tell 'em how to get to it?' Then she laughed. She had perhaps come from some other part of the country where minds are not quite so slow, and where the slow-minded person is treated as being deaf and shouted at.

Then, at last, he stuck his spade into the soil, and leaving it, slowly advanced to the gate and told us to follow a path which he pointed out, and when we got on the hill we would see Priors Dean before us.

And that was how we found it. There is a satirical saying in the other villages that if you want to find the church at Priors Dean you must first cut down the nettles. There were no nettles or weeds of any kind, only the small ancient church with its little shingled spire standing in the middle of a large green graveyard with about a dozen or fifteen gravestones scattered about, three old tombs, and, close to the building, an ancient yew tree. This is a big, and has been a bigger, tree, as a large part of the trunk has perished on one side, but as it stands it measures nearly twenty-four feet round a yard from the earth. This, with a small farmhouse, in old times a manor house, and its outbuildings and a cottage or two, make the village. So quiet a spot is it that to see a human form or hear a human voice comes almost as a surprise. The little antique church, the few stones, the dark ancient tree – these are everything, and the effect on the mind is strangely grateful – a sense of enduring peace, with something of that solitariness and desolation which we find in unspoilt wildernesses.

W. H. Hudson (1841–1922)
Hampshire Days (1903)

And here's how Edward Thomas saw the same village a decade or so later.

The Manor Farm

The rock-like mud unfroze a little and rills
Ran and sparkled down each side of the road
Under the catkins wagging in the hedge.
But earth would have her sleep out, spite of the sun;
Nor did I value that thin gilding beam
More than a pretty February thing
Till I came down to the old Manor Farm,
And church and yew tree opposite, in age
Its equals and in size. The church and yew
And farmhouse slept in a Sunday silentness.
The air raised not a straw. The steep farm roof,
With tiles duskily glowing, entertained
The midday sun; and up and down the roof
White pigeons nestled. There was no sound but one.
Three cart-horses were looking over a gate
Drowsily through their forelocks, swishing their tails
Against a fly, a solitary fly.

The Winter's cheek flushed as if he had drained
Spring, Summer, and Autumn at a draft

And smiled quietly. But 'twas not Winter –
Rather a session of bliss unchangeable
Awakened from farm and church where it had lain
Safe under tile and thatch for ages since
This England, Old already, was called Merry.

Edward Thomas (1878–1917)

At around the same time, Josephine Tozier, an American who took her fellow countrymen on tours of England, spent an enjoyable day at Selborne.

One of the eccentricities of the British railway system is the aversion the officials display to calling out the name of a station. At the extreme end of each small platform, hidden among brilliant invitations to 'Use Pear's Soap ' or 'Take Beecham's Pills,' the name of the town is shyly concealed by a modest gray sign. My party almost refused to follow me, when I began to pull down the bags at Alton.

The town of Alton saves itself from hopeless dullness only by the pretty curve its High Street describes. I have read somewhere that Mrs Gaskell was building a house in Alton when she died, yet the place itself possesses no visible attractions. Alton, situated in the centre of a hop-growing region, is a brewing town. The solemn brick Georgian houses look comfortable and ugly. Public houses, mere drinking-places, supply all the picturesque element by their names: the French Horn, the Hop Poles, the Jug of Ale, and the pretentious Star, 'patronised by Royalty.'

The green once passed, and the homely little town behind us, we become aware of the charm which induced Mrs Gaskell to choose Alton as a dwelling-place. The road branches where we leave the last houses; one way leads us over low hills to our destination, the other is a shaded road to Chawton, where lived Jane Austen's brother, who inherited the manor-house, and the cottage in which that gentle authoress spent the last years of her life.

Over the hills and far away goes the road to Selborne, past fields where festoons of the hop-vines make bowers of green. The highway winds up and down for five miles through copse and farmlands. We see noisy rooks gleaning the fields, and men ploughing with oxen; these last a rare sight in England. From the high points of the road we look down into the sunny valley on the little village of Chawton, and see the noonday smoke rising from the cottages. At the top of the last steep hill on our drive, the long, low ridge before us is pointed out to us as the 'Hanger,' and nestling at its base lies the village of Selborne.

None of the party, excepting the writer, has ever before seen an English village inn. They are at first inclined to be disappointed because 'The Queen's Arms' does not more exactly resemble the comic opera counterfeit. When the bedrooms are assigned us, the Matron discovers we fill the house. 'A whole inn to ourselves! Could anything be more perfect!'

We were lucky in coming to Selborne in July. Then occur the most festive days of the summer, the flower-show, and the county policeman's dinner. The squire's hospitality is responsible for the policeman's dinner. It is his entertainment. The constabulary is a valuable and imposing institution in rural England. During the hop-picking season Selborne and the country for miles around is overrun by rough men and women from the dregs of the London streets, who come to work in the hop-fields. That muscular member of the county police who keeps the peace in Selborne has proved himself such a terror to the evil-doers among these hordes that the squire, with a desire to show his appreciation for the protection afforded his village by this athletic policeman, once a year gives a dinner in his name to all the members of the constabulary for miles around.

The County Constabulary is a very important institution, but the annual dinner of the County Constabulary is a much more important institution. We were greatly disappointed, being females all, and Americans as well, to find that the invited guests did not come in uniform. The men came therefore in those spick and span garments in which every Englishman manages to array himself on Sunday.

After the meal was over came games at The Wakes. We had fortunately received an invitation to be present. We sat on the lawn under the glorious old trees and watched the game of cricket, which we did not understand in the least; a tug of war pleased us better, it came quite within our limits of comprehension. The host of the occasion wandered about talking with old and young. We were exceedingly interested in the relations between the classes here displayed. It was a novel sight for republicans, no equality, no condescension, yet not the slightest sign of servility.

Josephine Tozier (1853–?)
Among English Inns (1904)

I suppose we should not be surprised by the fictional Sherlock Holmes's take on the Hampshire countryside, somewhat north of Selborne, but Hampshire none the less.

By eleven o'clock the next day we were well upon our way to the old English capital. Holmes had been buried in the morning papers all the way down, but after we had passed the Hampshire border he threw them down, and began to admire the scenery. It was an ideal spring day, a light blue sky, flecked with little fleecy white clouds drifting across from west to east. The sun was shining very brightly, and yet there was an exhilarating nip in the air, which set an edge to a man's energy. All over the countryside, away to the rolling hills around Aldershot, the little red and grey roofs of the farm steadings peeped out from amidst the light green of the new foliage.

'Are they not fresh and beautiful?' I cried, with all the enthusiasm of a man fresh from the fogs of Baker Street. But Holmes shook his head gravely.

'Do you know, Watson,' said he, 'that it is one of the curses of a mind with a turn like mine that I must look at everything with reference to my own special subject. You look at these scattered houses, and you are impressed by their beauty. I look at them, and the only thought which comes to me is a feeling of their isolation, and of the impunity with which crime may be committed there.'

'Good heavens!' I cried. 'Who would associate crime with these dear old homesteads?'

'They always fill me with a certain horror. It is my belief, Watson, founded upon my experience, that the lowest and vilest alleys in London do not present a more dreadful record of sin than does the smiling and beautiful countryside.'

Sir Arthur Conan Doyle (1859–1930)
The Copper Beeches (1892)

And indeed Holmes's suspicions are confirmed by the following ballad, based on a true crime, the murder of Fanny Adams. The horrible murder was committed in 1867 near Alton and reported in the London newspapers. The ghastly mutilation of the child was recorded in Baker's diary: 'Saturday August 24th. Killed a young girl. It was fine and hot':

The Execution of Frederick Baker – a ballad

You tender mothers pray give attention
To these few lines I will now relate;
From a dreary cell, now to you I'll mention
A wicked murderer now has met his fate.
This villain's name it is Frederick Baker
His trial is over and his time has come,
On the gallows high he has met his maker
To answer for that cruel deed he'd done.

cho: Prepare for death, wicked Frederick Baker,
 For on the scaffold you will shortly die,
 Your victim waits for you to meet your maker;
 She dwells with angels and her God on high

On that Saturday little Fanny Adams
Near the hop-garden with her sister played,
With hearts so light, they were filled with gladness,
When that monster, Baker, towards them strayed;
In that heart of stone not a spark of pity
As he those halfpence to the children gave,
But now in gaol in Winchester city
He soon will die and fill a murderer's grave.

He told those children to go and leave him
With little Fanny at the garden gate.
He said, 'Come with me,' and she, believing
In his arms he lifted her as now I state.
'O do not take me, my mother wants me,
I must go home again please sir,' she cried,
But on this earth she never saw them,
For in that hop-garden there, the poor girl died.

When the deed was done and that little darling
Her soul to God her Maker it had flown,
She could not return to her mother's bidding
He mutilated her, it is well known.
Her heart-broken parents in anguish weeping
For vengeance on her murderer cried,
Her mother wrings her hands in sorrow
O would for you, Dear Fanny, I had died.

The jury soon found this monster guilty,
The judge on him this awful sentence passed:
Saying, 'Prepare yourself, for the cruel murder
You have committed, your die is cast.
And from your cell you will mount the scaffold,
And many thousands will you behold,
You will die the death of a cruel murderer,
And may the Lord have mercy on your soul!

What visions now must haunt his pillow
As in his cell he does lie the while?
She calls to him, 'O you wicked murderer
'Tis I your victim calls, that little child!
The hangman comes; hark the bell is tolling
Your time has come, you cannot be saved,'
He mounts the scaffold and the drop is falling
And Frederick Baker fills a murderer's grave.

P G Wodehouse's Hampshire village life sparkles with amusement but
he also bases his diversion on historical fact. While in England the
prolific novelist lived in Hampshire, at Emsworth, which is *Belpher*.

Chapter I

In as much as the scene of this story is that historic pile, Belpher Castle, in the county of Hampshire, it would be an agreeable task to open it with a leisurely description of the place, followed by some notes on the history of the Earls of Marshmoreton, who have owned it since the fifteenth century. Unfortunately, in these days of rush and hurry, a novelist works at a disadvantage. He must leap into the middle of his tale with as little delay as he would employ in boarding a moving tramcar...

Chapter VII

The first requisite of an invading army is a base. George, having entered Belpher village and thus accomplished the first stage in his forward movement on the castle, selected as his base the 'Marshmoreton Arms.' Selected is perhaps hardly the right word, as it implies choice, and in George's case there was no choice. There are two inns at Belpher, but the 'Marshmoreton Arms' is the only one that offers accommodation for man and beast, assuming – that is to say – that the man and beast desire to spend the night. The other house, the 'Blue Boar,' is a mere beerhouse, where the lower strata of Belpher society gather of a night to quench their thirst and to tell one another interminable stories without any point whatsoever. But the 'Marshmoreton Arms' is a comfortable, respectable hostelry, catering for the village plutocrats. There of an evening you will find the local veterinary surgeon smoking a pipe with the grocer, the baker, and the butcher, with perhaps a sprinkling of neighbouring farmers to help the conversation along. On Saturdays there is a 'shilling ordinary' – which is rural English for a cut off the joint and a boiled potato, followed by hunks of the sort of cheese which believes that it pays to advertise – and this is usually well attended.

On the other days of the week, until late in the evening, however, the visitor to the 'Marshmoreton Arms' has the place almost entirely to himself.

It is to be questioned whether in the whole length and breadth of the world there is a more admirable spot for a man in love to pass a day or two than the typical English village. The Rocky Mountains, that traditional stamping-ground for the heart-broken, may be well enough in their way; but a lover has to be cast in a pretty stern mould to be able to be introspective when at any moment he may meet with an annoyed cinnamon bear. In the English village there are no such obstacles to meditation. It combines the comforts of civilisation with the restfulness of solitude in a manner equalled by no other spot except the New York Public Library. Here your lover may wander to and fro unmolested, speaking to nobody, by nobody addressed, and have the satisfaction at the end of the day of sitting down to a capitally cooked chop and chips, lubricated by golden English ale.

Belpher, in addition to all the advantages of the usual village, has a quiet charm all its own, due to the fact that it has seen better days. In a sense, it is a ruin, and ruins are always soothing to the bruised soul. Ten years before, Belpher had been a flourishing centre of the South of England oyster trade. It is situated by the shore, where Hayling Island, lying athwart the mouth of the bay, forms the waters into a sort of brackish lagoon, in much the same way as Fire Island shuts off the Great South Bay of Long Island from the waves of the Atlantic. The water of Belpher Creek is shallow even at high tide, and when the tide runs out it leaves glistening mud flats, which it is the peculiar taste of oysters to prefer to any other habitation. For years Belpher oysters had been the mainstay of gay supper parties at the 'Savoy,' the 'Carlton' and Romano's. Dukes doted on them; chorus girls wept if they were not on the bill of fare. And then, in an evil hour, somebody discovered that what made the Belpher oyster so particularly plump and succulent was the fact that it breakfasted, lunched and dined almost entirely on the local sewage. There is but a thin line between popular homage and execration. We see it in the case of politicians, generals and prize-fighters; and oysters are no exception to the rule. There was a typhoid scare – quite a passing and unjustified scare, but strong enough to do its deadly work; and almost overnight Belpher passed from a place of flourishing industry to the sleepy, by-the-world-forgotten spot which it was when George Bevan discovered it. The shallow water is still there; the mud is still there; even the oyster-beds are still there; but not the oysters nor the little world of activity which had sprung up around them. The glory of Belpher is dead; and over its gates Ichabod is written. But, if it has lost in importance, it has gained in charm; and George, for one, had no regrets. To him, in his present state of mental upheaval, Belpher was the ideal spot.

P G Wodehouse (1881–1975)
Damsel in Distress (1919)

A very different Hampshire is imagined by Richard Adams in his novel *Watership Down*, in which a small group of rabbits, possessing their own culture, language and mythology, escape the destruction of their warren and seek a place to establish a new home, encountering perils and temptations along the way. Richard Adams lived his last twenty-eight years in Whitchurch.

Nuthanger is like a farm in an old tale. Between Ecchinswell and the foot of Watership Down and about half a mile from each, there is a broad knoll, steeper on the north side but falling gently on the south – like the down ridge itself. Narrow lanes climb both slopes and come together in a great ring of elm trees which encircles the flat summit. Any wind – even the lightest – draws from the height of the elms a rushing sound, multifoliate and powerful. Within this ring stands the farmhouse, with its barns and out-buildings. The house may be two hundred years old or it may be older, built of brick, with a stone-faced front looking south towards the down. On the east side, in front of the house, a barn stands clear of the ground on staddle-stones; and opposite is the cow-byre.

Richard Adams (1920-2016)
Watership Down (1972)

You could hardly get more of a contrast between *Watership Down* and the next subject in this anthology.

Basingstoke is one of the most derided towns in England. Its reputation is as an over-developed eyesore of numbing dullness. Its very name lends itself to mockery. Basingrad,

Basingjoke, Bazingsmoke, Boringstoke and even more ironic Amazingstoke are variants thought up and used by its own residents, not always with affection. Though it is best known for its bewildering succession of pointless roundabouts, the curse of the town is its ridiculous, often hostile 'Modernist' architecture, much of it illustrated and described on Joe Tozer's witty website *(It's Basingstoke not Boringstoke)*. The most notorious feature is the so-called 'Great Wall of Basingstoke', a huge retaining wall, built in the 1960s, for 'the great mass of concrete poured over the razed remains of the old market town'. Also of note are the 'Hanging Gardens of Basingstoke', a misfired attempt at horticulture on the top of a 1970s steel-and-glass block, and the 'Costa del Basingstoke', a gaily-coloured apartment complex in the style of a 'Costa' resort ('however as Basingstoke has no beach it has to make do with a view over the town's enormous car park'). The town's most risible attraction is surely the prominent sculpture that locals have dubbed the 'Wote Street Willy'. Said to be an image of a mother and chid, it is actually 'the largest phallus on public display in Britain'. One thinks also of the 'Toy Town' tower that looms over Festival Place, and wonders if it, too, is a phallic reference. A town that treats itself as a joke can hardly expect to be taken seriously by outsiders.

Rupert Willoughby
Basingstoke and its contribution to World Culture (2011)

As you might expect of a place suffering from such a reputation, Basingstoke is not widely described in the annals of history, but I like this footnote. Cosimo III of Medici was so miserably incompetent a ruler of his huge estates, reducing his people to penury, that he was encouraged to travel; wherever he went in Europe he was welcomed amiably and with signs of honour, which he seemed partly to expect and at the same time resent.

Intending to sleep that night at Basingstoke, his highness departed for that place, and travelling through an open and desolate country, took refreshment at the small village of Sutton, then continuing his journey through a country chiefly devoted to pasture, and in some parts woody, he discovered, two miles from Basingstoke, a troop of horse consisting of fifty-four men, excellently mounted, of the royal regiment of my Lord Aubry de Vere, Earl of Oxford, commanded by his lieutenant. They came by the king's orders, to attend upon and be at the disposal of his highness, as was intimated to him by the commander, who, dismounting, came up to the carriage. His highness in reply, accepted only a small party, whom he sent to meet the baggage, and dismissed the rest. He then alighted to examine the military more closely, inspecting every file of the company, the officers of which wore a red sash, with gold tassels. This regiment of the Earl of Oxford is composed of eight companies of seventy men each; they receive from the king half a ducat a day, this is paid them every two months, which being of twenty-eight days each, they have seven payments annually. In each of these companies the colonel has the privilege of keeping two places vacant, and of appropriating the emolument to himself, which amounts to more than fourteen pounds sterling every week.

His highness having arrived early at Basingstoke, walked on foot through the town, which is wretched, both in regard to the buildings, the greater part of which are of wood, and the total absence of trade; so that the gratification of his curiosity did not compensate for the fatigue of walking even a few paces. Whilst his highness was viewing the church, which is a small and very indifferent building, the mayor and two other officers came with the insignia of magistracy, to wait upon him; but his highness civilly declined this public demonstration of respect.

On the morning of the 14th, which was Palm Sunday, his highness attended at the Benediction, and after he had privately heard Mass, with his suite, every thing was arranged for his departure for Egham. The whole troop was in readiness to march with his highness, but he accepted only the same convoy as before, which was useful for the security of the baggage, refusing all the rest, as serving no other purpose than to display the formality of a public reception. Nevertheless they all insisted upon accompanying him out of the district, where, having halted, they took leave after two salutes. We travelled fourteen miles through a country nearly level, and entirely open, appropriated to pasturage, as is all the rest of the territory of Hampshire, through which we passed, and dined at Okested, a small village.

Conte Lorenzo Magalotti
Travels of Cosimo lll, Grand Duke of Tuscany, through England during the reign of King Charles II 1669 (translation published 1821)

One of the few accounts of what it was like to live in Basingstoke, before it was taken in hand by the developers who ruined it, comes from the autobiography of the cricket commentator John Arlott, who was born here in 1914.

The background to it all was Basingstoke; nothing like the sprawling Basingstoke of today but a friendly, bumbling country town of some 12,000 people, in which almost everyone knew almost everyone else. It is worth recalling that, when the idea of making it a 'New Town' was broached, that wise man George Willis, having listened to the arguments – often most passionate on both sides – observed that no one could argue from knowledge because never before had there been such an exercise as this proposed rapid conversion of a small town into a large one. No one could tell what the outcome would be, he said, but if Basingstoke submitted to being the material for such an experiment, then, experiment or no, it would be irreversible. He was, obviously, correct, but he was far too nice a man to have felt any pleasure in his grave at being right about the dire outcome he had half prophesied. The essential weakness of the plan lay in the fact that the people who came in to settle the place were strangers. It was no surprise that they felt warmth and nostalgia for their original homes when they found themselves in the monotonous duplication of houses which were all too soon described as 'the slums of the future'. Much of the damage was by unwitting official vandalism. The former town had four buildings of distinction: all dwelling houses, of no great size, and obstructing no reasonable development; all four were demolished in the construction of the blur which is 'modern' Basingstoke.

The old place – like so many in everyone's childhood memories – was at its best in the period about Christmas, when the lights from the shop windows shimmered across

239

the – invariably – rain-shiny streets. Moreover, all the shops – even those of the same type – stocked different varieties of their goods; there simply was less standardisation. Hosts of representatives from small firms prowled those shops, of which each owner wanted something 'different from them down the road'. So the term 'window-shopping' had real meaning. The market-place in particular was splendid, with its naphta flares, its varieties of meat, fish, fruit, shoes, cheap clothes, sweets, while the cheapjacks hoarsely provided the background of sound.

Of course, it was not in the least sophisticated. Especially on Sunday evenings, as the motorists drove back to London from the coast, a considerable proportion of the population was not merely content, but delighted, to watch the variety of cars, motorcycles, and all types of horse-drawn carts, traps and, at times, wagons – such as some of the village cricket teams used for short journeys to away matches – as they made their noisy but varied way along the main road of the town which ran through the market place, where the connoisseurs of traffic matters used to congregate.

The business area of the town, with the exception of the railway complex, consisted of Winchester Street and its continuation into London Street, plus the upper, or southern halves of Wote Street and Church Street, and the terminus of the old Basingstoke canal, facing the Barge Inn; a late-night resort for drunks, later to become the bus-station. The little side streets, like Potters Lane and Victoria Street, were lined with tiny terraces which, at the time they were knocked down, housed old people who were moved into 'modern' homes a mile or two out of town: as a result, they lost sight of their old friends and gossips, shops and pubs and, in many cases, simply faded away in loneliness. It was not a happy result; more a plan for anonymity. Those councillors who had controlled the town in earlier days were reactionary and, with the exception of George Willis, mainly Tory tradesmen; but they had character and, therefore, they produced a Basingstoke of some character, quite unlike the impersonality created by those who later 'planned' and moved on.

John Arlott (1914–91)
Basingstoke Boy (1990)

As with any county, Hampshire has her fair share of ruined buildings. With her usual wit, Jane Austen here praises Henry VIII for his part in their creation. She was only fifteen at the time.

> Nothing can be said in his vindication, but that his abolishing Religious Houses & leaving them to the ruinous depredations of time has been of infinite use to the landscape of England in general, which probably was a principal motive for his doing it.

Jane Austen (1775–1817)
The History of England (1791)

She might have had in mind the Holy Ghost Chapel, at Basingstoke, a ruin to which Gilbert White confesses to have contributed:

> When a schoolboy, more than fifty years ago, he [the author] was eye-witness, perhaps a party concerned, in the undermining a portion of that fine old ruin at the north end of Basingstoke town, well known by the name of *Holy Ghost Chapel.*
>
> Very providentially the vast fragment which these thoughtless little engineers endeavoured to sap did not give way so soon as might have been expected; but it fell the night following, and with such violence that it shook the very ground, and, awakening the inhabitants of the neighbouring cottages, made them start up in their beds as if they had felt an earthquake. The motive for this dangerous attempt does not appear: perhaps the more danger the more honour, thought the boys; and the notion of doing some mischief gave a zest to the enterprise. As Dryden says upon another occasion,
> 'It look'd so like a sin it pleas'd the more.'

Gilbert White (1720–93)
The Antiquities of Selborne
Letter XXVI

Going back to our earliest ruins, here is W. H. Hudson again, this time appreciating not the architecture of the Victorians, but the interior decoration of the Romans.

...The old Romans must have felt this instinctive pleasure of the eye very keenly when they took such great pains over their floors. I was strongly impressed with this fact at Silchester when looking at the old floors of rich and poor houses alike which have been uncovered during the last two or three years. They seem to have sought for the effect of mosaic even in the meaner habitations, and in passages and walks, and when tesserae could not be had they broke up common tiles into small square fragments, and made their floors in that way. Even with so poor a material, and without any ornamentation, they did get the effect sought, and those ancient fragments of floors made of fragments of tiles, unburied after so many centuries, do actually more gratify the sight than the floors of polished oak or other expensive material which are seen in our mansions and palaces.

W. H. Hudson (1841–1922)
Hampshire Days (1903)

The ruins of Netley Abbey, east of Southampton, caught the attention of many, beginning, here, with Horace Walpole, that proponent of the Gothic.

But how shall I describe Netley to you? I can only, by telling you it is the spot in the world for which Mr Chute and I wish. The ruins are vast and contain fragments of beautiful fretted roofs, pendant in the air, with all variety of Gothic patterns of windows, topped round and round with ivy. Many trees have sprouted up among the walls, and only want to be increased by cypresses. A hill rises above the abbey, enriched with wood. The fort in which we would build a tower for habitation remains with two small platforms. This little castle is buried from the abbey in a wood, in the very centre, on the edge of the hill; on each side breaks in the view of the Southampton sea, deep blue glistening with silver and vessels; on one side terminated by Southampton, on the other by Calshot Castle; and the Isle of Wight rising above the opposite hills – in short, they are not the ruins of Netley but of Paradise. Oh, the purpled abbots! What a spot they had chosen to slumber in! The scene is so beautifully tranquil, yet so lively, that they seem only to have retired into the world.

A little later, Thomas Gray (1716-1771) describes how 'the ferryman who rowed me [to Netley], told me that he would not for all the world pass a night at the Abbey, there were such things seen near it!'

The American novelist, and sometime US consul in Liverpool, Nathaniel Hawthorne, visited the ruins with his wife, Sophia, in the 1850s.

The remains of the Abbey stand in a sheltered place, but within view of Southampton Water; and it is a most picturesque and perfect ruin, all ivy-grown, of course, and with great trees where the pillars of the nave used to stand, and also in the refectory and the cloister court; and so much soil on the summit of the broken walls, that weeds flourish abundantly there, and grass too; and there was a wild rose-bush, in full bloom, as much as thirty or forty feet from the ground. S– [Sophia] and I ascended a winding-stair, leading up within a round tower, the steps much foot-worn; and, reaching the top, we came forth at the height where a gallery had formerly run round the church, in the thickness of the wall. The upper portions of the edifice were now chiefly thrown down; but I followed a foot-path, on the top of the remaining wall, quite to the western entrance of the church. Since the time when the Abbey was taken from the monks, it has been private property; and the possessor, in Henry VIII's days, or subsequently, built a residence for himself within its precincts out of the old materials. This has now entirely disappeared, all but some unsightly old masonry, patched

into the original walls. Large portions of the ruin have been removed, likewise, to be used as building-materials elsewhere; and this is the Abbey mentioned, I think, by Dr Watts, concerning which a Mr William Taylor had a dream while he was contemplating pulling it down. He dreamed that a part of it fell upon his head; and, sure enough, a piece of the wall did come down and crush him. In the nave I saw a large mass of conglomerated stone that had fallen from the wall between the nave and cloisters, and thought that perhaps this was the very mass that killed poor Mr Taylor. The ruins are extensive and very interesting; but I have put off describing them too long, and cannot make a distinct picture of them now. Moreover, except to a spectator skilled in architecture, all ruined abbeys are pretty much alike. As we came away, we noticed some women making baskets at the entrance, and one of them urged us to buy some of her handiwork; for that she was the gypsy of Netley Abbey, and had lived among the ruins these thirty years. So I bought one for a shilling. She was a woman with a prominent nose, and weather-tanned, but not very picturesque or striking.

Nathaniel Hawthorne (1804–64)
Passages from the English notebooks

And here the rector-poet Bowles takes the sobering metaphorical route. In 1789 his *Fourteen Sonnets*, published in 1789, were enormously popular and admired by Coleridge and Wordsworth.

Netley Abbey

Fall'n pile! I ask not what has been thy fate;
But when the winds, slow wafted from the main,
Through each rent arch, like spirits that complain,
Come hollow to my ear, I meditate
On this world's passing pageant, and the lot
Of those who once majestic in their prime
Stood smiling at decay, till bowed by time
Or injury, their early boast forgot,
They may have fall'n like thee! Pale and forlorn,
Their brow, besprent with thin hairs, white as snow,

They lift, still unsubdued, as they would scorn
This short-lived scene of vanity and woe;
Whilst in their sad looks smilingly they bear
The trace of creeping age, and the pale hue of care!

William Lisle Bowles (1762–1850)

But not all the visitors are enamoured.

Somewhere among the cables and the gantries lay the ruins
of a Cistercian Abbey, and next to it Netley Hospital, once
half a mile long and still too small to accommodate the daily
shipments from Flanders. I wasn't interested in the Abbey; I
think ruins are overrated, particularly the sort with a few feet
of crumbling wall and all the rest but a heap of stones in the
grass. Netley Hospital has two wings left and a green tower.
It remains in use as a convalescent home. When it was built
in 1914 it had a special jetty at the end of the garden for the
boats bringing in the casualties. They were loaded into coal
trucks, Jack said, and shunted up the front-drive between
the rhododendron bushes. He said the wounded were so
numerous that they lay in rows in the corridors. We shook our
heads and looked sorrowful, but really it went in one ear and
out the other. It's all too long ago.

Beryl Bainbridge (1932–2010)
English Journey or the Road to Milton Keynes (1984)

Bedales School has left its alternative mark on a corner of Hampshire
as well as on the lives of its many pupils. It was created by the genius
of John Hayden Badley in 1893, as a corrective to the sporting and
classical life at Rugby School where he had been both a scholar and a
teacher. He believed that education should be a matter of Hand, Head
and Heart and at Bedales the children are encouraged to rise early to
bake bread for the school, and help at lambing time on the farm, as
well as drawing, acting, designing and academic work. Oswald Powell,
Badley's second master, reports that it was lightly spoken of in its early
days as the 'children of cranks taught by amateurs'. Over the years, it
attracted to the area a succession of thoughtful, creative people, both
as teachers and as parents. As can be seen from the following two

extracts, it suited some of its pupils better than others. Firstly, we hear from John Rothenstein (1901–92), who went on to be director of the Tate Gallery from 1938–64.

I was sent in the autumn term, 1912, to Bedales, which was in some respects a peculiar school, although its peculiarities are not those generally attributed to it. I do not remember why I was sent there...

Bedales is a co-educational school, the most successful of its kind in England...[It] first opened in 1893 in an old house on Bedales Hill, near Lindfield in Sussex, as a school for boys. Five years later four girls joined the sixty boys already there. In 1900 the school – by then numbering sixty-eight boys, seven girls and a staff of nine – was moved to an estate of some hundred and twenty acres by the village of Steep near Petersfield in Hampshire. Therefore at the time of my own entry something of the fervour and of the prejudices, too, engendered during the early years, were still strong among these older boys. The 'Early Christians', so to say, among them could be distinguished by certain outward signs: they affected sandals, and coats that looked as though they had been made at home or else in some remote fishing village, and they showed a predeliction for cold baths, a vegetable diet, for brown bread, and in season and out of it for fresh air, the colder the better. The outlook expressed by these outward signs was in politics Liberal or Socialist, but Socialist according to Morris rather than Marx. This was partly due to the fact that Bedales, however pronounced its departures from the traditional pattern, was very much a 'public school' and therefore very English in the cast of thought that prevailed there. Marx therefore would have repelled not only, as at other schools, on account of his 'foreignness', but even more as standing for something which at Bedales aroused peculiar antipathy, namely a dogmatic creed...

...the old 'activists' won recruits from time to time among their juniors, usually from boys and girls from the wealthier, more conventional homes, to whom the high idealism that existed at Bedales made a particular appeal. In spite of the influence of the 'activists' and the periodic adhesion to their number of these recruits, the general tendency of the school was in the direction of a closer approximation to the conditions that prevailed in other public schools. There was no abandoment of the founder's ideals, but they began to be given a more flexible interpretation; the carrot and the sandal were fast becoming anachronisms. From what I hear about development at Bedales since my own time, I understand that this tendency has grown even more pronounced. If Bedales has gone a long way to meet the world it has also, in a modest way, modified it. Ideas and practices which seemed evolutionary or eccentric at the time of its foundation have won wide acceptance, and to an appreciable degree as a result of Bedales' pioneering.

I was not a success at Bedales: I gained little in the course of my years there, and gave less. This was not chiefly due to defects in the school so much as the fact that it was not the right school for me nor I the right boy for it. When I arrived there its particular form of idealism was one which made no fresh appeal to me: I had already become familiar with it ... through my Hampstead environment. I trust that it will not be considered immodest if I say that I already possessed, in however rudimentary a form, some of the qualities which it was the mission of Bedales to implant. I was capable, for example, of forming independent opinions; I was fairly tolerant of the opinions of other people, fairly free from national or class prejudice, benevolently disposed towards my fellow men, ready to co-operate with them, and appreciative of fine craftsmanship. The possession of these qualities was not due to personal merit: it just so happened that they were qualities fairly common among those with whom I was brought up... Drawing – which I cultivated with ease, as well as some crafts and intellectually peripheral subjects, which were deemed to rank with such crucial subjects as science and languages – masked my ignorance of these. Whether the depths of my ignorance were suspected I do not know: what I do know is that I was never told that I was wasting my own time and the time of my teachers; and never warned that I would be wise to reflect and that unless I showed improvement I had better go elsewhere – preferably to a coach.

It would be wrong to suggest that my years at Bedales were wretched, but I was vaguely oppressed by a sense of something being fundamentally amiss – I had not the wit to see that the want of application on my own part and of critical firm direction on that of my teachers was making nonsense of my presence there. There were, on the contrary, many aspects of school life that I enjoyed. First my friends... Then there was the surrounding country, which we were encouraged to explore. In front, seawards, were the South Downs, the great smooth dome of Butser Hill – a calm presence always felt – their most prominent feature. Behind, a wooded hillside rose up steeply. The main school building itself, a great square stucco-face block, built in a species of suburban-Edwardian-institutional style, was far from beautiful, yet pleasant enough to live in. The adjacent Hall, where all public functions took place, from the very secular religious services...to variety shows staged by the boys and girls, was a fine place, built of oak and red brick, in the arts-and-crafts style with which at home in the Cotswolds I had already become familiar, with something of the look of an urbanised barn.

It may be considered singular, at least by those who do not know Bedales, that I do not include among the pleasures of life the presence of girls.

The girls at Bedales lived in conditions very different from those prevailing, for example, at co-educational American schools and universities. At such institutions girls are enrolled as a matter of course. At Bedales it was otherwise. Their presence was an audacious experiment, and the school authorities were under a particularly heavy responsibility towards the girls and their parents...That the authorities should have taken strong precautions against relationships that might have resulted in illegitimate births and other undesirable consequences was entirely understandable, but, speaking for myself, the safeguards imposed were destructive of almost all the pleasure that I might otherwise have taken in the proximity of the girls. I speak for myself only, because there was singularly little discussion among the boys about the girls, but I suspect that my own feelings were fairly widely shared. However justified such measures might have been, their effect, so far as I was concerned, was to make my relationship with girls constrained and uneasy, and it was with surprise that I discovered, during the holidays, that my relationships with girls from conventional schools, however strict, were by comparison natural and relaxed. But in our remote corner of Gloucestershire girls, or for that matter boys of my own age, were very few.

...It remains to say something of the remarkable man whose convictions brought Bedales into being: John Haden Badley. He was born in 1865, educated at Rugby and Cambridge, and came under the influence of progressive educationists such as Montessori and Frobel and of Fabian Socialism. He came to regard education as 'not concerned primarily with intellectual development...with the exercise of memory or reasoning powers, but the development of the creative intelligence...the formation of interests, purposes and ideals.'

John Rothenstein (1901–92)
Summer's Lease (1965)

And now Jocelyn Brooke, who confessed that 'not content with the English names [of flowers], I memorised many of the Latin and Greek ones as well. Some of these (at the age of 8) I conceitedly incorporated in a school essay... The Headmaster read the essay aloud to the school (no wonder I was unpopular)'. He continued as a botanist, wrote novels and published some eighteen books in his last twenty years.

At Bedales...on Saturday and Sunday afternoons we would set off on our bicycles – Mr Bickersteth (the biology master), myself, and one or two other enthusiasts – for Harting or Selborne, or over the downs towards Winchester, in search of some unfound rarity. And after the long torrid hours spent wading through marshes, or climbing over chalk-downs, we would arrive back, sweating, our vascula crammed with specimens. Perhaps we had found the Frog Orchid on Wardown, or the Violet Helleborine on Selborne Hanger; or I had seen sundew or bog asphodel for the first time in Woolmer Forest. It was seldom that the vasculum didn't contain something which made the journey worth-while and exciting. Arriving back at school, we would bathe, then eat an enormous tea; and happiness would blossom in my mind like some brilliant, alien flower which has established itself in homely surroundings, where its splendour is still a source of surprise, almost of suspicion. It was as though one should suddenly come upon the Military Orchid on a waste patch in some dingy suburb, among Mugwort and Goosefoot and all the squalid weeds bred by indifference and neglect.

After tea, I would return to the Lab., to put our specimens in water, and to gloat, once again, on the fabulous lineaments of the military and the lizard.

Jocelyn Brooke (1908–66)
The Military Orchid (1948)

Edward Thomas came here in 1906 so that his son Merfyn could go to Bedales. To defray the costs his wife, Helen, taught at the school. It was here that Thomas became a poet, and many of his poems are about places which can be identified around the village of Steep. Here it is 'The pub with no name', whose enigmatic empty sign is explained.

Up in the Wind

...

Once on a time 'tis plain that 'The White Horse'
Stood merely on the border of waste
Where horse and cart picked its own course afresh.
On all sides then, as now, paths ran to the inn;
And now a farm-track takes you from a gate.
Two roads cross, and not a house in sight
Except 'The White Horse' in this clump of beeches.
It hides from either road, a field's breadth back;
And it's the trees you see, and not the house,
Both near and far, when the clump's the highest thing
And homely, too, upon a far horizon
To one that knows there is an inn within.

... 'Did you ever see
Our signboard?' No. The post and empty frame
I knew. Without them I could not have guessed
The low grey house and its one stack under trees
Was not a hermitage but a public-house.
'But can that empty frame be any use?
Now I should like to see a good white horse
Swing there, a really beautiful white horse,

Galloping one side, being painted on the other.'
'But would you like to hear it swing all night
And all day? All I ever had to thank
The wind for was blowing the sign down.
Time after time it blew down and I could sleep.
At last they fixed it, and it took a thief
To move it, and we've never had another:
It's lying at the bottom of our pond.'

Edward Thomas (1878–1917)

Eleanor Farjeon, the writer and children's author, became a very close friend of the poet, and his wife Helen, a friendship which really began when the Thomases lent her their house in Froxfield, Wick Green, one Easter.

Eleanor fell deeply in love with Edward, who was drawn to her knowledge and love of literature, her intelligence and wit. She became his willing unpaid typist and he relied on her for assistance for the rest of his life, until his death in the trenches in 1917. She was horrified to discover that her mother had feared they were having an affair.

... It stood, with his little study in the garden, on the ridge above the Leg o' Mutton Hill where the Sarsen stone stands now that is his monument.

'May we ask some friends?' we enquired.

'Ask whom you like and do what you like in the house,' said Edward, and then in his gravest tone, 'only be careful not to dance the floors down.'

We did not know him well enough then to suspect his gravity; and visualising some sort of jerry-built cottage, we promised to be particularly careful.

Bertie and I had never had such a chance to make free before, to invite a party to a house of our own. We had no idea of its size, but we knew that the Thomas family numbered five, and that many of our friends were hardened campers. We immediately inaugurated a comprehensive house-party: the Corders, the Baxes, the Antoniettis, Myra, Godwin and Rosalind, and her sister Joan Thornycroft, whom we knew less well than Rosalind, were among the invited, and others I can't remember. They were asked indiscriminately for the whole

251

Easter week-end, or as much of it as they could manage. We had no time to get replies from everybody, but before I and Paul Corder (the vanguard) took train for Petersfield, we knew that only Olga of the Antoniettis would presently join us, and that Clifford and Dolly Corder had fallen out of the party. Our knapsacks heavy with food, we began the long trek from the station to Steep, and thence to the top of Stonor Hill, ignorant of how many were coming, or for how long, or how many beds there were to accommodate them. The country was entirely unknown to us. Leaving Steep behind we began to mount, and the beechen beauty of Stonor hanger took our breath away; so, when we reached the summit, did the house. It had been built for the Thomases by the craftsman Geoffrey Lupton, an Old Bedalian (the Thomas children were young Bedalians). I can't better Robert Eckert's description of the place in his life of Edward. Lupton, a disciple of William Morris, had 'planned to build the house almost entirely by hand, from the oak, to be seasoned, sawed, and planed near by, to the bricks, and the great nails, hinges, and hasps to be forged in the village. Native oak planks were to be used for the floor, native stone for the thresholds. He suggested the house should be long and low, facing south, with the living-room to the east, and with windows on all sides except the north.' The house was built on ground owned by Lupton, not far from his own house 'at the edge of a plateau, overlooking a deep and densely wooded coomb, reached by a path that wound beside a stream up through the hanger. On top, 400 feet above the sea, was a wide view of the South Downs.' How many times I was to climb that glorious hanger, with Baba shuffling her feet among the beechmast, and hear Edward's 'Coo-ee!', at the end of his day's work, ring across the coomb from his study, while ours rang back lustily, I could not foresee. Dazed with delight, I wound upwards for the first time under the young beech-leaves, to the house at the top which Paul might have built himself. For he, a musician like his father, was also a disciple of the Morris way of life, a splendid carpenter, a metal-worker, and a weaver of stuffs. Dance the floors down indeed! We had our first laugh, unpacked our provision, took stock of the beds, and waited for Bertie, Myra, and Olga to join us in the evening. We three girls shared the biggest bedroom, the boys took the children's rooms; in the five succeeding days these became dormitories. Friends appeared and disappeared, some for the whole time, some for a night or two. Lovely Joan Thornycroft, on a walking-tour with a friend, arrived one evening, and next day vanished again. When beds gave out our newcomers slept on couches or the floor. It was soon plain that our food-stocks wouldn't last; on Saturday we raided the local shop for its entire supplies of bread and fruit and groceries. We cooked in shifts, and ate at random. Edith, Helen Thomas's daily help from the village, washed up and made beds in a state of continuous giggle.

We fell in love with the painting of a charming little girl – one of Edward's children we presumed. We walked and talked, and ransacked the bookshelves for indiscriminate reading... Godwin and Rosalind joined us. Arnold has come...

Myra has retired to a sunny nook outside with a volume of Lafcadio Hearn, and is heard wailing, 'I can't bear it, I can't bear it!' We rush to her aid, and find her in semi-hysteria – 'No! if it happens again I can't bear it!' Bertie snatches the book from her limp hand and insists on reading aloud a ghastly incident about a lonely valley inhabited by evil things with faces as bald as eggs: 'A timid traveller, crossing the haunted valley by night, sees a woman weeping with her face in her hands. He entreats her to tell him what her trouble is, she removes her hands from her face, and is featureless – as bald as an egg. Shrieking with fear he flies, trying to find a way out of the horrible place – he meets a travelling tinker who asks him roughly what's the matter with him – he babbles the story – 'and, oh sir! The woman's face was as bald as an egg!' 'Hey! Was it anything like this?' The tinker wipes his face with his hand from forehead to chin, and presents to the gibbering traveller a face as bald as...Stop! I can't bear it, wails Myra. At the denouement we are all hysterical, and Myra completely collapsed...For some time afterwards –'Hey! Was it anything like this?' was a password among us.

Paul storms in from a walk, announcing indignantly that high on the tallest pine-tree in the Stonor gorge hangs a sign-board warning trespassers of prosecution. His indignation takes fire, sentence is pronounced on the notice-board – after lunch it shall be cut down! We flock to the turn on the road from which it is visible, high out of reach. Bertie, Paul, and Godwin scramble down to the base of the tree in the coomb.

Thirty foot of bare pine-trunk challenges them. Paul makes the first attempt, slides down defeated after a very few feet, and is followed by Bertie, who gets only a little higher. Last, Godwin clasps the trunk with his mighty arms and knees, scales the tree-trunk like a giant monkey on a stick, panting heavily as he nears his goal, cheered by the girls looking down from the upper road – he arrives, hangs on by one arm in mid-air, wrenches off the offending board, and slides down again! We bear the trophy home triumphantly, chop it up, and after tea make a bonfire of it. May the fumes suffocate Squire Trevor-Battye, arch-enemy of ancient Rights of Way...

Godwin – all of us inert in the afternoon (why do I remember this pointless moment so distinctly?) – stirs, stretches, and yawns amiably, 'Let's go to the end of the ridge and sneer at Harry Roberts's horses'. We troop obediently after him, from some high point stare across some distant valley, sneer at the unseen horses of a man we don't know, troop back again, and relapse into inertia... Arnold Bax, one of our earliest comers and longest stayers, had arrived straight from Majorca, where he and Clifford with Gustav Holst and Balfour Gardiner had been holiday-making. He brought with him a jet-black cigar of great length and girth, resembling a lumpy stick of liquorice. Installed on the mantelpiece, it became our aim to get it smoked before we left. The men took turns at it several times a day. When Paul paled and succumbed, when Bertie, Arnold, and even Godwin had cried enough, Olga and I weighed in with a few puffs; but the cigar from Majorca defeated us in the end. I think it was left on the mantelpiece as a memento.

One by one the visitors faded away. With Edith's help we left things orderly, and in May Edward wrote from Wick Green the only letter beginning 'My dear Miss Farjeon'.

My dear Miss Farjeon,

I have just got home after a rather tiring time of work in London, and feel I must write and say what a pleasant feeling you have left here. My wife and I are grateful for it, and so is Edith. We all 3 want you to come again...

Eleanor Farjeon (1881–1965)
Edward Thomas: The Last Four Years (1958)

And here is one of Thomas's last poems, conjuring up the experience of living at Wick Green, on the edge of the beech hanger, from which they had had to move in 1913 because the rent was too much.

Wind and Mist

They met inside the gateway that gives the view,
A hollow land as vast as heaven. 'It is
A pleasant day, sir.' 'A very pleasant day.'
'And what a view here! If you like angled fields
Of grass and grain bounded by oak and thorn,
Here is a league. Had we with Germany
To play upon this board it could not be
More dear than April has made it with a smile.
The fields beyond that league close in together
And merge, even as our days into the past,
Into one wood that has a shining pane
Of water. Then the hills of the horizon–
That is how I should make hills had I to show
One who would never see them what hills were like,'
'Yes. Sixty miles of South Downs at one glance.
Sometimes a man feels proud of them, as if
He had just created them with one mighty thought.'
'That house, though modern, could not be better planned
For its position. I never liked a new
House better. Could you tell me who lives in it?'
'No one.' 'Ah – and I was peopling all
Those windows on the south with happy eyes,
The terrace under them with happy feet;
Girls–' 'Sir, I know. I know. I have seen that house
Through mist look lovely as a castle in Spain,
And airier. I have thought: " 'Twere happy there
To live." And I have laughed at that
Because I lived there then.' 'Extraordinary.'
'Yes, with my furniture and family
Still in it, I, knowing every nook of it
And loving none, and in fact hating it.'
'Dear me! How could that be? But pardon me.'
'No offence. Doubtless the house was not to blame,
But the eye watching from those windows saw,

255

Many a day, day after day, mist – mist
Like chaos surging back – and felt itself
Alone in all the world, marooned alone.
We lived in clouds, on the cliff's edge almost
(You see), and if clouds went, the visible earth
Lay too far off beneath and like a cloud.
I did not know it was the earth I loved
Until I tried to live there in the clouds
And the earth turned to cloud.'
'You had a garden
Of flint and clay, too.' 'True; that was real enough.
The flint was the one crop that never failed.
The clay first broke my heart, and then my back;
And the back heals not. There were other things
Real, too. In that room at the gable a child
Was born while the wind chilled a summer dawn:
Never looked grey mind on a greyer one
Than when the child's cry broke above the groans.'
'I hope they were both spared.' 'They were. Oh yes!
But flint and stone and childbirth were too real
For this cloud-castle. I had forgot the wind.
Pray do not let me get on to the wind.
You would not understand about the wind.
It is my subject, and compared with me
Those who have always lived on the firm ground
Are quite unreal in this matter of the wind.
There were whole days and nights when the wind and I
Between us shared the world, and the wind ruled
And I obeyed it and forgot the mist.
My past and the past of the world were in the wind.
Now you may say that though you understand
And feel for me, and so on, you yourself
Would find it different. You are all like that
If once you stand here free from wind and mist.
You would believe the house-agent's young man
Who gives no heed to anything I say.
Good morning. But one word. I want to admit
That I would try the house once more, if I could;
As I should like to try being young again.'

Edward Thomas (1878–1917)

Here is a small selection of writings on Hampshire's larger houses.

Between Winchester and Southampton, the Reverend John Keble, writing in 1858, describes how:

Cranbury Park is on a hill, intersected by various springs, and where the peaty ground soon gives way to gravel. The house, a large red brick one, built round a court, so that it looks low in proportion to its width, is on the level ground at the top, flat as it fronts to the south, but in the rear descending rapidly. In fact, on that side the grounds have the air of cresting the hill, and there is a group of exceedingly tall pine-trees which are a land-mark of the country on all sides, though the tallest of them was blown down a few years ago. Near them is one of the old-fashioned orangeries, with a great deal of wall and very little glass, and near it stands the sundial of Newtonian fame.

Cranbury was once the home of Sir Isaac Newton, who devised and calculated the sundial which still exists.

And here Philip Guedalla, biographer of the nineteenth-century Prime Minister Lord Palmerston, gives us a glimpse of Palmerston's birth and early life at Broadlands, a great classical house of the late eighteenth century near Romsey.

On an autumn day in 1784 the Viscount had his heir... they named the baby Henry John – Henry after his father, and John as pure flight of fancy. There was a christening Ball, and the Mara came down from the Opera to sing at a concert for them in her thin voice. After that the world went on much as before... The blind procession of the Eighteenth Century went slowly on ...and the child in Hampshire began to grow behind the far-too-Grecian portion of Broadlands, although one visitor found him a trifle 'washy'. The little town beyond the gates enjoyed the interminable leisure of a small country market and the park was majestic with that irregular interruption of green grass with large English trees, which indicates a stately dedication to complete uselessness...

Whilst a hard winter still delayed the hot summer of 1789, Lady Palmerston had put her Viscount's heir into breeches.

The boy was above four years old, 'quite stout, with a fine high colour'; and he came down to dessert now in the solemn dining-room at Broadlands, where the side-board that lived so kindly in Sir Joshua's memory stood in its long recess between the two grave urns on their pedestals. The deep drawing-room, where his mother sat in a soft gleam of satinwood, was still sacred; and he rarely kept still enough to watch the visitors as they commented with polite ecstasy upon 'Mr Adams's' (or was it Mr Kent's) gingerbread and snippets of embroidery, and medallions by the accomplished Kauffman looked down on them from the bright gilt of the ceiling. The boy was growing; and his first scrawls strayed cheerfully across the lines they ruled for him. There were two little sisters and a small brother now, and a black pony with an alarming reputation...

When the boy was six, with interests that (to judge from his earliest letters) were mainly dental, his papa went on his travels again and ventured his person on French territory...

He came back to find his country slightly disturbed by the proximity of France... Lord Palmerston's neighbours at Southampton and Lymington took the loyal fever and warranted by their votes that the Revolution should never come upstream to Broadlands, where the children were still playing with the black pony under the great trees. His heir, at seven, corresponded profusely with his mother, although a fastidious eye at home once judged his letters too bad to send. His zeal for correspondence even impelled a formal acceptance of her invitation 'to goble up mince-pyes or whatever else there is for dinner' on Christmas Day, addressed to 'Viscountess Palmerston in her dressing room upstairs, Broadlands', and sealed in glorious, if slightly grubby, emulation of a grown-up seal...

In the next year Lord Palmerston took the road for Italy. This time he carried his family with him; and his eldest son retained a loving memory of cheap and plentiful oranges and of miracles of *charcuterie* at Bologna, which put all English sausages to shame. At nine the boy was touring on the Continent with an Italian master. They fetched a wide circuit into Switzerland by way of Munich; and from Berne he sent the anxious intelligence that a double tooth had lost its 'stoping'. In the next year he was home again at Broadlands in charge of his Italian and a French governess, whose ministrations soon bore fruit in terrifying letters all in French and signed '*Henri Temple*'. The pony pawed; sometimes a pony phaeton rolled behind; and the boy kept house for his little sisters with Signor Gaetano and Madamoiselle.

Philip Guedalla (1889–1944)
Palmerston (1926)

From 1936–1973, James Lees-Milne worked for the National Trust. After being invalided out of the army in 1941, he rejoined the National Trust as 'an unqualified historic buildings secretary'. At that time the Trust had half-a-dozen historic houses open to the public, but the social changes which the war produced encouraged many country-house owners to pass responsibility for their maintenance to the Trust. As secretary he combined 'hard labour and sheer fun', travelling and visiting owners of large, cold, emptied mansions, reduced by the state of the country. Thanks to his extensive diaries, which are both witty and disarmingly honest, we have a prolific account of these visits.

December 16 1944
...I continued to Roche Old Court, one mile off the Andover-Salisbury road, close to the Pheasant Inn. The little manor house, fourteen rooms in all, is of red brick with stone dressings. Chettle says the date is circa 1620 because the brick is in English bond. In front of it are an old brick wall and several old farmbuildings, including a tithe barn of timber post construction, circa 1400. The house inside has much early plain wainscoting, and stairs of William and Mary period. The owner, Major Trevor Cox, M.P., was at Eton with me. Was at Hill's house. Says he remembers me. I vaguely remember him. Eton is an unfailing bond between those who were educated there, and an irritation to those who were not. He is not going bald like me, but grey about the whiskers.

...

I arrived at the Vyne at 5.30. Mrs Chute, grey-haired, once doubtless a pretty woman, now like a superannuated school-girl, received me. As school-girls pick shyly at their pinafores, so she picked at her skirt. We had tea in the Henry VIII linenfold panelled parlour. He, Charles Chute, a brother of Jackie Chute,

259

came in later. He is tall and better looking than his brother, and lacks any charm whatever. Highly educated, a scholar at Eton, winner of several firsts, he is pedagogic although not a schoolmaster. Rather abrupt, contradictory and snubbing. I did not care for either – much. He hates Horace Walpole, and has little use for his own forebear, John Chute, Horace's friend. Thinks them both, and me too I have little doubt, 'scugs'.

Sunday, 17th December
During the night it poured with rain. Water dripped through my bedroom ceiling, so I put my sponge bowl to catch the drips. Before breakfast, at 8.45 precisely, a sort of school bell rang, and we all trooped into the chapel for prayers, that is to say, the Chutes, I, the headmaster and mistresses of the school billeted here – the boys are now on holiday – the matron, followed by five servant girls in uniform. Mr Chute read the prayers, and the schoolmaster alone read the responses in so loud and aggressive a voice that I guessed he hated him. A sort of sparring match ensued. However it was all over in ten minutes. I liked it, but it is the first time I have ever attended Protestant prayers in a country house. The schoolmaster, rather sulky and surly, and the mistresses, singularly dreary, attend every meal. The mistresses exhale a forced, bumbling bonhomie. There is one perky little Irish woman, at whose lamentable jests it is customary to roar. I joined in the chorus out of politeness.

The Vyne is a very wonderful house. Yet I was a trifle disappointed. The rooms are awfully dark. The John Chute staircase, though a tour-de-force, is too narrow to be magnificent. The early Renaissance panelling is of great historical importance, yet ugly. The Webb fire-places look out of place, and the Webb portico is top-heavy. It does not belong to the façade, upon which it has been stuck like a postage stamp upon a piece of string. Mr Chute conducted me through practically every room. The Chapel is superb, with traces of early Renaissance in the friezes of the stall canopies, stained glass and coloured tiles.When I left, worn down by the Chutes, I decided I hated country houses and never wished to see another. I drove at 4.15 to Bramley Church and looked at the fine Banks monument there, which is almost as good as the superb Chaloner Chute one at the Vyne. Yes, I think the Chutes were Parliamentarians which accounts for their puritanism today. Then to Stratfield Saye. Found Gerry and his very handsome son and daughter-in-law (to whom I was introduced, titles and all mentioned by Gerry) cutting branches and clearing the shrubbery at the conservatory side of the house. A vast improvement has already been made. I can think of no house needing improvements that has fallen into better hands. We had tea in the dining-room, a beautiful room with a ceiling taken from Wood's book on Palmyra. From the window the landscape with water is just like the Vyne's.

James Lees-Milne (1908–97)
Prophesying Peace: Diaries 1944–45

Saturday, 5th October 1946
...I motored Christopher home to Froyle and stayed the night with him and Betty. It was fun. She is gay as a cricket, brisk and noisy. Him I got to understand for the first time. He is not censorious or grim as I previously thought, but delightful, with a sardonic humour. How quickly one reverses one's unfavourable opinion of people when one gets to know them. They are leaving their cottage-like house, with its very good furniture, after seven years' stay, for Scotney Castle.

Sunday, 6th October
Motored to Rotherfield Park this morning: Reptonish (actually by Parkinson) house, built about 1820, but added to in the same fashion by the Scott family throughout the last century. It has octagonal towers and pinnacled turrets, a Windsor Castle round tower in stone and flint, a red brick square tower with cupola, and presents a romantic, Germanic air. The park, sloping towards the main road, is an admirable specimen of picturesque layout. There are beech avenues to the north of the house in the form of a cross, dating from the eighteenth century. The Gerald Cokes were lunching.We motored to tea at Stratfield Saye... The fire seems to have caused but little damage. The house, full of fascinating and historic treasures, is being rearranged with Gerry's unerring taste.

11th January 1947

Motored to stay with Maud Russell at Mottisfont [Abbey]. Lunched en route at Winchester and went round the City Mill, our property, a dull little affair. Then to the glorious Cathedral. Particularly admired the fifteenth-century tombs of Cardinal Beaufort and William Wykeham, with fine, soaring pinnacles of stonework. This is a marvellous century for architecture, notably the nave here. What could be greater than this aspirant, congruous structure, all of a piece? Pouring with rain all day. Stopped at Sparsholt to look at Vaine Cottages, both extremely unimportant. The Trust does own some low-grade properties...

Sunday, 12th January

(Mottisfont) At first glance this is a beautiful old house of mellow red brick, the south front having been made symmetrical in George II's reign. The river Test running close beside it, swiftly. A pretty Georgian stable block to the west. Verdant lawns and massive old trees striding to the water's edge. Yet it is not a wholly satisfactory house and is moreover spooky. Built upon and out of the remains of a priory, the house comprises the nave of the church, the north nave wall wholly surviving. This makes me feel slightly uncomfortable. Maud Russell said that in altering floors they dug up several skeletons and reinterred them. (This she whispered to me softly in French while we were looking at a piscine in the larder in the cook's presence.) There are only three living rooms of any size in spite of Mottisfont being a large house. The dining-room is Palladian. The south-east drawing-room has a pretty rococo frieze, now picked out in gold. Mrs R ripped out the large hall – it too was Palladian, I see from old photographs – and Rex Whistler perpetrated a ridiculous and flimsy Gothick chiaroscuro trompe-l'oeil. It is too slight and too pretty. Mrs R has papered all the staircases and a long landing on the first floor in dull marble, rather sombre, but suitable. A curious house because the living-rooms are all on the first floor, and the offices on the ground floor, which is not a basement however.

This morning I walked through the village with Mr Baker and along the mown grass by the river. He talked of Herbert Baker, no relation, and of Lutyens, both of whom were his friends, chiefly Lutyens. He admitted that Lutyens was always vitriolic about Baker, and Baker Christian-like and charitable about Lutyens. The furniture in the house is all desirable but gives the impression of having been collected in a hurry. The decoration too seems unfinished. The house has the sparse tidiness of a newcomer, not the cluttered untidiness of accumulated centuries.

James Lees-Milne (1908–97)
Caves of Ice: Diaries 1946-7

On the western edge of Hampshire near Andover, Weyhill lies at the crossroads of many ancient tracks. As well as old drovers' roads, the Harrow Way, which was used to move tin from the mines in Cornwall and gold from Ireland, crossed Weyhill on its way to the ports in Kent and thence to Europe. Trade had been carried on here even before the Normans arrived.

Weyhill was famous in the past for its fair, second only to that of Winchester. Piers Plowman knows it in the later C14, Defoe mentions it, Cobbett still writes of it in 1822 and Hardy fictionalises it in *The Mayor of Casterbridge*.

Nikolaus Pevsner (1903–83)
Buildings of England: Hampshire (1967)

By the time William Cobbett visited in the early nineteenth century this was one of the largest fairs in the country, with over 100,000 sheep a day, large numbers of pigs, horses and cattle being traded. The hop fair saw the Farnham hop growers arriving in mass, travelling via Alton and joining up with growers from Bentley, Binstead and Froyle. There was a cheese fair too, and it was also the place for hiring skilled and unskilled workers.

By 1870 the fair had dwindled.

Piers Plowman discusses trading there in the fourteenth century.

Leaf by leaf – I learned lying,
And wily weighing – was my first lesson.
To Weyhill and Winchester – I went in Fair-time

With all manner of merchandise – as my master bade me.
Unless the grace of guile – had gone with my dealing
The stuff had lain seven years unsold – so God help me!
Then I practised my primer – in a party of drapers,
And learned to stretch the selvege – so that it looked longer.
With striped silks – I studied a lesson.
I pierced them with a packneedle – and plaited them together,
And put them in a press – and pinned them fast,
Till ten yards or twelve – told thirteen in total.

William Langland (1330?–1400?)
from *The Vision of Piers Plowman* (c1365)

Here William Cobbett is visiting the fair after the 'Panic of 1825', a stock market crash that started in the Bank of England, arising in part out of speculative investments in Latin America. He has the 'loan-mongers', bankers like Alexander Baring, a Hampshire man, firmly in his sights for causing such misery among the decent ordinary farmers.

Wednesday, 11 October 1826
When quarters are good you are apt to lurk in them; but really it was so wet that we could not get away from Burghclere till Monday evening. Being here, there were many reasons for our going to the great fair at Weyhill, which began yesterday, and, indeed, the day before at Appleshaw. These two days are allotted for the selling of sheep only, though the horse-fair begins on the 10th. To Appleshaw they bring nothing but those fine curled-horned and long-tailed ewes, which bring the house-lambs and the early Easter lambs; and these, which, to my taste, are the finest and most beautiful animals of the sheep kind, come exclusively out of Dorsetshire and out of the part of Somersetshire bordering on that county.

To Weyhill, which is a village of half a dozen houses on a down just above Appleshaw, they bring from the down-farms in Wiltshire and Hampshire, where they are bred, the South Down sheep; ewes to go away into the pasture and turnip countries to have lambs, wethers to be fatted and killed, and lambs (nine months old) to be kept to be sheep. At both fairs there is supposed to be about two hundred thousand sheep. It was of some consequence to ascertain how the price of these had been affected by 'late panic,' which ended the respite of 1822; or by the 'plethora of money' as loan-man Baring called it. I can assure this political doctor, that there was no such 'plethora' at Weyhill yesterday, where, while I viewed the long faces of the farmers, while I saw consequences of ruin painted on their countenances, I could not help saying to myself, 'the loan-mongers think they are cunning; but, by –, they will never escape the ultimate consequences of this horrible ruin!' The prices, take them on a fair average, were, at both fairs, just about one-half what they were last year.

...The sales of sheep, at this one fair (including Appleshaw), must have amounted, this year, to a hundred and twenty or thirty thousand pounds less than last year! Stick a pin there, master 'Prosperity Robinson,' and turn back to it again anon! Then came the horses; not equal in amount to the sheep, but of great amount. Then comes the cheese, a very great article; and it will have a falling off, if you take quantity into view, in a still greater proportion. The hops being a monstrous crop their price is nothing to judge by. But all is fallen. Even corn, though, in many parts, all but the wheat and rye have totally failed...

William Cobbett
Rural Rides

It is at Weydon (Weyhill) Fair that the drunken events which precipitate the action in Thomas Hardy's 1886 novel, *Mayor of Casterbridge,* take place.

...That the man and woman were husband and wife, and the parents of the girl in arms, there could be little doubt. No other than such relationship would have accounted for the atmosphere of stale familiarity which the trio carried along with them like a nimbus as they moved down the road.

The wife mostly kept her eyes fixed ahead, though with little interest – the scene for that matter being one that might have been matched at almost any spot in any county in England at this time of the year; a road neither straight nor crooked, neither level nor hilly, bordered by hedges, trees and other vegetation, which had entered the blackened-green stage of colour that the doomed leaves pass through on their way to dingy, and yellow, and red. The grassy margin of the bank, and the nearest hedgerow boughs, were powdered by the dust that had been stirred over them by hasty vehicles, the same dust as it lay on the road deadening their footfalls like a carpet; and this, with the aforesaid total absence of conversation, allowed every extraneous sound to be heard.

For a long time there was none, beyond the voice of a weak bird singing a trite old evening song that might doubtless have been heard on the hill at the same hour, and with the self-same trills, quavers, and breves, at any sunset of that season for centuries untold. But as they approached the village sundry distant shouts and rattles reached their ears from some elevated spot in that direction, as yet screened from view by foliage. When the outlying houses of Weydon-Priors could just be descried, the family group was met by a turnip-hoer with this hoe on his shoulder, and his dinner-bag suspended from it.

Henchard, in a drunken state, sells his wife to a stranger and now refreshed, departs Weydon Fair.

... He stood up, found that he was in fairly good condition for progress, unencumbered. Next he shouldered his tool basket, and found he could carry it. Then lifting the tent door he emerged into the open air. Here the man looked around with gloomy curiosity. The freshness of the September morning inspired and braced him as he stood. He and his family had been weary when they arrived the night before, and they had observed but little of the place; so that he now beheld it as a new thing. It exhibited itself as the top of an open down, bounded on one extreme by a plantation, and approached by a winding road. At the bottom stood the village which lent its name to the upland, and the annual fair that was held thereon. The spot stretched downward into valleys, and onward to other uplands, dotted with barrows, and trenched with the remains of prehistoric forts. The whole scene lay under the rays of a newly risen sun, which had not as yet dried a single blade of the heavily dewed grass, whereon the shadows of the yellow and red vans were projected far away, those thrown by the felloe of each wheel being elongated in shape to the orbit of a comet. All the gypsies and showmen who had remained on the ground lay snug within their carts and tents, or wrapped in horse-cloths under them, and were silent and still as death, with the exception of an occasional snore that revealed their presence. But the Seven Sleepers had a dog; and dogs of the mysterious breeds that vagrants own, that are as much like cats as dogs, and as much like foxes as cats, also lay about here. A little one started up under one of the carts, barked as a matter of principle, and quickly lay down again. He was the only positive spectator of the hay-trusser's exit from Weydon Fair-field.

Twenty years have passed and the wife he sold returns to Weyhill in search of Henchard, her former husband.

They walked with joined hands, and it could be perceived that this was the act of simple affection. The daughter carried in her outer hand a withy basket of old-fashioned make; the mother a blue bundle, which contrasted oddly with her black stuff gown.

Reaching the outskirts of the village, they pursued the same track as formerly, and ascended to the fair. Here, too, it was evident that the years had told. Certain mechanical improvements might have been noticed in the roundabouts and highfliers, machines for testing rustic strength and weight, and in erections devoted to shooting for nuts. But the real business of the fair had considerably dwindled. The new periodical great markets of neighbouring towns were beginning to interfere seriously with the trade carried on here for centuries. The pens for sheep, the tie-ropes for horses, were about half as long as they had been. The stalls of tailors, hosiers, coopers, linen-drapers, and other such trades had almost disappeared, and the vehicles were far less numerous. The mother and daughter threaded the crowd for some little distance, and then stood still.

The wife, now 'widowed', will find her former husband Mayor of Casterbridge.

Thomas Hardy (1848–1921)
Mayor of Casterbridge (1886)

Chapter 6
Chalk Streams and Cricketers

There are the most beautiful streams about I ever saw – full
of Trout.

John Keats (1795-1821)
Letter to Fanny Brawne from Winchester, August 1819

More than three quarters of all the world's chalk streams, a unique
ecosystem which is ideal for dry-fly fishing, are to be found in England,
with arguably the finest in Hampshire itself. Amongst fishermen the
reputation of the Test and the Itchen rivers is superb, and despite
the competing needs of water companies, who are always pushing to
extract the water from the chalky aquifer for the big cities on the coast,
and the threat from agricultural pollution, the rivers are still teeming
with fish – in particular trout. The ultimate sport is the hard-to-catch
wild brown trout.

Often wide and always fairly shallow, these rivers flow over pale
flinty gravel and are largely crystal clear because of their lack of clay and
silt. Fish are visible and carefully stalked by fishermen, who minimise
their presence and attempt to present the fish with a tempting fly by
means of a cast from afar.

For those without the hunting instinct or the desire, an afternoon
sitting by a chalk stream is a chance to enter a different, watery world.
Whether listening to the purling water, watching out for otters and
water voles, kingfishers, herons and egrets, or staring into the depths
– where caddisflies and minnows, miller's thumbs and sticklebacks go
about their busy lives – the echoes of *Jeremy Fisher* and *The Wind in the
Willows* are never far away.

On dry ground, country sportsmen have hunted the usual
astonishing variety of animals with guns and dogs, but unique to the
county is Hambledon Cricket Club, one of the world's oldest and known

as 'the cradle of cricket'. The HCC was the ruling body for the game in the mid-eighteenth century, handing over to the MCC in 1787, and it still plays on the same downland pitch it did then, on Ridge Meadow. Back then, the tiny village of Hambledon fielded a team which beat the England XI more often than they lost to it. The county also gave England one of cricket's most resonant and poetic voices, that of John Arlott, longtime commentator for the BBC's Test Match Special.

...

At the little village of Totton, the first on the way, we crossed the clear-flowing and troutful Test – grown into quite a river there – by two stone bridges, one old and gray, the other comparatively modern. The view from this spot looking up the valley is very charming. From the reedy river-side to the gently sloping hills stretch forth level luxuriant meadows of a rich restful green. Here and there in these we noticed the meek-eyed cattle were standing lazily about looking half asleep, just slowly and methodically whisking their tails now and then to keep the flies off, a very picture of dreamy contentment. The dominant note of the prospect was perfect tranquillity – a tranquillity that infused itself somehow into us, and causing us to loiter there indulging in general slothfulness; it is a good thing to be slothful sometimes in this eager world.

James John Hissey
On Southern English Roads (1846)

First published in 1676 in its complete version, *The Compleat Angler* is one of the most famous books on fishing, and was compiled over the lifetime of its author, a devoted fisherman. Izaak Walton, born in Stafford, was a draper and farmer whose love of fishing made him many friends all over the country, a number whose biographies he wrote – including the poet John Donne. Though he spent much of his fishing life in Staffordshire, he lived his last years in Hampshire, died in his daughter's house in Winchester and was buried in the cathedral.

Hampshire exceeds all England for swift, shallow, clear, pleasant brooks and stores of trouts...there are also, in divers rivers, especially that relate to or be near to the sea (as Winchester, or the Thames about Windsor) a little trout called Samlet or Skegger Trout (in both of which places I have caught twenty or forty at a standing) that will bite as fast and as freely as Minnows: these be by some taken to be young Salmons, but in those waters they never grow to be bigger than a herring.

Izaak Walton (1594–1683)
The Compleat Angler (1653)

Stockbridge is the most famous of the world's fisheries. Its repute rests on portly and perspicacious trout, which have fatter bodies, and cooler heads than any other known fish: on its lovely succession of deeps and shallows, racing rapids and swinging stretches, all as though arranged to give the dry fly man every variety of shot: and in the art with which nature has been assisted and seconded in this fine fishery. I do not intend to give that dullest thing in the world, a description of the water, meaningless to those that have not seen it, and inadequate to those who have. The very names of the different reaches seem to tell their own story. They have a classical ring about them: Sheepbridge, Maschine Shallow, the Black Lake, North Head – is it fancy which makes me think that such words would convey an essence of sport, even to one who cared nothing for fishing. Surely not: they stir the heart, just as whether we know them or not, and whether they denote our special pursuit or one of which we think little, we cannot hear unmoved such names as Belvoir or the Black Mount or Cloutsham or Sprouston Dub or Broomhead.

John Waller Hills (1867–1928)
Summer on the Test (1921)

With the Itchen flowing beneath the walls of the college, many a Wykehamist has fallen for the charms of fly-fishing as an escape from the regimented life of a shoolboy. Here, Sir Edward Grey, future Foreign Secretary, whose love of the Itchen lasted a lifetime, describes the beginnings of his passion. Even at the height of the First World War, Grey would often leave the House of Commons, take the train to Winchester, and walk to his cottage on the banks of the river at Itchen Abbas.

There must have been about a fortnight of the trout fishing season left when I first went to Winchester in September 1876, but I was not then in a position to take advantage of it. In these weeks I did not even think of fishing; everything about me was so strange; but there were not really any hardships, and as the sense of strangeness wore away, as knowledge came of what might and what might not be done without offending against customs and unwritten laws of opinion, I soon began to rejoice in the comparative freedom of a larger world, in the greater scope of work and games, in the anticipation of all that was before me. I made many plans during the winter for the opening of the next fishing season. The trout could be watched in the Itchen much more easily than in northern streams; they were there before our eyes. On mild autumn days we could watch them feeding, and numbers of them were larger than any I had ever hooked. Warnings were given abundantly that these trout were not to be caught easily, that with few exceptions no one at school ever had caught any: the traditions were of general failure to which there had been one or two remarkable exceptions, but even in naming these, hints were not wanting that it was very unlikely that any one would succeed again. Nevertheless the trout were there plain to be seen, taking flies, and nothing but experience could have destroyed my hopes or confidence. So on the opening day of the season, at the beginning of March, I hurried as soon as possible into the water meadows. Surely no one ever fished the Itchen with greater anticipation and with less chance of success. I must have been a strange uncomfortable figure, in a large white straw hat, a black coat, trousers and thin ungreased boots, splashing in the meadow (which was under water at the time), and stumbling in haste into the unfamiliar maze of runnels and water cuts. None of these drawbacks were fatal to success. The real obstacle was that I knew nothing, and had heard nothing of the dry fly, and was setting to work with a whippy double-handed rod of some thirteen feet in length, and three flies, probably a March-brown, a coch-y-bondhu and a Greenwell's glory, which I generally used in those days. I remember making straight for a particular spot, which I had often marked in winter as a likely-looking place; it was one where the current flowed from me under the further bank and made a ripple. There was no thought of looking for a rise, but the water was fished steadily. No trout showed a sign of paying any attention to my flies, and at the end of the allotted hour I left the river, wet and unsuccessful, but keen and reluctant to leave off. The same thing happened day after day, nothing occurred to break the monotony of failure, and my friends ceased even to ask whether I had caught anything: but it was at any rate a drawn battle, for I had no more thought of leaving off fishing than the trout had of taking my March-browns and other wet flies. At last one day at the very bottom of the water a trout did take my fly at the end of a long line down stream, but it was a tiny thing, hopelessly under the limit of size for the Itchen, one which might have been counted amongst northern dozens, but could not be brought home alone. During those early days of the season hardly any other anglers were out, and I saw nothing hooked; but as time went on, one or two local anglers, who understood the Winchester trout, began to fish, and, by watching them and asking a few questions I came to understand their method. Some flies were then bought from Hammond, who was in those days the great authority upon the Itchen; they were not tied with a divided wing, as is the rule now, but it was possible to make them float, especially the hare's ears, and it was with one of Hammond's flies that I had my first success. This was a long time in coming, for it was not till June that I caught a trout of reasonable size, and that was the only one I caught during my first season. I can see the place and the rise of that trout now, and recall the anxiety and excitement after it was hooked! It was indeed a morning never to be forgotten: all the deferred hope, all the keenness of many weeks, found satisfaction and reward in a moment, the great gulf between failure and success was passed, and I stood on the right side. I had seen now how the thing could happen, and I was sure it would happen again.

The trout weighed a little over a pound, and was hooked with a red quill gnat. It was carried home proudly by hand, for I had no landing-net in those days; and though there was no more success for me that season, it was henceforth possible to give a willing answer to the question whether I ever caught anything.

A small annual payment gave us the right to fish in about half a mile of the river on the part know as 'Old Barge', and the Winchester trout here had ways of their own, the result no doubt of special education. Day tickets, as well as season tickets, were issued for this piece of water, and I have seen as many as eleven rods fishing it at once, the average number of rods in the season being probably four or five a day. The effect upon the trout was curious but logical. They had become very difficult to catch, or else none would have survived; there were plenty of them, and it was only partly true to call them shy. As a matter of fact, it was not nearly so hard to approach them as it is on many waters much less fished; nor did they take offence very readily at clumsy casts. It was possible to go on casting for hours over rising trout without putting them down, but it would be a mistake to infer that they were indifferent to bad fishing. I suppose habit had made them patient of many faults in angling, which would have been resented at once by fish of less experience. The presence of a figure on the bank, the coming and going of the gut and of an artificial fly, became to most of these trout incidents inseparable from their feeding time. These things must have seemed to them attendant on every natural rise of fly, features not altogether welcome possibly, but on pain of complete starvation not to be treated with indiscriminating fear. To the end I never was quite sure on what success depended most on this wonderful piece of water. Fine gut and a perfectly floated fly and exact casting must have been of use here as everywhere, but these alone were not enough. A Winchester trout might disregard them all, and there was no magic attraction for it in the first cast; on the contrary, I came to look upon it as an exception, if a trout rose at my fly before it had been often fished over.

Perseverance and continuous rapid work seemed to have most effect. There was one man who understood those fish better than anyone else, and who caught far more; he fished nearly every day, and from watching him long and often I became aware of certain peculiarities in his style. Of course he knew the water very well and generally managed to be at a very good place when the rise began, and once there his plan was to stick to his fish and to cast quickly. He dried his fly harder and more rapidly than any one I ever saw, and brought it floating over the fish oftener in a given space of time. His rod and line used to make a very busy sound in the air, as he dried his fly. It was not pretty fishing to watch, but when he made a cast, the line went out straight and accurate, and he once to my knowledge landed in one day from this much-fished part of the river seven brace of trout, all above the limit of size. We used to find him fishing when we came out, and to leave him fishing when we had to go in, but his plan was always the same, to move very little, to watch the river closely when the fish were not rising, to cast quickly and incessantly while the rise lasted, and to change from one fish to another, rather than from place to place, all day. He was also a very silent angler, as if his business was solely with the trout, and what he was, besides being the best resident fisherman at Winchester, remained unknown to me. I was so struck by his success in fishing that it never occurred to me to ask about anything else.

One or two of the men who fished this portion of 'Old Barge' occasionally, were anglers of renown. There was, for instance, the late Mr Francis Francis, at that time probably the best known of all authorities on angling; my recollection of his fishing on the Itchen is that he used a double-handed rod, and threw a small fly with it more accurately than it seemed easy to do with so large an instrument. Sometimes too, but not often, we saw on 'Old Barge' the greatest angler I have ever met. One could not say which was the more instructive, to watch his fishing or to listen to his talk; no one had more information to give, no one was more generous in giving it; his knowledge seemed the result not only of observation and experience, but of some peculiar insight into the ways of trout. In the management of rod and tackle he displayed not only skill but genius. Such at any rate is my recollection of what I heard and saw in days long ago, and I gather from many tributes, which have appeared in print since then, that the genius of the late Mr Marryat was widely recognised, and most highly estimated, and most willingly deferred to by those who knew him best.

To enable our school fishing at Winchester to be understood, it is necessary to give some account of hours, for the management of time was most important. As a rule school arrangements did not set us free till twelve o'clock, and my object of course was to be by the water and fishing as soon as possible afterwards. My house – fortunate in all other respects – was unfortunate in being the farthest but one from the river. To have gone there and back after school was over would have been to lose at least ten minutes. This clearly could not be endured; nor must more precious time be lost in putting together a rod. It was necessary to make arrangements by which one could rush from school at twelve o'clock without a moment's delay, with a rod and tackle ready for immediate use, and with things of some kind on one's feet and legs, which, even when the water was 'out', would with ordinary care keep a dry inside in the water meadows. Wet feet may be wholesome enough under proper conditions, but even at the age of fourteen it is not good to eat dinner and spend several sedentary hours in wet boots and socks on every afternoon. By various expedients, all these difficulties were satisfactorily overcome, and if nothing untoward happened 'up to books' to delay one, and if 'dons' were punctual in getting work over, it was possible by running to begin fishing at about five minutes past twelve. Here let me explain how fortunate this was for us, - and by 'us' is meant those few of us who cared for fishing, the rest being unconscious of the special good fortune of having this hour from twelve to one o'clock free. It is, on the whole, the most likely hour in which to find trout rising. In cold weather it is often too early; in warm weather it is sometimes too late, but in the best of the fly fishing season, and indeed in any month of the season, on water where there is no May-fly, it is often the best hour of the rise in the day – using the word 'day' as distinct from 'evening'. If I were force to choose one hour, and only one, in which to fish daily throughout the season, it would be this hour from twelve to one o'clock. Soon after one o'clock we had to leave the water to go up to house for dinner. It was a compulsory meal for which one might be rather – but not very – late without notice being taken, and the adjustment of this point in one's mind, when fish were rising, was a very distressing business. There are ways my feet have often trod, but in which I have seldom gone at a walking pace; they are those which are the shortest from different parts of the river to the house in which I once was, and many many times have I sped along them, sometimes full of the joy of success, sometimes in exasperation and despair, but nearly always rather late, a rod at full length trembling and shaking in the air as I ran. The best method of making a good use of this hour on 'Old Barge' was to choose quickly an unoccupied place where fish were rising, and to stick to it. There would, as a rule, be no success at first, and the trout would go on feeding, apparently with a fixed determination to pay no attention to an artificial fly, but every now and then one of them would lose his head or make a mistake and be hooked. To land one fish not below the limit of size was satisfactory; a brace was a real success. The result of the best hour which I ever had was two brace and a half, but that was very exceptional. It happened at the end of May, on a day when the water was made rough by a strong wind up stream, and when there was a great rise of full-sized duns, which the trout were taking greedily. On whole school days it was impossible to get a full hour's fishing in the afternoon, and though there was more time on half-holidays, it was very seldom that there was a rise at that time. In the same meadow as this part of 'Old Barge', there was another stream, known to the outside world as the mill pond. It was a very dull bit of water with hardly any current, and though it held larger trout than the main river, they did not rise till comparatively late in the season, and then generally in the evening only. These trout were in their habits altogether different from those in 'Old Barge'. It once happened to me to have a great triumph and land one of them, which weighed three pounds and a quarter. This fish took a grey quill gnat at about five o'clock one afternoon, but as a rule, all we could do on the mill pond was to see occasionally the first signs of the beginning of the evening rise. In summer we could fish early in the evening, but we had to be indoors punctually at eight o'clock, and this was just too soon in June and July to let us have much chance, either in 'Old Barge' or the mill pond, though we saw other and freer anglers coming to the water as we left it. There was more discipline to be learnt in this way than in any other at school. To have a passion for fishing, to spend an hour by the river evening after evening watching intently for a rising trout, and invariable to tear oneself away just as the rise began was a curious experience. There were other parts of the Itchen, where we used to fish – on 'New Barge' along the old towing path, and from one side under the old elm trees at St Cross, but these places were farther away, and we generally went there on free afternoons, and then only when, after finding no trout rising in 'Old Barge', we roamed about in the vain hope that they might be rising somewhere else.

These Winchester trout taught us about the necessity of using fine gut and small flies, and of floating the fly accurately over a rising fish; but they did more than that, they taught us to expect success only as the result of patience and hard work. This was a valuable lesson, which made the fishing in other waters seem easy by comparison. A day on private water, where a feeding trout might reasonably be expected to rise to the first accurate cast was a glorious delight; something to be thought about for days beforehand and remembered long afterwards. In fly fishing, except on very rare days, or on waters that are really over-stocked and little fished, hard work is needed to make a good basket; and to have been used to work hard and to expect little is the best of training. The record of trout above the limit of size (three-quarters of a pound) caught by me on the water described at Winchester, was in 1877 one trout, in 1878 thirteen trout, in 1879 thirty-two trout, in 1880 seventy-six trout, figures which show how severe the training was at first, and how my dry fly education progressed under it.

Sir Edward Grey (1862–1933)
Fly Fishing (1899)

And here, from an historical novel by the Cornish author 'Q' – Sir Arthur Quiller-Couch, what sounds like an idyllic afternoon's activity:

...we panted, until evening released us to wander forth along the water-meadows by the Itchen and bathe, and having bathed to lie naked amid the mints and grasses for a while before returning in the twilight. This bathing went on, not in one or two great crowds, but in groups, often in pairs only, scattered along the river-bank almost all the way to Hills; it being our custom again at Winchester (and I believe it still continues) to socius or walk with one companion; and only at one or two favoured pools would several of these couples meet together for the sport. On the evening of which I am about to tell, my companion was a boy named Fiennes, of about my own age, and we bathed alone, though not far away to right and left the bank teemed with outcries of laughter and naked boys all silvery as their voices in the dusk.

With all this uproar the trout of Itchen, as you may suppose, had gone into hiding, but doubtless some fine fellows lay snug under the stones, and – the stream running shallow after the heats – as we stretched ourselves on the grass, Fiennes challenged me to tickle for one; it may be because he had heard me boast of my angling feats at home. There seemed a likely pool under the further bank; convenient except that to take up the best position beside it I must get the level sun full in my face. I crept across however, Fiennes keeping silent, and laid myself flat on my belly, and peered down into the pool, shading my eyes with one hand. For a long while I saw no fish, until the sun rays, striking aslant, touched the edge of a golden fin very prettily bestowed in a hole of the bank, and well within the overlap of a green weed. Now and again the fin quivered, but for the most part my gentleman lay quiet as a stone, head to stream, and waited for relief from these noisy Wykehamists. Experience, perhaps, had taught him to despise them; at any rate, when gently – very gently – I lowered my hand and began to tickle he showed neither alarm nor resentment. 'Is it a trout?' demanded Fiennes in an excited whisper from the further shore. But of course I made no answer, and presently I supposed he must have crept off to his clothes, for some way upstream I heard the second master's voice warning the bathers to dress and return, and with his usual formula *Ite domum saturae venit Hesperus ite capellae*; being short-sighted he missed to spy me, and I felt, rather than saw or heard, him pass on, for with one hand I shaded my eyes while with the other I tickled.

Yet another two minutes went by, then with a jerk I had my trout, my thumb and forefinger deep under his gills; brought down my other clutch upon him and, lifting, flung him back over me among the meadow grass, my posture being such that I could neither hold him struggling nor recover my own balance save by rolling over sideways on my shoulder-pin; which I did and running to him, where he gleamed and doubled, flipping the grasses, caught him in both hands and held him aloft.

Sir Arthur Quiller-Couch (1863–1944)
Sir John Constantine (1906)

This poet, another Wykehamist, who tells us that 'The lines were composed on an evening journey from Oxford to Southampton, the first time I had seen the Itchen since I left school.'

To the River Itchin (1789)

Itchin! When I behold thy banks again,
Thy crumbling margin, and thy silver breast,
On which the self-same tints still seem to rest,
Why feels my heart a shivering sense of pain!
Is it, that many a summer's day has past
Since, in life's morn, I carolled on thy side!
It is, that oft since then my heart has sighed
As Youth, and Hope's delusive gleams, flew fast!
Is it, that those who gathered on thy shore,
Companions of my youth, now meet no more!
Whate'er the cause, upon thy banks I bend,
Sorrowing; yet feel such solace at my heart,
As at the meeting of some long-lost friend,
From whom, in happier hours, we wept to part.

William Bowles (1762–1850)

Charles Kingsley, a Christian Socialist, professor of modern history at Cambridge and canon of Westminster, was moved to write his most famous work, *The Water Babies*, a moral fable of a child chimney-sweep, as a critique of child labour and a satire on the closed minds of scientists. He was vicar in Eversley, near Basingstoke, from 1834. The first chapter is mostly set in Harthover Place, the principal model for which is thought to be the magnificent Jacobean Bramshill House, home of Sir John Cope, in north Hampshire. Kingsley is said to have written part of *The Water Babies* while staying at the Plough Inn at Itchen Abbas on a fishing holiday.

Or was it such a salmon stream as I trust you will see among the Hampshire water-meadows before your hairs are gray, under the wise new fishing-laws, when Winchester apprentices shall covenant, as they did three hundred years ago, not to be made to eat salmon more than three days a week; and fresh-run fish shall be as plentiful under Salisbury spire as they are in Holly-hole at Christchurch; in the good time coming, when folks shall see that, of all Heaven's gifts of food, the one to be protected most carefully is that worthy gentleman salmon, who is generous enough to go down to the sea weighing five ounces, and to come back next year weighing five pounds, without having cost the soil or the state one farthing.

Charles Kingsley (1819–1875)
The Water Babies (1863)

Though King Arthur is only very slenderly mentioned in Gildas or Geoffrey of Monmouth and though it is generally allowed, now, by historians that such a figure did exist, the search for the precise location of Camelot may be fruitless. Evidence is produced for multiple sites in the West of England and Wales; is Wither here offering Alresford, site of the Bishop of Winchester's fish pond, as an unusually easterly site?

George Wither was born in Bentworth near Alton. Living in troubled times, he was active as poet and satirist and also as republican pamphleteer. In the Civil War he was captured by a troop of Royalist horse, owing his life to the intervention of Sir John Denham on the ground that so long as Wither lived he himself could not be accounted the worst poet in England.

from **Fair Virtue Mistresse of Phil Arete (1622)**

Two pretty rills do meet, and meeting make
Within one valley, a large silver lake...
... pleasant was that pool, for near it then
Was neither rotten marsh, nor boggy fen;
It was not overgrown with boisterous sedge,
Nor grew there rudely then along the hedge,

A bending willow, nor a prickly bush,
Nor broad-leav'd flag, nor reed, not knotty rush.
But here, well ordered, was a grove of bowers;
There grassy plots set round about with flowers.
Here you might (through the water) see the land
Appear, strew'd o'er with white or yellow sand.
Yon deeper was it and the wind, by whiffes,
Would make it rise and wash the snow-white cliffs,
On which oft pluming sat (unfrighted then)
The gaggling wild goose, and the snow-white swan;
With all those flocks of fowls, which to this day,
Upon those quiet waters breed and play.
...for though those excellencies wanting be,
Which once it had; it is the same that we
By transposition name the Ford of Arle;
And out of which along a chalky marle,
That river trills whose waters wash the fort
In which brave Arthur kept his royal court.
North-east not far from this great pool there lies
A tract of beechy mountains that arise
With leisurely-ascending to such height
As from their tops the warlike Isle of Wight
You in the ocean's bosom may espy,
Though near two hundred furlong thence it lie.

George Wither (1588–1667)

And here the North Hampshire River Lodon serves, as often, as a metaphor for the course of life. Thomas Warton was poet laureate in 1785-90, a friend of Dr Johnson and a historian of English Poetry; he assembled a miscellany of doggerel by Oxford wits and called it *The Oxford Sausage*.

To the River Lodon

'Ah! what a weary race my feet have run
Since first I trod thy banks with alders crowned,
And thought my way was all thro' fairy ground,
Beneath thy azure sky and golden sun;
Where first my muse to lisp her notes begun!

While pensive Memory traces back the round,
Which fills the varied interval between;
Much pleasure, more of sorrow, marks the scene.
Sweet native stream! those skies and suns so pure
No more return, to cheer my evening road!
Yet still one joy remains, that, not obscure,
Nor useless, all my vacant days have flowed,
From youth's gay dawn to manhood's prime mature;
Nor with the muse's laurel unbestowed.

Thomas Warton (1728–90)

In a letter to Daines Barrington, Gilbert White tells of the vital task
performed by river reeds in rural life in the eighteenth century.

I shall make no apology for troubling you with a detail of a
very simple piece of domestic oeconomy, being satisfied that
you think nothing beneath your attention that tends to utility:
the matter alluded to is the use of rushes instead of candles,
which I am well aware prevails in many districts besides this;
but as I know there are countries also where it does not obtain,
and as I have considered the subject with some degree of
exactness, I shall proceed in my humble story, and leave you to
judge of the expediency.

The proper species of rush for this purpose seems to be
the juncus effuses, or common soft rush, which is to be found
in most moist pastures, by the sides of streams, and under
hedges. These rushes are in best condition in the height of
summer; but may be gathered, so as to serve the purpose well,
quite on to autumn. It would be needless to add that the largest
and longest are best.

Decayed labourers, women, and children, make it their
business to procure and prepare them. As soon as they are cut
they must be flung into water, and kept there; for otherwise
they will dry and shrink, and the peel will not run. At first a
person would find it no easy matter to divest a rush of its peel
or rind, so as to leave one regular, narrow, even rib from top
to bottom that may support the pith: but this, like other feats,
soon becomes familiar even to children; and we have seen an
old woman, stone-blind, performing this business with great

283

dispatch, and seldom failing to strip them with the nicest regularity. When these unci are thus far prepared, they must lie out on the grass to be bleached, and take the dew for some nights, and afterwards be dried in the sun.

Some address is required in dipping these rushes in the scalding fat or grease; but this knack is to be attained by practice. The careful wife of an industrious Hampshire labourer obtains all her fat for nothing; for she saves the scummings of her bacon-pot for this use; and, if the grease abounds with salt, she causes the salt to precipitate to the bottom, by setting the scummings in a warm oven. Where hogs are not much in use, and especially by the sea-side, the coarser animal oils will come very cheap. A pound of common grease may be procured for four pence; and about six pounds of grease will dip a pound of rushes; and one pound of rushes may be bought for one shilling: so that a pound of rushes, medicated and ready for use, will cost three shillings. If men that keep bees will mix a little wax with the grease, it will give it a consistency, and render it more cleanly, and make the rushes burn longer: mutton suet would have the same effect.

A good rush, which measured in length two feet four inches and an half, being minuted, burnt only three minutes short of an hour: and a rush still of greater length has been known to burn one hour and a quarter.

These rushes give a good clear light. Watch-lights (coated with tallow), it is true, shed a dismal one, 'darkness visible'; but then the wicks of those have two ribs of the rind, or peel, to support the pith, while the wick of the dipped rush has but one. The two ribs are intended to impede the progress of the flame, and make the candle last.

In a pound of dry rushes, avoirdupois, which I caused to be weighed and numbered, we found upwards of one thousand six hundred individuals. Now suppose each of these burns, one with another, only half an hour, then a poor man will purchase eight hundred hours of light, a time exceeding thirty-three entire days, for three shillings. According to this account each rush, before dipping, costs 1/33rd of a farthing , and 1/11th afterwards. Thus a poor family will enjoy 5 1/2 hours of comfortable light for a farthing. An experienced old housekeeper assures me that one pound and a half of rushes completely supplies his family the year round, since working people burn no candle in the long days, because they rise and go to bed by daylight.

Little farmers use rushes much in the short days, both morning and evening in the dairy and kitchen; but the very poor, who are always the worst economists, and therefore must continue very poor, buy an halfpenny candle every evening, which, in their blowing open rooms, does not burn much more than two hours. Thus have they only two hours' light for their money instead of eleven.

Gilbert White (1720–93)
Letter XXVI to Daines Barrington,
Natural History of Selborne (1789)

In *The Sporting Magazine* in 1825, Nimrod (aka Charles James Apperley), the nineteenth-century sportsman and writer declared, 'I never hunt in Hampshire when I can help it, that is to say when I can hunt in a better county, for to ride a good hunter over a bed of flints is a misery.' Plenty did, however, including the Prince of Wales, later George IV, who leased Kempshott Park near Basingstoke in 1788–95, even going so far as to form the Kempshott Hunt, of which he was Master. Here is a breathless account of the county's hunting activity at that time.

At the Winchester races, cock-fighting, which was part of the programme, was generally recognised as a fashionable amusement, and in the *Racing Calendars* accounts of the mains fought will be found. The horses who ran for the king's plates must have been very different from the wretched cat-legged creatures we now too frequently see start, as they carried twelve stone, and the winner was the best of three four-mile heats. By advertisements in the county paper it appears that hairdressers used to come down from London, and stay during the race week at the Black Swan Hotel, Winchester.

Mr Stephen Terry of Dummer, sportsman living in Hants, was at Eton in 1791, and a contemporary of Beau Brummel. He began hunting on a pony about 1785, and says he can remember at least twenty different packs hunting in Freefolk Wood. On one occasion, when he had run his fox from the Holt to Waverley Abbey, the hounds entered the pleasure-grounds, and he followed them, riding over the well-kept lawn, and was surprised by hearing the gardener blame him, saying, 'Why neither my master nor my mistress ever ride there.' He merely replied, 'Don't they? Why I never saw better riding in all my life; but we shall lose our fox owing to these nasty stinking violets.' Lord Stawell kept hounds up to 1796. He once found a fox in Farnham Holt, which he ran to ground at Hurstbourne Park! In 1788, the Prince of Wales lived at Kempshot and while there had a pack of stag-hounds, which were afterwards turned into fox-hounds. At this time the prince was a very hard liver, and suffered much from gout. Nanny Stevens of Dummer, a stout, strong woman, was his nurse, and even helped him in and out of his bath, while his lazy valet did nothing but brush his clothes and look on. Mrs Fitzherbert visited the prince at Kempshot, and, while she was there, Mr Ridge's hounds, with Joe Hall and Phil Gosling, came over from Kilmiston. Lady Jersey, in hunting costume, joined the field, and Charles James Fox was at the breakfast booted and spurred, but he was so gouty that he could neither walk nor ride. In February 1793, the prince's establishment underwent an alteration. They hunted stag no more, but took to fox instead. George IV kept his honeymoon with Queen Caroline, April 1795, at Kempshot. In this month the prince was in treaty for Penton Lodge, near Andover; but in October he went to the Grange, and paid £5000 for stock and fixtures; the beer alone was estimated at £500, so large a stock had Mr Drummond in his cellar; and often, no doubt, amidst the domestic troubles of his after days, did the prince look back with a sad satisfaction and sorrow on the privacy and tranquil enjoyments of the sojourn at the Grange. While there he joined many parties, and was very intimate with Lord Rodney and Mr Charles Graeme, who then lived at Dean House, Kilmiston. William IV was a prince middy at Portsmouth, and occasionally came up to Kempshot, but he could not ride at all to hounds. Mr Chute of the Vine had a long career as a master of hounds with a pack of harriers about 1791, which, after some time, he turned into fox-hounds, and the country took the name of the Vine from the estate he occupied. Mr Terry was staying at the Vine with Mr Chute in the year 1796, and on Easter Tuesday they had a run with a celebrated hound called Spanker. Some foxes had been bred in a drain which ran under the drawing-room, so they found directly. It was a very sunny day, but they had a straight twelve miles to ground at Chilton Wood, and they did not dig. Spanker remained with the fox. On the fifth day after the run, as he had not returned to the kennel, Mr Terry, setting out in search, found Spanker alive at the earth, with the dead fox between his paws. This staunch hound was kept at Dummer until he recovered. Mr Chute was a wonderfully good kennel huntsman; his hounds were renowned for their great strength and their good noses, and he always bred them for those two qualities. His kennel, however, appears to have been useful rather than ornamental, for in Mr George Tattersall's able work, entitled *Sporting Architecture*, 'Where was a more miserable hole in the shape of a kennel for fox-hounds, than that in which the Vine pack was lodged in the late Mr Chute's time, and yet I never saw hounds freer from disease, nor able to stand their work better, than those hounds were. There was not even a grass ground, nor any yard at all so large as his own dining-room, and the sub-soil was strong clay.' Mr Chute was one of the last of the pigtails, and always wore it tied in proper form with black ribbon; his coat and waistcoat were open, and his shirt fronts got up with broad plaits. A year or two only before his death the pigtail was sacrificed. General Pole, who was a great friend, was present when the dreadful deed was done in Fox the hairdresser's shop. The fatal snip was given, and thus ended one of the last, if not the very last, of the pigtails.

The writer is here referring to the British army's adoption of a single pigtail as its standard dress for long hair, but the fashion died out in about 1800.

Aesop (pseud.)
Sporting reminiscences of Hampshire: from 1745 to 1862 (1864)

Nikolaus Pevsner reminds us of the danger of the sport when he writes in his architectural notes on Hampshire:

'Obelisk on Farley Down. Erected by Sir Paulet St John c1740 to record the leap into a chalk pit 25ft deep of a horse during foxhunting. The horse had his mount on his back.'

Far older than horseback fox hunting was the tradition of deer hunting, captured here in fiction and then non-fiction in the county.

'A hart royal is not meat for Roundheads, although the king's servants may feast on them.'

'That's truly said. Well, now I must see your woodcraft. You shall be leader of the chase.'

'Think you we can harbour a stag about here?'

'Yes, in this month, no doubt.'

'Let us walk on,' said Edward. 'The wind is fresh from the eastern quarter; we will face it if you please – or rather, keep it blowing on our right cheek for the present.'

''Tis well,' replied Oswald; and they walked for about half an hour.

'This is the slot of a doe,' said Edward in a low voice, pointing to the marks; 'yonder thicket is a likely harbour for the stag.' They proceeded, and Edward pointed out to Oswald the slot of the stag in the thicket. They then walked round, and found no marks of the animal having left his lair.

'He is here,' whispered Edward; and Oswald made a sign for Edward to enter the thicket, while he walked to the other

side. Edward entered the thicket cautiously. In the centre he perceived, through the trees, a small cleared spot, covered with high fern, and felt certain the stag was lying there. He forced his way on his knees till he had a better view of the place, and then cocked his gun. The noise induced the stag to move his antlers, and discover his lair. Edward could just perceive the eye of the animal through the heath; he waited till the beast settled again, took steady aim, and fired. At the report of the gun another stag sprung up and burst away. Oswald fired and wounded it, but the animal made off followed by the dogs. Edward who hardly knew whether he had missed or not, but felt almost certain that he had not, hastened out of the thicket to join the chase, and, as he passed through the fern patch, perceived that his quarry lay dead. He then followed the chase, and, being very fleet of foot, soon came up with Oswald, and passed him without speaking. The stag made for the swampy ground, and finally took to the water beyond it, and stood at bay. Edward then waited for Oswald, who came up with him.

'He has soiled,' said Edward, 'and now you may go in and kill him.'

Oswald, eager in the chase, hastened up to where the dogs and the stag were in the water, and put a bullet through the animal's head.

Edward went to him, assisted him to drag the stag out of the water, and then Oswald cut its throat, and proceeded to perform the usual offices.

Captain Marryat (1792–1848)
Children of New Forest (1847)

...There is an old keeper, now alive, named Adams, whose great-grandfather (mentioned in a perambulation taken in 1635), grandfather, father and self, enjoyed the head keepership of Wolmer-forest in succession for more than an hundred years. This person assures me, that his father has often told him, that Queen Anne, as she was journeying on the Portsmouth road, did not think the forest of Wolmer beneath her royal regard. For she came out of the great road at Lippock, which is just by, and reposing herself on a bank smoothed for that purpose, lying about half a mile to the east of Wolmer-pond, and still called Queen's-bank, saw with great complacency and satisfaction the whole herd of red deer brought by the keepers along the vale before her, consisting then of about five hundred head. A sight this, worthy the attention of the great sovereign! But he further adds that, by means of the Waltham blacks [poachers, who often blacked their faces for disguise], or, to use his own expression, as soon as they began blacking, they were reduced to about fifty head, and so continued decreasing till the time of the late Duke of Cumberland. It is now more than thirty years ago that his highness sent down an huntsman, and six yeoman-prickers, in scarlet jackets laced with gold, attended by the stag-hounds; ordering them to take every deer in this forest alive, and convey them in carts to Windsor. In the course of the summer they caught every stag, some of which showed extraordinary diversion; but, in the following winter, when the hinds were also carried off, such fine chases were exhibited as served the country people for matter of talk and wonder for years afterwards. I saw myself one of the yeoman-prickers single out a stag from the herd, and must confess that it was the most curious feat of activity I ever beheld, superior to anything in Mr Astley's riding-school. The exertions made by the horse and deer much exceeded all my expectations; though the former greatly excelled the latter in speed. When the devoted deer was separated from his companions, they gave him, by their watches, law, as they called it, for twenty minutes; when, sounding their horns, the stop-dogs were permitted to pursue, and the most gallant scene ensued.

...Our old race of deer-stealers are hardly extinct yet: it was but a little while ago that, over their ale, they used to recount the exploits of their youth; such as watching the pregnant hind to her lair, and, when the calf was dropped, paring its feet with a penknife to the quick to prevent its escape, till it was large and fat enough to be killed; the shooting at one of their neighbours with a bullet in a turnip-field by moonshine, mistaking him for a deer; and the losing a dog in the following extraordinary manner: Some fellows suspecting that a calf new-fallen was deposited in a certain spot of thick fern, went, with a lurcher, to surprise it; when the parent hind rushed out of the brake, and, taking a vast spring with all her feet close together, pitched upon the neck of the dog, and broke it short in two.

Gilbert White (1720–93)
Letters VI & VII to Thomas Pennant,
Natural History of Selborne (1789)

Peter Hawker was a celebrated diarist, author and sportsman. His sporting exploits were considered worthy of report in *The Times*. Hawker published his *Advice to Young Sportsmen* in 1814, a popular work having nine imprints in his lifetime with the latest paper edition printed in 1975. He served under the Duke of Wellington during the Peninsular War, received a serious thigh wound and was consequently declared unfit. He was made Lieutenant Colonel of the North Hampshire militia in 1821 and ultimately became deputy lieutenant for the county.

1810 September. – Longparish. My wound having sufficiently recovered to enable me to go out for a few hours a day on horseback, I took out my certificate for killing game, and on the 1st I killed 36 partridges and 2 hares, besides 1 brace of birds lost. We sprung a covey near Furgo Farm out of which I killed a brace with each barrel, and several of those that flew off pitched, and ran on the thatch of Furgo barn. In the evening I killed and bagged five successive double shots.

N.B. – The most I heard of being killed in our neighbourhood by anyone else was seven brace by Captain Haffendon. Some parties from Longparish have been out and killed nothing.

30th – N.B. My wounds are so far healed, that I am able to walk as sound as ever I did in my life, but have yet to recruit myself in general health, being at present very nervous and weak.

Game bagged in month of September 1810: 210 partridges, 6 hares, 4 quails, 3 landrails, 2 wild ducks. Total, 227 head.

October 26th – Went to shoot with Mr Wakeford, at Tytherly House, and killed 3 hares, 2 pheasants, and 1 partridge. We shot with spaniels, and soon after began were joined by a sheep dog, who forsook his flock to spend the day with us, and rendered us more service than any one of the cry; he kept well in bounds while we were beating; ran the pheasants off their legs the moment we found them, and pressed the hares so hard that he obliged most of them to leave the hedgerows within shot.

29th – 4 partridges, 1 woodcock, and 1 pheasant, besides two snipe at one shot. The cock was the first I had seen or heard of this season. I killed him with a snap shot in high covert, and never knew that he fell till John found him dead. In addition to my day's shooting I had famous sport with the harriers, which I met in the field, and followed with my old shooting pony. I found them two hares sitting, one of which I started, was in at the death of, and brought home in my game bag.

November 2nd – 4 snipes and 1 jack snipe. I was extremely ill and nervous, and shot infamously bad, or I should have killed ten couple.

Peter Hawker (1786–1853)
Diary 1802–53

In looking for a metaphor for the fruitless rivalries of a wasteful parliamentary committee, Trollope's mind lights upon a bloody and gruesome hunting tradition.

There is a sport prevalent among the downs in Hampshire to which, though not of a high degree, much interest is attached. Men and boys, with social glee and happy boyish shouts, congregate together on a hill-side, at the mouth of a narrow hole, and proceed, with the aid of a well-trained bull-dog, to draw a badger. If the badger be at all commendable in his class this is by no means an easy thing to do. He is a sturdy animal, and well fortified with sharp and practised teeth; his hide is of the toughest; his paws of the strongest, and his dead power of resistance so great as to give him more than an equal chance with the bull-dog. The delighted sportsmen stand round listening to the growls and snarls, the tearings, gnawings, and bloody struggles of the combatants within. 'Well done, badger! Well done, bull-dog! Draw him, bulldog! Bite him, badger!' Each has his friends, and the interest of the moment is intense.

The badger, it is true, has done no harm. He has been doing as it was appointed for him to do, poor badger, in that hole of his. But then, why were badgers created but to be drawn? Why, indeed, but to be drawn, or not to be drawn, as the case may be? See! the bull-dog returns minus an ear, with an eye hanging loose, his nether lip torn off, and one paw bitten through and through. Limping, dejected, beaten, glaring fearfully from his one remaining eye, the dog comes out; and the badger within rolls himself up with affected ease, hiding his bloody wounds from the public eye.

So it is that the sport is played in Hampshire; and so also at Westminster – with a difference, however. In Hampshire the two brutes retain ever their appointed natures. The badger is always a badger, and the bull-dog never other than a bull-dog. At Westminster there is a juster reciprocity of position. The badger when drawn has to take his place outside the hole, and fight again for the home of his love; while the victorious bull-dog assumes a state of badgerdom, dons the skin of his enemy, and, in his turn, submits to be baited.

The pursuit is certainly full of interest, but it is somewhat deficient in dignity.

Anthony Trollope (1815–1882)
Three Clerks (1857)

From his home in Froxfield, Edward Thomas looked down the precipitous beech hanger, hiding as it did for him, in this poem, something dark and deathly.

The Combe

The Combe was ever dark, ancient and dark.
Its mouth is stopped with bramble, thorn, and briar;
And no one scrambles over the sliding chalk
By beech and yew and perishing juniper
Down the half precipices of its sides, with roots
And rabbit holes for steps. The sun of Winter,
The moon of Summer, and all the singing birds
Except the missel-thrush that loves juniper,
Are quite shut out. But far more ancient and dark
The Combe looks since they killed the badger there,
Dug him out and gave him to the hounds,
That most ancient Briton of English beasts.

Edward Thomas (1787–1917)

Leaving blood sports behind, here is Aesop's early account of the glories of the Hambledon Cricket Club.

Hampshire might almost be called the birthplace of cricket, as for many years it could not only beat any other county, but was generally successful even against All England. The Hambledon Club, whose first recorded matches date from 1772, maintained the credit of the county by a long series of victories. Its matches were generally played on Broad Halfpenny Windmill or Stoke Downs. In 1787 (August 14, 15, 16), at Bishopsbourne Paddock, the seat of Sir Horace Mann, they beat All England, winning by 266 runs; and in June, 1788, on Stoke Down, they again beat All England by one innings and 76 runs. Amongst the names of the giants of those days are Nyren, who kept the Bat and Ball Inn, near Broad Halfpenny Down, and afterwards the George Inn at Hambledon. Nyren catered for the cricket meetings. In the *Hants Chronicle*, July 6, 1778, is the following advertisement : 'Nyren hopes the air of Stoke Down will, with the ladies, stand in the place of Marbres, Aspiques, Blanc-Manges: for good appetites there will be a quantity of beef, ham, chickens, tarts, &c,' James Aylward, who lived at Corhampton, was a crack man, and amongst the others of the old club were Richard Purchase of Liss, Hogsflesh of Southwick,

Taylor of Ropley and Alresford, Richard Aubrey-Veck of Bishop's Waltham, William Barber of Horndean, Noah Mann of North chapel, Thomas Brett of Catherington, Peter Stewart of Hambledon, landlord of the Green Man Inn, John Freeman tie of Alresford, David Harris of Crookham, Edward Aburrow of Hambledon, George Leer, also of Hambledon, Thomas Lord of Westmeon, John Wells of Wrecclesham, and William Beldham, also of the same place, who died aged ninety-seven. The true old Hambledon Club broke up about 1791, though it would appear that it existed in some form or other until the year 1825. Amongst the players we find old John Small, Lumpy (the best slow bowler of that day), since then Brown, the fastest bowler then known, Beagley, Carter, &c some of whom were paid ten shillings per day by the club as bowlers. Members of the committee of the noblemen and gentlemen met at the Star and Garter, in Pall-Mall, in February, 1774, to settle the laws of cricket. The Duke of Dorset, the Earl of Tankerville, the Earl of Winchelsea, and Lord Frederick Beauclerk, frequently played with the Hambledon Club, and Sir Horace Mann was very active in getting up an eleven to play against them. As early as 1787, Alresford had an excellent eleven, and a match on Tichborne Down against Odiham with Beldham is reported. In those days matches were not played entirely for the love and honour of the game, as now, but for large sums of money. The match in July, 1778, of the Hambledon Club against All England, was for one thousand guineas. And not for money only was the game played, as I find in the *Hants Chronicle* that a match was played on July 14th, 1783, for eleven pairs of white corded dimity breeches and eleven handsome striped pink waistcoats. In the month of September of this year, Kent and Hants played for four days. In July, 1793, a match was played on Stoke Down between twenty-two of Hertfordshire and Essex, who got forty-seven runs only in each innings, and an eleven of England, who were, in fact, nearly all Hambledon Club men, and they got one hundred and fifteen, thus winning by a single innings and twenty-one runs.

Aesop (pseud.)
Sporting reminiscences of Hampshire: from 1745–1862 (1864)
Speaking of himself in the third person, here John Arlott describes the

sporting pleasures of his youth in early twentieth-century Basingstoke, which led on to his professional career as a sports journalist. Arlott was also a poet and attracted the attention of John Betjeman, himself a cricket fan, who became a mentor for his literary ambitions.

What we [Arlott and his schoolfellows] had watched was the beginning of the fast leg-stump attack which, when it was used in Australia during the immediately following 1932-33 season, was called 'bodyline'... It felt like having been present at the making of history which, after a fashion, it was; significantly it was lassoing a boy into the most absorbing and profound of games. He was only too willing to be captured, though it never occurred to him that he would ever be close enough to it to live within its ambit.

In complete contrast to all this was the ordinary club cricket played for Old St Michael's, which had once been the choir team of the local parish church. It was indeed so remote a contrast that it seemed barely to belong to the same game. Yet it was educative in allowing the opportunity to experiment on live victims with all the basic tools of the game: pace, swing, finger-spin, wrist spin; even, as an interval in laborious struggles in the field, a terrible attempt at wicket-keeping. The nearest approach to success – with some degree of satisfaction – lay briefly in a burst of bowling as fast as possible; later, in off-spinners; but, most of all, in going in and, through a state of almost strokeless resistance – if indeed it was even as positive as resistance – not getting out. It was, though, a most companionable existence. Old St Michael's had no ground of their own – the nearest approach was the meadow behind the 'Rising Sun' pub across the road. Yet playing on a fresh ground each week was to be among old friends – for fixtures were arranged with a home match which saved travelling, and ended near their own pub...

[Basingstoke] was a place of do-it-yourself entertainment. Musical comedies, and sometimes straight plays, were mounted by amateurs. At soccer, Basingstoke once won the Hampshire League, and their 'blood' matches with Thorneycrofts engendered immense, but orderly, partisan enthusiasm. Basingstoke and North Hants played the best class of club cricket. The occasional match for them as an odd, picked-up body, only too anxious for a game, was a bonus for J. A. but no indication that he belonged on that level. The swimming baths were primitive enough, but a warm-weather pleasure; the two cinemas, a glimpse of a distant – surely not real – world.

John Arlott (1914–1991)
Basingstoke Boy: the Autobiography (1989)

A vital feature of the county is its coastline, which brings fishermen and sailors to its shores.

We had a long and steep descent to Bursledon Bridge, where we crossed the wide tidal river, the Hamble, on a picturesque wooden bridge. Bursledon is an exceedingly pretty spot, hemmed in by wooden hills from the progressive modern world and all its ugliness. It was full of brightness and movement that morning. The river, gleaming with light as it flowed on, was enlivened by sundry white-winged yachts and floating fishing craft; these with the waving woods around, combined to give an inspiriting feeling of freshness and life to the scene.

James John Hissey
On Southern English Roads

And John Betjeman himself, observant master of the poignant.

Youth and Age on Beaulieu River, Hants

Early sun on the Beaulieu water
Lights the undersides of oaks,
Clumps of leaves it floods and blanches,
All transparent glow the branches
Which the double sunlight soaks;
To her craft on Beaulieu water
Clemency the General's daughter
Pulls across with even strokes.

Schoolboy-sure she is this morning
Soon her sharpie's rigg'd and free.
Cool beneath a garden awning
Mrs Fairclough, sipping tea
And raising large long-distance glasses
As the little sharpie passes,
Sighs our sailor girl to see:

Tulip figure, so appealing,
Oval face, so serious-eyed,
Tree-roots pass'd and muddy beaches.
On to huge and lake-like reaches
Soft and sun-warm, see her glide –
Slacks the slim young limbs revealing,
Sun-brown arm the tiller feeling –
With the wind and with the tide.

Evening light will bring the water,
Day-long sun will burst the bud,
Clemency, the General's daughter,
Will return upon the flood.
But the older woman only
Knows the ebb-tide leaves her lonely
With the shining fields of mud.

Not far away, Jane Austen enjoyed the nautical atmosphere when living
with her brother Frank at Southampton.

We had a little water party yesterday; I and my two nephews
went from the Itchen ferry up to Northam, where we landed
… and walked home, and it was so much enjoyed that I had
intended to take them to Netley today; the tide is just right for
our going immediately after noonshine, but I am afraid there
will be rain; if we cannot get so far, however, we may perhaps
go round from the ferry to the quay.

I had not proposed doing more than cross the Itchen
yesterday, but it proved so pleasant, and so much to the
satisfaction of all, that when we reached the middle of the
stream we agreed to be rowed up the river; both boys rowed a
great part of the way, and their questions and remarks, as well

as their enjoyment, were very amusing.

Jane Austen
Letter to Cassandra, 24 October 1808

But the reality of the water, and making a living from it, is somewhat less enchanting.

The trawler, wallowing like a black hippo among swans, had an arrangement of rusted iron bedsprings attached to her bows. She looked as if she had sailed the China Seas. For all that, I liked her better than the prissy, white boats moored about her. Some of them had net curtains, and one had a painting hanging in the wheelhouse of an elephant on the rampage. The trawler is owned by Jack Pallot and his son, Chris. They fish in her all year round but in August they concentrate on clams. Jack and I had an interesting chat about clams, though they themselves spend uneventful lives in the mud at the bottom of the river. How they got here in the first place is curious. They were taken on board in New York, in the days of the ocean liners, to be served up in restaurants. When the ships returned to Southampton and the kitchens were cleaned out ready for the next voyage, the left-over clams were dumped from the portholes. They were only discovered ten years ago. A new power-house was built further up the Solent and Jack believes that the heating up of the water deluded the clams into thinking this was Florida. The clam's shell is kept shut by abductor muscles. You have to use a knife to prise one open. In season the muscles relax to allow ova and sperm to shoot into the water. The bits of jelly float to surface and in fourteen days the shell has formed. Then it sinks to the bottom, buries itself in mud for five years, and dies, possibly from boredom.

We fished for them further up the Itchen. The bedsprings, chained together and jack-knifed into the rough semblance of a trough, were flung into the river and dragged behind the bows. This is called dredging. After a few minutes the trough was winched higher to rinse the silt and the dirt from the catch. I didn't think this was particularly successful; when the trough was heaved into the bows I was spattered with mud from head to foot. Later the mud turned into a sort of woad, powder-blue and indelible. It was my job to throw out the lumps of old iron, shreds of rubber, pieces of broken glass which had been dredged up with the clams. There was even a collection of small clay pipes, the sort they used to give away with a plug of tobacco. I was hoping for human bones but was disappointed. The French will buy most of this morning's catch. They're partial to clams. Though fussy about size. It must be a generous mouthful yet manageable enough to swallow whole. For some reason a clam is not a pretty sight when cut in half. I enjoyed dredging and said so. Chris, wiping the mud from his eye, told me I'd get fed up with it in a week.

Beryl Bainbridge (1932–2010)
English journey or the road the Milton Keynes (1984)

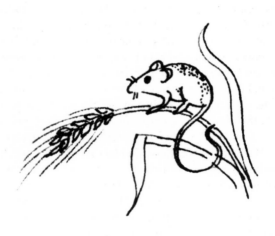

Chapter 7
Gilbert White and the Green Laboratory

I forgot to mention that, in going from Hawkley to Greatham, the man who went to show me the way, told me at a certain fork, 'that road goes to Selborne.' This put me in mind of a book, which was once recommended to me, but which I never saw, entitled *The History and Antiquities of Selborne* (or something of that sort), written, I think, by a parson of the name of White, brother of Mr White, so long a bookseller in Fleet Street. This parson had, I think, the living of the parish of Selborne. The book was mentioned to me as a work of great curiosity and interest... I shall now certainly read this book if I can get it. By the bye, if all the parsons had, for the last thirty years, employed their leisure time in writing the histories of their several parishes, instead of living, as many of them have, engaged in pursuits that I need not here name, neither their situation nor that of their flocks would, perhaps, have been the worse for it at this day.

William Cobbett
Rural Rides

G ilbert White was not in fact vicar of Selborne, but its assistant curate. Born here in 1720, he was a fellow of Oriel College, Oxford, but spent as much time as he could in the village, dwarfed by the majestic beech hangers which surround it. His *Natural History of Selborne* records the life of the village in minute, scientific detail, yet he writes affectionately, emotionally and with humour about this subject so close to his heart. His aim was to reveal the bounty of Providence, and the book is an unparalleled celebration of his time and place. He was not interested in the English village as either rustic idyll or rural squalor, but as an ecosystem. The first of his kind, he is, without doubt, the father of nature writing.

Visitors flock to the village of Selborne to visit White's house museum, The Wakes, and to get a glimpse of this green laboratory of his, the place he observed, minutely, until his death in 1793. Modest like himself, the village does not trumpet its hero; there is no need, for to this day, every part of it declares his wonderful engagement with nature.

As will be seen, all manner of other people have evoked Hampshire's exquisite natural heritage – from a Foreign Secretary to a farmer's son. But first a wonderful, playful biographical sketch of Gilbert White himself, from the pen of Virginia Woolf.

'...there is somewhat in most genera at least, that at first sight discriminates them, and enables a judicious observer to pronounce upon them with some certainty.' Gilbert White is talking, of course, about birds; the good ornithologist, he says, should be able to distinguish them by their air – 'on the ground as well as on the wing, and in the bush as well as in the hand.' But when the bird happens to be Gilbert White himself, when we try to discriminate the colour and shape of this very rare fowl, we are at a loss. Is he, like the bird so brightly coloured by hand as a frontispiece to the second volume, a hybrid – something between a hen that clucks and a nightingale that sings? It is one of those ambiguous books that seem to tell a plain story, the *Natural History of Selborne*, and yet by some apparently unconscious device of the author's has a door left open, through which we hear distant sounds, a dog barking, cart wheels creaking, and see, when 'all the fading landscape sinks in night', if not Venus herself, at least a phantom owl.

His intention seems plain enough – it was to impart certain observations upon the fauna of his native village to his friends Thomas Pennant and Daines Barrington. But it was not for the benefit of those gentlemen that he composed the sober yet stately description of Selborne with which the book opens. There it is before us, the village of Selborne, lying in the extreme eastern corner of the county of Hampshire, with its hanger and its sheep walks and those deep lanes 'that affright ladies and make timid horsemen shudder'. The soil is part clay, part malm; the cottages are of stone or brick; the men work in the hop gardens and in the spring and summer weed the corn. No novelist could have opened better.

Selborne is set solidly in the foreground. But something is lacking; and so before the scene fills with birds, mice, voles, crickets and the Duke of Richmond's moose, before the page is loud with the chirpings, bleatings, lowings, and gruntings of their familiar intercourse, we have Queen Anne lying on the bank to watch the deer driven past. It was an anecdote, he casually remarks, that he had from an old keeper, Adams, whose great-grandfather, father and self were all keepers in the forest. And thus the single straggling street is allied with history, and shaded by tradition. No novelist could have given us more briefly and completely all that we need to know before the story begins.

The story of Selborne is a vegetable, an animal story. The gossip is about the habits of vipers and the love interest is supplied chiefly by frogs. Compared with Gilbert White the most realistic of novelists is a rash romantic. The crop of the cuckoo is examined; the viper is dissected; the grasshopper is sought with a pliant grass blade in its hole; the mouse is measured and found to weigh one copper halfpenny. Nothing can exceed the minuteness of these observations, or the scrupulous care with which they are conducted. The chief question in dispute – it is indeed the theme of the book – is the migration of swallows. Barrington believed that the swallow sleeps out the winter; White, who has a nephew in Andalusia to inform him, now inclines to migration; then draws back. Every grain of evidence is sifted; none is obscured. With all his faculties bent on this great question, the image of science at her most innocent and most sincere, he loses that self-consciousness which so often separates us from our fellow-creatures and becomes like a bird seen through field-glasses busy in a distant hedge. This is the moment then, when his eyes are fixed upon the swallow, to watch Gilbert White himself.

We observe in the first place the creature's charming simplicity. He is quite indifferent to public opinion. He will transplant a colony of crickets to his lawn; imprison one in a paper cage on his table; bawl through a speaking trumpet at his bees – they remain indifferent; and arrive at Selborne with Aunt Snooke's aged tortoise seated beside him in the post-chaise. And while thus engaged he emits those little chuckles of delight, whose half-conscious burblings and comments which make him as 'amusive' as one of his own birds. '...But their inequality of height,' he muses, pondering the abortive match between the moose and the red deer, 'must always have been a bar to any commerce of an amorous kind.' 'The copulation of frogs,' he observes, 'is notorious to everybody...and yet I never saw, or read, of toads being observed in the same situation.' 'Pitiable seems the condition of this poor embarrassed reptile,' he laments over the tortoise, yet 'there is a season (usually the beginning of June) when the tortoise walks on tip-toe' along the garden path in search of love.

And just as the vicarage garden seemed to Aunt Snooke's tortoise a whole world, so, as we look through the eyes of Gilbert White, England becomes immense. The South Downs, across which he rides year after year, turn to 'a vast range of mountains'. The country is very empty. He is more solitary at Selborne than a peasant to-day in the remotest Hebrides. It is true that he has – he is proud of the fact – a nephew in Andalusia; but he has no acquaintance at present among the gentlemen of the Navy; and though London and Bath exist, of course – London indeed boasts a very fine collection of horns – rumours from those capitals come very slowly across wild moors and roads which the snow has made impassable. In this quiet air sounds are magnified. We hear the whisper of the grasshopper lark; the caw of rooks is like a pack of hounds 'in hollow, echoing woods'; and on a still summer evening the Portsmouth gun booms out just as the goat-sucker begins its song. His mind, like the bird's crop that the farmer's wife found stuffed with vegetables and cooked for her dinner, has nothing but insects in it and tender green shoots. This innocent, this unconscious happiness is conveyed, not by assertion, but much more effectively by those unsought memories that come of their own accord. They are all of hot summer evenings – at Oxford in Christ Church quadrangle; riding from Richmond to Sunbury with the swallows skimming the river. Even the strident voice of the cricket, so discordant to some, fills his mind 'with a train of summer ideas, of everything that is rural, verdurous and joyful'. There is a continuity in his happiness; the same thoughts recur on the same occasions. 'I made the same remark in former years as I came the same way annually.' Year after year he was thinking of the swallows.

But the landscape in which this bird roams so freely has its hedges. They shut in, but they protect. There is what he calls, so aptly, Providence. Church spires, he remarks, 'are very necessary ingredients in the landscape.' Providence dwells there – inscrutable, for why does it allot so many years to Aunt Snooke's tortoise? But all-wise – consider the legs of the frog – 'How wonderful is the economy of Providence with regards to the limbs of so vile an animal!' In another fifty years Providence would have been neither so inscrutable nor as wise – it would have lost its shade. But Providence about 1760 was in its prime; it sets all doubts at rest, and so leaves the mind free to question practically everything. Besides Providence there are the castles and seats of the nobility. He respects them almost equally. The old families – the Howes, the Mordaunts – know their places and keep the poor in theirs. Gilbert White is far less tender to the poor – 'We abound with poor,' he writes, as if the vermin were beneath his notice – than to the grasshopper whom he lifts out of his hole so carefully and once inadvertently squeezed to death. Finally, shading the landscape with its august laurel, is literature – Latin literature, naturally. His mind is haunted by the classics. He sounds a Latin phrase now and then as if to tune his English. The echo that was so famous a feature of Selborne seems of its own accord to boom out *Tityre, tu patulae recubans...* It was with Virgil in his mind that Gilbert White described the women making rush candles at Selborne.

So we observe through our field-glasses this very fine specimen of the eighteenth-century naturalist. But just as we think we have got him named he moves. He sounds a note that is not the characteristic note of the common English clergyman. 'When I hear fine music I am haunted by passages therefrom night and day; and especially at first waking, which by their importunity, give me more uneasiness than pleasure.' Why does music, he asks, 'so strangely affect some men, as it were by recollection, for days after a concert is over?'

307

It is a question that sends us baffled to his biography. But we learn only what we knew already – that his affection for Kitty Mulso was not passionate; that he was born at Selborne in 1720 and died there in 1793; and that his 'days passed with scarcely any other vicissitudes than those of the seasons.' But one fact is added – a negative, but a revealing fact; there is no portrait of him in existence.

He has no face. That is why perhaps he escapes identification. His observation of the insect in the grass is minute; but he also raises his eyes to the horizon and looks and listens. In that moment of abstraction he hears sounds that make him uneasy in the early morning; he escapes from Selborne, from his own age, and comes winging his way to us in the dusk along the hedgerows. A clerical owl? A parson with the wings of a bird? A hybrid? But his own description fits him best. 'The kestrel or wind-hover,' he says, 'has a peculiar mode of hanging in the air in one place, his wings all the time being briskly agitated.'

Virginia Woolf (1882–1941)
'White's Selborne' (1939) from *The Captain's Death Bed
and Other Essays* (1950)

We begin with trees. In this letter, we see vintage Gilbert White, conveying the fragile interdependence of the human and the natural world.

Letter II: To Thomas Pennant
In the centre of the village, and near the church, is a square piece of ground surrounded by houses, and vulgarly called the Plestor. In the midst of this spot stood, in old times, a vast oak, with a short squat body, and huge horizontal arms extending almost to the extremity of the area. This venerable tree, surrounded with stone steps, and seats above them, was the delight of old and young, and a place of much resort in summer evenings; where the former sat in grave debate, while the latter frolicked and danced before them. Long might it have stood, had not the amazing tempest of 1703 overturned it at once, to the infinite regret of the inhabitants, and the vicar, who bestowed several pounds in setting it in its place again;

but all his care could not avail; the tree sprouted for a time, then withered and died. This oak I mention to show to what a bulk planted oaks also may arrive: and planted this tree must certainly have been.

On the Blackmoor estate there is a small wood called Losel's, of a few acres, that was lately furnished with a set of oaks...

In the centre of this grove there stood an oak, which, though shapely and tall on the whole, bulged out into a large excrescence about the middle of the stem. On this a pair of ravens had fixed their residence for such a series of years, that the oak was distinguished by the title of the Raven-tree. Many were the attempts of the neighbouring youths to get at this eyry: the difficulty whetted their inclinations, and each was ambitious of surmounting the arduous task. But, when they arrived at the swelling, it jutted out so in their way, and was so far beyond their grasp, that the most daring lads were awed, and acknowledged the undertaking to be too hazardous. So the ravens built on, nest upon nest, in perfect security, till the fatal day arrived in which the wood was to be levelled. It was in the month of February, when those birds usually sit. The saw was applied to the butt, the wedges were applied into the opening, the woods echoed to the heavy blows of the beetle or mallet, the tree nodded to its fall; but still the dam sat on. At last, when it gave way, the bird was flung from her nest; and, though her parental affection deserved a better fate, was whipped down by the twigs, which brought her dead to the ground.

Gilbert White (1720–93)
The Natural History of Selborne (1789)

29th September 1822
Uphusband
I see that some plantations of ash and hazel have been made along here; but, with great submission to the planters, I think they have gone the wrong way to work, as to the mode of preparing the ground. They have planted small trees, and that is right; they have trenched the ground, and that is also right; but they have brought the bottom soil to the top; and that is wrong, always; and especially where the bottom soil is gravel or chalk, or clay...

This country, though so open, has its beauties. The homesteads in the sheltered bottoms with fine lofty trees about the houses and yards, form a beautiful contrast with the large open fields. The little villages, running straggling along the dells (always with lofty trees and rookeries) are very interesting objects, even in the winter. You feel a sort of satisfaction, when you are out upon the bleak hills yourself, at the thought of the shelter, which is experienced in the dwellings in the valleys.

William Cobbett (1763–1835)
Rural Rides (1822–26)

Edward Thomas, who called himself an 'inhabitant of earth', lived at Steep some ten miles south of Selborne, and was a pioneering ecological poet, a man whose engagement with the natural world seems somehow prophetic of the century to come. Like Thomas Hardy, he evoked a landscape of association. Despite only writing poetry for two years before his death in the trenches in Arras in April 1917, he had a deep influence on the poets of the twentieth century. Ted Hughes wrote, 'He was the father of us all.'

Aspens

All day and night, save winter, every weather,
Above the inn, the smithy, and the shop,
The aspens at the cross-roads talk together
Of rain, until their last leaves fall from the top.

Out of the blacksmith's cavern comes the ringing
Of hammer, shoe, and anvil; out of the inn
The clink, the hum, the roar, the random singing –
The sounds that for these fifty years have been.

The whisper of the aspens is not drowned,
And over lightless pane and footless road,
Empty as sky, with every other sound
Not ceasing, calls their ghosts from their abode,

A silent smithy, a silent inn, nor fails
In the bare moonlight or the thick-furred gloom,
In tempest or the night of nightingales,
To turn the cross-roads to a ghostly room.

And it would be the same were no house near.
Over all sorts of weather, men, and times,
Aspens must shake their leaves and men may hear
But need not listen, more than to my rhymes.

Whatever wind blows, while they and I have leaves
We cannot other than an aspen be
That ceaselessly, unreasonably grieves,
Or so men think who like a different tree.

Edward Thomas (1878–1917)

Flora Thompson, best known for her later novel *Lark Rise to Candleford*, lived in a dreary little terraced house in Liphook (according to Diana Athill). Her self-taught interest in nature was influenced by Gilbert White and Selborne, which was just down the road. She must have visited the magnificent yews of nearby Kingley Vale, some of which are thought to be over 2,000 years old.

… What an essentially English tree the yew is, whether seen, as here, in some ancient churchyard, carved into quaint shapes of walls and arbours and fabulous birds and beasts in some historic garden, or in its wild native state upon the Downs. Perhaps it is seen at its best in the latter setting. All about the South Downs it grows lavishly, its red stems and glossy dark foliage striking a rare note of colour against the pale turf and pearly chalk-tints of the hills, where even the skies have a paler blue and the clouds are more snowy than elsewhere.

Some of these wild yews of the hills must be tremendously old; not that they ever attain the girth of trunk or circumference of shade they have been known to do in more sheltered positions, but the gnarled toughness of the stems, six or eight twined together to form a trunk, and the grotesque, wind-tortured boughs, all bending one way from the sea, bear the plain impress of centuries.

Flora Thompson (1876–1947)
Peverel Papers: Nature Notes 1921–27 (1986)

The Selborne yew, here commemorated by the poet Anthony Rye, was one of the largest, finest and oldest in the British Isles, but was felled by the Great Storm of 1987. Rye lived much of his life in Selborne at Sparrow's Hanger (land owned once by Gilbert White) and published three volumes of poetry.

The Selborne Yew

Come under this famous yew – ancient yew:
This and England like twin seedlings grew,
Yet the Conqueror's self coeval knew
No such strength compact of means so few.

Time in the circle of these boughs we see
Turned to a monolith or stone-hard tree,
And yet its course upon it seems to be
Moulten, like a river's, written free.

Like a river whose deep hidden throes
Seam the swelling surface as it goes,
With long thrusts and blind convulsive flows,
To the ocean whence its power arose.

To this day, any observant driver on the A3 will notice the Canadian maples mentioned here.

Now the bushes are of full size again. Bracken has grown up and filled the rents made by bomb-practice. The heather has returned in waves, a purple sea. Very soon all will be as it had been for countless ages before the war broke out, and only the avenue of maple trees the Canadians planted by the roadside will mark any difference between that heath and a score of others by the same roadside.

The Canadian military camp was on Bramshott Common, and even today signs of it can still be detected there. Three hundred Canadian servicemen who died of wounds in the First World War are buried in Bramshott churchyards.

Flora Thompson (1876–1947)
Peverel Papers: Nature Notes 1921–27 (1986)

Letter XLVI: to Daines Barrington
There is a steep abrupt pasture field interspersed with furze close to the back of this village, well known by the name of the Short Lithe, consisting of a rocky dry soil, and inclining to the afternoon sun. This spot abounds with the field-cricket; which, though frequent in these parts, is by no means a common insect in many other countries.

As their cheerful summer cry cannot but draw the attention of a naturalist, I have often gone down to examine the oeconomy of these *grylli* and study their mode of life: but they are so shy and cautious that it is no easy matter to get a sight of them; for, feeling a person's footsteps as he advances, they stop short in the midst of their song, and retire backward nimbly into their burrows, where they lurk till all suspicion of danger is over.

Letter XLVII: to Daines Barrington
While many other insects must be sought after in fields and woods, and waters, the house-cricket, resides altogether within our dwellings, intruding itself upon our notice whether we will or no. This species delights in new-built houses, being, like the spider, pleased with the moisture of the walls; and besides, the softness of the mortar enables them to burrow and mine between the joints of the bricks or stones, and to open communications from one room to another. They are particularly fond of kitchens and bakers' ovens, on account of their perpetual warmth.

Tender insects that live abroad either enjoy only the short period of one summer, or else doze away the cold uncomfortable months in profound slumbers; but these, residing as it were in a torrid zone, are always alert and merry: a good Christmas fire is to them like the heats of the dog-days.

Though they are frequently heard by day, yet is their natural time of motion only in the night. As soon as it grows dusk, the chirping increases, and they come running forth…

Gilbert White (1720–93)
The Natural History of Selborne (1789)

Edward Thomas penned his first poem at the age of 36, when living in Steep where the family had moved, from London, to be close to Bedales School where their children were educated. Shortly before moving, in 1913, impatient for the end of winter, and perhaps seeking to hurry the departure of his cyclical depression, he cycled from Clapham to Somerset looking for signs of spring. Here he is in Hampshire.

Soon after leaving Farnham, the road actually touched the river, and horses can walk through it parallel to the road and cool their feet; and just past this, I entered Hampshire. More often the river was midway between my road and the terrace, touching an old farmhouse of brick and timber in the plashy meadows, or turning a mill with a white plunge of water under sycamores. But the gayest and most spring-like sign was the fresh whitewash on every fruit tree in an orchard by the wayside; it suggested a festival. The poles were being set up in the hop gardens. The hedges enclosing them had been allowed to grow up to a great height for a screen against wind, and to make a diaphanous green wall. Many were the buildings related to hops, whose mellow brickwork seemed to have been stained by a hundred harvests.

Bentley, the first village in Hampshire, seemed hardly more than a denser gathering, and all on the right hand, of the houses that had been scattered along since Farnham, with the addition of two inns and of a green which a brooklet crosses and turns into a pond at the road's edge. After Bentley the road ascended, the place of houses was taken by trees, chiefly lines of beeches connected with several embowered mansions at some distance, one of pale stone, one of dark brick. Several rookeries inhabited these beeches. Froyle House, perhaps the chief in this neighbourhood, stood near where the road is highest, and yet closest to the river a many-gabled pale house next to a red church tower among elms and black-flamed cypresses. Up to the church and house a quarter of a mile of grass mounted, with some isolated ancient thorns and many oaks, which in one spot near the road gathered together into a loose copse. The park itself ran with not too conspicuous or regular a boundary into hop gardens and ploughland. A low wall on a bank separated it from the road, and where a footpath had to pass the wall the stile was a slab of stone pierced by two pairs of foot-holes, approached up the bank by three stone steps. It was here, and at eleven, that I first heard the chiffchaff saying, 'Chiff-chaff, chiff-chaff, chiff-chaff, chiff!' A streamlet darted out of the park towards the Wey, and on the other side of the road, and below it, had to itself a little steep coomb of ash trees. An oak had been felled on the coomb side, and a man was clearing the brushwood round it, but the small bird's double note, almost as regular as the ticking of a clock, though often coming to an end on the first half, sounded very clear in the coomb. He sang as he flitted among the swaying ash tops in that warm, cloudy sun. I thought he sang more shrilly than usual, something distractedly. But I was satisfied. Nothing so convinces me, year after year, that spring has come and cannot be repulsed, though checked it may be, as this least of songs. In the blasting or dripping weather which may ensue, the chiffchaff is probably unheard; but he is not silenced. I heard him on March 19 when I was fifteen, and I believe not a year has passed without my hearing him within a day or two of that date. I always expect him and always hear him. Not all the blackbirds, thrushes, larks, chaffinches, and robins can hide the note. The silence of July and August does not daunt him. I hear him yearly in September, and well into October the sole summer voice remaining save in memory. But for the wind I should have heard him yesterday. I went on more cheerfully, as if each note had been the hammering of a tiny nail into winter's coffin.

My road now had the close company of the railway, which had crossed the river. The three ran side by side on a strip not more than a quarter of a mile in breadth; but the river, small, and not far from its source, was for the most part invisible behind the railway. Close to the railway bank some gypsies had pitched a tent, betrayed by the scarlet frock of one of the children. But in a moment scarlet abounded. The hounds crossing road and railway in front of me were lost to sight for several minutes before they reappeared on the rising fields towards Binsted Wyck. The riders, nearly all in scarlet, kept coming in for ten minutes or so from all hands, down lanes, over sodden arable land, between hop gardens, past folded sheep. Backwards and forwards galloped the scarlet before the right crossing of the railway was taken. The fox died in obscurity two miles away.

Edward Thomas (1878–1917)
In Pursuit of Spring (1914)

As well as his epistolary *Natural History of Selborne*, Gilbert White's journals are a source of wondrous information. The theme of birds continues.

Apr. 28, 1779
Five long-legged plovers, *charadrius bimantopus,* were shot at Frinsham-pond. There were three brace in all. These are the most rare of all British birds. Their legs are marvellously long for the bulk of their bodies. To be in proportion of weight for inches the legs of the *Flamingo* should be more than 10 feet in length.

May 1, 1779
A pair of Creepers (*certhia*) build at one end of the parsonage-house at Greatham, [near Selborne] behind some loose plaster. It is very amusing to see them run creeping up the walls with the agility of a mouse. They take great delight in climbing up steep surfaces, & support themselves in their progress with their tails, which are long, & stiff & inclined downwards.

Gilbert White (1720–93)
Naturalist's Journal

Letter XX: to Thomas Pennant
There is no bird, I believe, whose manners I have studied more than that of the *caprimulgus* (the goat-sucker), as it is a wonderful and curious creature: but I have always found that though sometimes it may chatter as it flies, as I know it does, yet in general it utters its jarring note sitting on a bough; and I have for many an half hour watched as it sat with its under mandible

quivering, and particularly this summer. It perches usually on a bare twig, with its head lower than its tail, in an attitude well expressed by your draughtsman in the folio British Zoology. This bird is most punctual in beginning its song exactly at the close of day; so exactly that I have known it strike up more than once or twice just as the report of the Portsmouth evening gun, which we can hear when the weather is still. It appears to me past all doubt that its notes are formed by organic impulse, by the powers of the parts of its windpipe, formed for sound, just as cats purr. You will credit me, I hope, when I tell you that, as my neighbours were assembled in an hermitage on the side of a steep hill where we drink tea, one of these churn-owls came and settled on the cross of that little straw edifice and began to chatter, and continued his note for many minutes: and we were all struck with wonder to find that the organs of that little animal, when put in motion, gave a sensible vibration to the whole building! This bird also sometimes makes a small squeak, repeated four or five times; and I have observed that to happen when the cock has been pursuing.

Gilbert White (1720–93)
The Natural History of Selborne (1789)

We started this morning coming through the Duke of Buckingham's park, at Avington, which is close by Easton, and on the same side of the Itchen. This is a very beautiful place. The house is close down at the edge of the meadow land; there is a lawn before it, and a pond supplied by the Itchen, at the end of the lawn, and bounded by the park on the other side. The high road, through the park, goes very near to this water; and we saw thousands of wild-ducks in the pond, or sitting round on the green edges of it, while, on one side of the pond, the hares and pheasants were moving about upon a gravel walk on the side of a very fine plantation. We looked down upon all this from a rising ground, and the water, like a looking-glass, showed us the trees, and even the animals.

This is certainly one of the very prettiest spots in the world.

William Cobbett (1763–1835)
Rural Rides (1822–26)

Letter IV: to Daines Barrington

Your observation that 'the cuckoo does not deposit its egg indiscriminately in the nest of the first bird that comes its way, but probably looks out a nurse in some degree congenerous, with whom to intrust its young' is perfectly new to me; and struck me so forcibly, that I naturally fell into a train of thought that led me to consider whether the fact was so, and what reason there was for it. When I came to recollect and enquire, I could not find that any cuckoo had ever been seen in these parts, except in the nest of a wagtail, the hedge-sparrow, the titlark, the white-throat, and the red-breast, all soft-billed insectivorous birds ... this proceeding of the cuckoo, of dropping its eggs as it were by chance, is such a monstrous outrage on maternal affection, one of the first great dictates of nature, and such a violence on instinct, that, had it only been related of a bird in the Brazils, or Peru, it would never have merited our belief.

Letter X: to Daines Barrington

From what follows, it will appear that neither owls nor cuckoos keep to one note. A friend remarks that many (most) of his owls hoot in B flat: but that one went almost half a note below A. The pipe he tried their notes by was a common half-crown pitch pipe, such as masters use for tuning of harpsichords; it was the common London pitch.

A neighbour of mine, who is said to have a nice ear, remarks that the owls about this village hoot in three different keys, in G flat, or F sharp, in B flat and A flat. He heard two hooting to each other, the one in A flat, and the other in B flat.

Query: Do these different notes proceed from different species, or only from various individuals; for, about Selborne wood, he found they were mostly in D: he heard two sing together, the one in D, the other in D sharp, who made a disagreeable concert: he afterwards heard one in D sharp, and about Wolmer-forest some on C. As to nightingales, he says that their notes are so short, and their transitions so rapid, that he cannot well ascertain their key. Perhaps in a cage, and in a room, their notes may be more distinguishable. This person has tried to settle the notes of a swift, and of several other small birds, but cannot bring them to any criterion.

Letter XVII: to Daines Barrington

The reptiles, few as they are, I am not acquainted with, so well as I could wish, with regard to their natural history. There is a degree of dubiousness and obscurity attending the propagation of this class of animals, sometimes analogous to that of the cryptogamia in the sexual system of plants: and the case is the same as regards some of the fishes: as the eel, etc.

The method in which toads procreate and bring forth seems to me very much in the dark. Some authors say that they are viviparous: and yet Ray classes them among his oviparous animals; and is silent with regard to the manner of their bringing forth...

The copulation of frogs (or at least the appearance of it; for Sammerdam proves that the male has no *penis intrans*) is notorious to everybody: because we see them sticking upon each other's backs for a month together in spring: and yet I never saw, or read, of toads being observed in the same situation. It is strange that the matter with regard to the venom of toads has not yet been settled. That they are not noxious to some animals is plain: for ducks, buzzards, owls, stone-curlews, and snakes, eat them, to my knowledge, with impunity. And I well remember the time, but was not eye-witness to the fact (though numbers of persons were), when a quack, at this village, ate a toad to make the country people stare; afterwards he drank oil.

Letter XXIII: to Daines Barrington

On September the 21st, 1741, being then on a visit, and intent on field-diversions, I rose before daybreak: when I came into the enclosures, I found the stubbles and clover-grounds matted all over with a thick coat of cobweb, in the meshes of which a copious and heavy dew hung so plentifully that the whole face of the country seemed, as it were, covered with two or three setting-nets drawn one over another. When the dogs attempted to hunt, their eyes were so blinded and hoodwinked that they could not proceed, but were obliged to lie down and scrape the incumbrances from their faces with their fore-feet, so that, finding my sport interrupted, I returned home musing in my mind on the oddness of the occurrence.

As the morning advanced the sun became bright and warm, and the day turned out one of those most lovely ones which no season but the autumn produces: cloudless, calm, serene, and worthy of the South of France itself. About nine an appearance very unusual began to demand our attention, a shower of cobwebs falling from very elevated regions, and continuing, without any interruption, till the close of the day. These webs were not single filmy threads, floating in the air in all directions, but perfect flakes or rags; some near an inch broad, and five or six long, which fell with a degree of velocity which showed they were considerably heavier than the atmosphere. On every side, as the observer turned his eyes might he behold a continual succession of fresh flakes falling into his sight, and twinkling like stars as they turned their sides towards the sun.

How far this wonderful shower extended would be difficult to say, but we know that it reached Bradley, Selborne, and Alresford, three places which lie in a sort of a triangle, the shortest of whose sides is about eight miles in extent.

At the second of these places there was a gentleman (for whose veracity and intelligent turn we have the greatest veneration) who observed it the moment he got abroad; but concluded that, as soon as he came upon the hill above his house, where he took his morning rides, he should be higher than this meteor, which he imagined might have been blown, like thistle-down, from the common above: but, to his great astonishment, when he rode to the most elevated part of the down, 300 feet above his fields, he found the webs in appearance still as much above him as before; still descending into sight in a constant succession, and twinkling in the sun, so as to draw the attention of the most incurious.

Neither before nor after was any such fall observed; but on this day the flakes hung in the trees and hedges so thick, that a diligent person sent out might have gathered baskets full. The remark that I shall make on these cobweb-like appearances, called gossamer, is, that, strange and superstitious as the notions about them were formerly, nobody in these days doubts but they are the real production of small spiders, which swarm in the fields in fine weather in autumn, and have a power of shooting out webs from their tails so as to render themselves buoyant, and lighter than air. But why these apterous insects should that day take such a wonderful aerial excursion, and why their webs should at once become so gross and material as to be considerably more weighty than air, and to descend with precipitation, is a matter beyond my skill. If I might be allowed to hazard a supposition, I should imagine that those filmy threads, when first shot, might be entangled in the rising dew, and so drawn up, spiders and all, by a brisk evaporation into the region where clouds are formed: and if the spiders have a power of coiling and thickening their webs in the air, as Dr Lister says they have, then, when they were become heavier than the air, they must fall.

Every day in fine weather, in autumn chiefly, I do see those spiders shooting out their webs and mounting aloft: they will go off from your finger if you take them into your hand. Last summer one alighted on my book as I was reading in the parlour; and, running to the top of the page, and shooting out a web, took its departure from thence. But what I most wondered at, was that it went off with considerable velocity in a place where no air was stirring; and I am sure that I did not assist it with my breath. So that these little crawlers seem to have while mounting, some loco-motive power without the use of wings, and to move in the air, faster than the air itself.

Letter XI: to Thomas Pennant
The most unusual birds I ever observed in these parts were a pair of hoopoes (*upupa*) which came several years ago in the summer, and frequented an ornamental piece of ground, which joins to my garden, for some weeks. They used to march about in a stately manner, feeding in the walks, many times in the day; and seemed disposed to breed in my outlet; but were frightened and persecuted by idle boys, who would never let them be at rest.

321

Letter IV: to Thomas Pennant

A certain swallow built for two years together on the handles of a pair of garden-shears, that were stuck up against the boards in an out-house, and therefore must have her nest spoiled whenever that implement was wanted: and, what is stranger still, another bird of the same species built its nest on the wings and body of an owl that happened by accident to hang dead and dry from the rafter of a barn. This owl, with the nest on its wings, and with eggs in the nest, was brought as a curiosity worthy of the most elegant private museum in Great Britain. The owner, struck with the oddity of the sight, furnished the bringer with a large shell, or conch, desiring him to fix it just where the owl hung: the person did as he was ordered, and the following year a pair, probably the same pair, built their nest in the conch, and laid their eggs.

Letter LXVI: to Daines Barrington

There is a wonderful spirit of sociality in the brute creation, independent of sexual attachment: the congregating of gregarious birds in the winter is a remarkable instance.

...But this propensity seems not to be confined to animals of the same species; for we know a doe still alive, that was brought up from a little fawn with a dairy of cows; with them it goes afield, and with them it returns to the yard. The dogs of the house take no notice of this deer, being used to her; but, if strange dogs come by, a chase ensues; while the master smiles to see his favourite securely leading her pursuers over a hedge, or gate, or stile, till she returns to the cows, who, with fierce lowings and menacing horns, drive the assailants quite out of the pasture.

Letter XXV: to Daines Barrington

The natural term of a hog's life is little known, and the reason is plain – because it is neither profitable nor convenient to keep that turbulent animal to the full extent of its time: however, my neighbour, a man of substance, who had no occasion to study every little advantage to a nicety, kept an half-bred Bantam sow, who was as thick as she was long, and whose belly swept on the ground, till she was advanced to her seventeenth year; at which period she showed some tokens of age by the decay of her teeth and the decline of her fertility.

For about ten years this prolific mother produced two litters in the year of about ten at a time, and once above twenty at a litter; but, as there were near double the number of pigs to that of teats, many died. From long experience in the world this female was grown very sagacious and artful: when she found occasion to converse with a boar she used to open all the intervening gates, and march, by herself, up to a distant farm where one was kept; and when her purpose was served would return by the same means. At the age of about fifteen her litters began to be reduce to four or five; and such a litter she exhibited when in her fatting-pen. She proved, when fat, good bacon, juicy and tender; the rind, or sward, was remarkably thin. At a moderate computation she was allowed to have been the fruitful parent of three hundred pigs: a prodigious instance of fecundity in so large a quadruped! She was killed in spring 1775.

Letter X: To Thomas Pennant
I have had no opportunity yet of procuring any of those mice which I mentioned to you in town. The person that brought me the last says they are plenty in harvest, at which time I will take care to get more, and will endeavour to put the matter out of doubt, whether it be a non-descript species or not...

...As to the small mice, I have further to remark, that though they hang their nests for breeding up amidst the straws of the standing corn, above the ground; yet I find that, in the winter, they burrow deep in the earth, and make warm beds of grass, but their grand rendezvous seems to be in the corn-ricks, into which they are carried in harvest. A neighbour housed an oat-rick lately, under the thatch of which were assembled near an hundred ... I suppose that they are the smallest quadrupeds in this island.

Letter LXVlII: to Daines Barrington
On the subject of rural economy, it may not be improper to mention a pretty implement of housewifery that we have seen no where else; that is, little neat besoms which our foresters make from the stalk of the *polytricum commune*, or great golden maiden-hair, which they call silk-wood, and find plenty in the bogs. When this moss is well combed and dressed, and divested of its outer skin, it becomes of a beautiful bright chestnut colour; and, being soft and pliant, is very proper for the dusting of beds, curtains, carpets, hangings, etc. If these besoms were known to the brushmakers in town, it is probable they might come much in use for the purpose above-mentioned.

Gilbert White (1720–93)
The Natural History of Selborne (1789)

Ketcher's Field is part of Lord Selborne's land on the edge of the village. Here, some two hundred and fifty years after Gilbert White wrote the above, David Rushton, a local resident, remembers his parents' farming of hops on the land.

The area around Ketchers Field was then, but not now, full of hop fields, and Mum and Dad took on many acres of hops during the growing season, in which there were five different stages that all had to be kept under control. For all those who have never seen a hop garden, they grow in long rows, like grapes, but go up very high, so all over the field are poles (as high as telegraph poles) supporting overhead wires. Each hop plant had a wire skewer, like a corkscrew, in the ground from which four climbing strings were tied and then attached to the overhead wire.

The work in the hop fields was, to me, mind-numbingly boring. Firstly we had to go to each plant (and there were literally thousands) and train two vines up every string. The climbing string was actually made of coconut husk and was ideal for vines to grip on. With four climbing strings to each plant, that meant eight strong vines had to be selected and trained up, and they had to go clockwise, following the sun, or they would unwind.

It was a long and laborious task and seemed never-ending. After all that had been done, the vines had to be 'seconded', which meant going over the whole lot again to make sure they had taken. Then there was another process, 'clearing', to cut away all the unwanted vines around the bottom of the plant from the climbing ones, then tying, which was going through the lot again tying a short length of string around the vertical four, a third of the way up, to tidy them, and by this time they were so high as to keep the light out, and finally 'stripping' the vines. This was stripping the leaves off from the tied section to the ground, and by the end I had green stained hands for weeks after, but when it was all done over a few months, they did look good.

Hop picking itself was a completely different affair. For a start, I was legally allowed two weeks off school and that in itself was good. To me it was a magic time, the time when summer began to give way to autumn and the mists gathered on the morning before the sun was hot enough to disperse it, and when the Gypsies came and erected their great bell-shaped tents in the field at the end of our garden! This was the time when the two Missionaries moved into another smaller version of our house that may have been purpose-built. The scene was now set for the great harvest.

West meadow was the field allotted to the Travelling families when they came for the hop-picking season – it was just on the other side of what I called my river, a drainage ditch at the end of our garden. Their arrival was like a fair coming to town. The lorries, some brightly painted, and horse-drawn Romany caravans, makes me wish now that I had got my first Brownie 127 camera many years earlier. When the families arrived they always brought with them a bit of mystique. Many of the pubs would have signs up saying 'Hop Pickers not Allowed', or sometimes 'No Travellers', but inevitably some always got in and Friday and Saturday nights were always very lively.

With us being the nearest house to them and our neighbours, Mr and Mrs Melluish and daughter Margaret, who was about my age, we got to know them better than most. Dad was certainly known by most of the Travellers either by word of mouth or by experience. One season, two or three had climbed our massive old pear tree about one o'clock on one Sunday morning to clear some of the crop; they had been out having a good evening. As Dad said he heard a general racket coming from up the pear tree, so Dad being Dad, he discharged both barrels of his shotgun into the air, which awoke the entire camp and certainly alarmed the occupants of the pear tree. They must have literally fallen out of that tree with cries of 'Lordy Sir, the man's got a gun, let's get out of the way' and words much more vivid than that, but after that incident we never had trouble again, and Dad was seen in a new light by many.

When the camp in West Meadow was full, it really was like something out of the old Wild West. The great tall round tents were ex-Army from one century or another, and what a lovely assortment of horses, as many breeds of horse that you could think of, all amazingly marked animals, rarely a one-coloured horse among them. They all had beautiful markings and were truly the Travellers' pride and joy. But the most amazing scenes were at night, when it got dark and all the cooking fires were alight, the glow from each fire lit up the faces of the occupying families as they sat around cooking or eating the evening meal. They also spoke in a language that you had to be quick to pick up on; they not only spoke rapidly but used a lot of phrases and words that ordinary folk would simply not understand.

A lot of the time, I didn't know what they were saying until I got to know them better. Some of their surnames were very unusual as well, such as Pidgeley, and their homes on wheels were works of art and contained all of their prize possessions and were always spick and span. With the arrival of the harvest pickers came the Missionaries. I used to look forward to their arrival with excitement. Every year they came and moved into the old Nissen hut to care for the spiritual and physical well-being of the Travellers. Nothing was too much trouble. They were always on hand for advice, help or just to lend a sympathetic ear. These two men were really dedicated to their

work and had been to other countries helping the poor and administering help and spreading the word of God.

The old hut had a sink and running water and that was about all, a few old chairs, a table and old paraffin lamps. I can always remember the smoky smell of them, and there would have been an outside toilet. The other thing that always stays with me was the outside cooking kiln. It was very similar to a modern barbecue, an open fire at the bottom with a grill across and brick chimney all in one. This old cooking place still stands as a monument to the Missionaries thanks to my Mum and Dad who, when the builders demolished the hut to build the Ketchers Little Field houses as they are now, persuaded them to keep the old fireplace. The Mission Hut chimney was finally left as a gift to the community.

I wonder how many of those children who came with their parents to pick hops can recall those men. I wonder if they recall the talks they gave to them, all seated on the grass in the evenings hearing about Jesus and his reason for being here, and how many can read and write because of them and became better people through their teachings? In later years, they used to have a big furniture lorry with the back converted into a cinema to show films. It would come round and then the entire camp would sit at the back of the lorry and watch these religious and educational films. I was one of them! I used to go over and sit with them as often as possible. The Missionaries had a special atmosphere or magnetic personality about them and I can remember one year when they left I was in tears. What dedicated people they must have been. With more people like that, there would be no trouble on this planet.

The actual hop-picking itself had a very carnival kind of atmosphere about it. We would all set off to whichever field we were harvesting and join the long line of hop-pickers wending their way along the lane on a fine misty morning with a slight chill on the air, and all the Travellers would have a lovely smell of smoke from their fires. Once in the field, now with the hops fully grown and very dark between the rows, the vines covered in green hops looking a bit like small pine cones and when touched they gave off a lovely aroma. I can still catch a whiff of hops today over a pint of good English bitter. We were all given a row or two, and these were ours. There was always a bit of argy-bargy as some bigger families would try and get more, even when picking it was not uncommon for someone to pinch a few of someone else's hops and many a row has been sparked off, even to the extent of blows being exchanged. The Travellers certainly had an endless vocabulary of colourful swear words up their sleeves.

At the start, each family had a big round numbered basket allotted to them, which held around seven bushels of hops, a bushel being the measuring unit. When the Tally Man (who also kept a record of how many bushels of hops each family picked, for later payment) blew his whistle, the pick was on and all across the end of the hop garden, vines would be pulled and countless hands would pluck at the hops in a feverish race to pick as many as possible. It was a bit like the start of a gold-rush, and in a sense it was, the actual picking aim was to pick mostly hops with as little leaf as possible, but some were more careful than others. I have seen baskets of lovely light green hops with hardly a leaf and another with about a quarter of the hops in leaf so the Tally Man had a difficult job to sort out the exact crop before each basket was emptied into a great hop-sack called a Surplus sack. These, when full, made a sort of giant bean bag upon which the smaller children would play until told off for squashing the hops or the sacks. These were picked up by the wagon and horse carts to be taken to the drying kiln.

Mum, Dad and I used to pick feverishly away, and strangely enough, I used to pluck hops left-handedly, although I am naturally a right-handed person. From the air it must have looked like a plague of locusts going through the green jungle, some moving faster than others, and each morning and afternoon picking would stop for a 10-minute break at the sound of the Tally Man's whistle. Then came the familiar cry of 'Tea-o!' this coming from the Missionaries at one end or the other of the hop field, and there they would have set up a huge urn of tea, and for next to nothing a piping hot cup of tea could be had. At dinner time, out would come the carefully packed sandwiches which we would sit down and eat with a great relish; my word, did they taste good!

Inevitably, when all the hops were harvested, the Travellers drifted away and the field at the end of our garden once again

Gilbert White and the Green Laboratory

became silent. All that was left would be charred circles where the fires had been and larger circles of crushed and brown grass where the tents had been. How quiet the place was once more.

David Rushton
'How the Barbecue Chimney came to be at Ketchers Field',
Northanger Parish Magazine (2016)

It's as well to remember how fragile and how precious is the natural world so beloved of White and the other writers in this chapter. *Carpe Diem!* Here White describes the effects of the eruption of the volcano, Skaptar-Jokull, in Iceland in 1783.

Letter CIX: to Daines Barrington
The summer of the year 1783 was an amazing and portentous one, and full of horrible phaenomena; for besides the alarming meteors and tremendous thunder-storms that affrighted and distressed the different counties of this kingdom, the peculiar haze, or smokey fog, that prevailed for many weeks in this island, and in every part of Europe, and even beyond its limits, was a most extraordinary appearance, unlike anything known within the memory of man. By my journal I find that I had noticed this strange occurrence from June 23 to July 20 inclusive, during which period the wind varied to every quarter without making any alteration in the air. The sun, at noon, looked as blank as a clouded moon, and shed a rust-coloured ferruginous light on the ground, and floors of rooms; but was particularly lurid and blood-coloured at rising and setting. All the time the heat was so intense that butchers' meat could hardly be eaten on the day after it was killed; and the flies swarmed so in the lanes and hedges that they rendered the horses half frantic, and riding irksome. The country people began to look with a superstitious awe at the red, louring aspect of the sun; and indeed there was reason for the most enlightened person to be apprehensive; for, all the while, Calabria and part of the isle of Sicily, were torn and convulsed with earthquakes; and about that juncture a volcano sprung out of the sea on the coast of Norway. On this occasion Milton's noble simile of the sun, in his first book of *Paradise Lost*, frequently occurred to my mind; and it is indeed

particularly applicable, because, towards the end, it alludes to a superstitious kind of dread, with which the minds of men are always impressed by such strange and unusual phaenomena.

...As when the sun, new risen,
Looks through the horizontal, misty air,
Shorn of his beams; or from behind the moon,
In dim eclipse, disastrous twilight sheds
On half the nations, and with fear of change
Perplexes monarchs (Milton Paradise Lost, 1)

Gilbert White (1720–93)
The Natural History of Selborne (1789)

Chapter 8
Military life

Over the centuries, Hampshire has witnessed the departure of countless military and naval expeditions to the Continent, but nothing approaches the preparations of the spring and early summer of 1944, when men and women from all over the Empire and Europe, and from the United States, gathered in secret for D-Day. From April 1 to D-Day – June 6 – a ten-mile coastal strip along the south coast, from The Wash in Norfolk to Land's End in Cornwall, was a restricted zone. On D-Day itself, around 156,000 troops were landed on Normandy's beaches, with troop ships leaving from Portsmouth and, in the case of the Americans, Southampton.

Even in times of peace, when soldiers and sailors aren't mobilising and funnelling through the county, Hampshire has a military aspect. Not far from Portsmouth and the ships of the navy, naval officers – both serving and retired – populate the villages of the Meon valley and around, while the north of the county is province of Aldershot garrison – 'Home of the British Army' – and the RAF base at Odiham. Certain place names – Cheriton, Basing House, Bramdean – are redolent of earlier fighting and echo with the bullets of the English Civil War (1642–49), when the armies of Parliament and the King faced one another, each to protect their own idea of our hallowed constitution.

...

The Civil War was fought more vigorously, widely and decisively in our county than in any other. Billettings and quarterings, skirmishes and battles affected every village and house: Basing, Warblington, Lymington, Havant, Aldershot, Titchfield, Whitchurch, Alresford, Odiham, Seven Barrows, Baughurst, Overton, Hurst Castle, Basingstoke, Kingsclere, Hackwood, Portsmouth, Winchester, Romsey,

Andover, Southampton, Petersfield, Fareham, Alton, Southwick and Bramdean. The entire county was involved, and the climax in 1644 was the decisive Battle of Cheriton where terrible slaughter 'broke all measures and upset the whole scheme of the king's counsels', after which the Parliamentarians were eventually victorious. The depredations of the surrounding land, however, meant that there was 'hardly anything left for man or beast'. The following excerpts give a flavour of the time.

During the siege of Basing House, scarcity of ammunition, as well as of provisions, caused difficulties for its owner the Royalist John Paulet, Marquis of Winchester, who had garrisoned it for the King. In the first year of the siege (12 October 1643) the King issued a warrant to the following effect:

To our right trusty and well-beloved Henry, Lord Percy, general of our ordnance for the present expedition. Our will and pleasure is, that you forthwith take order for sending to the Marquess of Winchester's House of Basing ten barrels of powder with match and bullets proportionable. And this shall be your warrant. Given at our Court at Oxford this twelfth day of October, 1643.

The Marquis responded:
My Lord. Understanding by a letter from Mr Secretary Nicholas, that his Majesty hath given a warrant for the issuing out of your magazine ten barrels of powder and double proportion of match, I therefore desire your Lordship to command carts for the conveying of the said powder from Oxford to this garrison, standing not only in great want of the same, but also daily expecting the enemy's approach, who are now at Farnham with a considerable force of horse and foot. I have dispatched this messenger who will attend the expedition. And if any arms have been brought into the magazine, I desire your favour in the furtherance of 100 muskets to be sent with this conveyance, and in so doing yon shall infinitely oblige, my Lord, your Lordship's most affectionate kinsman and humble Servant, Winchester. Basing Castle, 2nd November, 1643

For two long frustrating years Parliament attempted to take 'Loyalty House', as it was called, and eventually the Parliamentarians sent a summons to the Marquis:

My Lord, These are in the name and by the authority of the Parliament of England, the highest court of justice in this kingdom, to demand the House and Garrison of Basing to be delivered unto me, to be disposed of according to order of Parliament. And hereof I expect your answer by this drum, within one hour after the receipt hereof, in the mean time I rest; yours to serve you, Richard Norton.

The Marquis answered:
Sir, Whereas you demand the House and Garrison of Basing by a pretended authority of Parliament, I make this answer: That without the King there can be no Parliament, by His Majesty's commission I keep the place, and without his absolute command shall not deliver it to any pretenders whatever. I am, yours to serve you, Winchester.

When the house eventually fell to Cromwell, on October 14th 1645, among the captives were the architect Inigo Jones (1573–1652), who had introduced the classical style into England and the great Czech engraver Wenceslaus Hollar (1607–1677). Jones was taken from the house dressed only in a blanket, having been first stripped of his clothes.

Sir William Waller, a parliamentarian commander who had made early gains for Parliament in Hampshire, including Portsmouth, Winchester and Farnham in 1642, is here lauded for his surprise attack and victory against Sir Ralph Hopton at Alton in 1643.

A Narration of The Great Victory made public on December 16th 1643 (Through God's Providence) Obtained by the PARLIAMENTS Forces Under Sir William Waller, at ALTON in SURREY the 13 of this instant December 1643. Against the Cavaliers: Where were taken near a thousand prisoners, a thousand Arms, two hundred horse, with divers officers of great quality. As it was delivered by a Messenger sent by Sir WILLIAM WALLER, to the committee of safety of the kingdom, and divers of the house of Commons, and by them appointed to be forthwith printed and published.

Tuesday the Twelfth of this instant December, Sir William Waller in the afternoon, drew forth his Forces into a Battalia in Farnham-Park, about the number of Five thousand horse and foot, among which were the Regiment of Westminster, whose behaviour and valour in this service, is never to be forgotten: the manner of the businesse was exceedingly well carryed, both by *Sir William* and all the rest, for strictnesse of appearance, and likewise for secrecie, that the Enemy, nor no Malignant party, could have the opportunity to understand the least of their intentions: They were upon the march by seven of the clock in the night, and in an hours march obtained a Heath between Brunden and Farnham; and there after an hour's stay for the Foot, whose march were not so quick as the horse, they all willingly and cheerfully marcht together, till neer one of the clock in the night, in the way towards Basing; but on a sudden were appointed to face towards the South, and so towards Alton, passing exactly between the hills, till they obtained within half a mile of the said town, altogether undiscovered by the Enemy, our Scouts being so diligent, that not a person stirring in those passages was left at liberty to have any opportunity to inform the Enemy of our proceedings; and being now in the sight of the Town, about nine of the clock in the morning, we understood by the Scouts we took, That the Lord Craford was in the Town, who had there about Five hundred horse; the taking of which Scouts, some of them escaping, gave opportunity for the said Lord to shift for himself, who conceived himself and all the rest of his forces lost; yet he speedily drew forth about Three hundred of the horse Eastward, towards Winchester rode, where, unexpectedly, he met with some of our horse, and retreated back again into the Town, and fled Southward; our horse perceiving that, persued them, whilst our Foot made the woods ring with a shout; There were three or four of them slain in their flight, and being in narrow Lanes after half a miles pusuit, our men retreated againe, having taken about Thirty Horse, and some Prisoners; in the meane whiles the Foot were not idle, nor Sir William, whose rare exploits in this service may be registered with the rest of his valiant and Honourable Actions.

The horse were immediately appointed to make good all passages, so that the Enemy could not have the benefit of their accustomed running away, but were taken by our horse, our foot in the meantime behaving themselves like men, with great expedition; beat the Enemies out of the Works of the North-west and East parts of the Towne, and possest themselves thereof, where they displayed their Colours in the sight of their Enemies, then our men advanced speedily into the Market-place, and the Enemy being all Musquetiers drew themselves in to the works near the church, where they had double Trenches and a Half-Moone, and made the Church and a Barne there by their chiefest refuge, here grew then a very hot fight, which was continued neer two houres, by reason of a Malignant, who willingly fired his own Barne, and other houses, thereby to offend our men with the smoake; by reason of which smoake we lost about three men: the fire and smoak abating, our men fell close to their work againe, and forced the Enemy to retreat into the said Church and Barne, where they were all taken prisoners. The Towne being thus taken on all sides, the Enemy desired and obtained quarter: Yet being infected with Irish Rebels and their wonted treachery, one of them after quarter given, fired off a Pistoll in the said Church, against Major Shambrook; but by God's providence, was not killed therewith, but hurt in the thigh, and great hopes there is of his speedy recovery.

In this fight were taken prisoners 700 in the Church, neere 1000 in the Barne; above 100 in the field, with divers Irish men and women: also near 200 horse, 1000 arms, one Colonell, one Major, one Lieutenant Colonell, thirteen Captaines, three Coronets, one of which with the Princes Armes, another the Earl of Straffords, with divers other colours hid in the Church; there were slaine of the Enemie neere 40 amongst which was Colonell Richard Bolles: the Enemies word was *(Charles)* Ours *(Truth and Victory)*.

The mighty providence of God was seene in this, and as in many other mercies towards us: for in the Fight a certaine truth, there were not above five of our men slaine, and about six wounded, and about six scorched with powder, by reason of their owne negligence: This done, our worthy Major Generall caused the people of the said Towne to slight the Workes: took the prisoners, and tied them two by two with Match, and are now in Farnham Church and Castle, where they may hear better doctrine than they have heard at Oxford, or amongst the Irish Rebels.

Despite Sir William Waller's early taking of Winchester, by late 1643 the city was back in Royalist hands. It was not until Oliver Cromwell attacked in October 1645 that the city was finally secured for Parliament. Cromwell, leader of the Parliamentarians, was appointed Lord Protector of the Commonwealth of England Scotland and Ireland, which lasted from 1649–1660, in 1653.

6 October 1645
I came to Winchester the Lord's day 28th September. After some dispute with the Governor we entered the town. I summoned the castle; was denied; whereupon we fell to prepare batteries which we could not perfect (some of our guns being out of order) till the Friday following. Our battery was six guns, which being finished, after firing one round, I sent in for a second summons for a treaty; which they refused. Whereupon we went on with our work, and made a breach in the wall by the Black Tower; which after about 200 shot we thought stormable; and purposed on Monday morning to attempt it. On Sunday night about ten of the clock, the Governor beat a parley, desiring to treat. I agreed unto it, and sent Colonel Hammond and Major Harrison in to him, who agreed upon these enclosed articles...

Sir, this is the addition of another mercy. You see God is not weary in doing you good... His goodness in this is much to be acknowledged: for the castle was well-manned with six hundred and eighty horse and foot, there being near two hundred gentlemen, officers, and their servants; well victualled with fifteen hundred-weight of cheese, very great store of wheat and beer; near twenty barrels of powder, seven pieces of cannon; the works were exceedingly good and strong. It's very likely it would have cost much blood to have gained it by storm. We have not lost twelve men.

Oliver Cromwell (1599–1658)
Letter

...

From 1760–62, the great historian Edward Gibbon's studies were interrupted by a period of home defence with the Hampshire militia. Since the Civil War, the idea of a large standing army had been seen as dangerous by both sides of the political spectrum, and it was preferred to keep a small army for foreign wars, with the defence of England to be performed by local militias. As can be seen from his account, though Gibbon was annoyed by the disruption, he did his duty conscientiously and found the experience vital for understanding the military aspects of the Roman empire for his magnificent history *The Decline and Fall of the Roman Empire* (1776).

A national militia has been the cry of every patriot since the Revolution; and this measure, both in parliament and in the field, was supported by the country gentlemen or Tories, who insensibly transferred their loyalty to the house of Hanover: in the language of Mr Burke, they have changed the idol, but they have preserved the idolatry. In the act of offering our names and receiving our commissions, as major and captain in the Hampshire regiment (June 12, 1759), we had not supposed that we should be dragged away, my father from his farm, myself from my books, and condemned, during two years and a half (May 10, 1760 – December 23, 1762), to a wandering life of military servitude. But a weekly or monthly exercise of thirty thousand provincials would have left them useless and ridiculous; and after the pretence of an invasion had vanished, the popularity of Mr Pitt gave a sanction to the illegal step of keeping them till the end of the war under arms, in constant pay and duty, and at a distance from their respective homes. When the King's order for our embodying came down, it was too late to retreat, and too soon to repent. The south battalion of the Hampshire militia was a small independent corps of four hundred and seventy-six, officers and men, commanded by Lieutenant-Colonel Sir Thomas Worsley, who, after a prolix and passionate contest, delivered us from the tyranny of the Lord Lieutenant, the Duke of Bolton. My proper station, as first captain, was at the head of my own, and afterwards of the grenadier company; but in the absence, or even in the presence, of the two field officers, I was entrusted by my friend and my father with the effective labour of dictating orders, and exercising the battalion. With the help of an original journal, I could write the history of my bloodless and inglorious campaigns; but as these events have lost much of their importance in my own eyes, they shall be dispatched in a few words. From Winchester, the first place of assembly (June 4, 1760), we were removed, at our own request, for the benefit of a foreign education. By the arbitrary, and often capricious orders of the War Office, the battalion successively marched to the pleasant and hospitable town of Blandford (June 17); to Hilsea barracks, a seat of disease and discord (September 1); to Cranbrook in the Weald of Kent (December 11); to the seacoast of Dover (December 27); to Winchester camp (June 25, 1761); to the populous and disorderly town of Devizes (October 23); to Salisbury (February 28 , 1762); to our beloved Blandford a second time (March 9); and finally, to the fashionable resort of Southampton (June 2); where the colours were fixed till our final dissolution (December 23). On the beach at Dover we had exercised in sight of the Gallic shores. But the most splendid and useful scene of our life was a four months' encampment on Winchester Down, under the command of the Earl of Effingham. Our army consisted of the thirty-fourth regiment of foot and six militia corps. The consciousness of defects was stimulated by friendly emulation. We improved our time and opportunities in morning and evening field-days; and in the general reviews the South Hampshire were rather a credit than a disgrace to the line.

...But my principal obligation to the militia was the making me an Englishman, and a soldier. After my foreign education, with my reserved temper, I should long have continued a stranger to my native country, had I not been shaken in this various scene of new faces and friends: had not experience forced me to feel the characters of our leading men, the state of parties, the forms of office, and the operation of our civil and military system. In this peaceful service I imbibed the rudiments of the language and science of tactics, which opened a new field of study and observation... The disciplines and evolutions of a modern battalion gave me a clearer notion of the phalanx and the legion; and the captain of the Hampshire grenadiers (the reader may smile) has not been useless to the historian of the Roman Empire.

... On the 25th of June, 1765, I arrived at my father's house; and the five years and a half between my travels and my father's death (1770) are the portion of my life which I passed with the least enjoyment, and which I remember with the least satisfaction. Every spring I attended the monthly meeting and exercise of the militia at Southampton; and by the resignation of my father, and the death of Sir Thomas Worsley, I was successively promoted to the rank of major and lieutenant-colonel commandant; but I was each year more disgusted with the inn, the wine, the company, and the tiresome repetition of annual attendance and daily exercise.

Edward Gibbon (1737–1794)
Autobiography (1796)

...

All of Edward Thomas's extraordinary poetic *oeuvre*, written between 1914 and 1917 when he died, was composed in the shadow of war. He volunteered in July 1915.

The Owl

Downhill I came, hungry, and yet not starved;
Cold, yet had heat within me that was proof
Against the North wind; tired, yet so that rest
Had seemed the sweetest thing under a roof.
Then at the inn I had food, fire, and rest,
Knowing how hungry, cold, and tired was I.
All of the night was quite barred out except
An owl's cry, a most melancholy cry
Shaken out long and clear upon the hill,
No merry note, nor cause of merriment,
But one telling me plain what I escaped
And others could not, that night, as in I went.
And salted was my food, and my repose,
Salted and sobered, too, by the bird's voice
Speaking for all who lay under the stars,
Soldiers and poor, unable to rejoice.

Edward Thomas (1878–1917)

The poet Charles Hamilton Sorley was living in Aldershot when he wrote with a somewhat puritanical sense of duty to his mother and with less fervour to his friend Arthur Watts, before moving out to the Western Front in late May 1915. He was killed, less than five months later, during the final offensive of the Battle of Loos on 13 October

341

1915. Robert Graves considered that Sorley was 'one of the three poets of importance killed during the war', the others being Isaac Rosenberg and Wilfred Owen.

28 April 1915

I saw Rupert Brooke's death in the *Morning Post*. The *Morning Post*, which has always hitherto disapproved of him, is now loud in his praises because he has conformed to their stupid axiom of literary criticism that the only stuff of poetry is violent physical experience, by dying on active service. I think Brooke's earlier poems – especially notably 'The Fish' and 'Grantchester', which you can find in Georgian Poetry – are his best. That last sonnet-sequence of his, of which you sent me the review in the Times Lit. Sup., and which has been so praised, I find (with the exception of that beginning 'These hearts were woven of human joys and cares, Washed marvellously with sorrow' which is not about himself) overpraised. He is far too obsessed with his own sacrifice, regarding the going to war of himself (and others) as a highly intense, remarkable and sacrificial exploit, whereas it is merely the conduct demanded of him (and others) by the turn of circumstances, where non-compliance with this demand would have made life intolerable. It was not that 'they' gave up anything of that list he gives in one sonnet: but that the essence of these things had been endangered by circumstances over which he had no control, and he must fight to recapture them. He has clothed his attitude in fine words: but he has taken a sentimental attitude.

23 May 1915

...We profess no interest in our work; our going has lost all glamour in adjournment; a weary acceptance of the tyranny of discipline, and the undisguised boredom we feel toward one another, mark all our comings and goings: we hate our general, our C.O. and men; we do not hate the Germans: in short we are nearing the attitude of regular soldiers to the army in general...

Charles Hamilton Sorley (1895–1915)
The Letters of Charles Sorley *(1919)*

Cicely Fox Smith, who lived in Hampshire, was a productive writer, particularly of nautical verse and romantic novels. This is far from being her only poem encouraging the 1914–1918 war effort.

Speed the Plough

As I was a-walking on Chilbolton Down,
I saw an old farmer there driving to town,
A-jogging to market behind his old grey,
So I jumped up behind him and thus he did say:

'My boy he be fightin', a fine strappin' lad,
I gave he to England, the only boy I had;
My boy he be fightin' out over the foam,
An' here be I frettin' an' mopin' at home.

'An' if there be times when 'tis just about hard
Without his strong arm in the field an' the yard,
Why, I plucks up my heart then an' flicks the old grey,
An' this is the tune that her heels seem to say:

"Oh the hoof an' the horn, the roots an' the corn,
The flock in the fold an' the pigs in the pen,
Rye-grass an' clover, an' barns brimmin' over,
They feed the King's horses an' feed the King's men"

'Then I looks at my furrows to see the corn spring,
Like little green sword-blades all drawn for the King,
An' 'tis "Get up, old Bess, there be plenty to do,
For old chaps like me an' old horses like you."

'My boy be in Flanders, he's young an' he's bold,
But they will not have we, lass, for we be too old;
So step it out cheerful, an' kip up your heart,
For you an' me, Bess, we be doin' our part –

'Wi' the shocks an' the sheaves, the lambs an' the beeves,
The ducks an' the geese an' the good speckled hen,
Rye-grass an' clover, an' barns brimmin' over,
To feed the King's horses an' feed the King's men.'

Cicely Fox Smith (1882–1954)

Here, Edward Thomas records his departure for the Continent in early 1916. He died in the battle of Arras on April 7 1917, 'when a bullet stopped his song'.

January 20th 1916
Up at 5. Very cold. Off at 6.30, men marching in frosty dark to station singing 'Pack up your troubles in your old kit-bag'. The rotten song in the still dark brought one tear. No food or tea – Freezing carriage. Southampton at 9.30 and there had to wait till dusk, walking up and down, watching ice-scattered water, gulls and dark wood beyond, or London Scottish playing improvised Rugger, or men dancing to concertina, in a great shed between railway and water. Smith and I got off for lunch after Horton and Capt Lushington returned from theirs. Letter to Helen from 'South Western Hotel', where sea-captains were talking of the 'Black Adder' and of 'The Black Ball Line' that used to go to Australia. Hung about till dark – the seagulls as light failed nearly all floated instead of flying – then sailed at 7.

Edward Thomas (1878–1917)
Diary

...

Take a Highwayman's Heath, destroy every vestige of life with fire and axe, from the pine that has longest been a landmark, to the smallest beetle smothered in smoking moss. Burn acres of purple and pink heather, and pare away the young bracken that springs verdant from its ashes. Let flame consume the perfumed gorse in all its glory, and not spare the broom, whose more exquisite yellow atones for its lack of fragrance. In this common ruin be every lesser flower involved: blue beds of speedwell by the wayfarer's path, the daintier milkwort, and rougher red rattle down to the very dodder that clasps the heather, let them perish, and the face of Dame Nature be utterly blackened! Then: shave the heath as bare as the back of your hand, and if you have felled every tree, and left not so much as a tussock of grass or a scarlet toadstool to break the force of the winds; then shall the winds come from the east and from the west, from the north and from the south, shall raise on your shaven heath clouds of sand that would not edit a desert in the heart of Africa. By some such recipe the ground was prepared for that Camp of Instruction at Asholt. Then a due portion of this sandy oasis in a wilderness of beauty was mapped out into lines, with military precision, and on these were built rows of little wooden huts, which were painted a neat and useful black... But it may be at once conceded to the credit of the camp, that those who lived there thought better of it than those who did not, and that those who lived there longest were apt to like it best of all.

Juliana Horatia Ewing (1841–85)
The Story of a Short Life (1885)

Asholt is a variation on Aldershot, here described by the wife of an army officer who spent eight years in the town from 1869. The events she describes were recent, for in 1850 Aldershot was a small village with a church, a couple of large houses, a few cottages and a green. No traveller ever came, and soldiers were unheard of.

Mrs Ewing was less critical of the place than many. In Anthony Powell's *The Kindly Ones,* Nicholas Jenkins describes it as 'that uniquely detestable town'. Nikolaus Pevsner initially echoes this description: 'The army descended on Aldershot in 1854. It created miles of great dreariness.' But he adds briskly, 'The dreariness is being remedied now.'

From John Betjeman, an acute observation of our human foibles in Aldershot in the 1950s. The town is also commemorated in his poem, 'A Subaltern's Love Song', as the place where Miss Joan Hunter Dunn, object of the poet's desire, is 'Furnish'd and burnish'd by Aldershot sun'.

Aldershot Crematorium

Between the swimming-pool and cricket-ground
    How straight the crematorium driveway lies!
And little puffs of smoke without a sound
    Show what we loved dissolving in the skies,
Dear hands and feet and laughter-lighted face
And silk that hinted at the body's grace.

But no-one seems to know quite what to say
    (Friends are so altered by the passing years):
'Well, anyhow, it's not so cold today'—
    And thus we try to dissipate our fears.

'I am the Resurrection and the Life':
Strong, deep and painful, doubt inserts the knife.

John Betjeman (1906–84)

In the spring of 1944, Aldershot held thousands of soldiers headed for the Normandy Beaches. As sympathetically imagined by Alexander Baron, many of the men of the Wessex Regiment were from farming families in Somerset.

They gave themselves up to summer, and passed their days in a stupor of content, drugged with sunshine, anaesthetised by the scent of blossoming flowers, lazy and languid and enchanted by the richness that was coming to life all round them. The dizzy hours and days reeled past them as they slept in the sun, lulled by the drone of bombers and of bumble-bees. Private Oh-Three-Seven Smith was a little anxious.

'I reckon we'll be away before the harvest, Corporal,' he said.

'I reckon we will.' Corporal Shuttleworth was not very interested.

'Going to be a good harvest this year, Mister Hodge is thinking.'

'Is he?' said Shuttleworth. 'Leave me alone. I'm writing.' He was huddled on his bed with a writing pad on his knees. The blanket was littered with crumpled sheets of paper.

Oh-Three-Seven Smith pulled his beret on to the back of his head. 'I'll be off down there,' he said.

Shuttleworth looked up. 'Down where? Hodge's Farm again?'

'I promised Mister Hodge I would. It's been hard going getting the barley in in time.'

'Christ Almighty!' Shuttleworth exploded. 'It's been the hottest day in weeks, we've been marching our feet off all day. Look at the others...look at 'em...'

Most of the platoon were sprawling on their beds, with their boots off, smoking.

'And you go off,' he went on, 'to break your back working. It's knockin' off time now, Smithy. Lay down and give your feet a rest.'

'They'll be working for three hours yet in Ten-Acre Field,' said Oh-Three-Seven Smith, 'till it gets dark. There's a lot to do down there.'

'He's a mean bugger,' said one of the men as Private Smith went out, 'he kills himself workin' every night for a couple of bob.'

'It's not the money,' said Shuttleworth, 'he likes it. There's a lot of these swedebashers go down the farms every night to put some work in.'

There were, in fact, many men in the Fifth Battalion whose greatest pleasure was to work on the land whenever they could get out of the camp. They came from the farmlands of the western counties in which the battalion had originally been raised. Successive dilutions had flooded the battalion with men from all parts of the British Isles but there was still this core of countrymen, a kind of passive mass within the battalion of big, beefy, awkward lads with shy, red faces, whose names rarely made news or even figured on the charge sheets, who spent their evenings (when they were not out working) sitting quietly on their beds talking to each other, writing long letters or grubbing in the enormous parcels of food they were always receiving from home. They had the reputation of being miserly with money and generous with food. They were poor hands at gambling and past masters at rabbiting. They were easy to pick out in the dining hall, where they clenched their knives and forks in their fists and, bending low over their plates, shovelled vast quantities of food into their mouths humbly and absorbedly. They were good soldiers, enduring, uncomplaining, not without initiative but rarely inspired. Their speech was a delight to hear, broad-vowelled and leisurely, full of rich, rolling r's.

Oh-Three-Seven Smith made his way down the lane and along the main road past the village with the relaxed, unhurried gait of the countryman who saves his energy for the work to come.

He had been enjoying himself these last three weeks. It had been a race, down on Hodge's Farm, to get the last crops sown by the beginning of May, to get the barley in and drill the swedes and mangolds, to broadcast the grass and clover seeds for next year's hay and get it harrowed in.

They would be just about finishing the job off tonight, it gave him a pleasant feeling inside to think of a job like that accomplished. After that the evenings would be more leisurely; there would be a lull, during which tractors and equipment would get fresh coats of paint to protect them from the weather, the beams of the barns would be creosoted again, the mangolds ground for the bullocks and fresh stocks laid in of fertiliser and cattle feed.

And there would be time for talks with Mister Hodge. What a man that Mister Hodge was! Private Smith had never known a farmer like him; young, and full of science – he had been to one of those agricultural colleges – and always ready to teach. He could tell you all about the soil, chemistry, not the old stuff that the old men mumbled about in the corner chair down the pub, and all about every disease that every animal in the farmyard might ever get, and how to feed them, and how to look after poultry, and all about drainage – he would bend over a map and mark out lines on it just like an officer, and in a few weeks that field would be as dry and firm as you could want.

'Evenin', Mister Hodge.' He was taken by surprise. He had not expected to see Hodge coming down the road towards him, at this time of evening, when the sky was still pearly with sunlight. And Charlie Benbow with him, too.

'Hello, Tom. It's saved you a walk, meeting us. We've finished up in Ten-Acre; we're just going down to the Ploughman to celebrate. You'll come, won't you?'

Tom. He was a nice man, Mister Hodge, and his wife a nice woman; she laid a lovely supper in front of you. For the last five years Private Smith had grown unaccustomed to being called Tom. He only heard the name from his mother when he was home on leave. In the battalion, he was one of a tribe of Smiths, each of whom bore some distinguishing title. There was Sanitary Smith, the chief latrine-wallah (sometimes known by a more pungent and equally alliterative nickname), and Smith-In-The-Signals, and a score of other Smiths each of whom had been trained to accompany his surname with the last three digits of his Army number. So that when Tom Smith saw a finger jabbed at him and heard a voice bark, 'What's your name, you?' it had become a reflex for him to jerk to attention and answer, 'Oh-Three-Seven Smith, sir.'

It was nice, in the evening, to come out of camp and leave the saluting and the sentries behind you, and to sit in the kitchen at Hodge's place or in the public bar at the Ploughman among kindly farming folk who called you Tom. It was the next best thing to being at home with mother.

They were turning in through the door of the Ploughman, and settling themselves in their accustomed places at the plain wooden table. Private Smith preferred this dark, dingy, low-beamed little four-ale bar, with its sawdust-covered floor and the same dozen and a half farmhands gathered every night, to the gaudy, rowdy Horse and Hounds at the other end of the village, where most of the battalion flocked to crowd bawling round the strident piano and to woo the fancy women of the district. At the Horse and Hounds you poured beer down you till you had to spew it up; at the Ploughman you sat with friends and made your pint last.

Oh-Three-Seven Smith sipped his ale appreciatively and listened respectfully to the conversation of his seniors. Under their elbows on the table there were newspapers, with stories of thousands of bombers roaring over Europe, with headlines: KING'S MESSAGE TO HOME FLEET – GOD SPEED BEFORE BATTLE. But tonight, among his friends, Private Smith spoke not a word about bombers or battles, but talked happily about pigmeal and ribrollers, seed-harrows and granular fertiliser.

'You're getting busy up at the camp again, Tom,' remarked Mister Hodge. 'We could hear the rifles going all day on the range.'

'Ah,' said Tom, 'we're never finished training.'

'Balloon'll be going up soon, by the look of things,' said Charlie Benbow.

'Before the harvest,' said Tom. That was the only thing that worried him. He paid little heed to the battalion's warlike preparations; he never wondered what might be in store across the water; certainly he had never known the breath of fear. But sometimes he felt a little anxious because he would be taken away before the summer was at its height, and just when Mister Hodge, who had so much to teach him, was getting interested in him. 'I don't think I'll be with you for the harvet, Mister Hodge.'

Mister Hodge laughed heartily. 'Never you worry about that, Tom, lad,' he said. 'You'll have your own harvest to get in by then. Eh, lad? You deserve another pint for that. Drink up, Tom, boy, and I'll get you one.'

349

'I'll be sorry for all that, Mister Hodge,' said Tom solemnly. 'I've never been on a farm like yours before. All this science. It's a good thing for a farmer, knowledge.'

'There's always after the war,' said Mister Hodge. 'If your mother'll let you stay away for a year or two more, I'll be pleased to have you with me. Anyway, we shall be friends, shan't we, and write to each other? You're going to write when you're away, aren't you Tom?'

Tom blushed. 'If it's all right with you, Mister Hodge. Oh,' he said, as Charlie Benbow brought another pint along, 'I haven't finished the other one yet.'

They fell to talking about the war again. The newspapers told of fresh victories in Italy and of a great Russian offensive in the Crimea.

'Old Staylin,' chortled Charlie Benbow, wiping a spot of froth from his straggling moustache, 'he's the boy. He knows what he's doin' of all right. More than some of them over 'ere.'

'They say,' Tom butted in, eager to repeat a joke that was going the rounds of the Fifth Battalion and which represented almost the sum total of Tom's political knowledge, 'they say old Stalin's sent a telegram to Churchill, askin' if he sh'd stop at Calais or come on over here.'

They all laughed. Old Charlie thumped the table with his huge fist. 'Ah,' he said, 'he's the boy all right. Told 'em to burn the crops, 'e did. Burn the crops, 'e told 'em. An' they did.'

Tom laughed again, immoderately. He was light-headed with happiness. The talk flowed on around him, but he did not hear it. He was thinking only on Mister Hodge's words. 'There's always after the war...I'll be pleased to have you with me.' To be a free man, and to work here, with Mister Hodge and Old Charlie and the others. There was no war for Tom Smith, and no thought of tomorrow's battle in his mind; only after the war, and a job at Hodge's Farm.

He became attentive again. Mister Hodge was speaking to him about poultry. Tom's mother kept hens. Mister Hodge knew all about hens, and gave Tom regular advice about them, which was faithfully passed on to Mrs Smith in a series of long letters.

'Send your mother this, Tom,' said Mister Hodge, putting a pamphlet on the table. 'If she hasn't got it already it'll be of interest to her.'

'I'll copy it out, Mister Hodge,' said Tom sturdily, 'and keep this one for myself to learn from.'

He was light-footed with joy as he walked back to camp, later, in the cool dusk. A job with Mister Hodge. Science. Knowledge. It was a proud thing, knowledge.

He swung into camp.

'Good night, mate,' said the sentry.

' 'Night.'

Tom Smith was Oh-Three-Seven Smith once more.

...

The other candle-light burned on. Private Oh-Three-Seven Smith was writing to his mother. He peered at the pamphlet by his side and copied a phrase painstakingly; then turned back to the pamphlet.

Cod liver oil as a two per cent addition to any mash is worth while. It helps health, growth and fertility. Calcium in some form, as oyster or cockle shell, limestone grit or dust, or even crushed chalk, is necessary for bone and shell. There was the dull, spreading broo-oom of bombs exploding, and the hut quaked. Private Smith hardly noticed it. Although animal protein in the mash is required, experiments have shown that ten per cent is the maximum, and this may be reduced to five per cent by using fishmeal with five per cent of soya-bean meal.

Every battery in the area was firing now. The anti-aircraft barrage was a wall of sound through which the noise of the bombers' engines penetrated fitfully. Private Smith finished his letter and licked the envelope thoughtfully as shrapnel clattered on the corrugated iron roof of the hut.

He blew out his candle. 'Good night, Corporal,' he whispered across to Shuttleworth's bed. There was no reply. He pulled his blanket up over him. Outside, the raid was at its height. Private Oh-Three-Seven Smith rolled over, grunted, pushed his face against the straw-filled bolster, and fell asleep.

Alexander Baron (1917–99)
From the city, from the plough (1948)

The day that Private Oh-Three-Seven Smith would have waited for, were he lucky enough to survive, was VE Day, here described by Ralph

Dutton, owner and creator of the beautiful gardens at Hinton Ampner near Alresford.

The end of the war in Europe was now well insight; on 7th May the German government agreed to unconditional surrender, and it was announced the 8th May was to be celebrated as V.E. Day. It happened to synchronise with my two days' leave from the Foreign Office, so I was able to organise a celebration at Hinton. Feverishly we built as large a bonfire as was possible at short notice on a high point of the ridge between the villages of Hinton and Bramdean, and from the local pub I was able to obtain a barrel of beer. As it grew dark a large concourse from the two villages assembled and at 10.30 precisely the barrel was broached, and I set fire to the bonfire. It burned magnificently, the first flames of joy, as opposed to sorrow, that had lit the night sky for five and three-quarter years. From the ridge the dark landscape stretched away northward and southward into the invisible distance. The deep blue scene was suddenly broken by many little points of brilliant light where others all over the countryside were doing as we were, and celebrating the joyful end of the long succession of sombre days. It was a moving sight, as moving I think as the clamorous jubilations in the streets of London. About midnight as the fire died down and the barrel of beer gave out, we dispersed to our homes, I to Hinton where once again after so long an interval I slept in my own bedroom. The ten camp-beds had been removed and one of adult size found for me. That there was no carpet and only black-out over the windows was no hardship: I was home again at last.

Ralph Dutton (1898–1985)
Hampshire Manor (1968)

Chapter 9
Travelling and Leaving

In the present age of rushing to and from at steam-haste – not the slow post haste of old – when 'globe-trotting' has become quite commonplace, this simple chronicle of a leisurely driving tour of only a few hundred miles *On Southern English Roads* may seem almost an anomaly. On behalf, however, of quiet loving tourists like myself, who do not measure beauty by the mile, and who from pure pleasure choose to travel by road and behind horses just as our pre-railway forefathers did, I may quote a dictum of Ruskin's, 'A fool wants to shorten time and space, a wise man wants to lengthen both.'

James John Hissey
On Southern English Roads (1896)

How poignant has Hissey's plea become! The methods of progress described in this chapter – on foot with Boumphrey, riding as Cobbett recommends, Fiennes's side-saddle, Hissey's carriage and pair or Sturmey's autocar – compared, in their several ways, with the experience of today's travellers, seem enviable in their variety, in their pace and fascinate with what they tell us about the simplicity and emptiness of the past. Hampshire is less the focus in this final chapter than movement itself, though in the process aspects of the county are revealed. A motorcar is talk of the town in Stockbridge, a river doubles as a road, and in winter a lane becomes a stream. Edward Thomas meets an elderly labourer who lamely sets off against the north-east wind ten miles to Alton with his dog for company and Boumphrey is thrilled by traces of a Roman road. And in the final poem, Louis MacNeice presages the end as he takes the train 'bound for the dead leaves falling' and 'London's packed and stale and pregnant air', the gentle folds of Hampshire, her generals, admirals and knitting spinsters left to their genteel existence.

...

William Cobbett, social reformer, travelled to see the state of the countryside for himself, the better to press for reform and to oppose the authority of the landlords. Always excitable and appreciative of beauty, here he learns the meaning of the word picturesque.

I went through green lanes and bridle-ways till I came to the turnpike-road from Petersfield to Winchester, which I crossed, going into a narrow and almost untrodden green lane, on the side of which I found a cottage. Upon my asking the way to Hawkley, the woman at the cottage said, 'Right up the lane, sir: you'll come to a hanger presently: you must take care, sir: you can't ride down: will your horses go alone?'

On we trotted up this pretty green lane; and indeed, we had been coming gently and generally uphill for a good while. The lane was between highish banks and pretty high stuff growing on the banks, so that we could see no distance from us, and could receive not the smallest hint of what was so near at hand. The lane had a little turn towards the end; so that, out we came, all in a moment, at the very edge of the hanger!

And never, in all my life, was I so surprised and delighted!

I pulled up my horse, and sat and looked; and it was like looking from the top of a castle down into the sea, except that the valley was land and not water. I looked at my servant, to see what effect this unexpected sight had upon him. His surprise was as great as mine, though he had been bred amongst the North Hampshire hills. Those who had so strenuously dwelt on the dirt and dangers of this route, had not said a word about beauties, the matchless beauties of the scenery. These hangers are woods on the sides of very steep hills. The trees and underwood hang, in some sort, to the ground, instead of standing on it. Hence these places are called Hangers. From the summit of that which I had now to descend, I looked down upon the villages of Hawkley, Greatham, Selborne and some others.

From the south-east, round, southward, to the north-west, the main valley has cross-valleys running out of it, the hills on the sides of which are very steep, and, in many parts, covered with wood. The hills that form these cross-valleys run out from the main valley, like piers into the sea. Two of these promontories, of great height, are on the west side of the main valley, and were the first objects that struck my sight when I came to the edge of the hanger, which was on the south. The ends of these promontories are nearly perpendicular, and their tops so high in the air, that you cannot look at the village below without something like a feeling of apprehension. The leaves are all off, the hop-poles are in stack, the fields have little verdure; but, while the spot is beautiful beyond description even now, I must leave to imagination to suppose what it is when the trees and hangers and hedges are in leaf, the corn waving, the meadows bright, and the hops upon the poles!

From the south-west, round, eastward, to the north, lie the heaths, of which Woolmer Forest makes a part, and these go gradually rising up to Hindhead, the crown of which is to the north-west, leaving the rest of the circle (the part from north to north-west) to be occupied by a continuation of the valley towards Headley, Binstead, Frensham and the Holt Forest. So that even the contrast in the view from the top of the hanger is as great as can possibly be imagined. Men, however, are not to have such beautiful views as this without some trouble. We had had the view; but we had to go down the hanger. We had, indeed, some roads to get along, as we could, afterwards; but we had to get down the hanger first. The horses took the lead, and crept partly down upon their feet and partly upon their hocks. It was extremely slippery too; for the soil is a sort of marl, or, as they call it here, maume, or mame, which is, when wet, very much like grey soap. In such a case it was likely that I should keep in the rear, which I did, and I descended by taking hold of the branches of the underwood, and so letting myself down. When we got to the bottom, I bade my man, when he should go back to Uphusband, tell the people there that Ashmansworth Lane is not the worst piece of road in the world. Our worst, however, was not come yet, nor had we by any means seen the most novel sights.

After crossing a little field and going through a farmyard, we came into a lane, which was, at once, road and river...

(*after heading for Thursley via Headley and, because of an ignorant guide, Hindhead, Cobbett declared*)...Thus ended the most interesting day, as far as I know, that I ever passed in all my life. Hawkley-hangers, promontories, and stone-

roads will always come to my mind when I see, or hear of
picturesque views.

William Cobbett (1763–1835)
Rural Rides (1822–26)

Quite likely, it was in such hanger that Edward Thomas met the
inspiration for this poem, since he lived for sometime with the very
view which so delighted Cobbett.

Man and Dog

"'Twill take some getting.' 'Sir, I think 'twill so.'
The old man stared up at the mistletoe
That hung too high in the poplar's crest for plunder
Of any climber, though not for kissing under:
Then he went on against the north-east wind –
Straight but lame, leaning on a staff new-skinned,
Carrying a brolly, flag-basket, and old coat, –
Towards Alton, ten miles off. And he had not
Done less from Chilgrove where he pulled up docks.
'Twere best, if he had had 'a money-box,'
To have waited there till the sheep cleared a field
For what a half-week's flint-picking would yield.
His mind was running on the work he had done
Since he left Christchurch in the New Forest, one
Spring in the 'seventies, – navvying on dock and line
From Southampton to Newcastle-upon-Tyne, –
In 'seventy-four a year of soldiering
With the Berkshires, – hoeing and harvesting
In half the shires where corn and couch will grow.
His sons, three sons, were fighting, but the hoe
And reap-hook he liked, or anything to do with trees.
He fell once from a poplar tall as these:
The Flying Man they called him in hospital.
'If I flew now, to another world I'd fall.'
He laughed and whistled to the small brown bitch
With spots of blue that hunted in the ditch.
Her foxy Welsh grandfather must have paired
Beneath him. He kept sheep in Wales and scared

Strangers, I will warrant, with his pearl eye
And trick of shrinking off as he were shy,
Then following close in silence for – for what?
'No rabbit, never fear, she ever got,
Yet always hunts. Today she nearly had one:
She would and she wouldn't. 'Twas like that. The bad one!
She's not much use, but still she's company,
Though I'm not. She goes everywhere with me.
So Alton I must reach tonight somehow:
I'll get no shakedown with that bedfellow
From farmers. Many a man sleeps worse tonight
Than I shall.' 'In the trenches.' 'Yes. That's right.
But they'll be out of that – I hope they be –
This weather, marching after the enemy.'
'And so I hope. Good luck.' And there I nodded
'Good night. You keep straight on.' Stiffly, he plodded;
And at his heels the crisp leaves scurried fast,
And the leaf-coloured robin watched. They passed,
The robin till next day, the man for good,
Together in the twilight of the wood.

Edward Thomas (1878–1917)

Here, Priestley and Boumphrey are transported back through history. Priestley starts by leaving Winchester.

I never pass through these smaller Cathedral cities, on a fine day, without imagining I could spend a few happy years there, and never find myself compelled to spend a morning and afternoon in one without wishing the day was over and I was moving on. We climbed again into country so empty and lovely, so apparently incapable of earning its exquisite living, that people ought to pay just to have a glimpse of it, as one of the few last luxuries in the world for the ranging eye. And now the road straightened itself and made inexorably for Southampton.

...we rolled over the pleasant empty countryside of Hampshire, which, once your eyes have left the road, has a timeless quality. The Saxons, wandering over their Wessex, must have seen much of what we saw that morning. The landscape might have been designed to impress upon

359

returning travellers on the boat train out of Southampton, that
they were indeed back in England again.

J. B. Priestley (1894–1984)
English Journey (1935)

By a pleasant little village called St Mary Bourne I found a raised
causeway running through a hazel wood but never a sign of it
in the fields on either side. There is a real thrill in picking up a
section of road like this. You know from your map you are more
or less along the right line and you hunt about till a slight ridge
meets your eye. Very possibly it is only the remains of a bank or
something but you stick your walking stick into it, and if it is the
right thing, everywhere you prod you strike something hard a
few inches down. Across a few fields a modern road picked up a
line of it and ran with almost into Andover...

I picked up the Portway again the other side of Andover at
Hundred Acre Corner, by the aerodrome, and 5 miles ahead of
me I saw, almost on the line of the road, a tall hill with a clump
of Scotch pines on it, marked ROMAN CAMP on my map.
I made my way towards it, delighted to find that, for about a
mile, the modern road turned away and left me in comfort on
a broad grassy lane with turf to walk on, chaffinches to listen
to and blackthorn to look at. Miles and miles of the Roman
roads run along these grassy lanes at times, and I do strongly
recommend them to walkers.

G. M. Boumphrey
Along the Roman Roads (1935)

In Edward Thomas's poem, the path is infinitely puzzling. For what?
Where to? By whom? As with life, the work is to follow it to its
conclusion until it mysteriously ends, and to enjoy it on the way.

The Path

Running along a bank, a parapet
That saves from the precipitous wood below
The level road, there is a path. It serves
Children for looking down the long smooth steep,

Between the legs of beech and yew, to where
A fallen tree checks the sight: while men and women
Content themselves with the road and what they see
Over the bank, and what the children tell.
The path, winding like silver, trickles on,
Bordered and even invaded by thinnest moss
That tries to cover roots and crumbling chalk
With gold, olive, and emerald, but in vain.
The children wear it. They have flattened the bank
On top, and silvered it between the moss
With the current of their feet, year after year.
But the road is houseless, and leads not to school.
To see a child is rare there, and the eye
Has but the road, the wood that overhangs
And underyawns it, and the path that looks
As if it led on to some legendary
Or fancied place where men have wished to go
And stay; till, sudden, it ends where the wood ends.

Edward Thomas (1878–1917)

William Cobbett again, enjoying the rhythms and advantages of horseback travel, and the joys of friendship.

...The village of Uphusband, the legal name of Hurstbourn Tarrant, is, as the reader will recollect, a great favourite with me, not the less so certainly on account of the excellent free-quarter that it affords *[Cobbett often took hospitality here from his good friend, the farmer George Blount]*.
... Uphusband once more, and, for the sixth time this year, over the North Hampshire Hills, which, notwithstanding their everlasting flints, I like very much. As you ride along, even in a green lane, the horses' feet make a noise like hammering. It seems as if you are riding on a mass of iron. Yet the soil is good, and bears some of the best wheat in England. All these high and, indeed, all chalky lands are excellent for sheep. But on the tops of some of these hills are as fine meadows as I ever saw...
Here, at Avington, everything is in such beautiful order; the lawn before the house is of the finest green, and most neatly kept; and the edge of the pond (which is of several acres) is as

361

smooth as if it formed part of a bowling-green. To see so many wild-fowl, in a situation where everything is in the parterre-order, has a most pleasant effect on the mind; and Richard and I, like Pope's cock in the farm-yard, could not help thanking the duke and duchess for having generously made such ample provision for our pleasure, and that, too, merely to please us as we were passing along. Now this is the advantage of going about on horseback. On foot, the fatigue is too great, and you go too slowly. In any sort of carriage, you cannot get into the real country places. To travel in stagecoaches is to be hurried along by force, in a box, with an air-hole in it…

William Cobbett (1763–1835)
Rural Rides (1822–26)

As Celia Fiennes reminds us, all was not always easy on horseback, even if, in this extract, it allowed her to make her first acquaintance with the exotic oring (orange) tree.

…Ffrom thence its 6 miles to Rumsey, and the Road Runnes just by a fine house of one of my relations Sr John St Barbe's; the Rows of trees in the avenues runs just from ye Road to the front of the house… Here was fine flowers and Greens Dwarfe trees and oring and Lemon trees in Rows with fruite and flowers at once and some ripe; they are ye first oring trees that I ever Saw. Here are Stately woods and walks. …The Little raines I had in the morning … made the ways very slippery, and it being mostly on Chaulk way a Little before I Came to Alsford forcing my horse out of the hollow way his feete failed and he Could noe ways recover himself, and soe I was shott off his neck upon the Bank, but noe harm I bless God and as soon as he Could role himself up stood stock still by me, which I Looked on as a Great mercy – indeed mercy and truth all wayes have attended me. The next day I went to Alton 10 miles thence Ffarnham 9 miles more. This proved a very wet day, after an hours Rideing in the morning it never Ceased more or Less to raine.

Celia Fiennes (1662–1741)
Through England on a Side Saddle:
In the Time of William and Mary (1888)

Henry Sturmey was half of the duo which invented the Sturmey-Archer gear for the bicycle, on which he had initially intended to make his great journey.

I had often thought I should like to go over the longest straightway journey possible in this country viz. – the route from Land's End to John o' Groats but, as the years wore on, time prevented the accomplishment of the tour upon that popular means of progression – the bicycle. I became, however, possessed of an autocar. I held some hazy notion that if all went well I might get a very original, enjoyable and eventful journey out of a tour by autocar over a celebrated roadway... I decided to make it forthwith largely to prove the capability of my own vehicle and through it the practical utility of autocars in general, and so, if possible, to remove in some degree, the opinion I felt to be largely held by the British public that autocars were utterly unreliable things which 'broke down', 'exploded', or 'ran away' or did some other unexpected and undesirable thing about every five miles...

My original intention had been to tour along the South Coast, visiting several relatives on the way...

From Christchurch we entered the New Forest getting some of the most enjoyable driving of the whole trip. Everything was sweet and smiling. The sun was shining brilliantly, the roads for the most part excellent and broad, and the forest radiant in all the glory of autumn tinting, with here and there a wooded glade alternated by a clearing. I had not travelled many miles before I came across a gang of men engaged in bridge-making, evidently intending to put a new bridge across a little streamlet. They had cut through the road surface and destroyed the old bridge, and the temporary cartway went through the bed of the stream. At first I hesitated, but the men assured me it was not deep, and, fearing a deep layer of mud at the bottom, I dropped in the second speed and drove into the riverbed. However, the car came through all right, without any trouble, and a few miles further on, in one of the prettiest spots of the whole forest, a somewhat similar occurrence took place, the road way again being cut through for bridge-making. Here, however, the stream for the nonce was entirely dried up and the cart track had been taken wide into the valley through a mass of loose shingle at least a foot in depth and thoroughly well worked-up by the cartwheels. This looked awkward and I had my doubts as to getting through but when I got into the loose stuff, I dropped in the first speed, and we made fair progress. Just about the middle, however, in an extra deep quagmire of gravel, the engine commenced to slow down. Ashley and I were out like a shot on each side of the car, and, relieved of our weight, she just pulled through and struggled up on to the roadway again. From thence on we encountered several gravel carts, and I was struck by the extreme width between the wheels which was far greater than any other I had seen upon the vehicles in any other district; indeed, as the roads here were somewhat narrow, they gave us very little room to get by. Gradually the road ascended, and we left the forest, climbing over a series of wild, bare hills, deep in bracken. In spite of the gradients and the aforementioned difficulties of the roadway we covered the seventeen miles out of Bournemouth in 1hr 25mins and then a series of fresh loosely laid stones checked our way, and we had to go slowly for a mile or two until we ran into Lyndhurst. From thence to Totton the road was bumpy and, after having to stop the engine once to let a restive horse go by, we were taken on by a couple of scorchers in a trap who would insist upon racing us. However, about a mile settled them and they dropped away to the rear long before we reached Southampton, where I ran under the Bar Gate at 4.15, and made for the South Western Hotel, over roads which were slippery from the attention of watercarts, and tramways which required careful negotiation. However, the South-Western had no accommodation for the car, so I returned to the middle of the town, and made for the Dolphin where not only was the car safely and conveniently housed, but I also was made most comfortable. The run for the day was only thirty miles, but it was one of the pleasantest and most enjoyable of the trip...

I got away in mid-morning by the Winchester Road, rising steadily for several miles though magnificent woods of forest trees of a most picturesque character. The long climb was succeeded by an equally steady downgrade, and here I overtook a cyclist who evidently desired to show his contempt for the new vehicle, as he pedalled away gaily in front, sitting back in his saddle in a *negligee* attitude with his hands in his pockets until the car began to overhaul him, and then he suddenly discovered that he required to make up a cigarette, and so dismounted for the apparent purpose, though I had my own views as to the real reason for the stoppage. Leaving the main Winchester Road, I struck away to the left for Chilworth, running over a very broad road and rising through a fine series of woods and at times on the higher ground gaining lovely peeps of a fine expanse of forest radiant in autumn tints...

Romsey was reached in good time, and some fine running made along the valley of the Test over perfectly-level roads, somewhat narrow and winding, but with many pretty peeps of farm and river. At Mottisfont one slight hill was encountered, and the picturesque thatched cottages both here and at Houghton village, into which we soon ran, were strikingly interesting...

Mr and Mrs T., whose guest I was, turned up shortly after from a run with the hounds, indeed it seems that I narrowly missed coming across the pack, an encounter which I have no doubt would have caused considerable consternation among some of the mounts. In the afternoon the car was cleared of its luggage and petrol cans, and with friends on board, a short run into Stockbridge brought the day's drive up to 23 miles.

Of course, the autocar was the talk of the town and everyone in Stockbridge had something to say about it. Sunday was a glorious day, Monday ditto, beautifully fresh as to air, with a dead calm, but somewhat misty. After driving round the farm with my cousin behind a four-legged motor and strolling about getting snapshots with the camera, I made up a party for Stonehenge which, as yet, I had never seen but had often wished to visit, first of all calling at the post office at Stockbridge and wiring to Messrs. Carless, Capel and Co for a fresh supply of petrol as I found I should not have sufficient to carry me back to London. Then climbing a steep gradient out of Stockbridge, we ran through very pretty country following the course of a little stream winding in and out of somewhat narrow but very fair roadways through a series of villages known as 'The Wallops', bringing the villagers out in considerable excitement as we rode by. This was followed by some long steady climbs over roads somewhat loose in surface and made with broken flints which made me quake for the safety of my tyres.

Henry Sturmey
Through the Length and Breadth of the Land by Autocar (1899)

Before the use of the internal combustion engine, rivers proved no obstacle for wheeled traffic, as James John Hissey observes from his carraige and pair.

The charm of Ringwood is its river. The Avon here is wide and shallow; it spreads itself out and makes a great show. The river, too, forms a double sort of highway, for we noticed boats upon it, and two carts with drivers proceeding along its bed, the water being not quite as high as the axels. The river is manifestly an important local thoroughfare, we had never observed used as a road before.

James John Hissey
On Southern English Roads (1896)

Overshadowed by the Second World War, this poem marking the turn from summer to autumn, recalled from a railway carriage, seems to suggest an irrevocable change to the world order, hidden and ignored by the shaven lawns and silver dishes of middle-class life. The Irish poet Louis MacNeice published *Letters from Iceland* with W. H. Auden in 1937 and was associated also with Stephen Spender and Cecil Day-Lewis.

Autumn Journal (1938)

Close and slow, summer is ending in Hampshire,
    Ebbing away down ramps of shaven lawn where close-
    clipped yew
Insulates the lives of retired generals and admirals
    And the spyglasses hung in the hall and the prayer-
    books ready in the pew
And August going out to the tin trumpets of nasturtiums
    And the sunflowers' Salvation Army blare of brass
And the spinster sitting in a deck-chair picking up stitches

Not raising her eyes to the noise of the 'planes that pass
Northward from Lee-on-Solent. Macrocarpa and cypress
    And roses on a rustic trellis and mulberry trees
And bacon and eggs in a silver dish for breakfast
    And all the inherited assets of bodily ease
And all the inherited worries, rheumatism and taxes
    And whether Stella will marry and what to do with Dick
And the branch of the family that lost their money in Hatry
    And the passing of the Morning Post and of life's
    climacteric
And the growth of vulgarity, cars that pass the gate-lodge
    And crowds undressing on the beach
And the hiking cockney lovers with thoughts directed
    Neither to God nor Nation but each to each.
But the home is still a sanctum under the pelmets,
    All quiet on the Family Front,
Farmyard noises across the fields at evening
    While the trucks of the Southern Railway dawdle …
    shunt
Into poppy sidings for the night – night which knows no
    passion
    No assault of hands or tongue
For all is old as flint or chalk or pine-needles
    And the rebels and the young
Have taken the train to town or the two-seater
    Unravelling rails or road,
Losing the thread deliberately behind them –
    Autumnal palinode.
And I am in the train too now and summer is going
    South as I go north
Bound for the dead leaves falling, the burning bonfire,
    The dying that brings forth
The harder life, revealing the trees' girders
    The frost that kills the germs of laissez-faire;
West Meon, Tisted, Farnham, Woking, Weybridge,
    Then London's packed and stale and pregnant air.

Louis MacNeice (1907–63)

About the Editor

PHILIP ANGELL

Alastair Langlands has been rooted in the beech woods above Selborne for nearly fifty years, though he is a native of Galloway. An eloquent speaker and performer, he was also a passionate teacher of English, and has shepherded generations of young actors, artists and writers from Bedales School into lives of creativity. He bakes bread at dawn and is supported by a love of cricket, claret and Wagner's 'Ring Cycle'. He visits the theatre whenever possible and has never knowingly missed an opportunity for a swim.

Index

ELAND

61 Exmouth Market, London EC1R 4QL
Email: info@travelbooks.co.uk

Eland was started thirty years ago to revive great travel books which had fallen out of print. Although the list soon diversified into biography and fiction, all the titles are chosen for their interest in spirit of place. One of our readers explained that for him reading an Eland is like listening to an experienced anthropologist at the bar – she's let her hair down and is telling all the stories that were just too good to go into the textbook.

Eland books are for travellers, and for those who are content to travel in their own minds. They open out our understanding of other cultures, interpret the unknown and reveal different environments, as well as celebrating the humour and occasional horrors of travel. We take immense trouble to select only the most readable books and many readers collect the entire series of well over one hundred titles.

Extracts from each and every one of our books can be read on our website, at www.travelbooks.co.uk. If you would like a free copy of our catalogue, please order it from the website, email us or send a postcard.